D0961481

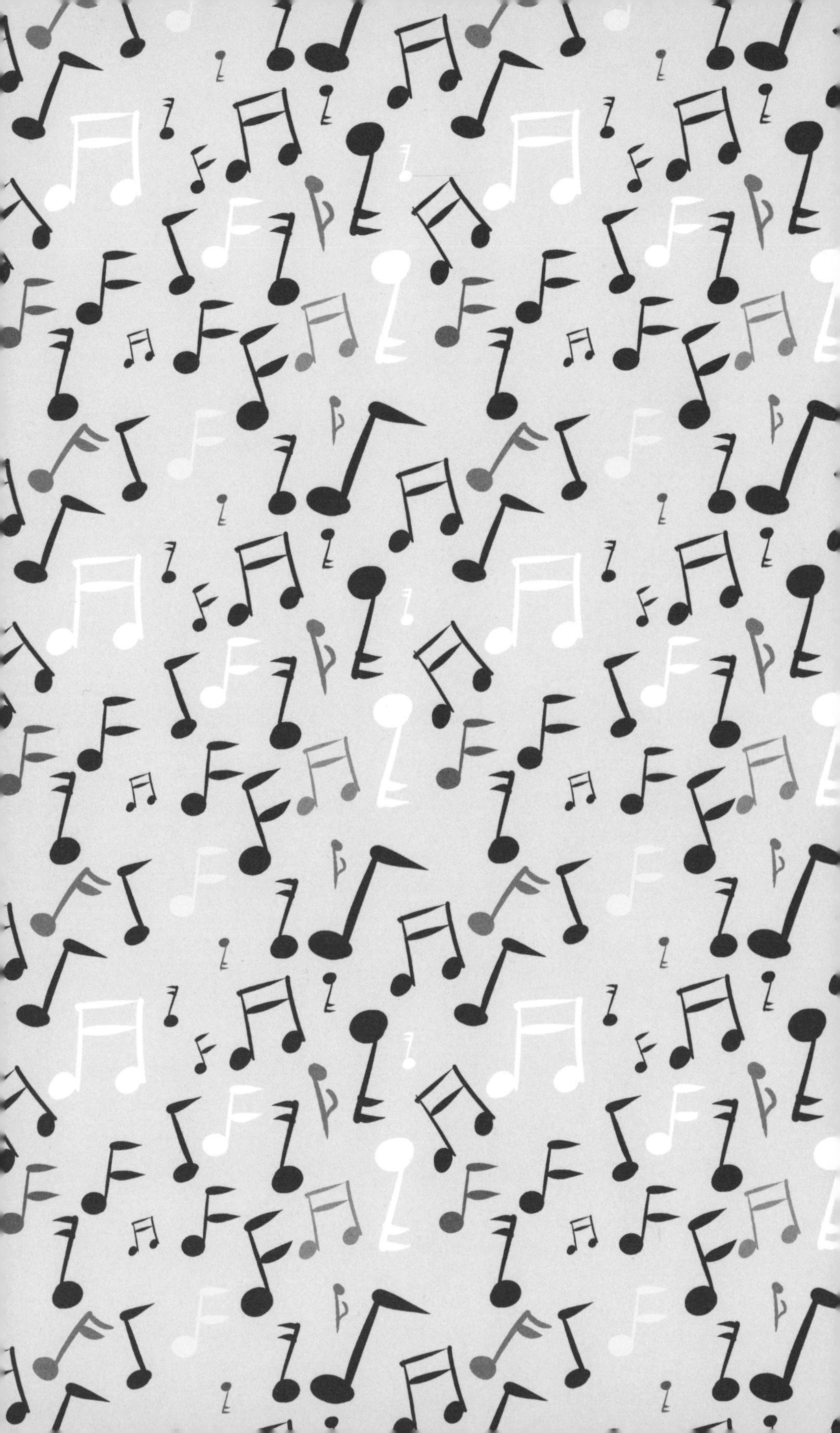

SHOWTIME AT THE APOLLO

PRAISE FOR THE ORIGINAL BOOK

"Mr. Fox has recaptured [the Apollo's] spirit."
—*New York Times*

"The essential book, mandatory for the most casual student
as well as the most ardent fan."
—**David Hinckley, *Daily News***

"The definitive history of Harlem's (and black America's) essential theater."
—*New York*

"*Showtime at the Apollo* is not only a history of that wonderful theater, but also a
fascinating insider's view of the Harlem music scene."
—**John Hammond**, legendary producer and talent scout who discovered Billie
Holiday, Aretha Franklin, and Bob Dylan, among many others

"I could almost feel and taste the Apollo again."
—**Doc Pomus**, Rock and Roll Hall of Fame inductee and classic
songwriter for musicians such as Elvis Presley

"A wonderful book."
—**Tavis Smiley**, PBS talk show host

"Ted Fox made the Apollo come alive for me again."
—**Jerry Wexler**, cofounder of Atlantic Records

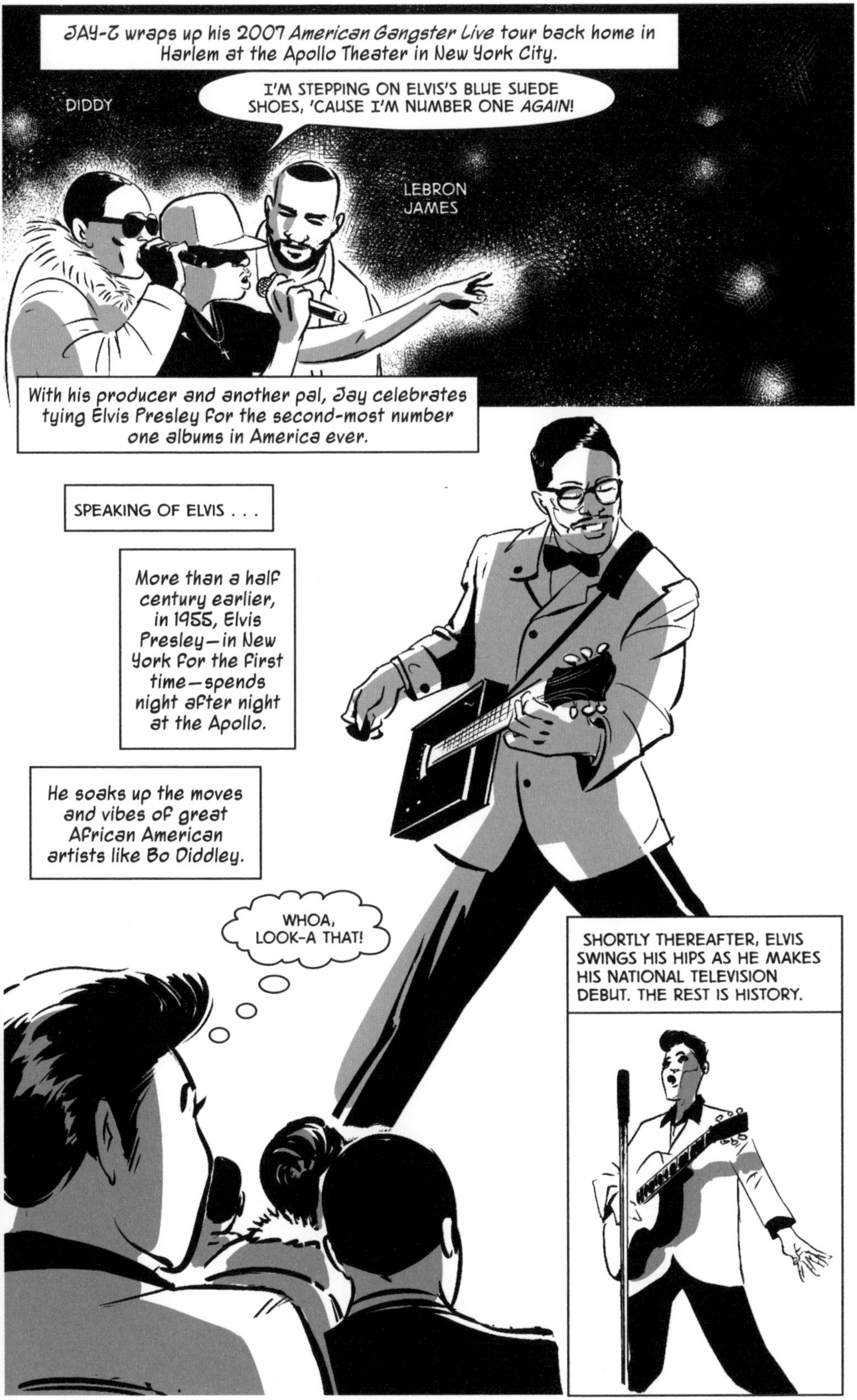
JAY-Z wraps up his 2007 American Gangster Live tour back home in Harlem at the Apollo Theater in New York City.
DIDDY
I'M STEPPING ON ELVIS'S BLUE SUEDE SHOES, 'CAUSE I'M NUMBER ONE AGAIN!
LEBRON JAMES
With his producer and another pal, Jay celebrates tying Elvis Presley for the second-most number one albums in America ever.
SPEAKING OF ELVIS . . .
More than a half century earlier, in 1955, Elvis Presley—in New York for the first time—spends night after night at the Apollo.
He soaks up the moves and vibes of great African American artists like Bo Diddley.
WHOA, LOOK-A THAT!
SHORTLY THEREAFTER, ELVIS SWINGS HIS HIPS AS HE MAKES HIS NATIONAL TELEVISION DEBUT. THE REST IS HISTORY.

CHRIS ROCK TAPES HIS HBO COMEDY SPECIAL *BIGGER AND BLACKER* AT THE APOLLO IN 1999.

PHARRELL WILLIAMS MAKES HIS APOLLO DEBUT IN JUNE 2014 AND JOINS THE THEATER'S BOARD OF DIRECTORS JUST FIVE MONTHS LATER!

APOLLO THEATER 03/09/12, A LIVE ALBUM BY BRUCE SPRINGSTEEN AND THE E STREET BAND, IS RELEASED IN 2014, AND IS THE FIRST ALBUM OFFICIALLY RELEASED THROUGH THE BRUCE SPRINGSTEEN ARCHIVES.

PAUL MCCARTNEY FINALLY GETS TO PLAY THE APOLLO ON DECEMBER 13, 2010, PERFORMING FOR A CELEBRITY-STUDDED AUDIENCE AT A LIVE SIRIUS XM RADIO BROADCAST.

I WANT TO TAKE A MOMENT . . . I JUST WANT TO JUST SOAK IN THE APOLLO . . .

THIS IS VERY SPECIAL FOR US BRITISH BOYS . . . THE HOLY GRAIL. I DREAMED OF PLAYING HERE FOR MANY A YEAR.

PAUL MCCARTNEY MAKES SURE TO TOUCH THE LEGENDARY TREE OF HOPE.

In fact, McCartney is checking off an item from his bucket list.

WHEN THE BEATLES FIRST FLY TO AMERICA IN FEBRUARY 1964, THEY PESTER NOTORIOUS PRODUCER PHIL SPECTOR TO TELL THEM ALL ABOUT THE APOLLO.

THE APOLLO IS THE FIRST PLACE WE WANT TO SEE WHEN WE GET TO AMERICA! *YEAH, YEAH, YEAH!*

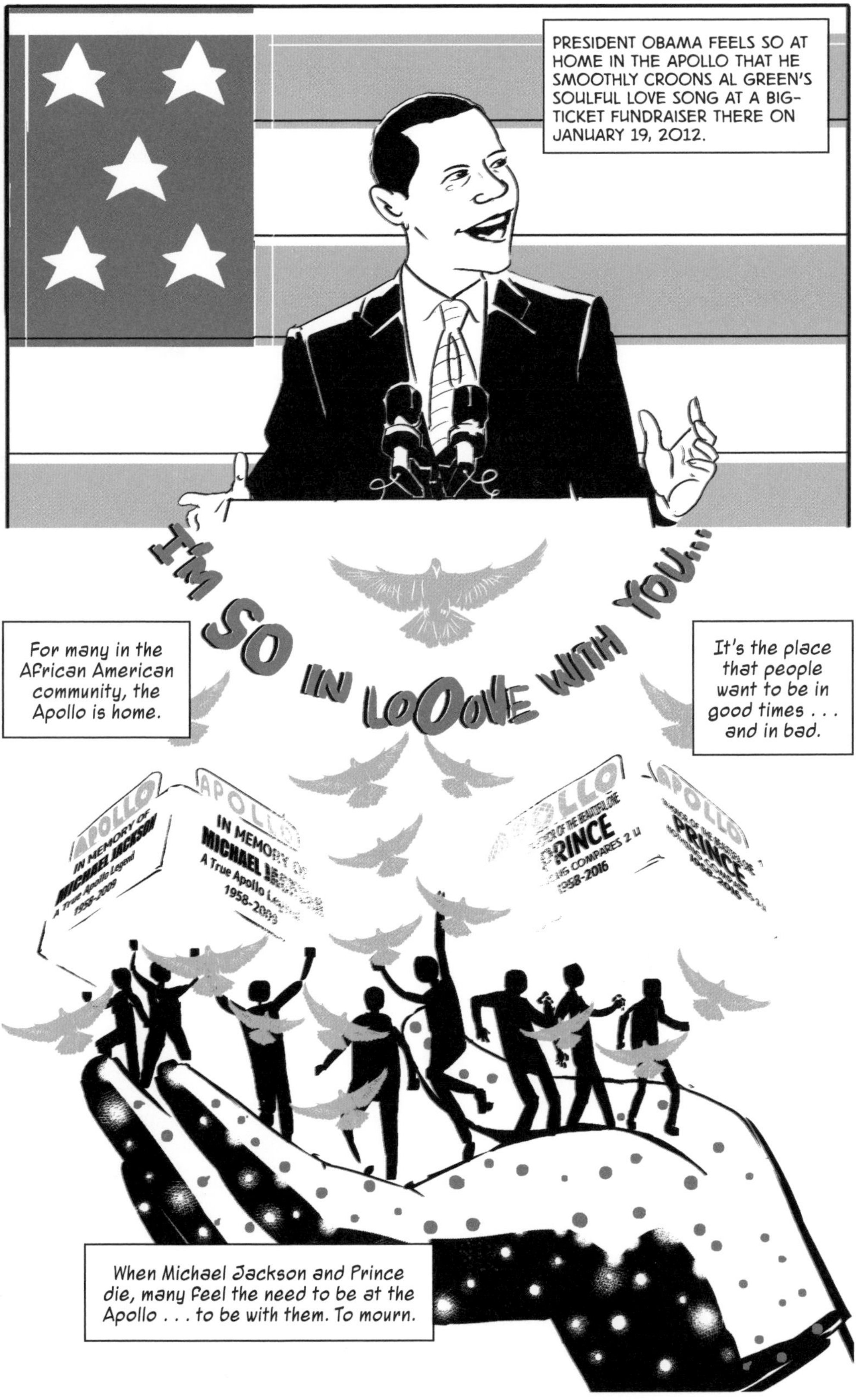
PRESIDENT OBAMA FEELS SO AT HOME IN THE APOLLO THAT HE SMOOTHLY CROONS AL GREEN'S SOULFUL LOVE SONG AT A BIG-TICKET FUNDRAISER THERE ON JANUARY 19, 2012.
I'M SO IN LOoOOVE WITH YOU...
For many in the African American community, the Apollo is home.
It's the place that people want to be in good times . . . and in bad.
APOLLO
IN MEMORY OF
MICHAEL JACKSON
A True Apollo Legend
1958-2009
PRINCE
1958-2016
When Michael Jackson and Prince die, many feel the need to be at the Apollo . . . to be with them. To mourn.

AND, FOR THE GODFATHER OF SOUL . . .

REST IN PEACE APOLLO LEGEND
THE GODFATHER OF SOUL
JAMES BROWN
1933–2006

"SOUL POWER!"

JAMES BROWN'S TWENTY-FOUR-CARAT GOLD COFFIN COMING HOME TO THE APOLLO

"SAY IT LOUD! I'M BLACK AND I'M PROUD!"

THE REVEREND AL SHARPTON, ONCE JAMES BROWN'S ROAD MANAGER AND SPIRITUAL ADVISOR, STANDS BY THE CASKET OF HIS GREAT FRIEND.

Brown's first funeral service is held at the Apollo on December 28, 2006, officiated by Reverend Sharpton.

BUT WHY HERE? WHY THE APOLLO?

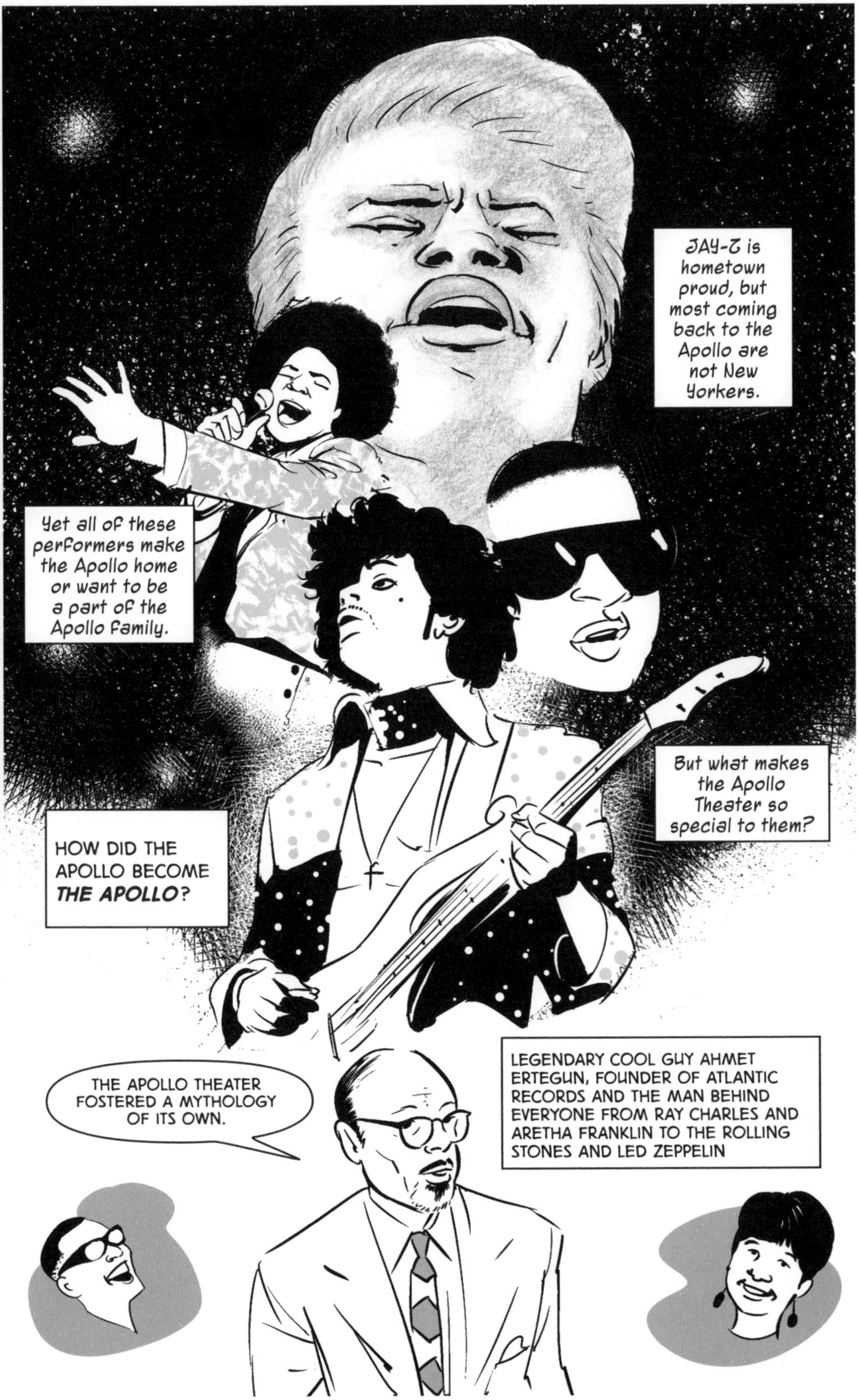
JAY-Z is hometown proud, but most coming back to the Apollo are not New Yorkers.
Yet all of these performers make the Apollo home or want to be a part of the Apollo family.
But what makes the Apollo Theater so special to them?
HOW DID THE APOLLO BECOME ***THE APOLLO***?
THE APOLLO THEATER FOSTERED A MYTHOLOGY OF ITS OWN.
LEGENDARY COOL GUY AHMET ERTEGUN, FOUNDER OF ATLANTIC RECORDS AND THE MAN BEHIND EVERYONE FROM RAY CHARLES AND ARETHA FRANKLIN TO THE ROLLING STONES AND LED ZEPPELIN

It is an epic tale.

A story of struggle and triumph, pathos and glee, spanning generations and many changes in society, culture, and style.

A tale made by and told by characters both heroic and quite ordinary.

A story of creativity, expression, hard work, and fun, triumphing again and again in the face of adversity and injustice . . .

And, ironically, it is the story of how that spells doom for the little theater . . .

. . . only to bring it to a celebratory comeback and rebirth.

The truth of the Apollo's great history is the stuff of which myths are made.

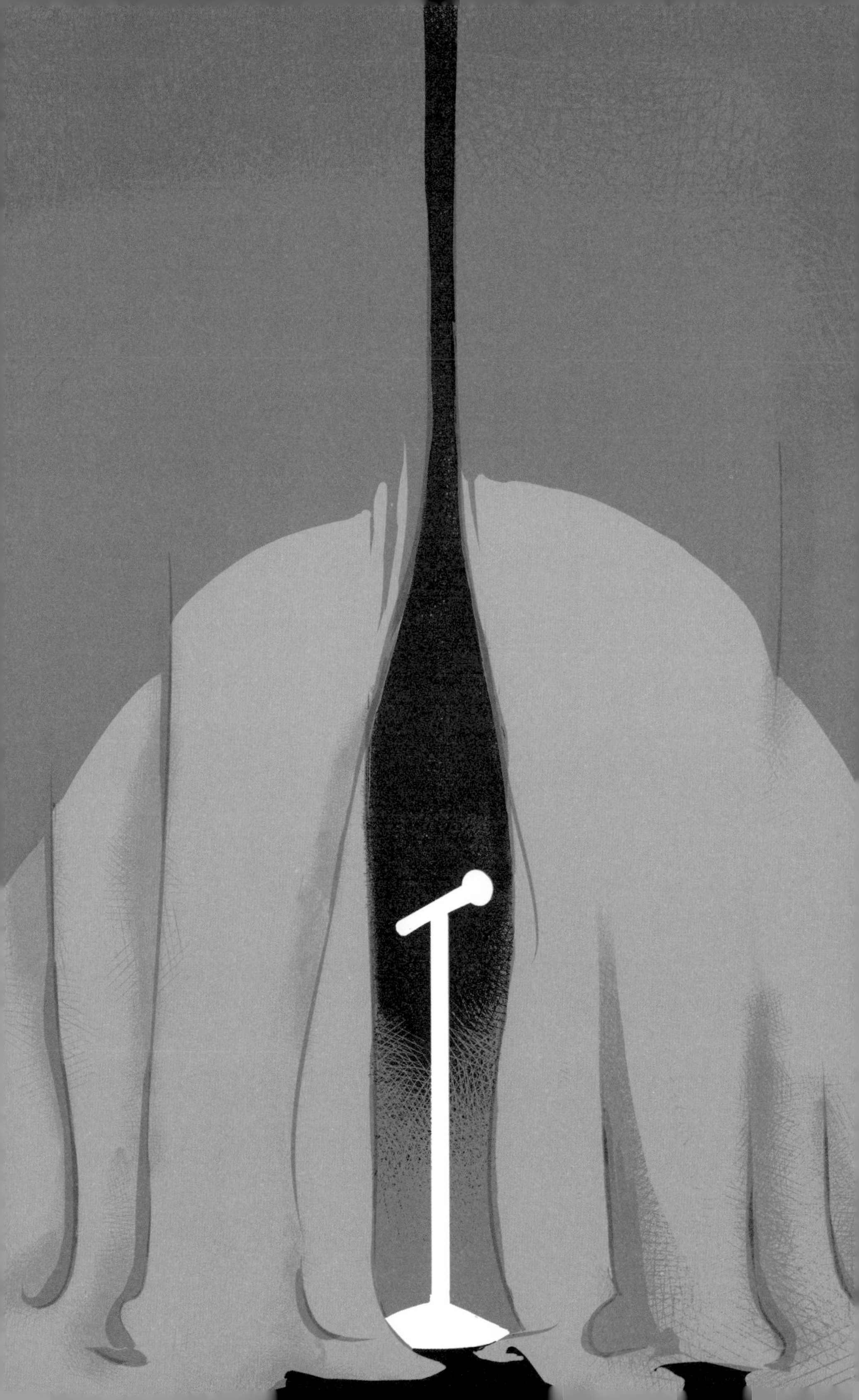

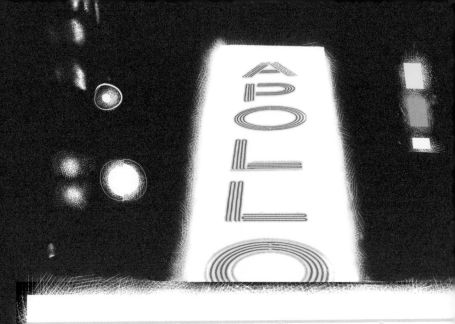

SHOWTIME AT

THE EPIC TALE OF HARLE

BY TED FOX ILLUST

THE APOLLO

LEGENDARY THEATER

ED BY JAMES OTIS SMITH

Abrams ComicArts   New York

To the women and men who lived the Apollo story and made it happen. —T.F.

To my mother. Thanks for all the music. —J.O.S.

ACKNOWLEDGMENTS

This book would not exist without the recollections and insights of the many participants in the Apollo story I have interviewed over the years, detailed in A Note on Sources and Methods.

Thank you, Jonelle Procope, and everyone at the Apollo Theater Foundation for your dedication and vision.

I'd like to thank James Otis Smith for his prodigious efforts to beautifully depict this epic tale. Thank you for bringing to life the scenes and images that heretofore only lived in my mind.

My representatives, Joan Hilty and Pete Friedrich of Pageturner, worked relentlessly to make this book a reality: They schooled me about the world of graphic novels, made the deal happen, coached me in my efforts to create the manuscript, pitched in when work needed to be done, interfaced on every aspect of its development, and rode herd on the entire process from beginning to end. You are the best.

To Charlie Kochman, editorial director at Abrams ComicArts (a.k.a. The Hardest Working Man in Publishing), thank you for your understanding, enthusiasm, and passion, your unflagging hard work on every aspect of this project, your attention to detail, your great ideas for improving the book—and for always doing what you said you'd do. Also at Abrams, managing editor Amy Vreeland did a magnificent, thorough job copyediting the manuscript, and art director Siobhán Gallagher's work yielded such a beautiful design. Thank you.

I give great thanks, and all my love, to my wife, Ann Derry. In addition to patiently serving as my consiglieri and counselor for all aspects of this project, she reviewed, edited, and talked me through every word and made this book immeasurably better in the process.

Thanks to my daughter, O. K. Fox, for hipping me to the world of graphic novels and comics. You are responsible for planting the seed that became this work. Thanks also, my dear, for introducing me to our mutual Purchase College alum Dean Haspiel at Zinefeast Vol. 1, which you founded at Purchase in 2013. In the world of comics and graphic novels, Dino is the man. He is the connection behind so much and between so many—and he still manages to create tremendous amounts of his own remarkable work when he isn't helping good people make good things happen. Thanks, Dino, for introducing me to Joan and Pete and James, and for being my guru whenever I have needed one.
—Ted Fox

Special thanks to Cav and Dino for getting things done.
—James Otis Smith

Editor: Charles Kochman

Book Production: Pageturner. Producer: Pete Friedrich.

Art assist: Mike Cavallaro, Nick Bertozzi, Gabrielle Gomez, Victoria Lau, and Stephen Gullo. Color assist: Frank Reynoso, Victoria Lau, Sally Han

Designer: Siobhán Gallagher

Managing Editor: Amy Vreeland

Production Manager: Erin Vanderveer

Cataloging-in-Publication Data has been applied for and may be obtained from the Library of Congress.

ISBN 978-1-4197-3138-9

Copyright © 2018 Ted Fox

Text by Ted Fox; illustrated by James Otis Smith

Adapted from *Showtime at the Apollo: The Story of Harlem's World Famous Theater* by Ted Fox, published by Holt, Rinehart, and Winston in 1983; Da Capo Press in 1993; and Mill Road Enterprises in 2003.

Published in 2018 by Abrams ComicArts®, an imprint of ABRAMS.

All rights reserved. No portion of this book may be reproduced, stored in a retrieval system, or transmitted in any form or by any means, mechanical, electronic, photocopying, recording, or otherwise, without written permission from the publisher.

Printed and bound in China

10 9 8 7 6 5 4 3 2 1

Abrams ComicArts books are available at special discounts when purchased in quantity for premiums and promotions as well as fundraising or educational use. Special editions can also be created to specification. For details, contact specialsales@abramsbooks.com or the address below.

Abrams ComicArts® is a registered trademark of Harry N. Abrams, Inc.

ABRAMS The Art of Books
195 Broadway, New York, NY 10007
abramsbooks.com

The Apollo Theater is located at 253 West 125th Street, New York, NY, 10027

For tickets and to learn more about the Apollo, its upcoming events, broadcasts, livestreams, podcasts, and more, visit apollotheater.org

CONTENTS

PREFACE

People all over the world know the Apollo Theater. It's a legend. A mythical place. Busloads of visitors from around the world descend on the theater in New York City's Harlem, perhaps to take a tour or to experience for themselves the wild Wednesday Amateur Night shows they have seen on television. Apollo lore piques their curiosity, yet the story of how and why the theater became this fabled showplace is a tale that remains to be discovered.

Some of the Apollo's great African American artists, who were the bedrock of so much of the vital music and entertainment that we enjoy today, are unknown to new generations. Those men and women were the greatest stars in the black community at a time when it was difficult or impossible to "cross over" to white audiences. Any contemporary superstar would acknowledge the influence of these performers and hail them as the pioneers of the "urban" sound and look that dominates today's popular culture.

This ultimate cultural triumph did not come easily. It took decades. There was great fun, excitement, and joy along the way. But it was a struggle, too—and the Apollo Theater was a leader. That story—that epic tale—is essential to understanding our popular culture. Yet I believe it is a remarkably undertold and underacknowledged story. The Apollo has been in my life since I began to conceive what would become my book, *Showtime at the Apollo: The Story of Harlem's World Famous Theater*, originally published in 1983. That book remains the only full-scale history of Harlem's legendary showplace, and I'm honored that it has been called the definitive book on the Apollo. Now, in this graphic novel, through focused storytelling and James Otis Smith's amazing artwork, we can bring the tale to life in a whole new way.

As the Apollo marks its 85th anniversary in 2019, it is thriving—bursting with music, theater, and dance. It looks marvelous—an appropriate state for this iconic American cultural institution—thanks to substantial investments in renovations and upgrades. It is both a triumph and a challenge for the Apollo as it figures out how to keep its doors open in a fast-gentrifying neighborhood, while serving what is still the heart and soul of New York's African American community.

Entertainers—both black and white—now routinely sell out glittering arenas that seat tens of thousands and feature the latest in technology. Concert tickets cost hundreds of dollars. Spectacle is as important as substance in these rigorously choreographed stage shows. But behind much of today's extravaganza is the grit, imagination, creativity, innovation, and hard-earned soulfulness that the funky little theater on 125th Street gave the world. And the top stars and celebrities who still long to come back to the Apollo—from JAY-Z to Bruce Springsteen to President Obama to Paul McCartney—know it.

Working the Apollo, as readers will see, could be terribly difficult back in the day. An Apollo engagement meant doing thirty-one shows a week in its classic era, and some called the theater "the workhouse" or "the penitentiary." The atmosphere was sometimes threatening. Dressing room hustles and rip-offs were common. The physical condition of the struggling theater was often atrocious. By today's standards, no one was getting rich. In the earliest days, you could purchase a ticket for as little as a dime—and you could stay all day. Even in the mid-1970s, tickets topped out at six bucks.

Yet performers always looked forward to playing the Apollo—to them it was home.

It was home, too, for the people of Harlem, where a night out at the Apollo was something special. The Apollo was an indispensable part of the community. The theater's mainly African American audience sat at the center of the greatest city in the world, in the middle of the most important black neighborhood in the country, right on Harlem's main street, in the top black theater of all time. There they were at ease and invincible—even when it may have been difficult for them to feel that way in the wider world.

As the civil rights movement began to alter the nation's consciousness in the 1950s and '60s, other areas of opportunity became available to African American performers. The racist, segregated system the Apollo was forced to work within for so many years—and actively fought against—began to collapse, at least in part because of the Apollo's tenacity and its inspiring creative innovations. The eager and far-reaching acceptance of black culture as a cornerstone of the world's popular culture was the beginning of something brand-new then, if not now. There was triumph in that, but tragedy, too, capped by a stunning rebirth for the little theater that had done so much to make that happen.

This is that story.

Ted Fox

New York City

March 2018

A Quest

Today, the Apollo is celebrated and honored. But that wasn't always so.

YOUR AUTHOR, AGE TWENTY-FIVE, BACK IN THE DAY—MARCH 1980.

IT IS A BLEAK TIME IN NEW YORK CITY, BUT THE BEGINNING OF A QUEST FOR ME.

NEGLECTED BY THE CITY FOR YEARS, HARLEM IS STILL STRUGGLING TO RECOVER FROM THE HORRIBLE RIOTS AFTER THE BLACKOUT OF JULY 1977.

Exit 125 Street

THE CITY IS BROKE. CRIME IS RAMPANT. DRUGS ARE A SCOURGE.

HARLEM IS STRUGGLING.

THE APOLLO HAD BEEN SHUTTERED BY ITS OWNER, **BOBBY SCHIFFMAN**, IN 1976, AND SAT EMPTY AND NEGLECTED FOR YEARS.

BOBBY'S FAMILY HAD RUN THE APOLLO SINCE 1935, A YEAR AFTER ITS OPENING.

APOLLO
PARLIAMENT FUNKADELIC

THIS IS THE LATEST SPUTTERING ATTEMPT TO REVIVE THE DETERIORATING VENUE. THE THEATER SEEMS ON ITS LAST LEGS.

I KNOW THAT GUY.

BOBBY KNOWS EVERYBODY.

BOBBY GOLFS WITH **MARVIN GAYE**

BOBBY HUNTS WITH **REDD FOXX**

BOBBY HANGS OUT WITH **GLADYS KNIGHT**

BOBBY SCHIFFMAN IS A RIOT— A FABULOUS RACONTEUR WHO LOVES TELLING STORIES OF HIS TIME AT THE APOLLO. AND I LOVE HEARING HIS STORIES.

HE HOOKS ME.

BOBBY, I WANT TO WRITE A BOOK ABOUT THE APOLLO.

HMM, THIS LITTLE PISHER?

Still, he gives me his blessing and agrees to sit for extensive interviews.

He has one caveat:

WRITE ABOUT THE WAY THE APOLLO REALLY WAS, THE **GOOD** AND THE **BAD**.

Little of it seemed to have any value at the time.

!SOUL!

BOBBY AND HIS FAMILY KEPT SOME FILES AND OTHER MATERIALS, BUT WHEN THE APOLLO CLOSED IN 1976, PILES OF HISTORICAL PHOTOS, POSTERS, HANDBILLS, AND OTHER EPHEMERA WERE TOSSED OUT.

No one thought this material would matter.

I WANT TO KNOW MORE ABOUT THE APOLLO.

HI, I'M WRITING A BOOK ABOUT THE APOLLO THEATER.

I'D LIKE TO TALK TO SOMEONE ABOUT IT.

WHY, I CAN TELL YOU EVERYTHING YOU WANT TO KNOW ABOUT THE APOLLO!

Francis "Doll" Thomas, locally known as *"Mr. Apollo,"* is literally living in the nearly abandoned theater, in a rambling, loftlike apartment right over the lobby!

He worked in the Harlem showbiz scene for forty years before I was even born.

THE STORIES BEGIN.

Stories of good times . . .

I barely have to ask any questions.

They just spill out of Doll like a miraculously flowing fountain of knowledge . . .

3

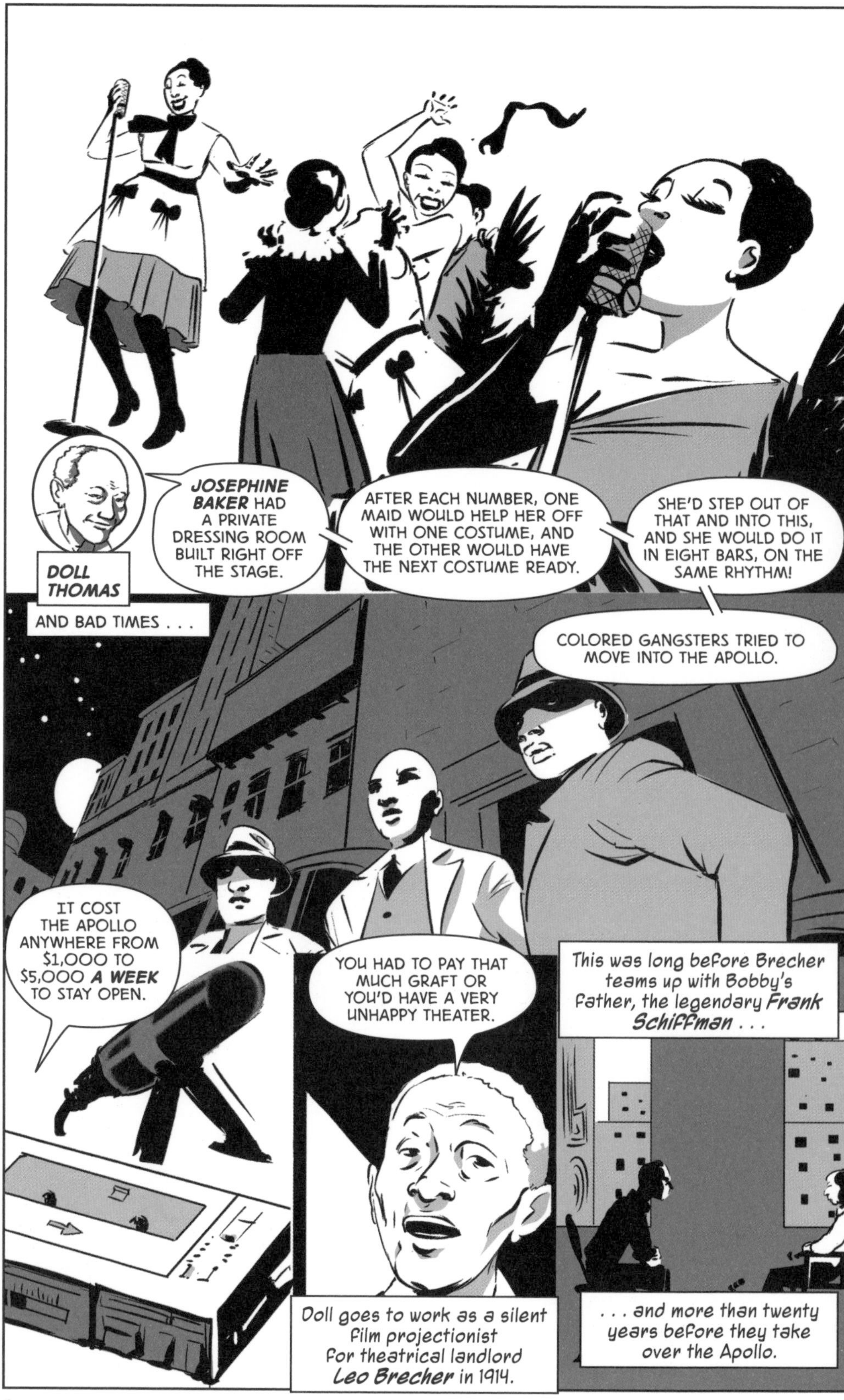

DOLL THOMAS
JOSEPHINE BAKER HAD A PRIVATE DRESSING ROOM BUILT RIGHT OFF THE STAGE.
AFTER EACH NUMBER, ONE MAID WOULD HELP HER OFF WITH ONE COSTUME, AND THE OTHER WOULD HAVE THE NEXT COSTUME READY.
SHE'D STEP OUT OF THAT AND INTO THIS, AND SHE WOULD DO IT IN EIGHT BARS, ON THE SAME RHYTHM!
AND BAD TIMES . . .
COLORED GANGSTERS TRIED TO MOVE INTO THE APOLLO.
IT COST THE APOLLO ANYWHERE FROM $1,000 TO $5,000 A WEEK TO STAY OPEN.
YOU HAD TO PAY THAT MUCH GRAFT OR YOU'D HAVE A VERY UNHAPPY THEATER.
Doll goes to work as a silent film projectionist for theatrical landlord Leo Brecher in 1914.
This was long before Brecher teams up with Bobby's father, the legendary Frank Schiffman . . .
. . . and more than twenty years before they take over the Apollo.

WHOA!

Doll has truly seen it all.

I start tracking down well-known artists who played the Apollo.

I can get five "contacts" for free if I sign up for a trial offer at an outfit called Celebrity Service.

That's how I learn *Dionne Warwick* has an apartment in the *Waldorf Towers* in New York City.

In those more trusting days, the switchboard puts me right through to her.

WHEN I TELL HER I'M WRITING A BOOK ON THE APOLLO, SHE SCREAMS SO LOUD I HAVE TO HOLD THE PHONE AWAY FROM MY EAR!

MAY I HAVE DIONNE WARWICK, PLEASE?

WHAAAT?!

She picks up herself!

I'VE BEEN WAITING MY WHOLE LIFE FOR SOMEONE TO TELL THAT STORY!

WHAT ARE YOU DOING RIGHT NOW?

THAT VERY AFTERNOON I SPEND THREE HOURS WITH DIONNE IN HER SUITE AS SHE TALKS AND TALKS AND TALKS ABOUT WHAT IT MEANS TO PERFORM AT THE APOLLO AND BE A PART OF ITS FAMILY . . .

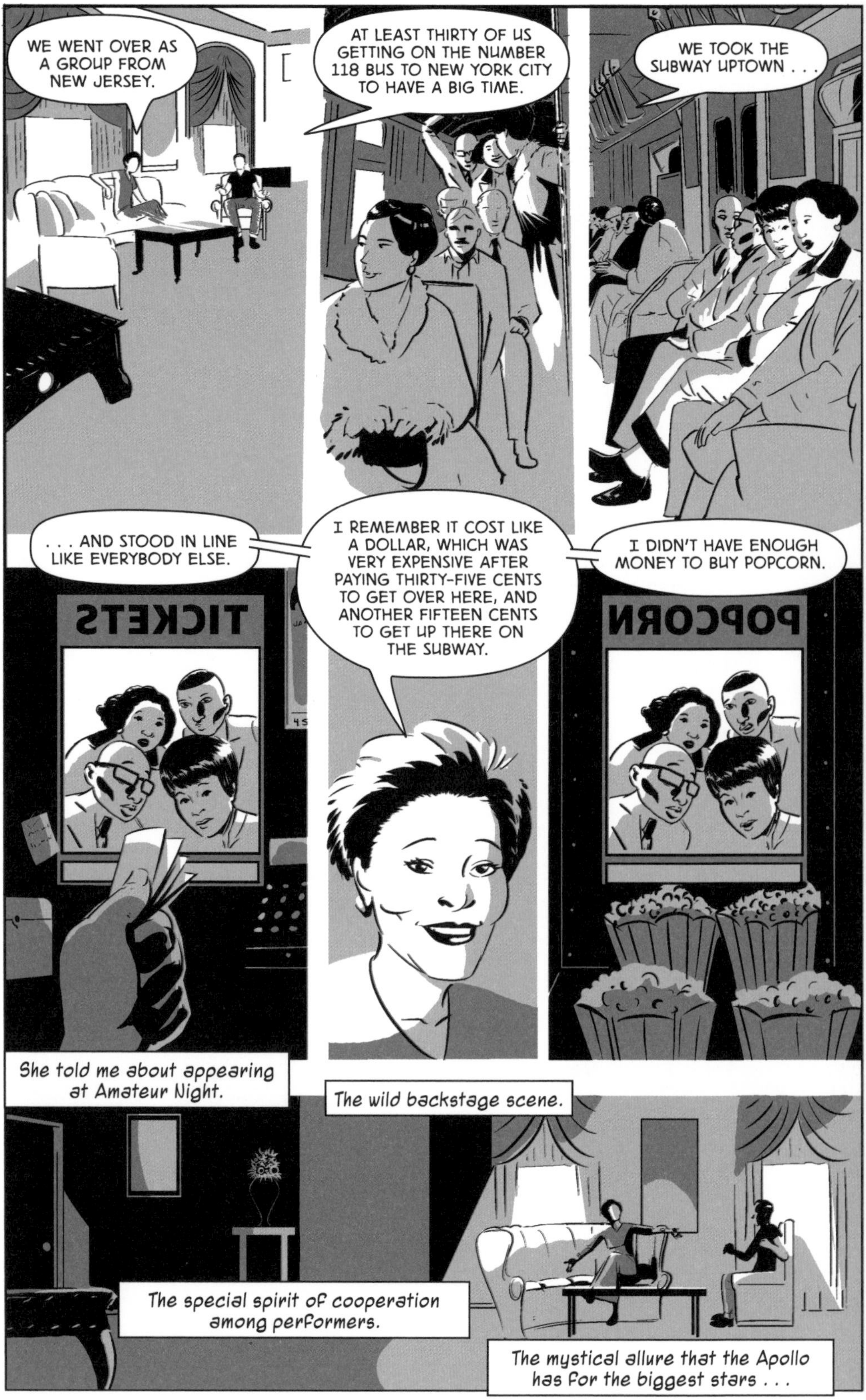
WE WENT OVER AS A GROUP FROM NEW JERSEY.
AT LEAST THIRTY OF US GETTING ON THE NUMBER 118 BUS TO NEW YORK CITY TO HAVE A BIG TIME.
WE TOOK THE SUBWAY UPTOWN . . .
. . . AND STOOD IN LINE LIKE EVERYBODY ELSE.
I REMEMBER IT COST LIKE A DOLLAR, WHICH WAS VERY EXPENSIVE AFTER PAYING THIRTY-FIVE CENTS TO GET OVER HERE, AND ANOTHER FIFTEEN CENTS TO GET UP THERE ON THE SUBWAY.
I DIDN'T HAVE ENOUGH MONEY TO BUY POPCORN.
TICKETS
POPCORN
She told me about appearing at Amateur Night.
The wild backstage scene.
The special spirit of cooperation among performers.
The mystical allure that the Apollo has for the biggest stars . . .

I COME OUT OF THE SCEPTER RECORDS OFFICE ON THE CORNER OF 54TH AND BROADWAY.

THERE'S A GUY WITH A T-SHIRT AND A PAIR OF JEANS AND A LEATHER JACKET AND SUPER-BLUE EYES.

IT'S *TOM JONES*.

WHERE ARE YOU GOING?

I'M GOING TO THE APOLLO.

CAN I—I—I— GO WITH YOU?!

OF COURSE!

THAT NIGHT, TOM JONES SANG AT THE APOLLO.

I THINK THAT WAS THE BEGINNING OF HIS CAREER.

HE KILLED THE AUDIENCE. IT WAS WONDERFUL.

HE SAID IN HIS ENTIRE LIFE, HE'D NEVER FELT ANYTHING LIKE THAT BEFORE.

HAVE YOU TALKED TO *SAMMY* YET?

I KNOW EXACTLY WHO SHE IS TALKING ABOUT.

UM, SAMMY DAVIS JR.?

I haven't talked to any other entertainers yet, and *Sammy Davis Jr.* is one of the biggest stars in the world at that time. But I don't even know if I can do this book yet. I have no deal. No agent. I haven't written a word.

NO. NO, I SURE HAVEN'T TALKED TO SAMMY YET.

WHY, HE'S AT THE *PLAZA*. I'M GOING TO CALL HIM RIGHT NOW!

WHAAAT?!

SAMMY, IT'S DIONNE. I'VE GOT THIS YOUNG GUY HERE, AND HE'S WRITING A BOOK ABOUT THE APOLLO THEATER . . .

THE VERY NEXT DAY IN **HIS** SUITE AT THE PLAZA HOTEL . . .

FOR HOURS, SAMMY DAVIS JR. REGALES ME WITH STORIES OF PLAYING THE APOLLO IN THE '40S WITH HIS FATHER AND UNCLE IN THE **WILL MASTIN TRIO** . . .

. . . TELLS ME HOW MUCH PRIDE HE FELT WALKING TO WORK FROM HIS FAMILY'S NEARBY APARTMENT . . .

. . . HOW DIFFERENT IT WAS PLAYING A TOUGH CROWD AT A BIG-TIME GANGSTER-RUN JOINT LIKE THE **COPACABANA** VERSUS THE APOLLO'S LEGENDARY **"WORLD'S TOUGHEST AUDIENCE . . ."**

BUT AT THE APOLLO, THEY'D BREAK YOUR **HEART**.

YOU DIDN'T GO INTO THE COPA LIGHTWEIGHT— THEY'D BREAK YOUR LEGS.

Sammy even shows me dance steps, sings, and kills me with impressions of Hollywood greats.

HAVE YOU TALKED TO **LIONEL HAMPTON** YET?

8

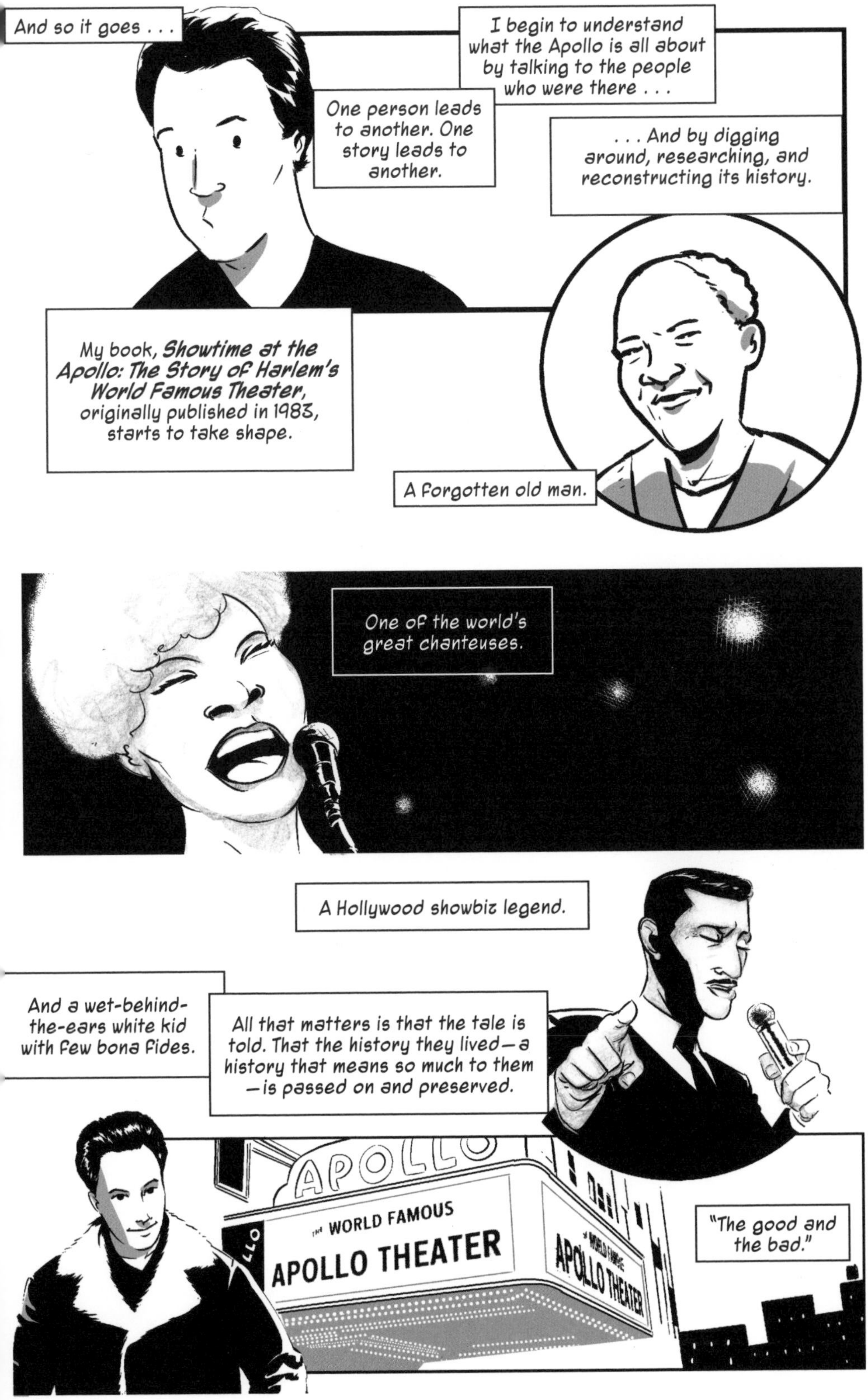
And so it goes . . .
I begin to understand what the Apollo is all about by talking to the people who were there . . .
One person leads to another. One story leads to another.
. . . And by digging around, researching, and reconstructing its history.
My book, *Showtime at the Apollo: The Story of Harlem's World Famous Theater*, originally published in 1983, starts to take shape.
A forgotten old man.
One of the world's great chanteuses.
A Hollywood showbiz legend.
And a wet-behind-the-ears white kid with few bona fides.
All that matters is that the tale is told. That the history they lived—a history that means so much to them—is passed on and preserved.
APOLLO
THE WORLD FAMOUS
APOLLO THEATER
"The good and the bad."

CHAPTER 1

The Apollo: Home

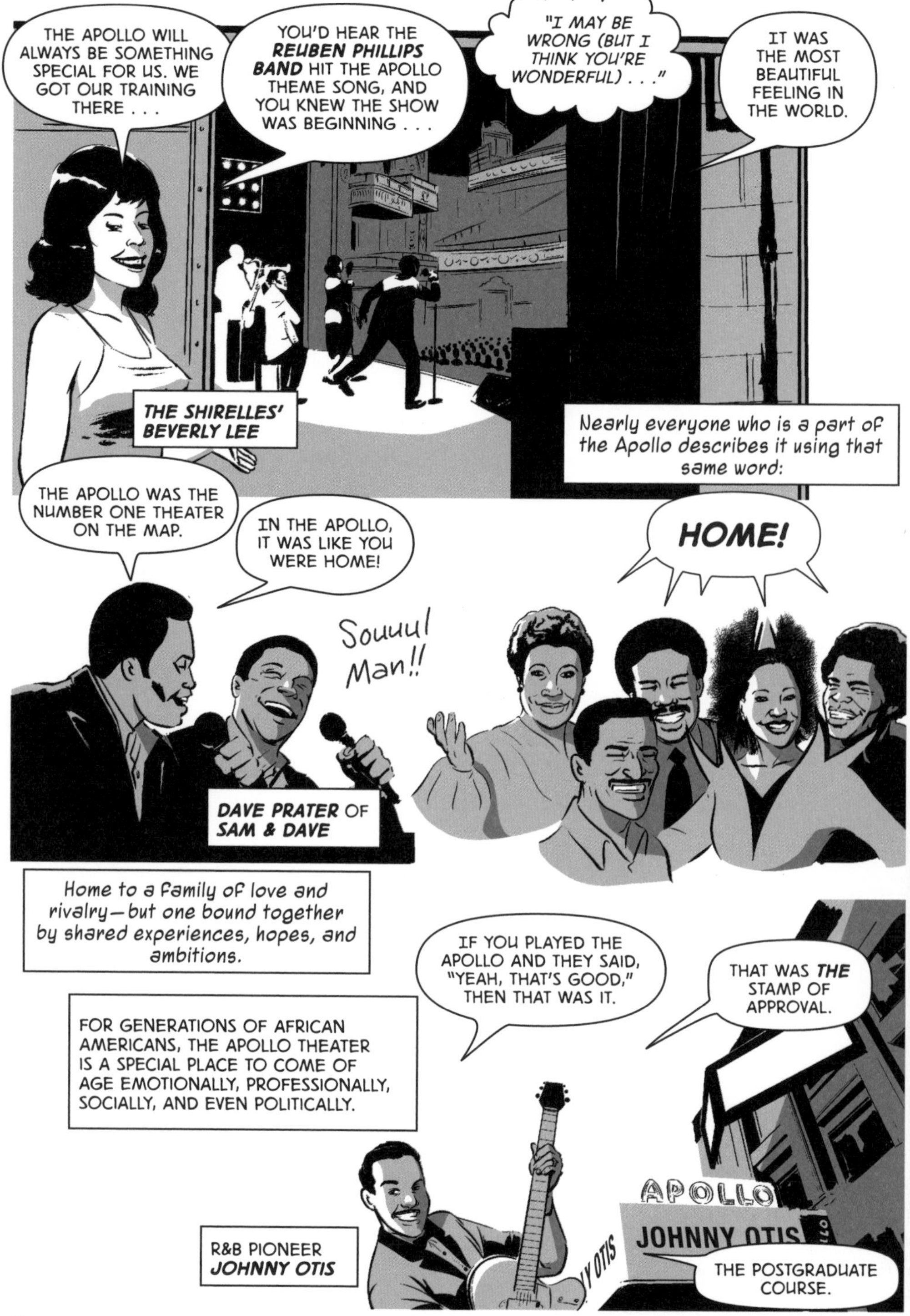

THE APOLLO WILL ALWAYS BE SOMETHING SPECIAL FOR US. WE GOT OUR TRAINING THERE . . .
YOU'D HEAR THE **REUBEN PHILLIPS BAND** HIT THE APOLLO THEME SONG, AND YOU KNEW THE SHOW WAS BEGINNING . . .
"I MAY BE WRONG (BUT I THINK YOU'RE WONDERFUL) . . ."
IT WAS THE MOST BEAUTIFUL FEELING IN THE WORLD.
THE SHIRELLES' BEVERLY LEE
Nearly everyone who is a part of the Apollo describes it using that same word:
THE APOLLO WAS THE NUMBER ONE THEATER ON THE MAP.
IN THE APOLLO, IT WAS LIKE YOU WERE HOME!
Souuul Man!!
DAVE PRATER OF **SAM & DAVE**
HOME!
Home to a family of love and rivalry—but one bound together by shared experiences, hopes, and ambitions.
FOR GENERATIONS OF AFRICAN AMERICANS, THE APOLLO THEATER IS A SPECIAL PLACE TO COME OF AGE EMOTIONALLY, PROFESSIONALLY, SOCIALLY, AND EVEN POLITICALLY.
IF YOU PLAYED THE APOLLO AND THEY SAID, "YEAH, THAT'S GOOD," THEN THAT WAS IT.
THAT WAS **THE** STAMP OF APPROVAL.
APOLLO
JOHNNY OTIS
R&B PIONEER **JOHNNY OTIS**
THE POSTGRADUATE COURSE.

WE SERVE WHITES only

It is also a refuge from the indignities and difficulties of working—of being—black in Jim Crow America.

THE APOLLO WAS THE APEX OF BLACK ENTERTAINMENT.

In the theater, one can be at ease and just be oneself among the Apollo family and within one's community.

IF YOU'RE A BLACK ENTERTAINER IN CHARLOTTE OR MISSISSIPPI, YOU HAVE GREAT CONSTRAINTS PUT UPON YOU . . .

. . . BUT COMING TO HARLEM AND THE APOLLO WAS AN EXPRESSION OF THE BLACK SPIRIT IN AMERICA. IT WAS A HAVEN.

THE APOLLO THEATER STOOD FOR THE GREATEST—THE CASTLE THAT YOU REACH WHEN YOU FINALLY MAKE IT.

AHMET ERTEGUN

11

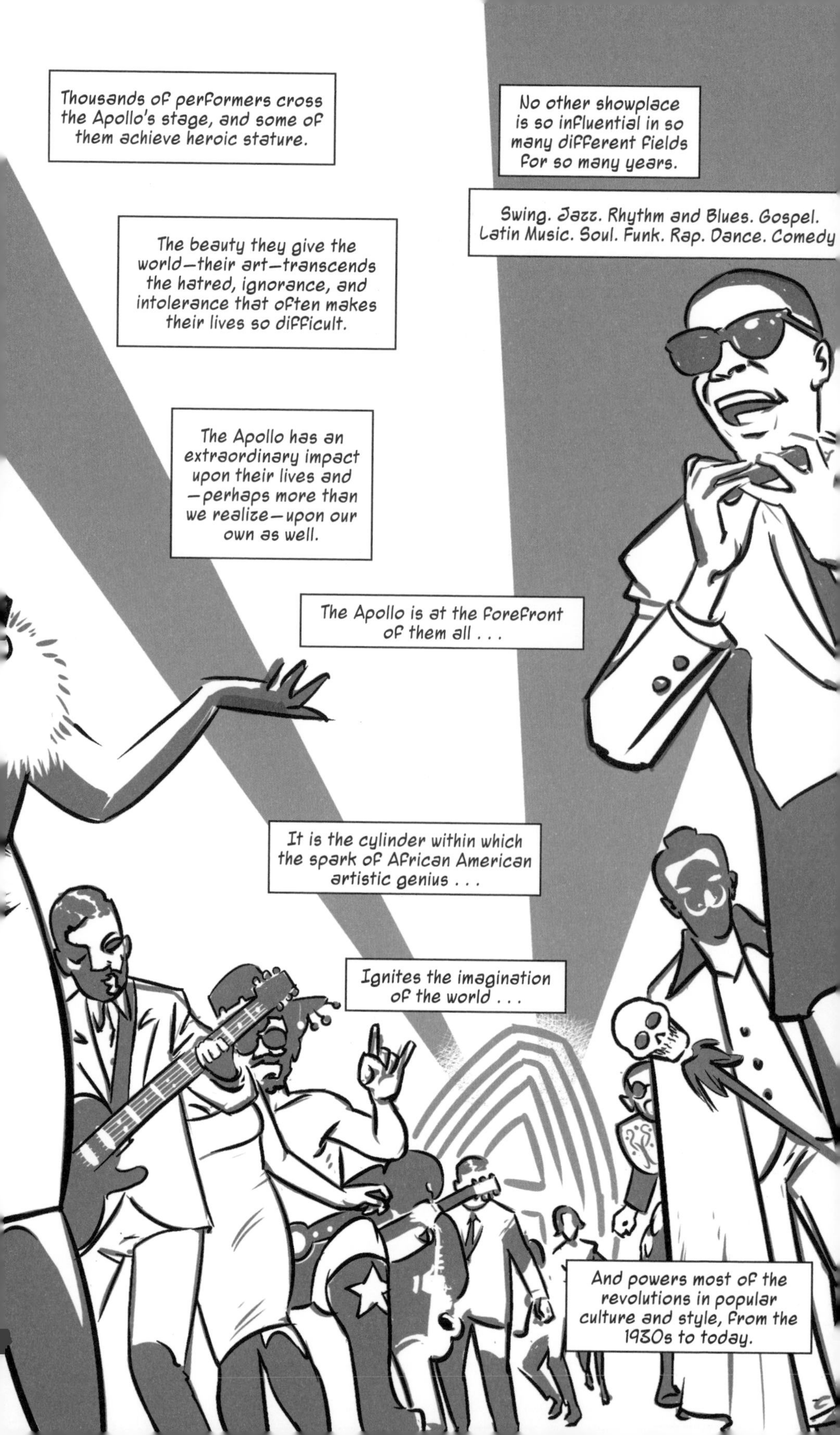
Thousands of performers cross the Apollo's stage, and some of them achieve heroic stature.
The beauty they give the world—their art—transcends the hatred, ignorance, and intolerance that often makes their lives so difficult.
The Apollo has an extraordinary impact upon their lives and—perhaps more than we realize—upon our own as well.
No other showplace is so influential in so many different fields for so many years.
Swing. Jazz. Rhythm and Blues. Gospel. Latin Music. Soul. Funk. Rap. Dance. Comedy
The Apollo is at the forefront of them all . . .
It is the cylinder within which the spark of African American artistic genius . . .
Ignites the imagination of the world . . .
And powers most of the revolutions in popular culture and style, from the 1930s to today.

THIS **HOME** HAS THIRTEEN DRESSING ROOMS ON FOUR FLOORS.

Within their tacky, cold, painted cement walls beats the heart of the Apollo Theater.

HERE **LOUIS ARMSTRONG** ENTERTAINS GUESTS AND WELL-WISHERS IN HIS UNDERWEAR.

JAMES BROWN HOLDS COURT.

ELLA FITZGERALD SETS OUT HER USUAL SPREAD.

ADVICE IS GIVEN AND LESSONS LEARNED. DEALS ARE MADE. SONGS, DANCE STEPS, AND COMEDY BITS ARE CREATED.

JEROME "LITTLE ANTHONY" GOURDINE OF LITTLE ANTHONY AND THE IMPERIALS

I DON'T CARE HOW BIG YOU THOUGHT YOU WERE, WHEN YOU FIRST CAME IN THE APOLLO, YOU WERE **NOBODY**.

IT DIDN'T MATTER IF YOU HAD NINE HIT RECORDS, YOU STAYED IN THE TOP DRESSING ROOM ON THE FOURTH FLOOR.

"ANTHONY! YOU'RE ON!"

There, performers can also measure their progress and their status.

HAD TO WALK ALL THE WAY DOWNSTAIRS.

REDD FOXX

R&B LEGEND **RUTH BROWN**

Once performers prove themselves, they are moved downstairs. And, if lucky, ultimately to the bright red star's dressing room on the first level off the stage.

THE APOLLO WAS SO WELL LOVED THAT EVEN THE PERFORMERS WHO WERE NOT WORKING USED TO SPEND A LOT OF TIME THERE.

THEY WOULD GET DRESSED UP, COME BACKSTAGE, AND SPEND THE DAY.

BACKSTAGE YOU'D FIND A CELEBRITY JUST SITTING IN THE WINGS WATCHING THE SHOW . . .

MUHAMMAD ALI

SUGAR RAY ROBINSON

One of the main roots of the Harlem grapevine is anchored in the Apollo. It's an excellent place to catch up on the latest showbiz gossip or hot Harlem news.

COMEDIAN/ACTOR **SCOEY MITCHELL**

I'M SURE A LOT OF WHITE PERFORMERS WANTED TO KNOW WHAT IT WAS THAT WAS SO SPECIAL ABOUT THIS PLACE.

IT WAS A COMING TOGETHER, A **COMMUNITY** O WHAT WE ALL HAD THERE.

THE APOLLO WAS THE GATHERING SPOT.

ENTERTAINERS WOULD COME TO RECEIVE THEIR MESSAGES.

SIT THERE ALL DAY AND ANSWER THAT PAY PHONE.

IF THINGS WEREN'T GOING WELL, YOU JUST STAYED THERE—WENT INTO THE DRESSING ROOM AND WENT TO SLEEP.

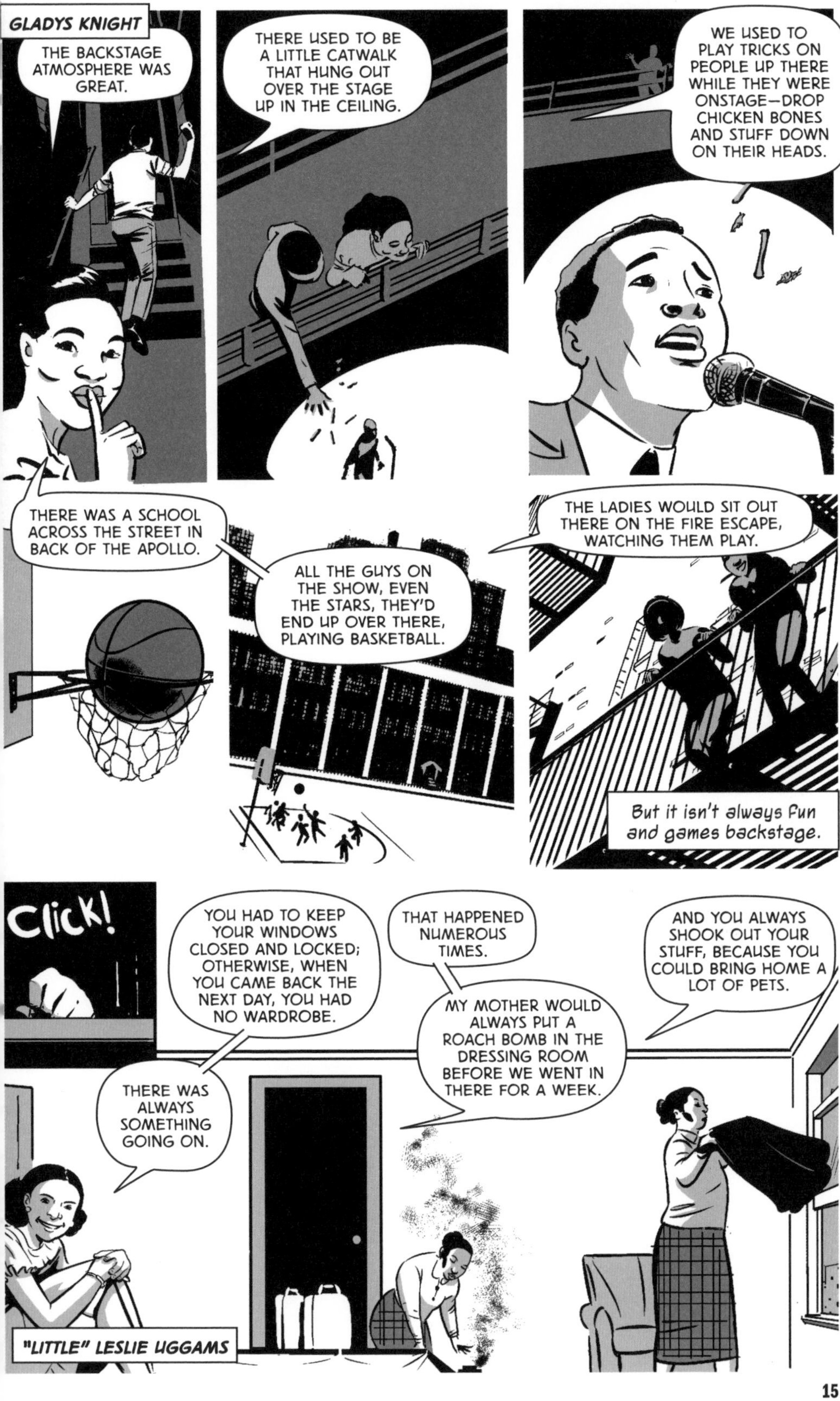
GLADYS KNIGHT
THE BACKSTAGE ATMOSPHERE WAS GREAT.
THERE USED TO BE A LITTLE CATWALK THAT HUNG OUT OVER THE STAGE UP IN THE CEILING.
WE USED TO PLAY TRICKS ON PEOPLE UP THERE WHILE THEY WERE ONSTAGE—DROP CHICKEN BONES AND STUFF DOWN ON THEIR HEADS.
THERE WAS A SCHOOL ACROSS THE STREET IN BACK OF THE APOLLO.
ALL THE GUYS ON THE SHOW, EVEN THE STARS, THEY'D END UP OVER THERE, PLAYING BASKETBALL.
THE LADIES WOULD SIT OUT THERE ON THE FIRE ESCAPE, WATCHING THEM PLAY.
But it isn't always fun and games backstage.
CLICK!
YOU HAD TO KEEP YOUR WINDOWS CLOSED AND LOCKED; OTHERWISE, WHEN YOU CAME BACK THE NEXT DAY, YOU HAD NO WARDROBE.
THERE WAS ALWAYS SOMETHING GOING ON.
THAT HAPPENED NUMEROUS TIMES.
MY MOTHER WOULD ALWAYS PUT A ROACH BOMB IN THE DRESSING ROOM BEFORE WE WENT IN THERE FOR A WEEK.
AND YOU ALWAYS SHOOK OUT YOUR STUFF, BECAUSE YOU COULD BRING HOME A LOT OF PETS.
"LITTLE" LESLIE UGGAMS

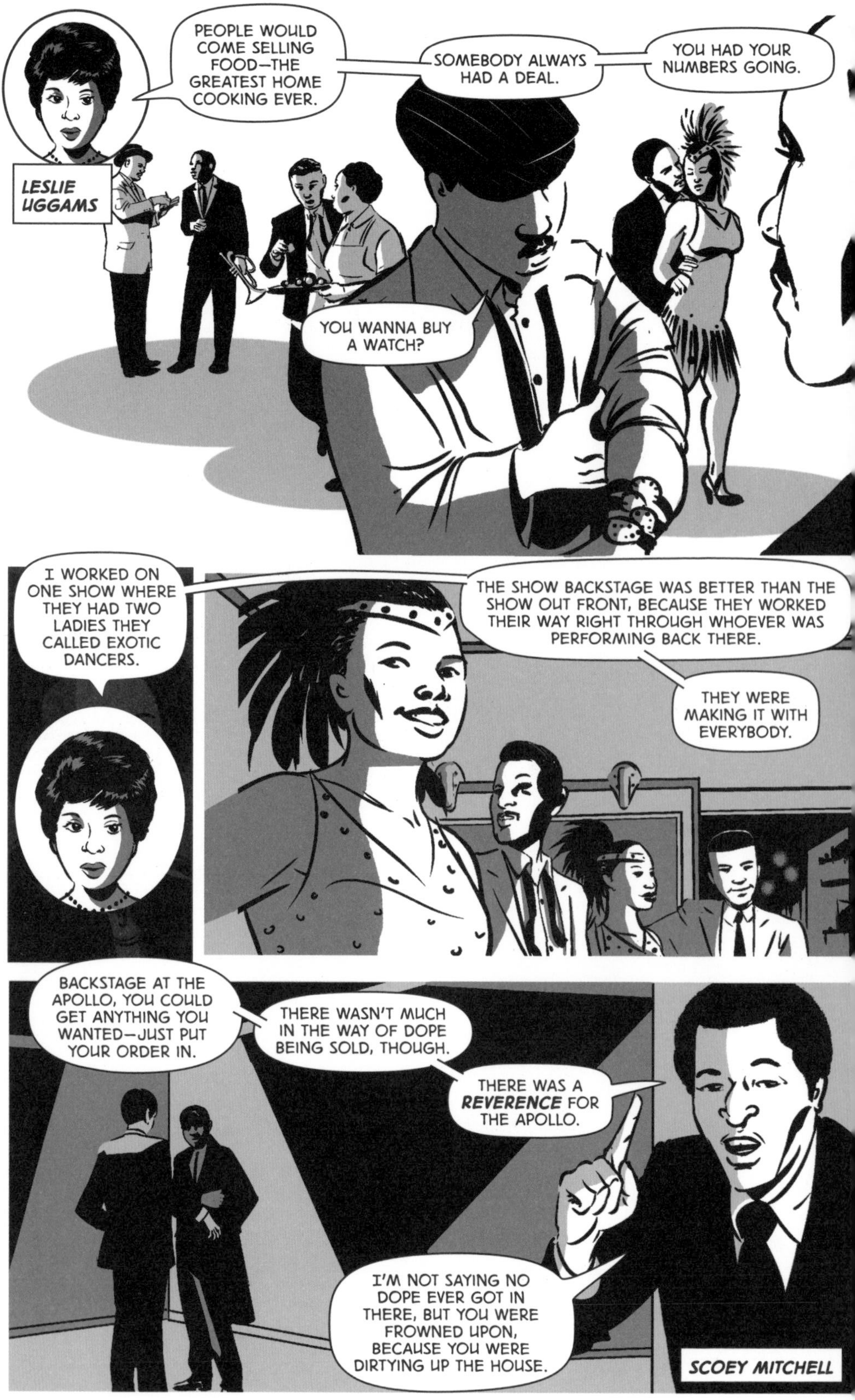
PEOPLE WOULD COME SELLING FOOD—THE GREATEST HOME COOKING EVER.
SOMEBODY ALWAYS HAD A DEAL.
YOU HAD YOUR NUMBERS GOING.
LESLIE UGGAMS
YOU WANNA BUY A WATCH?
I WORKED ON ONE SHOW WHERE THEY HAD TWO LADIES THEY CALLED EXOTIC DANCERS.
THE SHOW BACKSTAGE WAS BETTER THAN THE SHOW OUT FRONT, BECAUSE THEY WORKED THEIR WAY RIGHT THROUGH WHOEVER WAS PERFORMING BACK THERE.
THEY WERE MAKING IT WITH EVERYBODY.
BACKSTAGE AT THE APOLLO, YOU COULD GET ANYTHING YOU WANTED—JUST PUT YOUR ORDER IN.
THERE WASN'T MUCH IN THE WAY OF DOPE BEING SOLD, THOUGH.
THERE WAS A ***REVERENCE*** FOR THE APOLLO.
I'M NOT SAYING NO DOPE EVER GOT IN THERE, BUT YOU WERE FROWNED UPON, BECAUSE YOU WERE DIRTYING UP THE HOUSE.
SCOEY MITCHELL

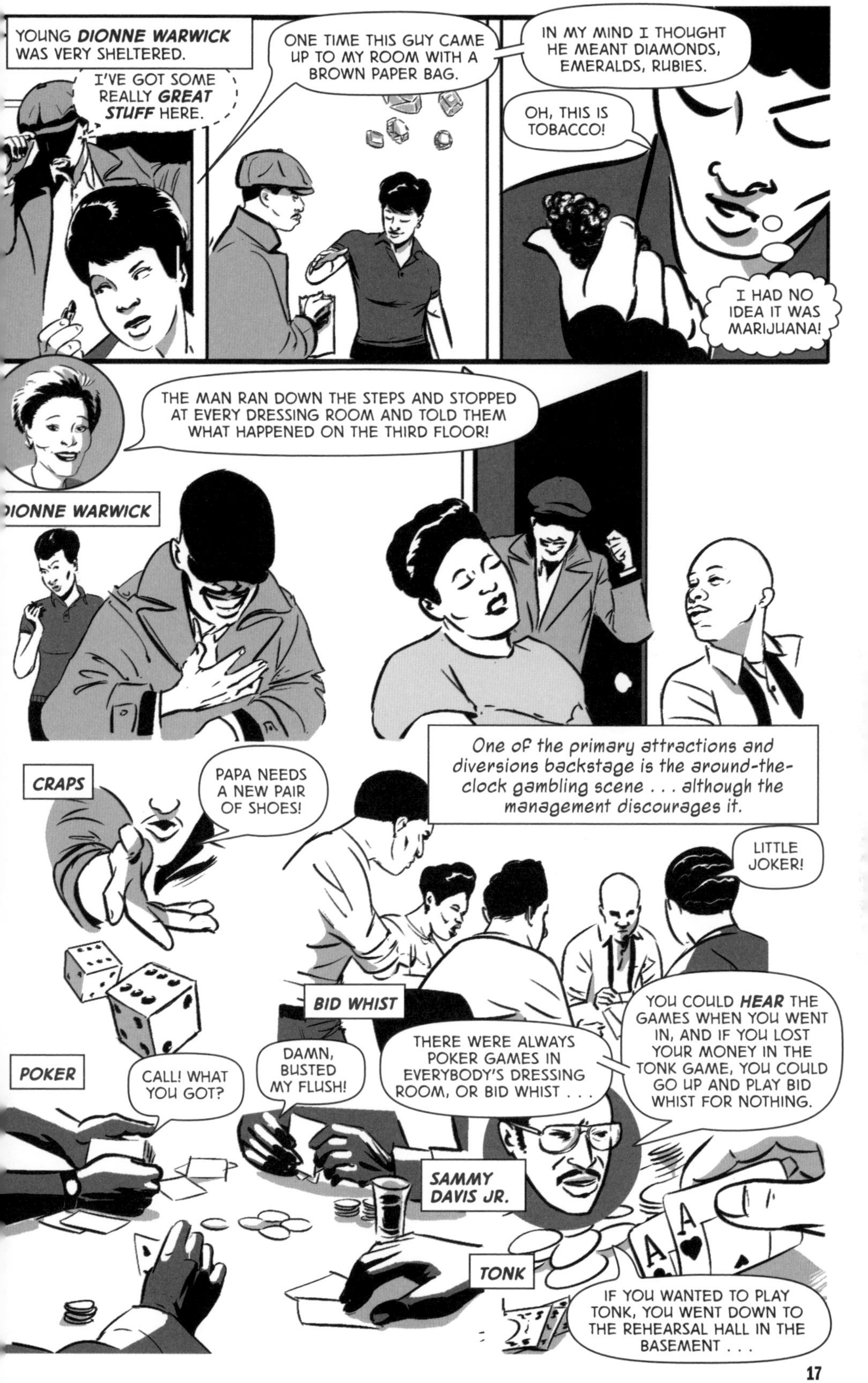
YOUNG DIONNE WARWICK WAS VERY SHELTERED.
I'VE GOT SOME REALLY GREAT STUFF HERE.
ONE TIME THIS GUY CAME UP TO MY ROOM WITH A BROWN PAPER BAG.
IN MY MIND I THOUGHT HE MEANT DIAMONDS, EMERALDS, RUBIES.
OH, THIS IS TOBACCO!
I HAD NO IDEA IT WAS MARIJUANA!
THE MAN RAN DOWN THE STEPS AND STOPPED AT EVERY DRESSING ROOM AND TOLD THEM WHAT HAPPENED ON THE THIRD FLOOR!
DIONNE WARWICK
One of the primary attractions and diversions backstage is the around-the-clock gambling scene . . . although the management discourages it.
CRAPS
PAPA NEEDS A NEW PAIR OF SHOES!
LITTLE JOKER!
BID WHIST
POKER
CALL! WHAT YOU GOT?
DAMN, BUSTED MY FLUSH!
THERE WERE ALWAYS POKER GAMES IN EVERYBODY'S DRESSING ROOM, OR BID WHIST . . .
YOU COULD HEAR THE GAMES WHEN YOU WENT IN, AND IF YOU LOST YOUR MONEY IN THE TONK GAME, YOU COULD GO UP AND PLAY BID WHIST FOR NOTHING.
SAMMY DAVIS JR.
TONK
IF YOU WANTED TO PLAY TONK, YOU WENT DOWN TO THE REHEARSAL HALL IN THE BASEMENT . . .

The main game is tonk, a fast-paced, big-betting, rummy-style card game normally played for two to five dollars a hand, but sometimes much more.

I'VE SEEN SOME GUYS LIKE REDD FOXX DAMN NEAR MISS THE SHOW, 'CAUSE THEY DIDN'T WANT TO LEAVE THE TABLE.

THEY'D COME OUT ON THE STAGE WITH HALF THEIR COSTUMES ON.

FIVE MINUTES, REDD . . .

I'LL BE RIGHT THERE!

COMEDIAN **REDD FOXX**

SANDMAN SIMS, DANCER, AMATEUR NIGHT EXECUTIONER, APOLLO FIXTURE

REDD, YOU'RE ON!

BE RIGHT THERE!

Rehearsal Hall

BEING BLIND DOESN'T STOP *RAY CHARLES* FROM PLAYING TONK, ASSISTED BY HIS VALET.

RAY CHARLES USED TO PLAY. HE HAD A GUY SITTING BY HIS SHOULDER TELLING HIM WHAT HE'S GOT, AND WHAT THE OTHERS PLAYED.

HE DOESN'T LIKE TO LOSE.

COMEDIAN **WILLIE LEWIS**

DAMN CHEATER! SHOW ME WHERE HE'S AT! POINT ME AT HIM!

THE STAGEHANDS CONTROL ACCESS TO THE DRESSING ROOMS, AS WELL AS THE LIGHTS, SOUND, AND SCENERY.

SMART ENTERTAINERS KEEP THE STAGEHANDS HAPPY.

ESPECIALLY IMPORTANT IS A GRUFF CHARACTER NAMED *WILLIAM SPAYNE*.

I REMEMBER THE FIRST TIME I SAW THAT MEAN OLD SPAYNE. HE GAVE ME THE DIRTIEST LOOK IN THE WORLD.

OTHERWISE, ONE'S ACT CAN DEVELOP MYSTERIOUS *TECHNICAL DIFFICULTIES* OR THE ACT'S GUESTS MIGHT BE KEPT *COOLING THEIR HEELS* IN THE BASEMENT WAITING ROOM.

COME HERE, ANTNEE. NOW HERE'S THE RULES.

LIKE A DRILL SERGEANT, SPAYNE WAS THE *LAW*.

SPAYNE COULD TELL YOU EVERYTHING ABOUT EVERYBODY.

THE APOLLO WAS A REAL FAMILY FEELING.

EVERYBODY WORKED FOR THE GOOD OF THE SHOW. EVERYONE WENT OUT AND DID THEIR BEST.

THINGS ABOUT THE PERSONAL LIVES OF SOME OF THE PEOPLE. PHILANDERINGS THAT WERE GOING ON. THE GOOD PEOPLE AND THE BAD.

RUTH BROWN IS THE "QUEEN OF R&B" IN THE 1950S.

HE WAS A *NEWSPAPER*!

LITTLE ANTHONY

Thanks to her string of hits such as "(Mama) He Treats Your Daughter Mean," her label, Atlantic Records, is dubbed "The House That Ruth Built."

I DIDN'T KNOW ANYTHING ABOUT SHOW BUSINESS WHEN I WENT IN TO THE APOLLO.

BUT THE REST OF THE ENTERTAINERS WOULD BE IN THE WINGS OR OUT IN THE AUDIENCE, AND THEY'D TELL YOU WHAT YOU WERE DOING *WRONG*, OR WHAT YOU *SHOULD DO*.

SEE, THE ENTERTAINERS *MADE* THE ACTS.

THIS IS HOW THE THEATER WAS BUILT—ON *SELF-HELP*. WE DIDN'T HAVE NO *CRITICS*.

Even though the work is difficult and the conditions often atrocious—some call the theater "the workhouse" or "the penitentiary" —performers always look forward to returning to the Apollo. To coming home.

DIONNE WARWICK

ARTISTS DIDN'T LOOK FORWARD TO THE FIVE SHOWS A DAY OR THE FILTHY DRESSING ROOMS.

BUT THEY DID LOOK FORWARD TO THE FEELING VERY MUCH.

THE THEATER WAS TERRIBLE: DRAFTY, DIRTY, SMELLY—*AWFUL*. AND WE *LOVED* EVERY MINUTE OF IT!

One of the keys to the Apollo's success is its *adaptability* and *nimbleness*.

A typical Apollo bill opens on Friday morning, with the entire retinue staying for a week—sometimes doing five shows a day, up to *thirty-one* shows a week.

JAMES BROWN AT APOLLO

LOUIS JORDAN
LITTLE WILLIE JOHN

SARAH VAUGHN

During any season, the Apollo offers all types of shows for all types of audiences, interspersed.

JACKIE WILSON

DINAH WASHINGTON

ONE WEEK YOU GO AFTER THE SARAH VAUGHAN FANS. ONE WEEK YOU GO AFTER THE JACKIE WILSON FANS. THE NEXT WEEK THE DINAH WASHINGTON FANS. THEN THE SPORTS FANS WITH JOE LOUIS. THEN THE CHURCH PEOPLE.

JOE LOUIS

YOU TRY TO NURTURE EVERY MARKET.

YOU COULDN'T TAP THE SAME PEOPLE EVERY WEEK; YOU WOULD DRAIN THEM DRY.

ADMIT ONE
ADMIT ONE

BOBBY SCHIFFMAN

WE USED TO SCHEDULE SOME OF OUR SHOWS TIMED WITH THE PAYOFF OF THE CITY EMPLOYEES EVERY OTHER WEEK.

AND THE WELFARE CHECKS WERE VERY IMPORTANT: IF THEY CAME OUT THE FIRST AND THIRD WEEKS OF THE MONTH, THAT'S WHEN WE WOULD SCHEDULE THE SHOWS THAT THE MORE ELDERLY PEOPLE WOULD BE INTERESTED IN.

IF YOU WERE SELLING FIVE TICKETS TO SOMEBODY FOR SIX DOLLARS APIECE IN A NORMAL THEATER, A GUY WOULD COME UP AND DROP A TWENTY-DOLLAR BILL AND A TEN TO BUY THEM.

WHEN I FIRST STARTED AT THE APOLLO, WE WERE CHARGING SEVENTY CENTS. THE HIGHEST PRICE I EVER CHARGED WAS SIX DOLLARS. I TRIED SEVEN FOR REDD FOXX ONCE, AND THEY STAYED AWAY IN DROVES.

REDD FOXX TONIGHT

WE KNEW THAT YOUNG PEOPLE WILL FIND THE MONEY ANYTIME.

IN THE APOLLO, THEY WOULD DROP SOMETHING LIKE A TEN-DOLLAR BILL, SIX DOLLARS IN QUARTERS, TEN DOLLARS IN DIMES. PEOPLE WERE *SCRATCHING* TO GET ENOUGH MONEY.

WE WERE IN BUSINESS NO MATTER WHAT. WE ALWAYS DID A SHOW— SOME OF THEM GREAT, SOME OF THEM FAIR, SOME OF THEM LOUSY— BUT WE DID A SHOW EVERY WEEK.

THE APOLLO CREATES ITS OWN STAGE SETS AND CHANGES THEM EVERY WEEK.

WE WERE *OUTRAGEOUS* PROMOTERS, AND WE USED TO DO EVERYTHING WE COULD TO MAKE THE STAGE SHOW AS GLAMOROUS AND AS ELEVATED AS WE POSSIBLY COULD.

The main reason for the Apollo's success is a firm belief in the old adage: "The show must go on!" Good old-fashioned showbiz *tenacity*.

PEOPLE WOULD COME TO THE APOLLO TO ESCAPE FROM REALITY—FANTASIZE THAT THEY WERE PART OF THE ELEGANT LIVING THEY WERE SEEING PORTRAYED.

THE $600 MOHAIR SUITS, THE FANCY SHOES, THE FANCY CARS, AND THE BEAUTIFUL WOMEN— THIS WAS THE GLAMOUR OF SHOW BUSINESS.

WE WOULD SPEND *HOURS* PLANNING HOW TO GLAMORIZE THE STAGE.

To ensure that the show goes on and keeps going on in the future, the Apollo nurtures new talents—some discovered on its legendary Amateur Night—who later become the stars who keep the theater packed, generation after generation.

I USED TO DO SEVEN OR EIGHT ACTS ON EVERY SHOW.

THE THREE OR FOUR ACTS AT THE TOP OF THE SHOW WERE THE ONES THAT SOLD THE TICKETS.

THOSE AT THE BOTTOM WERE THE ONES WE WERE GIVING THE OPPORTUNITY TO DISPLAY THEIR WARES.

JAMES BROWN WAS ONCE THE OPENING ACT FOR LITTLE WILLIE JOHN.

REDD FOXX USED TO PLAY THE THEATER ALL THE TIME FOR $300, $400, $500.

AL GREEN WAS ONCE AN OPENING ACT.

GLADYS KNIGHT WOULD ALWAYS BE AN OPENING ACT BECAUSE SHE WAS SO ANIMATED.

THE SPINNERS WERE A LOCAL ACT, AND EVERY TIME WE NEEDED AN OPENING ACT AND COULDN'T THINK OF SOMEONE TO PUT IN THERE, WE'D GO BUY THE SPINNERS.

THE **SCHIFFMANS**: PATRIARCH **FRANK**, SONS **BOBBY** AND **JACK**. THE THEATER IS RUN BY A WHITE JEWISH FAMILY, BUT THEY ARE ALWAYS UP ON THE LATEST IN BLACK ENTERTAINMENT.

ALL BOBBY SCHIFFMAN HAD TO DO WAS STICK HIS HEAD OUT THE DOOR, AND THERE WERE THREE RECORD SHOPS ON 125TH STREET BLARING THE NEW HIT RECORDS.

As something new comes along, the Apollo seizes it and brings it into the theater.

The ability to do this, while retaining its old clientele, for nearly fifty years, is an unmatched achievement in show business.

BOBBY WOULD ALSO CHECK WITH THE RECORD COMPANIES TO SEE WHO WAS HOT AND WHO WAS COMING UP.

AHMET ERTEGUN

TAKE THE LEGEND OF THE **ORIOLES**:

The myth says that, out of nowhere, they storm the Apollo with a new look and sound, levelling everything before them, and **rhythm and blues** is born.

In fact, the **Orioles** had been shaking things up in Baltimore for at least a year before they make it at the Apollo.

R&B REVOLUTIONARIES ARE ACTIVE IN OTHER CITIES AND VENUES, LIKE BANDLEADER **JOHNNY OTIS** IN THE BARREL HOUSE IN LOS ANGELES . . .

AND **FATS DOMINO** IN THE HIDEAWAY BAR IN NEW ORLEANS . . .

Yet the theater is not a fomenter of cultural revolutions; rather, it is a legitimizer—the Apollo is the **Establishment**.

APOLLO

JOHNNY OTIS
THE ORIOLES
FATS DOMINO

The Apollo often leads the way in finding and presenting the latest thing.

As revolutionaries, artists "fight" in various places around the country. But they all know the ultimate battle is conquering the Apollo.

23

FRANK SCHIFFMAN IS THE APOLLO'S FATHER FIGURE.

HE IS ALSO A CONTROVERSIAL FIGURE IN HARLEM.

He is, as we will see, a vicious competitor who tries to eliminate anyone invading his turf.

He is loved and hated, hailed as a *progressive genius*, and denigrated as a *lucky opportunist*.

FRANK SCHIFFMAN WAS MARVELOUS.

HE HAD TO SHOW A PROFIT, BUT AT THE SAME TIME HE WAS MAKING THESE ELABORATE SHOWS AVAILABLE FOR A REASONABLE PRICE.

HE HAD AN AWARENESS OF COMMUNITY PROBLEMS.

HAROLD "STUMPY" CROMER OF THE COMEDY DUO STUMP AND STUMPY

FRANK SCHIFFMAN WITH NEW YOR MAYOR FIORELLO LA GUARDIA

LEONARD REED, LEGENDARY SHOW PRODUCER, DANCER, COMEDIAN, MC—AND APOLLO MANAGER

HE WAS THE SMARTEST THEATER OPERATOR I EVER KNEW.

FRANK SCHIFFMAN KNEW BLACK SHOW BUSINESS. HE WAS A GENIUS.

EVERYBODY USED TO TALK ABOUT HIM: "CHEAP SON OF A BITCH. HE WON'T DO THIS AND HE WON'T DO THAT." I WOULD SAY, "THE MAN'S NOT CHEAP, HE'S A BUSINESSMAN."

IN TWO YEARS, I LEARNED MORE ABOUT SHOW BUSINESS FROM FRANK SCHIFFMAN THAN I LEARNED IN TWENTY YEARS OF KNOCKING AROUND THEATERS.

HOWEVER, JOHN BUBBLES—ONE OF THE GREATEST DANCERS OF HIS TIME, AND HALF THE DUO OF BUCK AND BUBBLES—IS SKEPTICAL OF SCHIFFMAN.

HE WAS JUST LUCKY TO GET A THEATER AND HAVE NEGRO ENTERTAINMENT. WHAT DID HE KNOW?

ESTRELLITA BROOKS-MORSE, WHO FORMED THE POPULAR COMEDY TEAM OF APUS AND ESTRELLITA WITH HER HUSBAND APUS BROOKS, REMEMBERS A MAN WHO WAS KIND BUT FIRM . . .

SOME PEOPLE SAY HE WAS A LITTLE ROUGH, BUT HE WAS "POP" TO ME. HE GAVE MANY PERFORMERS BREAKS.

HE'D ALWAYS GIVE YOU A DRAW ON YOUR PAY, HE'D NEVER SAY NO. ON OPENING DAY, THEY'D KEEP BUGGING HIM : "POP, CAN I HAVE A DRAW?"

ONLY THING HE KNEW WAS HOW TO GET PEOPLE AS CHEAP AS HE COULD, AND WORK THEM AS LONG AS HE COULD. HE MISUSED THE PEOPLE.

JOHN HAMMOND, WHO PRODUCED AND POPULARIZED BILLIE HOLIDAY, COUNT BASIE, BOB DYLAN, AND BRUCE SPRINGSTEEN, WAS A GOOD FRIEND OF FRANK'S AND CALLED HIM "A GENUINE SHOW BUSINESS PHENOMENON." BUT STILL SAYS:

Many credit Frank Schiffman with maintaining the Apollo's consistently high standard of performance.

FRANK HAD NO ARTISTIC TASTE WHATEVER. HE LOOKED AT A SINGER IN TERMS OF WOULD SHE DRAW OR WOULDN'T SHE. COULD HE MAKE A DECENT PROFIT OFF HER.

WHATEVER HIS TRUE MOTIVES, MOST KNOW POP SCHIFFMAN AS A KEY FACTOR IN THE DEVELOPMENT OF THE APOLLO'S SHOWS.

He has strong ideas about the way the acts should present themselves.

THE MORNING BEFORE THE WEEKLY SHOW WOULD START, POP WOULD STAND IN BACK, LEANING UP AGAINST THE WALL IN THE REHEARSAL HALL.

HE WOULD LOOK AT THE SHOW, AND WHATEVER HE DIDN'T LIKE, HE'D TAKE OUT.

WHEN YOU DID A JOKE, FRANK SCHIFFMAN COULD TELL YOU . . .

LOOK, DO IT THIS WAY.

IT'S NOT GOING TO GO OVER. BUT IF YOU TURN IT AROUND AND DO IT THIS WAY, IT'S GOING TO CLICK.

HE WAS RIGHT.

IN THE LATE '40S AND EARLY '50S, FRANK AND HIS ELDER SON, JACK, ROPE OFF A SECTION IN THE CENTER ORCHESTRA AND COMMUNICATE VIA WALKIE-TALKIE WITH THE STAGEHANDS AND LIGHT OPERATORS.

Frank keeps meticulous notes, sometimes using a little penlight to write in the darkened theater, and later types up file cards of every performer and every performance.

10/15/48 2500.00
8/28/49 2675.75
Unless a miraculous change takes 5/25/50 2500.00
place Billie's value to us is lost.
She has lost her public favor. She
seems unable to remain away from
stimulants.
Gave a good show. Very cooperative 7-28-51 $2500.00
in finale. Sang fairly well. No
misbehavior. Salary received is top value for her.
Behaved well. Gave adequate but not exciting performance. Was over-paid.
12/5/52 $2000.00 Terrible! She was sick, but she was also under the
of stimulants. Only a miracle can restore
worthwhile playing her again.

BOBBY AND JACK SCHIFFMAN DONATE SOME WONDERFUL MATERIAL TO THE SMITHSONIAN INSTITUTION IN 1996, INCLUDING MANY OF THE INDIVIDUAL ARTIST'S FILE CARDS.

SANDMAN SIMS REMEMBERS A MAN WHOSE OCCASIONAL DISPLAYS OF AFFECTION COULD BE THE KISS OF DEATH.

SCHIFFMAN WAS A VERY EDUCATED MAN, AND VERY QUIET. YOU HARDLY HEARD HIM, AND WHEN HE WAS AROUND, YOU WOULD NEVER KNOW HE WAS THERE.

IF YOU DID A BAD ACT, HE WOULD NEVER EMBARRASS YOU. HE WOULD ALWAYS COME AND PUT HIS ARMS AROUND YOU.

HE'D COME OVER JUST SO SOFT AND NICE AND YOU'D SEE HIM DO THAT HUGGIN', AND YOU KNEW THAT ACT WAS *THROUGH*.

HE'D SAY . . .

OH, MR. SIMS, YOUR ACT DIDN'T GO OVER TOO WELL. YOU BETTER GO BACK AND TRY AGAIN. YOU'RE NOT ON THE NEXT SHOW. I'M SORRY.

There was a saying backstage at the Apollo: "Don't send out your laundry until after the first show."

He'd either laugh— or fire them.

When Schiffman comes backstage after the show, he's greeted with . . .

HEY, MR. SCHIFFMAN. SHOULD WE SEND OUT OUR LAUNDRY?

BOBBY'S OLDER BROTHER, JACK, HELPS HIS FATHER RUN THE THEATER IN THE LATE '40S AND EARLY '50S.

But he soon moves on, eventually settling in Florida where he becomes involved in citrus management. He passes away there in 2009 at age eighty-seven.

MY BROTHER HAD BEEN ON THE JOB FOUR OR FIVE YEARS, AND I USED TO LISTEN WITH MY MOUTH OPEN TO THE MANNER IN WHICH HE AND MY DAD DEALT WITH SOME OF THE PERFORMERS.

BOBBY WAS ONE OF THE PEOPLE. HE HAD A GOOD RAPPORT WITH *EVERYBODY*.

HE COULD DEAL WITH THIS PERSON WHO'S STRUNG OUT ON DRUGS—HE STILL GOT THEM TO THE SHOW—OR DEAL WITH THIS PERSON WITH A DRINKING PROBLEM.

LEARNING THE ROPES FROM BOYHOOD, BOBBY SPENDS A GREAT DEAL OF TIME IN HIS FAMILY'S THEATER.

I WORKED WITH A HALF DAY OFF EVERY OTHER WEEK. FROM TEN IN THE MORNING TILL MIDNIGHT. THIRTY-FIVE DOLLARS A WEEK.

BOBBY BECOMES ACTIVE IN RUNNING THE APOLLO IN THE EARLY '50S. IN 1961, HE PERSUADES HIS FATHER TO LET HIM TAKE OVER.

HEY, DAD, I THINK IT'S TIME WE CHANGED CHAIRS. YOU BE MY ASSISTANT. LET ME RUN THE THEATER.

I'VE BEEN WAITING FOR YOU TO TELL ME THAT. I'LL BE GLAD TO DO IT.

LESLIE UGGAMS

AFTER BOBBY TAKES OVER, FRANK GOES INTO SEMIRETIREMENT. BUT HE CONTINUES TO KEEP AN EYE ON THINGS UNTIL HIS DEATH IN 1974 AT AGE EIGHTY.

APOLLO MANAGEMENT IS LIKE *FAMILY*, WELL KNOWN TO MANY.

I FELT WE WERE IMPORTANT, BUT THE REASON THE APOLLO SUCCEEDED WAS THE *PEOPLE OF THE COMMUNITY*, THE JOE ON THE STREET WHO CAME IN AND PLUNKED DOWN HIS MONEY.

IT WAS THE COMMUNITY OF HARLEM THAT MADE THE APOLLO FLOURISH.

BABIES IN THE APOLLO? WHY NOT? AND IT'S CHEAPER THAN A SITTER!

THE APOLLO IS A VITAL PART OF HARLEM'S MAIN DRAG, 125TH STREET.

W. 125 ST.
8 AVE.

W. 125 ST.
EIGHTH AVE.

A HOT SHOW AT THE APOLLO MEANS MONEY IN THE BANK FOR EVERYONE ON 125TH STREET.

Ka-ching!

BILLY ECKSTINE
REDD FOXX
COLES and ATKINS

SCHING!$

THE SCHIFFMANS CONSCIOUSLY TRY TO MAKE THE APOLLO A PART OF THE HARLEM COMMUNITY—AND KEEP THEM VESTED IN THE THEATER'S FATE.

THE COMMUNITY DOES FEEL BAD WHEN THE APOLLO HAS TROUBLES. BUT MORE OFTEN THAN NOT, THEY HAVE REASON TO FEEL GOOD.

I WANT THEM TO FEEL BAD WHEN A PERFORMER GIVES US THE SHAFT.

I WANT THEM TO FEEL BAD WHEN THE ROOF LEAKS.

I WANT THEM TO FEEL BAD WHEN WE CAN'T GET A FIRST-RUN FILM . . .

BOBBY SCHIFFMAN

GOOD NEWS!
MIRTH and MELODY
ARE BACK IN HARLEM
GALA RE-OPENING FRIDAY, AUG. 29th

MIDNIGHT SHOW Every SATURDAY
WED. Night AMATEUR BROADCAST

WORLD'S GREATEST COLORED SHOWS

HARLEM'S HIGH SPOT
APOLLO
125th St. near 8th Ave. · Tel. UNiversity 4-4490
ONE BIG WEEK ONLY — BEGIN. FRIDAY, AUGUST 29th

AMERICA'S FOREMOST QUARTETTE
4 INK SPOTS
and the Finest Cast Ever Assembl

WHEELER MORAN

SUNSET RO

PAULINE BRYANT
Ralph BROWN — John M
JOHNNY VIGAL — EDD
HARPER'S DAN
WHITEY'S

FOR YEARS, THE THEATER IS BILLED AS "HARLEM'S HIGH SPOT"—AND THAT IT IS.

28

CHAPTER 2

Harlem Before the Apollo

The story of the Apollo Theater begins much earlier than its opening in *1934*—years before 125th Street becomes the *Main Street* of America's greatest African American community.

BETWEEN THE END OF WORLD WAR I AND THE BEGINNING OF THE GREAT DEPRESSION, GROUNDBREAKING AFRICAN AMERICANS LEAD A FLOWERING OF CREATIVITY KNOWN AS THE *HARLEM RENAISSANCE*.

Harlem becomes fashionable to the city's white socialites and intelligentsia.

The white world takes note.

They can imagine no more exciting an evening than a raucous crawl through Harlem's swankiest clubs.

NO SMART NEW YORK PARTY IS CONSIDERED COMPLETE WITHOUT A SMATTERING OF HARLEM RENAISSANCE INTELLECTUALS.

COUNTEE CULLEN

LANGSTON HUGHES

ZORA NEALE HURSTON

LEGENDARY SPOTS SUCH AS THE COTTON CLUB FEATURE THE GREATEST AFRICAN AMERICAN ARTISTS OF THE DAY, LIKE *DUKE ELLINGTON*.

OR *FATS WALLER* AT *CONNIE'S INN*.

CLUBS THAT, ALONG WITH *SMALLS PARADISE* AND *BARRON WILKINS' EXCLUSIVE CLUB*, MAKE UP HARLEM'S *BIG FOUR*.

SMALLS PARADISE

BARRON WI XCLUSIVE

But while African American artists draw crowds of rich white "swells" to the top clubs, black customers are usually **barred** from entering these legendary nightspots.

AT THE COTTON CLUB, **W. C. HANDY**, THE "FATHER OF THE BLUES," IS TURNED AWAY BY THE CLUB'S GANGSTER MANAGER, **GEORGE "BIG FRENCHY" DE MANGE**, WHILE WHITE REVELERS INSIDE SOAK UP THE MUSIC HE HELPED TO INVENT.

I DON'T CARE WHO YOU ARE.

LENA HORNE BEGINS HER CAREER AT THE COTTON CLUB AS A SIXTEEN-YEAR-OLD CHORINE.

LENA HORNE

THE SHOWS HAD A PRIMITIVE, NAKED QUALITY THAT WAS SUPPOSED TO MAKE A "CIVILIZED" AUDIENCE LOSE ITS INHIBITIONS.

DUKE ELLINGTON, KENTUCKY CLUB HOUSE BAND, 1923–28; COTTON CLUB, 1928–31.

FLETCHER HENDERSON, ROSELAND BALLROOM HOUSE BAND, 1924–31.

CAB CALLOWAY, COTTON CLUB HOUSE BAND, 1931–34.

The best black orchestras are booked for lengthy engagements at some of the top spots in the heart of Harlem and down on **Broadway**.

Even where black people aren't overtly **kept** out, they're often **priced** out.

THE JAZZ AGE

Stride piano players such as *James P. Johnson*, *Willie "The Lion" Smith*, and their protégé, *Fats Waller*, are at the height of their popularity and influence in the early '20s.

The music is modern, sophisticated, and wild—nearly everything Prohibition-era hedonists desire.

THEY TAKE THE BASIC RAGTIME TUNES POPULAR SINCE THE TURN OF THE CENTURY . . .

THE FINAL INGREDIENT—SENSUALITY—IS PROVIDED BY CLASSIC FEMALE BLUES SINGERS SUCH AS *MAMIE SMITH* AND *BESSIE SMITH*.

. . . SEPARATE THE RAGTIME BEAT WITH A STEADY LEFT HAND . . .

. . . AND JAZZ UP THE MELODY WITH THE DEXTEROUS DIGITS OF THE RIGHT HAND.

MAMIE SMITH'S HISTORIC 1920 RECORDING, *"CRAZY BLUES,"* IS SELLING EIGHT THOUSAND RECORDS A WEEK.

CRAZY BLUES

It was called the first recording of an "actual blues performance by a Negro artist with Negro accompaniment."

JAZZ IS INVENTED BY BLACKS IN NEW ORLEANS. YET A WHITE GROUP FROM THAT TOWN, THE *ORIGINAL DIXIELAND JAZZ BAND*, MAKES THE FIRST JAZZ RECORDING IN 1917.

The band's New York debut generates national headlines and helps popularize jazz.

BANDLEADER *PAUL WHITEMAN* IS CROWNED THE *"KING OF JAZZ"* BY CAPITALIZING ON THE MUSIC OF BLACK JAZZ INNOVATORS.

In Harlem, this leads to a strange dichotomy: The music that Harlemites hear on their radios is often a white dilution of black jazz.

BUDDY BOLDEN

JOSEPH "KING" OLIVER

FREDDIE KEPPARD

Harlem's black music buffs buy and play their own records—and find plenty of ways to "dig" their own music among their own people.

FOR MOST OF HARLEM, THE PLACE TO REALLY LET LOOSE IS AT A *RENT PARTY* IN SOMEONE'S APARTMENT, WITH THE LIGHTS DOWN LOW, THE SOUL FOOD PILED HIGH, AND THE MUSIC BLARING.

The rent party tradition begins in the South, with church socials designed to raise money. In Harlem, the concept is refined—a quarter or a buck at a time.

WILLIE "THE LION" SMITH REMEMBERS THEM IN HIS MEMOIR, *MUSIC ON MY MIND.*

AN ENTIRE FAMILY WOULD WORK FOR DAYS PREPARING.

THERE'D BE PILES OF HOG MAWS, PICKLED PIGS' TAILS, PIGS' FEET, SOUTHERN-FRIED CHICKEN, MASHED POTATOES, CHITTERLINGS, POTATO SALAD, CORN BREAD, RED BEANS AND RICE, CRAB SOUP, AND SOMETIMES THEY'D EVEN COME UP WITH A CHINESE DINNER WITH PILES OF CHOP SUEY . . .

THEY WOULD CROWD A HUNDRED OR MORE PEOPLE INTO A SEVEN-ROOM RAILROAD FLAT, AND THE WALLS WOULD BULGE.

SOME OF THE PARTIES SPREAD TO THE HALLS AND ALL OVER THE BUILDING.

GALLONS OF GIN, BEER, WINE, WHISKEY, EGGNOG, AND BRANDY WERE AVAILABLE TO WASH DOWN ALL THOSE VITTLES . . .

WHEN THERE WASN'T A CRAP GAME, OR POKER, GOING IN THE BACK BEDROOM, THEY'D USE IT FOR A PLACE TO REST UP, OR SLEEP OFF, OR MAKE LOVE.

THE RENT PARTY WAS THE PLACE TO PICK UP ON ALL THE LATEST JOKES, JIVE, AND UPTOWN NEWS.

IT GOT TO BE A BIG BUSINESS. THEY WOULD ADVERTISE A HOUSE-RENT PARTY FOR A MONTH IN ADVANCE . . . THEY EVEN BUILT UP MAILING LISTS.

AFTER A RENT PARTY, HARLEMITES MIGHT END UP AT ONE OF THE JOINTS ON *"JUNGLE ALLEY"*—THE PRIME LOCALE FOR CLUBS PATRONIZED BY BLACKS, BUT ALSO FREQUENTED BY "SLUMMING" WHITES.

At spots such as *Pod's and Jerry's*, or *Mexico's*, the real action doesn't start until the early hours of the morning and goes until well after sunrise.

33

AFTER THEIR GIGS AT THE BIG CLUBS WRAP UP, JAZZ GREATS MEET THERE IN FURIOUS *"CUTTING CONTESTS,"* PITTING THEM AGAINST YOUNG HOPEFULS TESTING THEIR CHOPS.

I'MA TAKE ON HAWK!

BEN WEBSTER, DON BYAS, AND *COLEMAN HAWKINS*

Jungle Alley and the Big Four nightclubs are in what is then *black Harlem*—many blocks north of 125th Street.

125TH STREET IN 1927. *DOLL THOMAS* LIVES AND WORKS IN HARLEM THEN.

THERE WERE NO BLACKS ON 125TH STREET. EVEN IN 1927, THE NEIGHBORHOOD WAS STRICTLY WHITE.

IF BLACK FOLKS WANTED TO GO INTO THE THEATER THAT'S NOW THE APOLLO, THEY ENTERED FROM 126TH STREET. HAD TO GO UP THE BACK STAIRS TO THE BALCONY.

THEY JUST WOULDN'T SELL US AN ORCHESTRA SEAT. THEY WERE EITHER "SOLD OUT" OR THEY'D FLATLY REFUSE.

ON 125TH STREET, *FRANK'S LUNCHROOM*—WE COULDN'T GET SERVED IN THERE.

ACROSS THE STREET WAS *CHILD'S*. WE COULDN'T GET SERVED IN THERE.

NEXT DOOR WAS *LOFT'S CANDY SHOP*. COULDN'T GET SERVED IN THERE.

RIGHT DOWN THE STREET WAS *FABIAN'S SEAFOOD SHOP*. COULDN'T GET SERVED IN THERE EITHER.

ALL THE BARS AND EVERYTHING ELSE WAS THE SAME WAY.

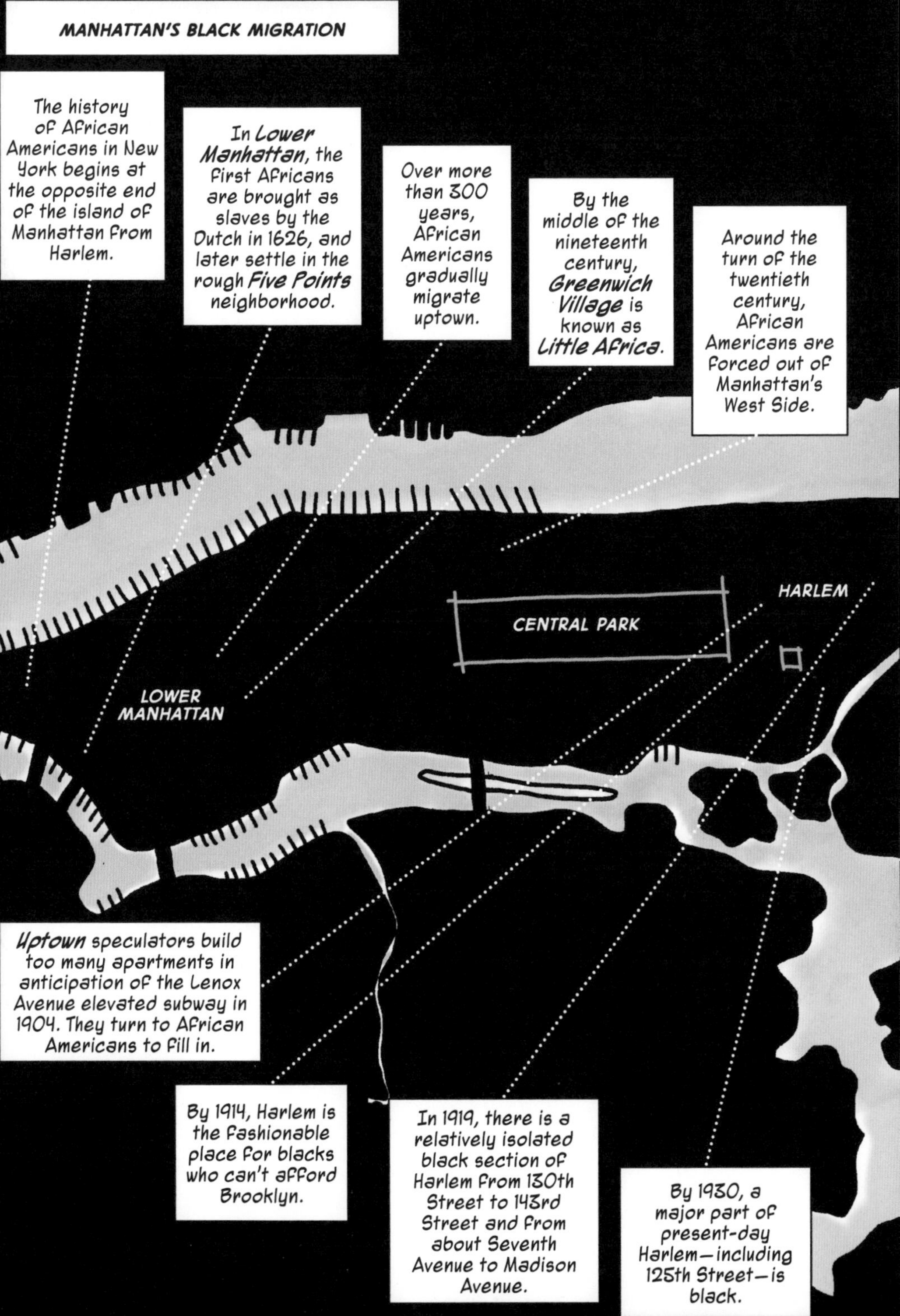
MANHATTAN'S BLACK MIGRATION
The history of African Americans in New York begins at the opposite end of the island of Manhattan from Harlem.
In *Lower Manhattan*, the first Africans are brought as slaves by the Dutch in 1626, and later settle in the rough *Five Points* neighborhood.
Over more than 300 years, African Americans gradually migrate uptown.
By the middle of the nineteenth century, *Greenwich Village* is known as *Little Africa*.
Around the turn of the twentieth century, African Americans are forced out of Manhattan's West Side.
HARLEM
CENTRAL PARK
LOWER MANHATTAN
Uptown speculators build too many apartments in anticipation of the Lenox Avenue elevated subway in 1904. They turn to African Americans to fill in.
By 1914, Harlem is the fashionable place for blacks who can't afford Brooklyn.
In 1919, there is a relatively isolated black section of Harlem from 130th Street to 143rd Street and from about Seventh Avenue to Madison Avenue.
By 1930, a major part of present-day Harlem—including 125th Street—is black.

ON 125TH STREET, IN 1914, THE FUTURE APOLLO THEATER OPENS AS **HURTIG & SEAMON'S MUSIC HALL.**

THE BLACK THEATRICAL SCENE IN HARLEM IS COMING UNDER THE CONTROL OF TWO MEN—ALTHOUGH THEY WON'T TAKE OVER THE APOLLO UNTIL 1935.

1 2 3 4 5 6 7 8 9 10

HURTIG & SEAMON'S MUSIC HALL

BACKSTAGE PASS

Issued to

A *vaudeville* house and *burlesque* joint, it presents mainly white shows to white audiences.

FRANK SCHIFFMA AND **LEO BRECH**

UP HERE, MR. BRECHER OWNED THE **ODEON** ON 145TH STREET AND THE **ODEON ANNEX** . . . PRIMARILY MOVIE THEATERS. HE OWNED THE **ROOSEVELT** AT 145TH AND FIFTH, THE **DOUGLAS** AT 142ND AND LENOX . . . AND OF COURSE THE **LAFAYETTE** AT 132ND AND SEVENTH.

THEY OWNED ALL THE THEATERS IN HARLEM.

I WENT TO WORK FOR MR. LEO BRECHER IN 1914, LONG BEFORE HE TIED UP WITH MR. SCHIFFMAN.

HE WAS VERY NICE, VERY SHREWD, AND VERY SMART.

BRECHER WAS THE LANDLORD FOR THE COTTON CLUB, WHICH WAS IN THE UPSTAIRS LOBBY OVER THE **DOUGLAS THEATER.**

LEO BRECHER

DOLL THOMA

IN THOSE DAYS, THE FILM PROJECTIONIST WENT DOWNTOWN AND GOT THE FILM **BEFORE** THE SHOW, AND TOOK THE FILM BACK **AFTER** THE SHOW.

The Austrian immigrant is the *money man.*

IF YOU HAD BOOKED A FILM THAT A RIVAL MOVIE HOUSE EXHIBITOR WANTED, HE HAD A GANG WAITING TO TAKE THE FILM AWAY FROM YOU.

THEY'D REMOVE THE FILM FROM THE BOX AND ROLL IT UP AND DOWN THE STREET!

SO MR. SCHIFFMAN CREATED A FILM DELIVERY SERVICE—THE FIRST ONE IN NEW YORK CITY—AND MET MR. BRECHER.

THEY FORMED ONE OF THE MOST AIRTIGHT AND SUCCESSFUL THEATER COMBINATIONS THAT THERE WAS, ESPECIALLY IN BLACK SHOW BUSINESS.

FILM DELIVERY

Brecher is content to

Frank Schiffman is a former schoolteacher who grew up on the Lower East Side, manages the

IN 1922, SCHIFFMAN AND BRECHER TAKE OVER THE *HARLEM OPERA HOUSE* ON 125TH STREET.

That's where the *Apollo* name first appears on 125th Street. A dozen years later, the name will be taken by its larger neighbor.

Just down the block from Hurtig & Seamon's, the Harlem Opera House features stage comedies and musicals featuring *Al Jolson* and the *Four Marx Brothers*.

A small competing theater over the lobby is variously known as **Hammerstein's Music Hall, Minsky's Burlesque** . . . and, finally, the **Apollo Burlesque**.

SCHIFFMAN AND BRECHER'S POWER UPTOWN BECOMES INDOMITABLE IN 1925 WHEN THEY ASSUME CONTROL OF THE GRANDDADDY OF ALL BLACK THEATERS, THE LAFAYETTE, ON SEVENTH AVENUE AND 132ND.

AND THEY WOULDN'T ALLOW ANY COMPETITION.

"DARKTOWN FOLLIES" AT THE LAFAYETTE, 1913

They inherit a theater with more than a decade's tradition as the *"Cradle of Stars."*

ACCORDING TO HARLEM RENAISSANCE WRITER *JAMES WELDON JOHNSON*:

The "Darktown Follies" drew space, headlines, and cartoons in the New York papers; and consequently it became the vogue to go to Harlem to see it . . .

The beginning of the nightly migration to Harlem in search of entertainment began.

Although until they take over, African Americans are admitted to the Lafayette only grudgingly—relegated to the balcony.

The Lafayette quickly becomes *the* theater in Harlem to see top black stars. A Lafayette debut is as important as an Apollo debut will soon become.

ETHEL WATERS, ONE OF THE GREATEST SINGERS AND ACTRESSES OF HER DAY, SPEAKS ABOUT HER 1918 LAFAYETTE DEBUT IN HER AUTOBIOGRAPHY.

I WAS ASKED TO APPEAR AT ONE OF THE SPECIAL SUNDAY-NIGHT SHOWS AT THE LAFAYETTE THEATER, THE *UPTOWN PALACE*. THOSE SUNDAY SHOWS WERE EVENTS.

HARLEM'S DICTYS GOT THEIR FIRST GANDER AT MY WORK THAT EVENING. THEY KNEW PERFORMERS, AND THEY DECIDED THAT I HAD A FUTURE BIGGER THAN MY PRESENT OR MY PAST.

Ethel Waters later becomes an Apollo favorite, too.

WHEN THE SONG-AND-DANCE TEAM OF *FORD LEE "BUCK" WASHINGTON* AND *JOHN "BUBBLES" SUBLETT* COME TO THE LAFAYETTE, THEY ARE ALREADY STARS.

JOHN BUBBLES

ANYTHING CONCERNING AN APPRECIATION OF LIFE, OR YOUR MOTHER OR FATHER, COULD NOT OCCUR TO THE MIND OF THE NEGRO.

AT THAT TIME, WHITES THOUGHT THE MOST IMPORTANT THINGS IN THE NEGRO WORLD WERE A BOTTLE OF GIN AND A PAIR OF DICE.

Buck and Bubbles, teenagers, newly arrived from Louisville, Kentucky, had been the first black act to play the Palace Theater on Broadway—the most famous vaudeville theater in the world then.

THE HOMESICK YOUNGSTER'S TEARS WERE REAL.

AT THE PALACE, I SANG A SONG CALLED "MAMMY O' MINE" WRITTEN BY A COLORED COMPOSER . . .

WHEN I SANG THAT VERSE, YOU COULD HEAR A PIN DROP.

I'M HEARTBROKEN FROM WHAT I'M GOING THROUGH.

WE WERE SUCH A HIT, MAN! THE MANAGER CAME RUNNING DOWN AFTER THE SHOW.

Mammy O' mine...

WHERE'S THE TWO COLORED BOYS?

THEY LOCKED US IN OUR DRESSING ROOM SO WE WOULDN'T GO AWAY!

FATS WALLER PLAYS PIANO AND ORGAN FOR THE SILENT MOVIES AT THE LINCOLN THEATER, OFTEN INJECTING HIS OWN OFFBEAT RIFFS, TO THE AMUSEMENT OF THE AUDIENCE.

Until about 1914, the *Lincoln* and the *Crescent* Theaters, in the heart of black Harlem, are the only two theaters in the city catering mainly to African Americans.

WHEN I WAS TWELVE OR THIRTEEN YEARS OLD, I WOULD STAND OUTSIDE THE LINCOLN THEATER BECAUSE FATS WALLER WAS PLAYING ORGAN THERE.

I DIDN'T HAVE ENOUGH GUTS TO GO INTO THE THEATER ON MY OWN.

YOUNG JOHN HAMMOND

FRANK SCHIFFMAN SEES THAT BLACK SHOW BUSINESS IS GOOD BUSINESS.

THE NEW YORK AGE

In all New York, Harlem was the last to show signs of business falling off.

He wants *in* on this action in his new neighborhood.

AT THE HEIGHT OF THE DEPRESSION, A CONFERENCE OF MOVIE EXHIBITORS TELLS HARLEM NEWSPAPER THE *NEW YORK AGE* . . .

THE NEW YORK AGE

Harlemites will not allow hard times to make hermits and recluses out of them, but will scrape up enough to take in their amusements.

From his headquarters at the Lafayette, Schiffman devotes himself to the development of black entertainment—and the elimination of his competitors.

SCHIFFMAN WAS *IMPOSSIBLE* TO COMPETE WITH.

HIS CONTRACTS WOULD SAY $1,000 A WEEK FOR A PLAYER—HE'D ACTUALLY PAY THEM $300, BUT AS LONG AS THEY COULD SHOW THAT PIECE OF PAPER AROUND TO HIS COMPETITOR—

THERE WAS A TAP DANCER NAMED EDDIE RECTOR, AND HE HAD ONE OF THESE PIECES OF PAPER THAT SAID $1,000.

EDDIE RECTOR IS THE SHOWBIZ PARTNER OF HARLEM LEGEND *RALPH COOPER*, WHO CREATES *AMATEUR NIGHT*.

SOMETIMES THE PLOY BACKFIRES.

HE HAD DRAWN PART OF IT, BUT WHEN HE CAME FOR THE REST, IT WASN'T THERE.

JOHN HAMMOND

USUALLY SCHIFFMAN COULD SWEET-TALK THESE PEOPLE.

BUT EDDIE CHASED SCHIFFMAN AROUND THE LAFAYETTE WITH A *GUN!*

SCHIFFMAN HAD TO CALL THE *POLICE.*

BESSIE SMITH PLAYED THE LAFAYETTE JUST ONCE AFTER SHE PLAYED THE ALHAMBRA. SHE HAD TO COME *CRAWLING* BACK TO DO IT.

IF YOU WANTED TO WORK BLACK THEATERS IN GENERAL, YOU HAD TO DEAL WITH SCHIFFMAN.

FRANK SCHIFFMAN HAD TO CLAW HIS WAY UP. SHOW BUSINESS WAS *ROUGH* IN THE OLD DAYS.

BESSIE SMITH

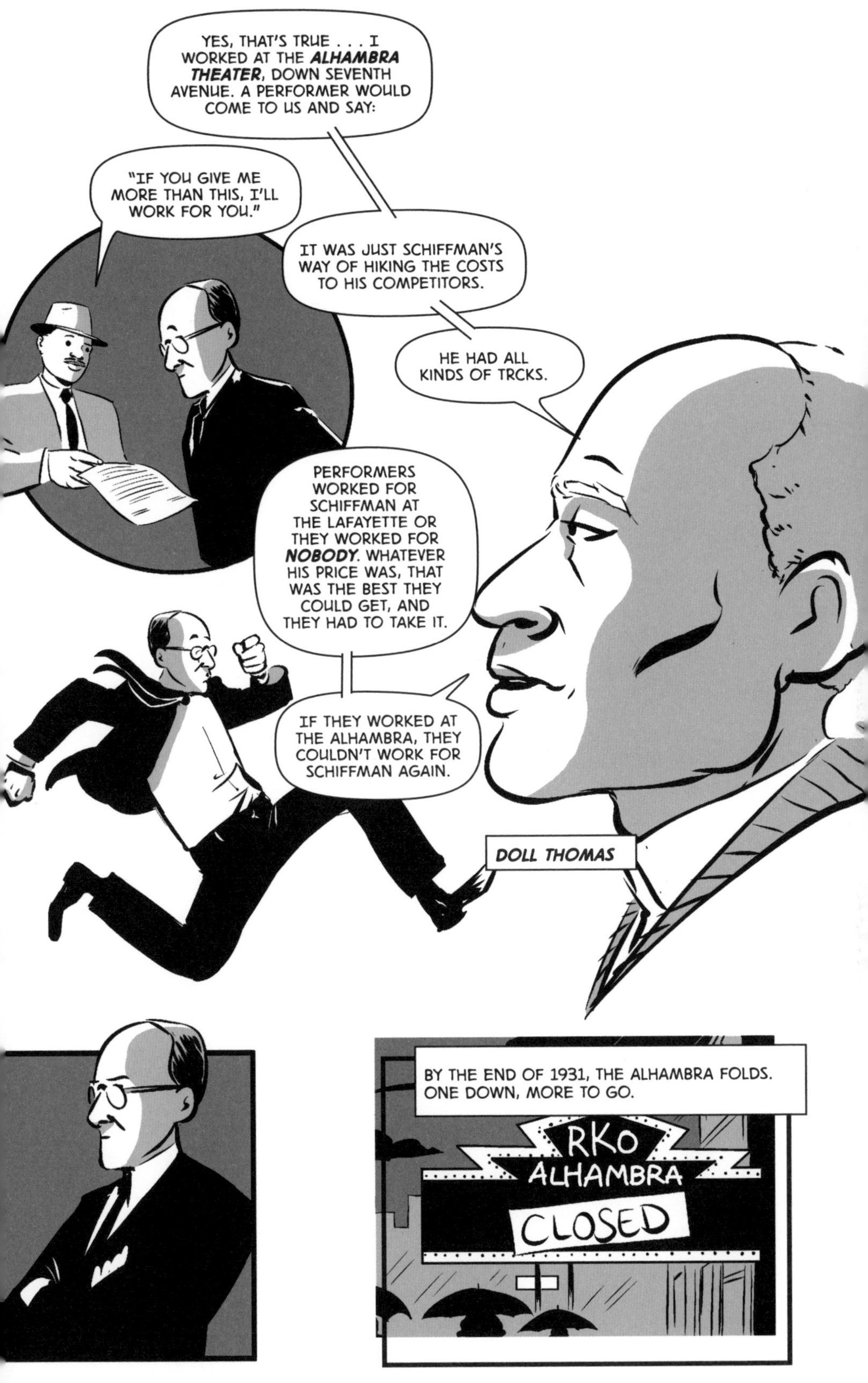

YES, THAT'S TRUE . . . I WORKED AT THE ***ALHAMBRA THEATER***, DOWN SEVENTH AVENUE. A PERFORMER WOULD COME TO US AND SAY:
"IF YOU GIVE ME MORE THAN THIS, I'LL WORK FOR YOU."
IT WAS JUST SCHIFFMAN'S WAY OF HIKING THE COSTS TO HIS COMPETITORS.
HE HAD ALL KINDS OF TRCKS.
PERFORMERS WORKED FOR SCHIFFMAN AT THE LAFAYETTE OR THEY WORKED FOR ***NOBODY***. WHATEVER HIS PRICE WAS, THAT WAS THE BEST THEY COULD GET, AND THEY HAD TO TAKE IT.
IF THEY WORKED AT THE ALHAMBRA, THEY COULDN'T WORK FOR SCHIFFMAN AGAIN.
DOLL THOMAS
BY THE END OF 1931, THE ALHAMBRA FOLDS. ONE DOWN, MORE TO GO.
RKO
ALHAMBRA
CLOSED

BY 1930, BURLESQUE THEATERS ARE IN TROUBLE. THEY ARE BECOMING PASSÉ AND INCREASINGLY THREATENED BY SEXY BROADWAY REVUES.

BARE LEGS— SHOCKINGLY, NO STOCKINGS!

BURLESQUE TAKES OFF ITS GLOVES AND ITS STOCKINGS AND FIGHTS BACK WITH BARE KNUCKLES AND KNEES AND MORE AND MORE BARE SKIN.

I PLAYED THE APOLLO WHEN IT WAS HURTIG & SEAMON'S, AS A CHILD STRIPPER. I WAS ABOUT FIFTEEN.

THE FIRST PART OF THE SHOW WOULD BE ALL WHITE.

BUT THE SECOND HALF WOULD BE A BLACK CHORUS LINE AND A BLACK COMEDIAN AND A BLACK SINGER—AND THEN THEY'D HAVE A BLACK STRIPPER.

ESTRELLITA BROOKS-MORSE

IT WASN'T VULGAR OR ANYTHING LIKE THAT. WE WERE WORKING TO BEAUTIFUL MUSIC, AND TAKING OFF PIECES BEAUTIFULLY. VERY **ARTISTIC**.

In 1933, newly elected Mayor *Fiorello La Guardia* begins a campaign against burlesque.

Hurtig & Seamon's is forced to go bankrupt.

SOON THE CITY FATHERS FEEL IT HAS GONE TOO FAR.

The little theater over the Harlem Opera House has to close, too.

In 1934, the landlord, *Sidney Cohen*, takes the Apollo name . . .

. . . and, with his manager, *Morris Sussman*, reopens the much larger Hurtig & Seamon's Burlesque as the new *125th Street Apollo Theatre*, featuring black entertainment for the newly black neighborhood.

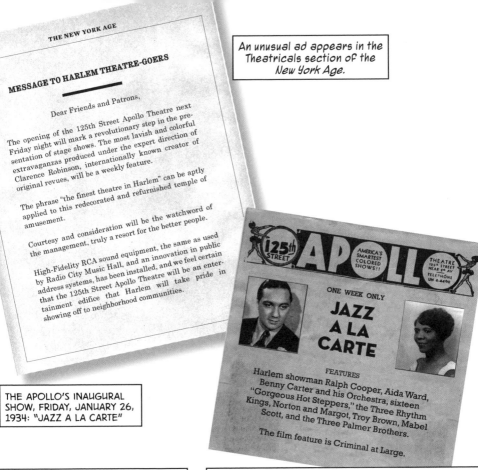

THE NEW YORK AGE

MESSAGE TO HARLEM THEATRE-GOERS

Dear Friends and Patrons,

The opening of the 125th Street Apollo Theatre next Friday night will mark a revolutionary step in the presentation of stage shows. The most lavish and colorful extravaganzas produced under the expert direction of Clarence Robinson, internationally known creator of original revues, will be a weekly feature.

The phrase "the finest theatre in Harlem" can be aptly applied to this redecorated and refurnished temple of amusement.

Courtesy and consideration will be the watchword of the management, truly a resort for the better people.

High-Fidelity RCA sound equipment, the same as used by Radio City Music Hall, and an innovation in public address systems, has been installed, and we feel certain that the 125th Street Apollo Theatre will be an entertainment edifice that Harlem will take pride in showing off to neighborhood communities.

An unusual ad appears in the Theatricals section of the New York Age.

125th STREET APOLLO

AMERICA'S SMARTEST COLORED SHOWS!!

THEATRE 125th STREET NEAR 8th AV TELEPHONE UN 4-4490

ONE WEEK ONLY

JAZZ A LA CARTE

FEATURES

Harlem showman Ralph Cooper, Aida Ward, Benny Carter and his Orchestra, sixteen "Gorgeous Hot Steppers," the Three Rhythm Kings, Norton and Margot, Troy Brown, Mabel Scott, and the Three Palmer Brothers.

The film feature is Criminal at Large.

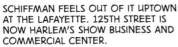

THE APOLLO'S INAUGURAL SHOW, FRIDAY, JANUARY 26, 1934: "JAZZ A LA CARTE"

SCHIFFMAN FEELS OUT OF IT UPTOWN AT THE LAFAYETTE. 125TH STREET IS NOW HARLEM'S SHOW BUSINESS AND COMMERCIAL CENTER.

EVEN RALPH COOPER'S NEWLY LAUNCHED WEDNESDAY AMATEUR NIGHT AT THE LAFAYETTE, ALONG WITH A PRICE REDUCTION TO AS LITTLE AS A DIME, CAN'T STANCH THE FLOW OF CUSTOMERS DOWN TO 125TH STREET.

SCHIFFMAN HALTS SHOWS AT THE LAFAYETTE . . .

. . . AND MOVES TO THE HARLEM OPERA HOUSE, JUST DOWN THE STREET FROM THE APOLLO, ON JUNE 9, 1934.

The Apollo and the Harlem Opera House are now the *only* black theaters left in Harlem.

The show business battle for 125th Street is brutal, but it occurs in the midst of a true horror—Harlem's first major *riot*.

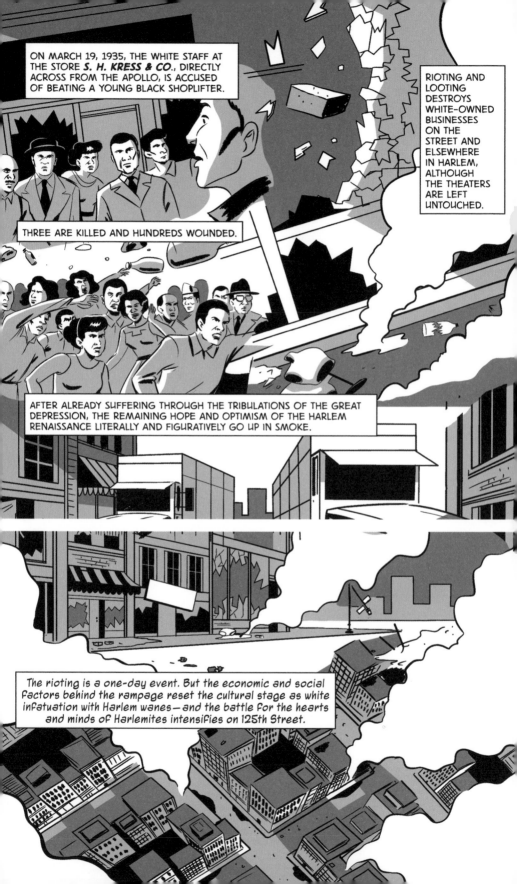

ON MARCH 19, 1935, THE WHITE STAFF AT THE STORE **S. H. KRESS & CO.**, DIRECTLY ACROSS FROM THE APOLLO, IS ACCUSED OF BEATING A YOUNG BLACK SHOPLIFTER.

RIOTING AND LOOTING DESTROYS WHITE-OWNED BUSINESSES ON THE STREET AND ELSEWHERE IN HARLEM, ALTHOUGH THE THEATERS ARE LEFT UNTOUCHED.

THREE ARE KILLED AND HUNDREDS WOUNDED.

AFTER ALREADY SUFFERING THROUGH THE TRIBULATIONS OF THE GREAT DEPRESSION, THE REMAINING HOPE AND OPTIMISM OF THE HARLEM RENAISSANCE LITERALLY AND FIGURATIVELY GO UP IN SMOKE.

The rioting is a one-day event. But the economic and social factors behind the rampage reset the cultural stage as white infatuation with Harlem wanes—and the battle for the hearts and minds of Harlemites intensifies on 125th Street.

AROUND THE TIME OF THE RIOT, **RALPH COOPER** TAKES HIS **WEDNESDAY AMATEUR NIGHT** TO **COHEN AND SUSSMAN'S APOLLO** AND BEGINS HIS INFLUENTIAL WMCA BROADCAST, **"AMATEUR NIGHT IN HARLEM**."

Schiffman fights back with his own *Tuesday Amateur Night,* broadcast on WNEW.

SIDNEY COHEN, HOWEVER, DOESN'T HAVE THE STOMACH, OR THE HEART, FOR THIS KIND OF BATTLE. SO HE TURNS TO AN OLD FAMILY FRIEND, **JOHN HAMMOND**, TO HELP HIM AT THE APOLLO.

I WOULD BOOK THE SHOWS, COHEN WOULD PUT UP THE CAPITAL, AND I WOULD HAVE A PERCENTAGE OF THE PROFITS.

I WAS ON MY WAY TO SIGN THE PAPERS.

I CALLED UP THE OFFICE ON 44TH STREET TO CONFIRM.

WE'RE TERRIBLY SORRY TO TELL YOU, BUT MR. COHEN HAS JUST HAD A HEART ATTACK. HE'S DEAD.

JUST LIKE **THAT**.

ON MAY 13, 1935, IT IS ANNOUNCED THAT THE APOLLO AND THE HARLEM OPERA HOUSE ARE MERGING.

EXCELLENT WORK, FRANK. YOU'VE BEEN A GOOD AND FAITHFUL MANAGER.

I'M GIVING YOU A HALF INTEREST IN THE APOLLO.

LEO BRECHER

But the **merger** is really a **takeover**.

The Harlem Opera House turns to **movies**.

And, Schiffman and Brecher move their operation to the Apollo.

FRANK SCHIFFMAN IS NOW CO-OWNER OF THE FINEST THEATER IN HARLEM—AND UNDISPUTED KING OF THE UPTOWN SCENE.

THE ONLY STAGE SHOW IN HARLEM

The Apollo changes its billing to "*The Only Stage Show in Harlem*" . . . and the legend begins.

CHAPTER 3
The 1930s: Swingin'

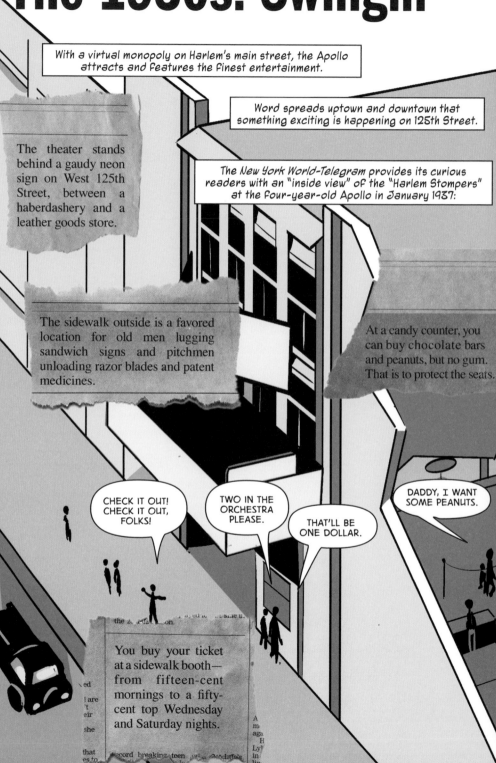

With a virtual monopoly on Harlem's main street, the Apollo attracts and features the finest entertainment.

Word spreads uptown and downtown that something exciting is happening on 125th Street.

The theater stands behind a gaudy neon sign on West 125th Street, between a haberdashery and a leather goods store.

The *New York World-Telegram* provides its curious readers with an "inside view" of the "Harlem Stompers" at the four-year-old Apollo in January 1937:

The sidewalk outside is a favored location for old men lugging sandwich signs and pitchmen unloading razor blades and patent medicines.

At a candy counter, you can buy chocolate bars and peanuts, but no gum. That is to protect the seats.

CHECK IT OUT! CHECK IT OUT, FOLKS!

TWO IN THE ORCHESTRA PLEASE.

THAT'LL BE ONE DOLLAR.

DADDY, I WANT SOME PEANUTS.

You buy your ticket at a sidewalk booth— from fifteen-cent mornings to a fifty-cent top Wednesday and Saturday nights.

The Apollo was once a burlesque house, and it still bears mementos of that colorful era.

The house seats 1,750 people. The roomy boxes next to the stage are generally inhabited by young men who appreciate the chorus line.

The stage itself is edged with applied pilasters of imitation marble, well chipped along the corners and tinted red, gilt, and blue.

The wallpaper has a recurring motif of a nude young woman.

OH MAMA!

On the rear wall hang three large oil paintings in ponderous frames, each featuring several square feet of female flesh.

The curtain is a startling crimson.

Enter through a narrow lobby lined with glistening mirrors and photographs of Harlem idols, all affectionately inscribed to the Apollo.

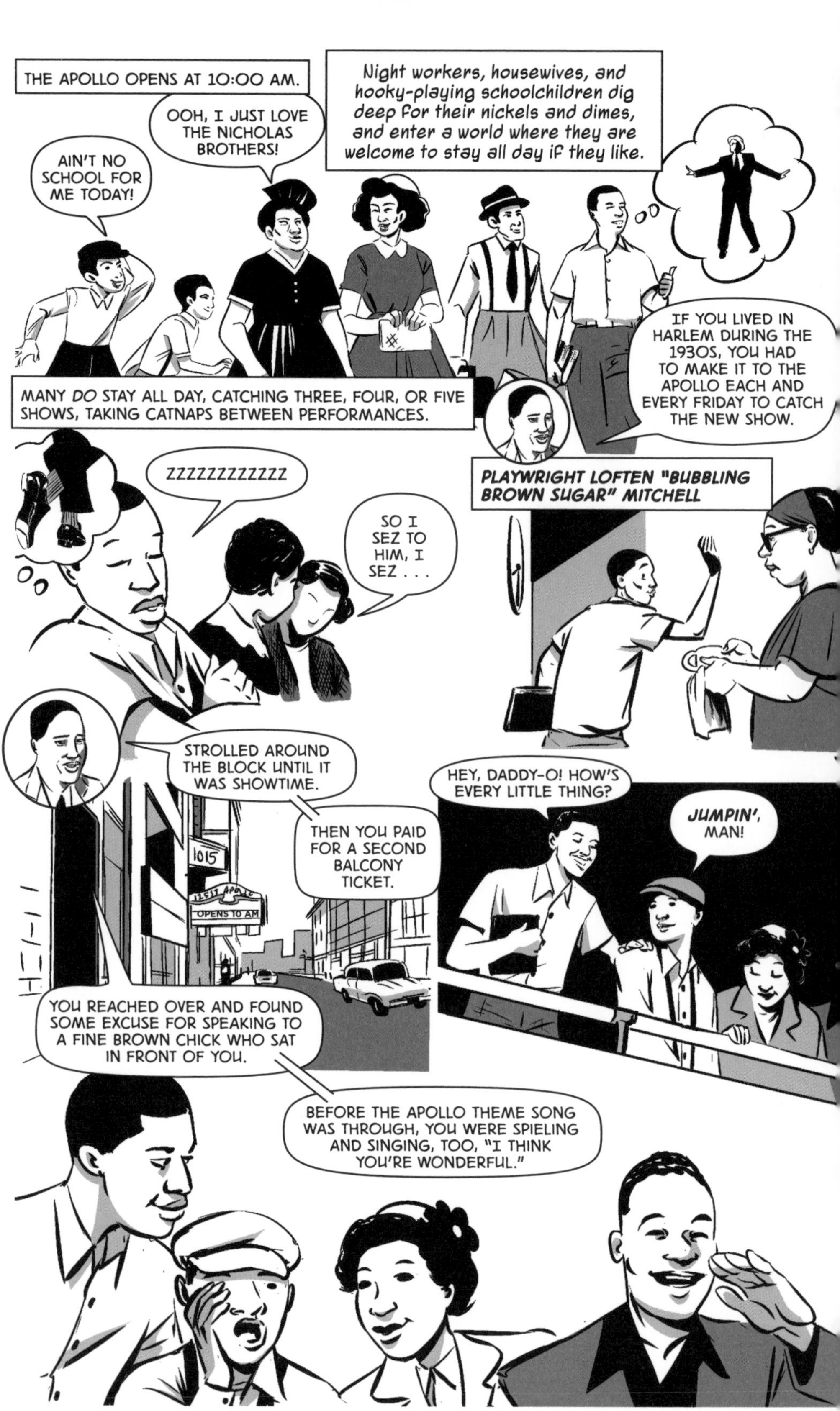

THE APOLLO OPENS AT 10:00 AM.
Night workers, housewives, and hooky-playing schoolchildren dig deep for their nickels and dimes, and enter a world where they are welcome to stay all day if they like.
AIN'T NO SCHOOL FOR ME TODAY!
OOH, I JUST LOVE THE NICHOLAS BROTHERS!
MANY DO STAY ALL DAY, CATCHING THREE, FOUR, OR FIVE SHOWS, TAKING CATNAPS BETWEEN PERFORMANCES.
IF YOU LIVED IN HARLEM DURING THE 1930S, YOU HAD TO MAKE IT TO THE APOLLO EACH AND EVERY FRIDAY TO CATCH THE NEW SHOW.
PLAYWRIGHT LOFTEN "BUBBLING BROWN SUGAR" MITCHELL
ZZZZZZZZZZZZ
SO I SEZ TO HIM, I SEZ . . .
STROLLED AROUND THE BLOCK UNTIL IT WAS SHOWTIME.
THEN YOU PAID FOR A SECOND BALCONY TICKET.
1015
OPENS 10 AM
HEY, DADDY-O! HOW'S EVERY LITTLE THING?
JUMPIN', MAN!
YOU REACHED OVER AND FOUND SOME EXCUSE FOR SPEAKING TO A FINE BROWN CHICK WHO SAT IN FRONT OF YOU.
BEFORE THE APOLLO THEME SONG WAS THROUGH, YOU WERE SPIELING AND SINGING, TOO, "I THINK YOU'RE WONDERFUL."

THE SHOW STRUCTURE IS ALWAYS BASICALLY THE SAME: FIRST A SHORT FILM, PERHAPS A BETTY BOOP CARTOON.

NEXT, A NEWSREEL, FOLLOWED BY A FEATURE FILM.

UNIVERSAL NEWS

THEN A PAUSE. SILENCE.

AT LAST, THE MASTER OF CEREMONIES ANNOUNCES, TO THE RISING APPLAUSE AND SCREAMS FROM THE AUDIENCE: "LADIES AND GENTLEMEN, IT'S SHOWTIME AT THE APOLLO!"

BA-BA-BOOM! THE BAND BREAKS INTO THE APOLLO THEME SONG, "I MAY BE WRONG (BUT I THINK YOU'RE WONDERFUL)," AND THE SHOW IS ROLLING.

THE BAND DOES A NUMBER WITH THE CHORUS LINE PERFORMING IN FRONT OF THEM.

THEN THE MC BRINGS ON A "SIGHT ACT" SUCH AS A TAP DANCER, ACROBAT, OR ANIMAL ACT . . .

. . . FOLLOWED BY A SINGER, THE CHORUS AGAIN, A COMEDY ACT, AND FINALLY THE FEATURED ATTRACTION OR BAND IN THE FINALE.

THE SHOWS, OR REVUES, LOOSELY REVOLVE AROUND A THEME.

★ Harlem Goes ★
HOLLYWOOD

HILLBILLY REVUE

VOODOO DRUMS

Modern Rhythm ♪♫

EBONY SHOWBOAT

THERE IS A NEW REVUE EACH WEEK. THIRTY-ONE SHOWS A WEEK: FOUR A DAY, PLUS AN EXTRA SHOW ON WEDNESDAY, SATURDAY, AND SUNDAY.

HALF HOUR!

WHAT?! DAMN! ARE YOU KIDDIN' ME? THE *HALF'S* ALREADY IN?!

MOST SHOWS RUN SIXTY TO NINETY MINUTES.

PERFORMERS OFTEN COMPLAIN THAT BY THE TIME THEY COME OFFSTAGE FROM ONE SHOW, THE BACKSTAGE BELL SIGNALING THIRTY MINUTES TO THE NEXT SHOW—THE HALF—HAS ALREADY RUNG.

MAKING THE SCENE AT THE APOLLO BECOMES THE ULTIMATE NIGHT ON THE TOWN . . .

. . . ESPECIALLY ON SATURDAY NIGHTS AND AT THE ANNUAL EASTER AND CHRISTMAS SHOWS, WHEN THE CROWDS REALLY "SHOW OUT."

The men appear in tight-belted, high-waisted coats, with freshly marcelled hair "conked" into beautifully rippling waves.

I HEAR COOP'S GOT SOME FINE SINGER WITH HIM.

YEAH, BILLIE SOMETHING, I THINK.

BABY, THAT NEW BARBER DID YOU RIGHT.

THANK YOU, DARLIN'. MMM, THAT PERFUME REALLY SENDS ME.

The women, fragrantly scented, gracefully glide through the lobby in tight slinky dresses, high heels, and veils.

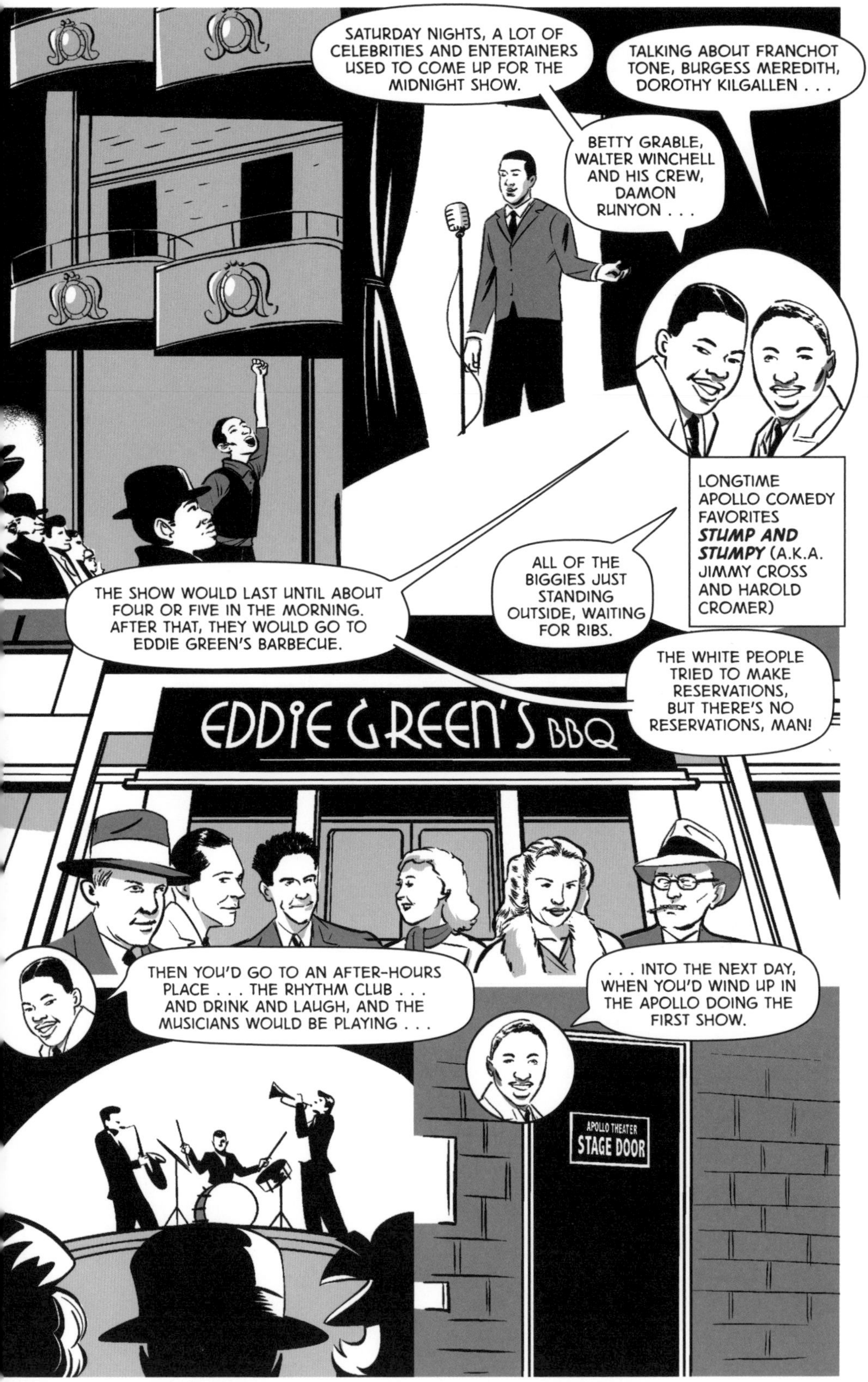
SATURDAY NIGHTS, A LOT OF CELEBRITIES AND ENTERTAINERS USED TO COME UP FOR THE MIDNIGHT SHOW.
TALKING ABOUT FRANCHOT TONE, BURGESS MEREDITH, DOROTHY KILGALLEN . . .
BETTY GRABLE, WALTER WINCHELL AND HIS CREW, DAMON RUNYON . . .
LONGTIME APOLLO COMEDY FAVORITES ***STUMP AND STUMPY*** (A.K.A. JIMMY CROSS AND HAROLD CROMER)
ALL OF THE BIGGIES JUST STANDING OUTSIDE, WAITING FOR RIBS.
THE SHOW WOULD LAST UNTIL ABOUT FOUR OR FIVE IN THE MORNING. AFTER THAT, THEY WOULD GO TO EDDIE GREEN'S BARBECUE.
THE WHITE PEOPLE TRIED TO MAKE RESERVATIONS, BUT THERE'S NO RESERVATIONS, MAN!
EDDIE GREEN'S BBQ
THEN YOU'D GO TO AN AFTER-HOURS PLACE . . . THE RHYTHM CLUB . . . AND DRINK AND LAUGH, AND THE MUSICIANS WOULD BE PLAYING . . .
. . . INTO THE NEXT DAY, WHEN YOU'D WIND UP IN THE APOLLO DOING THE FIRST SHOW.
APOLLO THEATER
STAGE DOOR

DOWNTOWN THEATERS SUCH AS THE PALACE, THE PARAMOUNT, AND THE ROXY ARE IN THE SAME CITY AS THE APOLLO, BUT THEY INHABIT DIFFERENT WORLDS.

Whites might come uptown for a night at the Apollo, but most of the black people who travel downtown are performers.

SOME PERFORMERS PLAY THE APOLLO AND ONE OF THE DOWNTOWN THEATERS SIMULTANEOUSLY, AN AWE-INSPIRING PRACTICE KNOWN AS **DOUBLING**.

Cab Calloway's piano player **Benny Payne** explains the routine in Calloway's autobiography.

STUMPY (A.K.A. HAROLD CROMER)

WE WERE ALREADY PLAYING FIVE SHOWS A DAY AT THE APOLLO. FOR FOUR DAYS, WE PLAYED **EIGHT** SHOWS A DAY: TWO SHOWS AT THE APOLLO, THEN WE GOT TAXICABS DOWNTOWN TO THE PARAMOUNT . . .

. . . BACK UPTOWN JUST IN TIME FOR THE NEXT SHOW AT THE APOLLO, JUMPED IN CABS AGAIN TO GET DOWNTOWN FOR THE SECOND PARAMOUNT SHOW, CAME BACK UPTOWN, THEN DOWNTOWN AGAIN, THEN BACK UPTOWN FOR THE MIDNIGHT SHOW AT THE APOLLO.

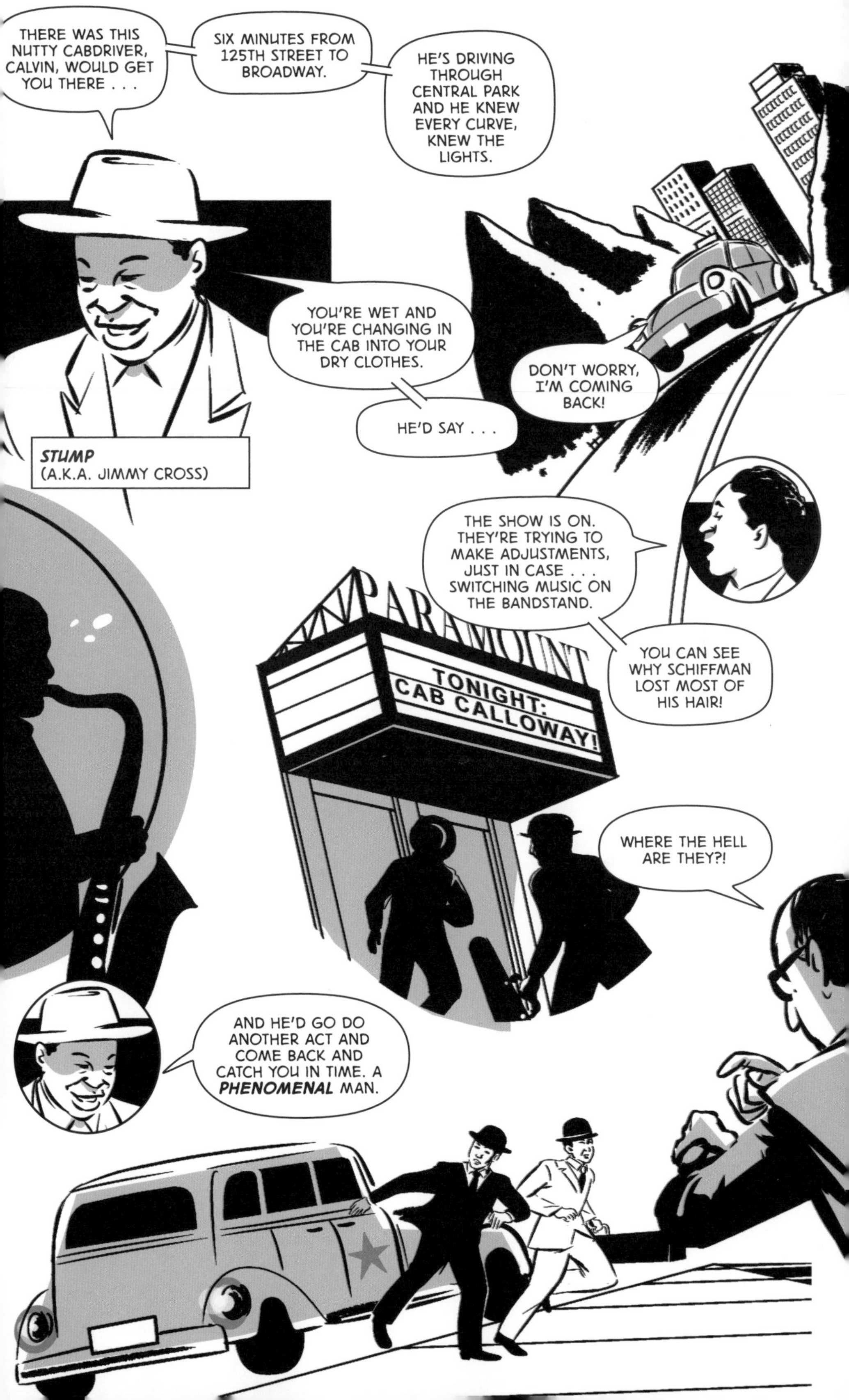

THERE WAS THIS NUTTY CABDRIVER, CALVIN, WOULD GET YOU THERE . . .
SIX MINUTES FROM 125TH STREET TO BROADWAY.
HE'S DRIVING THROUGH CENTRAL PARK AND HE KNEW EVERY CURVE, KNEW THE LIGHTS.
YOU'RE WET AND YOU'RE CHANGING IN THE CAB INTO YOUR DRY CLOTHES.
HE'D SAY . . .
DON'T WORRY, I'M COMING BACK!
STUMP
(A.K.A. JIMMY CROSS)
THE SHOW IS ON. THEY'RE TRYING TO MAKE ADJUSTMENTS, JUST IN CASE . . . SWITCHING MUSIC ON THE BANDSTAND.
PARAMOUNT
TONIGHT: CAB CALLOWAY!
YOU CAN SEE WHY SCHIFFMAN LOST MOST OF HIS HAIR!
WHERE THE HELL ARE THEY?!
AND HE'D GO DO ANOTHER ACT AND COME BACK AND CATCH YOU IN TIME. A *PHENOMENAL* MAN.

THE WEEKLY REVUES ARE CREATED BY A HANDFUL OF AFRICAN AMERICAN PRODUCERS— *CHARLIE DAVIS*, *ADDISON CAREY*, *LEONARD HARPER*, *TEDDIE BLACKMAN*, AND *CLARENCE ROBINSON*—WHO WORK WITH THE ACTS.

While one revue unfolds on the Apollo's stage, the following week's show is created, rehearsed, and readied in the theater's basement rehearsal hall.

THE APOLLO CHORUS GIRLS ARE CONSIDERED THE *BEST* LINE IN NEW YORK.

THE PRODUCTION SCHEDULE IS PROBABLY TOUGHEST ON THE CHORUS GIRLS, SAYS FORMER HOOFER CAROL CARTER . . .

THESE POOR GIRLS WOULD DO A SHOW, THEN GO DOWNSTAIRS TO THE REHEARSAL HALL, LEARN THE NEW NUMBERS, GET FITTED FOR COSTUMES—WHICH WERE MADE IN THE APOLLO'S OWN TAILOR SHOP— AND, BY THE TIME THEY HAD FINISHED REHEARSAL, THEY ONLY HAD FIVE OR TEN MINUTES TO GO UPSTAIRS.

THERE WAS A LITTLE EXIT IN THE REHEARSAL HALL SO YOU *WOULDN'T* HAVE TO GO OUT ON 125TH STREET—IN THE BACK, UP THE LITTLE STEPS AND THROUGH THE ALLEY, WHICH WOULD TAKE YOU TO 126TH STREET.

CAROL CARTER

TAKE A LEFT TURN TOWARD EIGHTH AVENUE RUN THROUGH THE STAGE DOOR . . .

. . . UPSTAIRS TO THE BIG DRESSING ROOM, AND GET INTO THEIR COSTUMES REAL FAST FOR THE NEXT SHOW!

THE MASTERS OF CEREMONY—ESPECIALLY *RALPH COOPER* AND *WILLIE BRYANT*—KEEP THE SHOWS MOVING AND LIVELY, PERFORMANCE AFTER PERFORMANCE, WEEK AFTER WEEK.

Some credit the Apollo with originating the modern-day concept of the master of ceremonies.

WILLIE BRYANT IS BELOVED BY ALL.

LEONARD REED, WHO, LIKE BRYANT, HAS A VERY LIGHT COMPLEXION, IS AN EARLY DANCE PARTNER OF BRYANT'S.

WILLIE WAS A GREAT SHOWMAN WHO COULD DO IT ALL. HE WAS ON THE BALL, BUT BITTER.

LEONARD REED

HE WAS PART NEGRO, AND DOWNTOWN THEY WOULDN'T LET HIM WORK. WILLIE WAS MADE TO STAY IN HARLEM. HE NEVER GOT THE CHANCE TO WORK IN PLACES THAT, SAY, BOB HOPE DID.

RALPH COOPER IS AN APOLLO ICON: SHOWMAN, BANDLEADER, HOOFER, COMEDIAN, MC, CREATOR OF AMATEUR NIGHT, AND MORE . . .

I WENT WHITE. WILLIE DIDN'T. I PLAYED ALL THE WHITE PLACES BY MYSELF . . .

WILLIE WAS A *GENIUS*. ONE OF THE GREATS IN SHOW BUSINESS THAT NEVER GOT ANYWHERE, BECAUSE OF HIS COLOR.

THE WHITE MAN ONLY LETS A FEW NEGROES THROUGH.

PLAYWRIGHT **LOFTEN MITCHELL** REMEMBERS RALPH COOPER IN THE *AMSTERDAM NEWS*—

THE GREATEST COMMENT ABOUT RALPH IS THAT HE USED TO WRITE OUT PASSES FOR US. WE KEPT THE PASSES FOR HIS AUTOGRAPH, THEN PAID OUR WAY INTO THE SHOW.

RALPH COOPER SERVED AS AN IDOL WHEN BLACK CHILDREN HAD PRECIOUS FEW.

AND IN THE DEPRESSION, THAT WAS REALLY *SOMETHING*!

RALPH COOPER AND FRANK SCHIFFMAN CALL A TRUCE.

All of Harlem assumes Schiffman resents Cooper for abandoning him back in 1934.

But Schiffman is far too smart to sacrifice a powerful attraction like Cooper out of personal pique.

Cooper, who is no fan of Schiffman, also knows they need each other.

55

RALPH COOPER BECOMES ONE OF HARLEM'S LEADING CELEBRITIES, THANKS TO THE SUCCESS OF AMATEUR NIGHT WHICH HE PIONEERS AT THE LAFAYETTE.

It don't mean a thing...

FOR MANY WHITES AROUND THE COUNTRY, THE APOLLO RADIO BROADCASTS ARE THEIR FIRST EXPOSURE TO THE NEW SOUNDS OF BLACK SWING MUSIC.

THROUGH COOPER'S WEDNESDAY "AMATEUR NIGHT IN HARLEM" RADIO SHOW, NOW BROADCAST LIVE FROM THE APOLLO OVER WMCA AND TWENTY-ONE OF ITS AFFILIATED STATIONS AROUND THE COUNTRY, THE APOLLO BECOMES NATIONALLY KNOWN.

Big bands have been the main force in music since the early '20s.

But a new musical form emerges by the time Duke Ellington hits in 1932 with the tune that gave the new sound a name.

WHITE BANDLEADERS ADOPT, REFINE, AND POPULARIZE THE *SWING* SOUND. BUT IT'S THE BLACK MUSICIANS IN THE SEMINAL BLACK ORCHESTRAS, WHO CREATE THE NEW MUSIC.

BENNY GOODMAN

THE DORSEY BROTHERS

ARTIE SHAW

FLETCHER HENDERSON

CAB CALLOWAY

ANDY KIRK

COUNT BASIE

DUKE ELLINGTON

CHICK WEBB

JIMMIE LUNCEFORD

DUKE ELLINGTON IS THE EPITOME OF URBAN SOPHISTICATION.

ELLINGTON AND COLLABORATOR BILLY STRAYHORN PRODUCE ETERNAL CLASSICS.

He, more than anyone else, has a right to be discouraged when the music became identified with white bandleaders. Yet he makes it work for him.

ELLINGTON HAS BEEN DEVELOPING AND HONING HIS SOUND FOR MANY YEARS BY THE TIME SWING BECOMES A NATIONAL PHENOMENON.

I MERELY TOOK THE ENERGY IT TAKES TO POUT, AND WROTE SOME BLUES.

WHILE DUKE ELLINGTON APPEALS TO HARLEMITES' SENSE OF STYLE, *COUNT BASIE* APPEALS TO THEIR SENSE OF EXCITEMENT.

HE BECOMES STRANDED ON TOUR IN KANSAS CITY IN THE EARLY '30S, AND SETTLES IN TO THE SCENE IN THE MIDWEST.

JOHN HAMMOND IS CAPTIVATED WHEN HE HEARS BASIE ON HIS CAR RADIO IN A LIVE BROADCAST FROM CHICAGO IN 1935.

Bill Basie is from New Jersey, and is greatly influenced by listening to Fats Waller play at Harlem's Lincoln Theater.

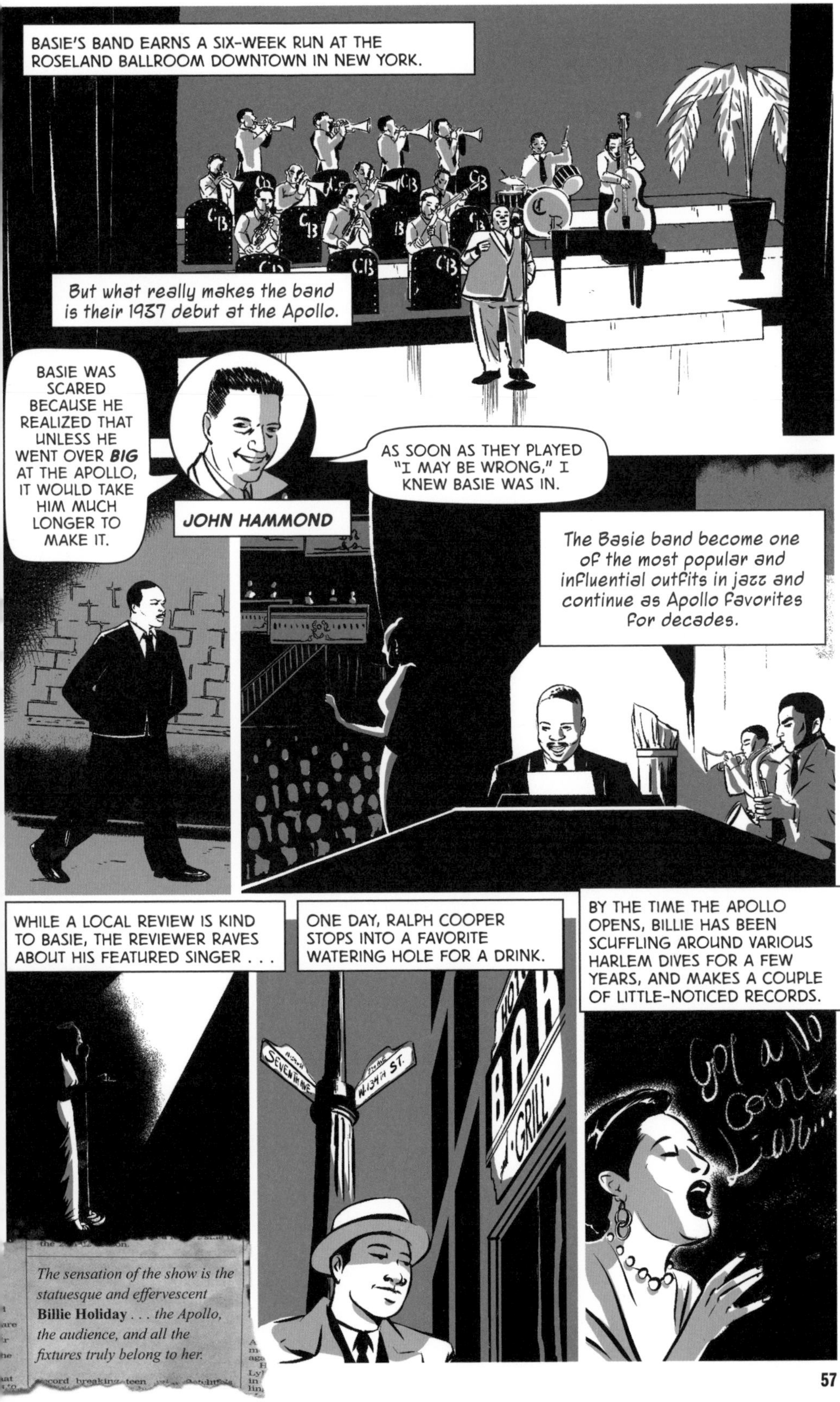
BASIE'S BAND EARNS A SIX-WEEK RUN AT THE ROSELAND BALLROOM DOWNTOWN IN NEW YORK.
But what really makes the band is their 1937 debut at the Apollo.
BASIE WAS SCARED BECAUSE HE REALIZED THAT UNLESS HE WENT OVER **BIG** AT THE APOLLO, IT WOULD TAKE HIM MUCH LONGER TO MAKE IT.
JOHN HAMMOND
AS SOON AS THEY PLAYED "I MAY BE WRONG," I KNEW BASIE WAS IN.
The Basie band become one of the most popular and influential outfits in jazz and continue as Apollo favorites for decades.
WHILE A LOCAL REVIEW IS KIND TO BASIE, THE REVIEWER RAVES ABOUT HIS FEATURED SINGER . . .
The sensation of the show is the statuesque and effervescent **Billie Holiday** *. . . the Apollo, the audience, and all the fixtures truly belong to her.*
ONE DAY, RALPH COOPER STOPS INTO A FAVORITE WATERING HOLE FOR A DRINK.
SEVENTH AVE
W. 134TH ST.
BAR
GRILL
BY THE TIME THE APOLLO OPENS, BILLIE HAS BEEN SCUFFLING AROUND VARIOUS HARLEM DIVES FOR A FEW YEARS, AND MAKES A COUPLE OF LITTLE-NOTICED RECORDS.
Got a No Count Liar...

COOPER LOVES BILLIE.

HE TOUTS HER TO FRANK SCHIFFMAN.

YOU NEVER HEARD SINGING SO SLOW, SO LAZY, WITH SUCH A DRAWL . . . IT AIN'T THE BLUES—I DON'T KNOW WHAT IT IS, BUT YOU GOT TO HEAR HER!

COOPER BUYS HER AN EVENING GOWN AND SLIPPERS.

HE PUTS HIS BAND THROUGH ITS PACES, FAMILIARIZING THEM WITH BILLIE'S ARRANGEMENTS.

THE APOLLO BOOKS HER FOR THE WEEK OF APRIL 19, 1935, ON A SHOW HEADLINED BY COOPER AND HIS ORCHESTRA.

In tiny type near the bottom of the bill, she is incorrectly listed as "Billie Halliday."

BILLIE IS NEARLY OVERCOME BY STAGE FRIGHT.

COMEDIAN PIGMEAT MARKHAM GENTLY NUDGES HER ON.

ONCE THE SPOTLIGHT HITS HER— LIKE MOONLIGHT—SHE REGAINS HER COMPOSURE.

What a little moonlight can do...

ENCORE!!

ENCORE!!

THEY WILL NOT LET HER GO WITHOUT AN ENCORE.

WOMEN ARE KEY TO THE SWING ERA, ALTHOUGH USUALLY AS FEATURED PERFORMERS IN THE BIG BANDS, NOT HEADLINERS.

Life in the male world of the big bands is tough for women.

Billie Holiday earns only seventy dollars a week with Count Basie, out of which she also has to maintain her wardrobe.

SOME, LIKE LENA HORNE, WHO LEAVES THE COTTON CLUB AND JOINS THE NOBLE SISSLE ORCHESTRA, HAVE MORE STAR POWER THAN THEIR BANDLEADERS.

NOBLE SISSLE

THE NONPAREIL IS **ELLA FITZGERALD**.

The story of her early days as a nervous amateur is frequently recounted— usually erroneously placing her at the Apollo's Amateur Night.

IN FACT, SHE IS DISCOVERED IN 1934 BY FRIENDS OF BANDLEADER **CHICK WEBB** AT AN AMATEUR-NIGHT PERFORMANCE AT SCHIFFMAN'S NEIGHBORING HARLEM OPERA HOUSE.

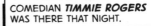

COMEDIAN **TIMMIE ROGERS** WAS THERE THAT NIGHT.

SHE DIDN'T KNOW THAT SHE COULD SING THAT WELL. SHE STARTED AS A **LINDY HOPPER** DANCING AT THE SAVOY BALLROOM.

SHE STOPPED THE SHOW COLD. THEY MADE HER TAKE AN ENCORE. SHE BROKE THE MOTHER *UP!*

The object of my affection...

ELLA IS INTRODUCED TO BANDLEADER CHICK WEBB, AND A CLASSIC PAIRING BEGINS.

WEBB IS A SUPERB DRUMMER WHOSE THUNDERING SOLOS ALSO ATTRACT A LARGE, SERIOUS JAZZ AUDIENCE.

Chick Webb has been thrilling the Lindy Hoppers at Harlem's *Savoy Ballroom* for years.

Chick is small and frail from an ongoing bout with tuberculosis, and he sits, hunchbacked, behind his massive drum set.

Chick's band with Ella Fitzgerald become Apollo favorites.

ELLA HELPS BRING CHICK NATIONAL PROMINENCE.

When Webb dies in 1939, she takes over the band and keeps it together for another three years.

Ella, on the other hand, is large, gawky, and plain-looking.

Two beautiful ugly ducklings, they are blessed with abundant talent, and they are drawn together in a bond of love, respect, and support.

FRANK SCHIFFMAN TELLS HIS SON JACK THAT THE MOST *MOVING* THING HE EVER HEARD WAS ELLA FITZGERALD SINGING "MY BUDDY" OVER WEBB'S CASKET.

My Buddy...

THE BIG BANDS ARE FEATURED ATTRACTIONS, BUT ALSO PLAY FOR ALL THE OTHER ACTS ON THE BILL.

ANDY KIRK'S CLOUDS OF JOY

BILL "BOJANGLES" ROBINSON

INSTEAD OF INJECTING YOURSELF, YOU'D SOFTEN DOWN, SO YOU COULD HEAR EVERY ONE OF THEIR STEPS.

I ENJOYED THE PERFORMERS THAT I BACKED UP.

WE ALWAYS HAD REGARD FOR THE ARTIST, WHATEVER HE WAS DOING.

WHEN WE DID *OUR* THING, THAT WAS WHEN WE'D FEATURE *OUR* MUSIC.

FOR THE FIRST FEW YEARS, ALL EXCEPT THE MIGHTIEST BIG BANDS PLAY IN THE *PIT.*

WHEN IT IS TIME FOR THE BAND'S SPECIALTY NUMBER, THE CURTAIN COMES DOWN, AND THE COMICS COME OUT TO COVER FOR THEM . . .

. . . AS THE BAND MEMBERS PICK UP THEIR INSTRUMENTS AND HEAD BACKSTAGE . . .

. . . TO THE FEATURED BANDSTAND ONSTAGE WHERE THEY PERFORM THEIR BIG NUMBER.

IN ANOTHER PRACTICE SOME CONDEMN AS DEGRADING, UNTIL THE LATE '40S MOST BLACK MALE COMICS WEAR EXAGGERATED BURNT-CORK "BLACKFACE" MAKEUP.

Many bandleaders find this degrading, and by the late '30s it is eliminated, and the stage is built out over the old pit.

Despite protests from the NAACP and others, the comics say they feel naked without it.

THE APOLLO BOASTS A VIRTUAL STOCK COMPANY OF THE *FINEST* COMEDIANS.

DUSTY FLETCHER

JOHN "SPIDER BRUCE" MASON

JOHNNY LEE LONG

JIMMIE BASKETTE

SPO-DEE-O-DEE

TIM "KINGFISH" MOORE

They're presented in sketches or skits involving up to a half dozen people or more.

I CALL THEM *LEBENSBILDER* . . . PICTURES OF LIFE.

FRANK SCHIFFMAN

DEWEY "PIGMEAT" MARKHAM PROBABLY PLAYS THE APOLLO MORE OFTEN THAN ANY OTHER PERFORMER INTO THE '70S.

During the '30s he is on the bill every week for four years.

HE IS MOST FAMOUS FOR THE *"HERE COME THE JUDGE"* ROUTINE.

INTRODUCED IN 1929, IT'S MADE NATIONALLY FAMOUS BY SAMMY DAVIS JR. IN THE LATE '60S.

MARKHAM ALSO CLAIMS TO HAVE INVENTED THE COMICAL DANCE MOVE *"TRUCKIN'."*

IT WAS THE BIGGEST THING IN THE COUNTRY!

THEN ONE DAY I SAW AN AL JOLSON MOVIE, AND THERE IN A BIG COLORED SEQUENCE WAS CAB CALLOWAY AND HIS BAND TRUCKIN' ALL OVER HEAVEN.

THERE WAS MY TRUCK GONE DOWN THE DRAIN, JUST LIKE *"HERE COME THE JUDGE."*

BUT OF ALL THE EARLY COMEDIANS, PROBABLY THE MOST BELOVED AND MOST SUCCESSFUL IS *JACKIE "MOMS" MABLEY*.

A regular for years at Connie's Inn, Moms starts at the Apollo in the early days at eighty-five dollars a week . . .

. . . becomes a headliner in black theaters and white nightclubs . .

A P O L L O

FEATURING "MOMS" MABLEY!

. . . and by the early '70s commands a salary of $8,500 a week at the Apollo.

LORETTA MARY AIKEN IS KNOWN TO EVERYONE AS "MOMS."

One of the early monologists, she delights the Apollo with folksy tales.

MY CHILDREN!

YEAH, MOMS, YOU RIGHT!

SHE PLAYS A SILLY, RANDY, BUT SAGE OLD BAT WHOSE *"MOMS' SHUFFLE"* IS ALMOST AS WELL KNOWN AS PIGMEAT'S *TRUCKIN'.*

AN OLD MAN CAN'T DO NOTHIN' FOR ME BUT BRING ME A MESSAGE FROM A YOUNG ONE.

MY SLOGAN IS, BY ALL MEANS DO WHAT YOU WANT TO DO, BUT KNOW WHAT YOU'RE DOIN'.

DANCE LEGEND *HONI COLES* IS ANOTHER KEY FIGURE WHO IS A PART OF THE APOLLO FOR MOST OF ITS HISTORY.

AT ONE TIME IN THE WORLD OF SHOW BUSINESS, THE TAP DANCER, OR HOOFER, WAS PROBABLY THE MOST IMPORTANT ACT ON THE AVERAGE BILL.

HE WAS THE BEST DRESSED, THE BEST CONDITIONED, THE MOST CONSCIENTIOUS PERFORMER ON ANY BILL.

In the early '30s, he develops a style known as "high-speed rhythm tap."

HE TALKS ABOUT THE EARLY DAYS OF DANCE AT THE APOLLO IN THE *AMSTERDAM NEWS:*

HE COULD OPEN THE SHOW, CLOSE IT, OR FILL ANY SPOT, ESPECIALLY THE TROUBLE SPOTS.

AND IN SPITE OF BEING THE LEAST PAID, HE WAS THE ACT TO "STOP THE SHOW."

COLES MEETS **CHOLLY ATKINS** WHILE TRAVELING WITH CAB CALLOWAY'S BAND.

After World War II, they form the team of Coles and Atkins.

But by that time the golden era of the dancers and the big bands has passed, making the duo "the last of the class acts."

FRANK SCHIFFMAN IS A TREMENDOUS FAN.

Through the '50s, Coles and Atkins traditionally reopen the Apollo, with Billy Eckstine, in August, after its usual summer break for renovations.

IN THE EARLY '60S, COLES BECOMES THE APOLLO'S **PRODUCTION MANAGER**.

Along with Atkins, he's an important mentor to all types performers until his death in 19

IN THE '30S, AND FOREVER THEREAFTER, **DANCE** IS A VITAL PART OF THE APOLLO EXPERIENCE.

SANDMAN SIMS

WANTA-BE TAP DANCERS, GONNA-BE TAP DANCERS, TRIED-TO-BE TAP DANCERS.

A LOT OF DANCERS WERE CHALLENGED RIGHT THERE ONSTAGE!

WHEN BIG-NAME DANCERS PLAYED THE APOLLO, THERE WAS NOTHING IN THE AUDIENCE BUT DANCERS WITH THEIR TAP SHOES.

UP IN THE BALCONY, DANCERS—AND THE FIRST SIX ROWS, YOU SAW NOTHING BUT TAP DANCERS.

HEY, MAN, YOU AIN'T DOING NUTHIN'.

LET ME COME UP THERE AND SEE WHAT YOU CAN REALLY DO.

COMPETITION FORCES DANCERS INTO MORE AND MORE ACROBATIC STUNTS, AS EACH ACT TRIES TO OUTDO THE OTHER.

Debilitating injuries short careers and sometimes leave dancers crippled.

PERHAPS THE MOST SPECTACULAR DANCE ACTS OF ALL TIME ARE THE **BERRY BROTHERS** AND THE **NICHOLAS BROTHERS**.

Known as "*flash acts*" because of their blinding speed and fancy steps, they are among only a handful of dance acts that can headline an Apollo show.

ONCE, TO TOP THE NICHOLAS BROTHERS IN A 1936 CHALLENGE MEET, ANANIAS BERRY DEVISES A FINALE WHERE HE AND BROTHER JIMMY LEAP FROM THE BANDSTAND . . .

. . . AS THE BAND PLAYS ITS FINAL NOTE, AND CRASH TWELVE FEET DOWN INTO TENDON-RIPPING SPLITS ON BOTH SIDES OF BROTHER WARREN . . .

. . . WHO ALSO DOES A SPLIT AFTER COMPLETING A TWISTING BACK SOMERSAULT.

THE BERRY BROTHERS BEGIN WITH ELLINGTON AT THE COTTON CLUB, TOUR ABROAD, HELP OPEN RADIO CITY MUSIC HALL IN 1932, AND ALSO WORK IN HOLLYWOOD.

HAROLD AND FAYARD NICHOLAS— EIGHT AND FOURTEEN—OPEN AT THE COTTON CLUB.

Ananias, weakened by years of bodily abuse in pursuit of his art, dies in 1951. He is just thirty-nine.

The boys, clad in top hats and evening clothes, become the darlings of Harlem.

WHEN THEY DEBUT AT THE APOLLO ON MARCH 2, 1934, THEY HAVE ALREADY MADE THE FILM *KID MILLIONS* WITH EDDIE CANTOR—WHICH WOULD COME OUT LATER THAT YEAR— AND STARRED IN THE ZIEGFELD FOLLIES ON BROADWAY.

THE NICHOLAS BROTHERS ARE AN ALL-AROUND ACT, COMBINING WILD AIRBORNE SPLITS WITH TASTY TAPPING AND SINGING.

HAROLD EVEN DOES IMITATIONS OF CAB CALLOWAY AND LOUIS ARMSTRONG.

HOWEVER, THE ONES TO WHOM ALL THE APOLLO'S DANCERS OWE THE GREATEST DEBT ARE *BILL "BOJANGLES" ROBINSON* AND *JOHN BUBBLES*.

BILL ROBINSON BEGINS HIS CAREER AS A "PICK"—FROM THE DEROGATORY TERM FOR A SMALL BLACK CHILD: *PICKANINNY*.

STARDOM DOESN'T COME UNTIL THE SMASH HIT 1928 STAGE PRODUCTION OF LEW LESLIE'S *BLACKBIRDS*, WHEN BOJANGLES IS FIFTY YEARS OLD . . .

SUDDENLY, HARLEM WAS CRAZY ABOUT BOJANGLES.

THE LEGENDARY *ETHEL WATERS*

These fast-stepping black children are employed as surefire *showstoppers* to bolster the white star's vaudeville act.

EVERYBODY IN HARLEM SAID BOJANGLES WAS A MAGNIFICENT DANCER.

BO, BO!

THE YEAR SCHIFFMAN TAKES OVER THE APOLLO, BOJANGLES ACHIEVES HIS GREATEST FAME, STARRING WITH AND COACHING SHIRLEY TEMPLE IN THE FILM *THE LITTLE COLONEL*.

JOHN BUBBLES INVENTS *RHYTHM TAP*—THE STYLE HONI COLES MASTERS AND SPEEDS UP.

BUBBLES AND PARTNER *FORD L. "BUCK" WASHINGTON* BRING "DOWNTOWN" STYLE TO THE APOLLO.

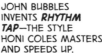

Buck and Bubbles are already headliners on Broadway In 1935, Bubbles is George Gershwin's personal choice to play Sportin' Life in *Porgy and Bess*.

WE WERE AN "AW!" ACT. WE WALKED ON THE STAGE UPTOWN IN A DOWNTOWN STYLE, THEY LOOKED AT US AND SAID, "AW!"

AT THE SAME TIME, BUCK PLAYS STOP-TIME ON THE PIANO IN THE LAZIEST MANNER IMAGINABLE.

HE FALLS OFF THE STOOL, REMEMBERING TO REACH UP FROM THE FLOOR JUST IN TIME TO PLUNK ONE NOTE EVERY SIXTEEN BARS.

DANCER PAUL DRAPER DESCRIBES THEM IN MARSHALL AND JEAN STEARNS'S BOOK, *JAZZ DANCE*:

PAUL DRAPER

BUBBLES HAS A CASUAL APPROACH TO THE COMPLICATED STEPS HE EXECUTES. HIS NONCHALANT MANNER CONTRADICTS THE INCREDIBLE THINGS HIS FEET ARE DOING.

YOU THINK HE IS JUST GOING TO STROLL AROUND THE STAGE, WHEN PRESTO, HE'LL TOSS OFF A BURST OF SIGHT AND SOUND THAT YOU JUST CAN'T BELIEVE.

DURING THE 1930S, THERE ARE AS MANY AS FIFTY TOP DANCE ACTS PLAYING REGULARLY AT THE APOLLO . . .

. . . ALONG WITH DOZENS OF OTHER COMEDIANS, SINGERS, EVEN ACROBATS CONTRIBUTING TO FRANK SCHIFFMAN'S TREASURED *VAUDEVILLE-VARIETY FORMAT*.

And, the Apollo continues the process of "nurturing" them, begun in the 1920s at the Lafayette.

SCHIFFMAN HAS A CIRCLE OF COLLEAGUES IN NIGHTCLUBS AND THEATERS WHO BREAK IN ACTS FOR THE APOLLO.

SANDMAN SIMS

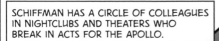

HE WOULD TAKE YOU OUT AND HOLD YOU AWHILE. GROOM YOU AND WORK YOU AROUND TILL YOU GOT A REAL GOOD ACT. BUILD YOUR ACT UP, AND BRING IT BACK TO THE APOLLO.

SOME CHARACTERIZE THE ARRANGEMENT LESS CHARITABLY.

THE APOLLO HAD A WORKING ARRANGEMENT WITH THE HOWARD THEATER IN WASHINGTON, THE ROYAL IN BALTIMORE, AND THE EARLE IN PHILLY.

IF YOU WANTED TO PLAY THE APOLLO, YOU HAD TO GET BOOKED FOR THE LOWER PRICE AT THE OTHER THEATERS.

JOHN HAMMOND

ACCOUNT OF APOLLO-THEATRE 4/8/39

Postal Telegraph

No doubt, Schiffman, the wily competitor, has a financial motive—and the theater owners regularly share contract prices, box office numbers, and critical reviews.

THE STRING OF BLACK THEATERS AND CLUBS ACROSS THE COUNTRY—SOMETIMES CALLED THE *CHITLIN CIRCUIT*—HAS A LONG HISTORY THAT PREDATES THE APOLLO.

Most of the performers who make it to the Apollo—and before that, the Lafayette—have to first learn the ropes, make a living, and prove themselves by playing a string of motley theaters around the country.

In the '20s, it is known as the Theatre Owners' Booking Association circuit—*T.O.B.A.*, or Toby Time.

Among African American performers, those initials come to stand for "tough on black asses."

LEONARD REED STARTS PLAYING THE CIRCUIT IN 1923 AS A CHARLESTON-STYLE DANCER . . .

THE GRAND THEATER IN CHICAGO WAS THE FIRST ON THE T.O.B.A. CIRCUIT. THEN, THE GLOBE IN ST. LOUIS, THE LINCOLN IN KANSAS CITY, THEN OKLAHOMA CITY, MUSKOGEE, AND THE ELLA B. MOORE THEATER IN DALLAS.

MOST OF THE THEATER OWNERS WERE WHITE, EXCEPT FOR THREE WOMEN WHO OWNED THEATERS IN OKLAHOMA CITY, TULSA, AND DALLAS.

FROM DALLAS TO HOUSTON, GALVESTON, SHREVEPORT, AND THEN TO MOBILE AND BIRMINGHAM TO ATLANTA.

THE T.O.B.A. CIRCUIT ENDED IN WASHINGTON, DC, AT THE MID-CITY, BLUE MOUSE, AND THE FOUR ACRES THEATERS—THAT WAS A SPLIT WEEK.

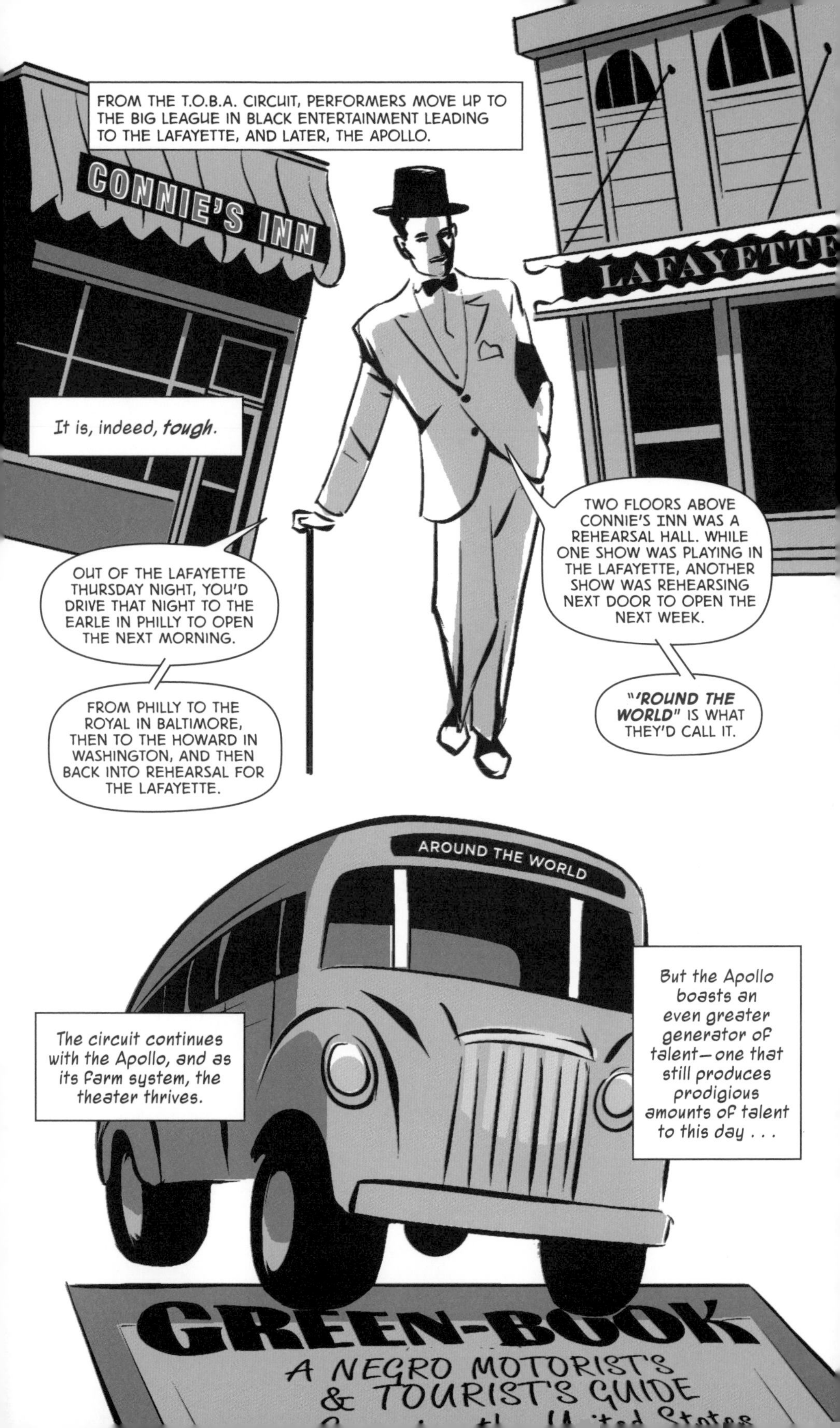
FROM THE T.O.B.A. CIRCUIT, PERFORMERS MOVE UP TO THE BIG LEAGUE IN BLACK ENTERTAINMENT LEADING TO THE LAFAYETTE, AND LATER, THE APOLLO.
CONNIE'S INN
LAFAYETTE
It is, indeed, *tough*.
TWO FLOORS ABOVE CONNIE'S INN WAS A REHEARSAL HALL. WHILE ONE SHOW WAS PLAYING IN THE LAFAYETTE, ANOTHER SHOW WAS REHEARSING NEXT DOOR TO OPEN THE NEXT WEEK.
OUT OF THE LAFAYETTE THURSDAY NIGHT, YOU'D DRIVE THAT NIGHT TO THE EARLE IN PHILLY TO OPEN THE NEXT MORNING.
FROM PHILLY TO THE ROYAL IN BALTIMORE, THEN TO THE HOWARD IN WASHINGTON, AND THEN BACK INTO REHEARSAL FOR THE LAFAYETTE.
"***'ROUND THE WORLD***" IS WHAT THEY'D CALL IT.
AROUND THE WORLD
The circuit continues with the Apollo, and as its farm system, the theater thrives.
But the Apollo boasts an even greater generator of talent—one that still produces prodigious amounts of talent to this day . . .
GREEN-BOOK
A NEGRO MOTORIST'S
& TOURIST'S GUIDE

CHAPTER 4

Amateur Night and the Apollo Audience

AMATEUR NIGHT, THE GREAT APOLLO TRADITION THAT HAS PRODUCED SO MUCH TALENT, COMES TO TELEVISION IN 1987 ON THE POPULAR LATE-NIGHT SERIES *SHOWTIME AT THE APOLLO*.

The long-running show keeps Amateur Night alive for new generations.

IT'S FUN AND EXCITING!

HOST
STEVE HARVEY

WE LOVE THE IDEA OF HELPING DISCOVER GREAT NEW TALENT.

AND WE GET A SLIGHTLY PERVERSE PLEASURE SEEING A HAPLESS AMATEUR BOOED OFFSTAGE.

However, the TV broadcast reflects a very different era.

Now, the sky's the limit, and urban music and urban popular culture rule.

Top stars emerge from everywhere, thanks to the Internet.

But back in the pre-television days, it's a very different environment for generations of African American hopefuls.

The legend of Amateur Night at the Apollo builds over decades, from thousands of individual stories . . .

JAMES BROWN, MEET SANDMAN SIMS.

I GAVE HIM A PAIR OF WHITE SNEAKERS.

IN THE '50S, JAMES BROWN CAME TO NEW YORK, AND HE DIDN'T HAVE NO SHOES, NOTHING TO DANCE IN, NOTHING TO SING IN.

SOME OTHER GUY GAVE HIM A PAIR OF PANTS. ANOTHER GUY GAVE HIM A SHIRT TO DO THE AMATEUR SHOW THAT NIGHT.

Harlem or Bust?

LEONARD REED IS THE APOLLO'S MANAGER AT THE TIME.

HE **BEGGED** ME TO PUT HIM ON THE AMATEUR HOUR.

NO, WE'RE FILLED UP!

I'M BETTER THAN ANYBODY ON THE SHOW! I'M BETTER THAN LITTLE WILLIE JOHN!

OK, WE'LL SEE . . .

I Criiiiied.. I Criiiiied..

HE **RIPPED** THAT SHOW APART!

THROUGHOUT THE APOLLO'S HISTORY, THE INNER CITIES, FACTORY TOWNS, AND DUSTY CROSSROADS OF AMERICA ARE FILLED WITH DREAMERS.

THESE COMMUNITIES OFFER LITTLE TO STIMULATE YOUNGSTERS WITH IMAGINATION, AND—DARE THEY HOPE IT—TALENT.

WHILE STARSTRUCK WHITE KIDS TRADITIONALLY HEAD FOR HOLLYWOOD OR BROADWAY . . .

. . . THEIR BLACK COUNTERPARTS BUCK THE ODDS AND BEAT A PATH FOR HARLEM AND THE WEDNESDAY NIGHT AMATEUR SHOW AT THE APOLLO.

THEY KNOW THEY WILL FACE THE TOUGHEST AND MOST DEMANDING AUDIENCE IN THE WORLD . . .

. . . A CROWD NOTORIOUS, ESPECIALLY ON AMATEUR NIGHT, FOR ITS VOCAL AND SOMETIMES PHYSICAL DEMONSTRATIONS OF DISPLEASURE.

THEY KNOW ABOUT *PORTO RICO*, THE CRAZY STAGEHAND WHO SERVES AS THE AUDIENCE'S HIT MAN AND EXECUTIONER.

THEY KNOW THEY MIGHT NOT EVEN PASS THE PRE-SHOW AUDITION, MUCH LESS WIN THE CONTEST.

THEY HAVE FAITH IN THEMSELVES, AND THEY KNOW THE APOLLO AUDIENCE IS AN ASTUTE JUDGE OF TALENT AND THE MOST APPRECIATIVE AUDIENCE IN THE WORLD.

AND, OF COURSE, THEY KNOW THAT FOUR FIRST-PLACE WINS GUARANTEES A WEEK'S PROFESSIONAL ENGAGEMENT AT THE THEATER.

YET THEY SHOW UP AND TRY—AN ESTIMATED 15,000, JUST IN THE FIRST TWENTY YEARS OF AMATEUR NIGHT AT THE APOLLO.

IF THEY CAN PLEASE THE AUDIENCE AT THE APOLLO, THEY CAN PLEASE ANY CROWD.

THE GREAT SOUL STAR *JOE TEX* IS KNOWN AS JOE ARRINGTON JR. IN 1955 WHEN HE DECIDES TO TAKE HIS CHANCE.

NEWLY ARRIVED FROM BAYTOWN, TEXAS, JOE SETTLES IN A DINGY ROOMING HOUSE, GETS A JOB IN A CLOTHING STORE, AND FILLS HIS EVENINGS SINGING ON STREET CORNERS WITH HIS BUDDIES.

HEMPSTEAD, LONG ISLAND.

YOU'RE GREAT, MAN! YOU OUGHTA GIVE THE APOLLO A TRY.

NAW . . .

SORRY, THERE'S A THREE-MONTH WAITING LIST.

ALL I WANT IS A *CHANCE.*

AUDITIONS

WE'LL SEND YOU A POSTCARD WHEN IT'S YOUR TURN. COME BACK NEXT MONDAY AND SIGN UP.

THE BASEMENT REHEARSAL HALL WAS ORIGINALLY A WHITE CLUB—JOE WARD'S COCONUT GROVE, SAID TO BE THE SITE OF LOUIS ARMSTRONG'S FIRST NEW YORK GIG.

When the Coconut Grove closed in 1930, it became the Rathskeller. Hence the leftover fake stone buttresses, exposed wood beams, and Germanic cityscapes.

OK, KID, OK! I'LL GIVE YOU A SHOT TONIGHT. BE HERE AT TEN SHARP.

THERE BOBBY SCHIFFMAN JUST HAPPENS TO SIT NEXT TO JOE, AND HE GETS AN EARFUL.

MAN, I'M GOING TO BE AT THE APOLLO TONIGHT! I'M GOING TO BE ON AMATEUR NIGHT! CHECK ME OUT!

WAITING TO GO ON, JOE SPOTS A SHORT, POLISHED TREE STUMP SITTING ON A PEDESTAL.

It is the remains of the fabled *Tree of Hope*—a chestnut tree that once stood outside the stage doors for the Lafayette Theater and Connie's Inn . . .

Before the tree is cut down to widen Seventh Avenue in 1933, it is a favorite gathering place for out-of-work performers.

The tree becomes a lucky charm for entertainers.

MANY GET A PIECE OF THE TREE OF HOPE WHEN IT IS CUT DOWN.

BOOKING AGENTS REALIZE IT IS A GOOD, INFORMAL HIRING HALL, AND MANY JOBS ARE LANDED THERE.

Ralph Cooper brings the largest chunk to the Apollo.

WAIT JUST A MINUTE, YOUNG MAN. YOU FORGOT TO TOUCH THE TREE OF HOPE!

IT BECOMES A SACRED AMATEUR NIGHT TRADITION— AMATEURS MUST TOUCH THE STUMP BEFORE GOING ON.

Joe wins the twenty-five-dollar first prize that night, then three more times, and gets a week's professional booking.

HENRY GLOVER OF KING RECORDS CATCHES JOE AT THE APOLLO AND SIGNS HIM.

Joe Tex goes on to become James Brown's labelmate and rival, and boasts million-selling hits such as "Hold What You've Got" and "Skinny Legs and All."

ALSO NEWLY ARRIVED IN NEW YORK, YOUNG PEARL BAILEY—WHO WOULD ONE DAY BOAST THE APOLLO BOX OFFICE RECORD—DECIDES TO GIVE AMATEUR NIGHT A TRY IN 1934.

So she heads down the street to the Apollo.

She first tries the Harlem Opera House's amateur contest, but arrives too late.

ERSKINE HAWKINS'S BAMA STATE COLLEGIANS

WHEN THE HAND WAS HELD OVER THE HEADS, I WON . . . FOR "IN MY SOLITUDE," ARRANGEMENT HOMEMADE.

IN HER AUTOBIOGRAPHY, THE RAW PEARL, PEARL BAILEY REMEMBERS BEING LUCKY IN MORE WAYS THAN ONE . . .

FOR THERE—THAT NIGHT—A YOUNG GIRL WALKED ON STAGE, OPENED HER MOUTH, AND THE AUDIENCE THAT HAD STARTED TO SNICKER ENDED UP CHEERING.

HER NAME WAS ELLA FITZGERALD. SHE WON, AND THAT VOICE WILL GO DOWN IN HISTORY.

I'M GRATEFUL I DIDN'T GO DOWN THE STREET TO THE OPERA HOUSE. I DOUBT I WOULD HAVE MADE IT THERE.

IT IS IMPOSSIBLE TO SAY WHICH AMATEUR NIGHT TRIUMPH IS THE MOST SIGNIFICANT.

SHE IS ONLY SIXTEEN YEARS OLD, A SINGER IN THE CHOIR AT THE MOUNT ZION BAPTIST CHURCH IN NEWARK, NEW JERSEY.

THE *COOTIE WILLIAMS* BAND WITH LEAD VOCALIST *EDDIE "CLEANHEAD" VINSON*

I REMEMBER HER STANDING BEHIND US, TREMBLING, SCARED TO COME ON.

But a leading contender surely is *Sarah Vaughan*'s in October 1942.

SARAH VAUGHAN DID "BODY AND SOUL." I'LL NEVER FORGET THAT. SHE BROKE THE HOUSE UP!

BILLY ECKSTINE—THE "FABULOUS MR. B"—IS IN THE APOLLO THAT EVENING CASHING HIS PAYCHECK FROM THE *EARL HINES* BAND.

GO ON OUT THERE, EVERYTHING'S GONNA BE ALL RIGHT. DO YOUR BEST, DON'T BE AFRAID.

Body and Sooooooul...

HE DECIDES TO STAY AND CATCH THE AMATEUR SHOW.

IT WAS LIKE A GRADE-B MOVIE . .

I RUSHED BACKSTAGE AND TOLD HER SHE MUST TRY OUT FOR THE EARL HINES BAND!

The "Divine Sarah" wins Hines over, too, and goes on to become one of the most important female jazz vocalists of all time.

Apollo Amateur Night Winners Hall of Fame

SARAH VAUGHN

PEARL BAILEY

GLADYS KNIGHT

RUTH BROWN

LESLIE UGGAMS

JIMI HENDRIX

DIONNE WARWICK

MICHAEL JACKSON

SCREAMIN' JAY HAWKINS

BILLY WARD OF THE DOMINOES

KING CURTIS

FRANKIE LYMON

BILL KENNY OF THE INKSPOTS

WILSON PICKETT

JAMES BROWN

"OF THE MAJOR BLACK ATTRACTIONS THAT ARE WORKING TODAY, 30 TO 40 PERCENT WERE LAUNCHED AT THE APOLLO'S AMATEUR NIGHT." —*BOBBY SCHIFFMAN*, 1975

OF COURSE, NOT EVERY CONTESTANT IS A BUDDING JAMES BROWN OR SARAH VAUGHAN.

NORMAN MILLER IS THE STAGEHAND IN CHARGE OF SOUND.

BUT ON WEDNESDAY NIGHTS HE BECOMES PORTO RICO, THE CRAZED, WILDLY DRESSED NEMESIS OF EVERY TERRIFIED AMATEUR AND THE SAVIOR OF THE DISQUIETED APOLLO CROWD.

GET OFF THE STAGE! *BOOOO!*

SHOOT HIM OFF!

But the audience knows that justice will be done—and calling in their own executioner becomes part of the Wednesday night ritual.

Legend has it that at one early Amateur Night show, Miller—his soundman's sensitive ears abused by a struggling crooner's singing attempt—runs onstage, fires a cap pistol, and chases the wretched amateur off.

ANOTHER AMATEUR NIGHT FIXTURE, DAVID "POP" JOHNSON, SITS IN THE SAME BOX EVERY WEDNESDAY NIGHT.

The audience loves it, and a new *Apollo tradition* is born.

In 1947, he claims he hasn't missed a show in thirteen years.

BLOW YOUR WHISTLE, POP!

When an amateur displeases him, he drapes a white handkerchief over his head.

Blowing his whistle summons Porto Rico.

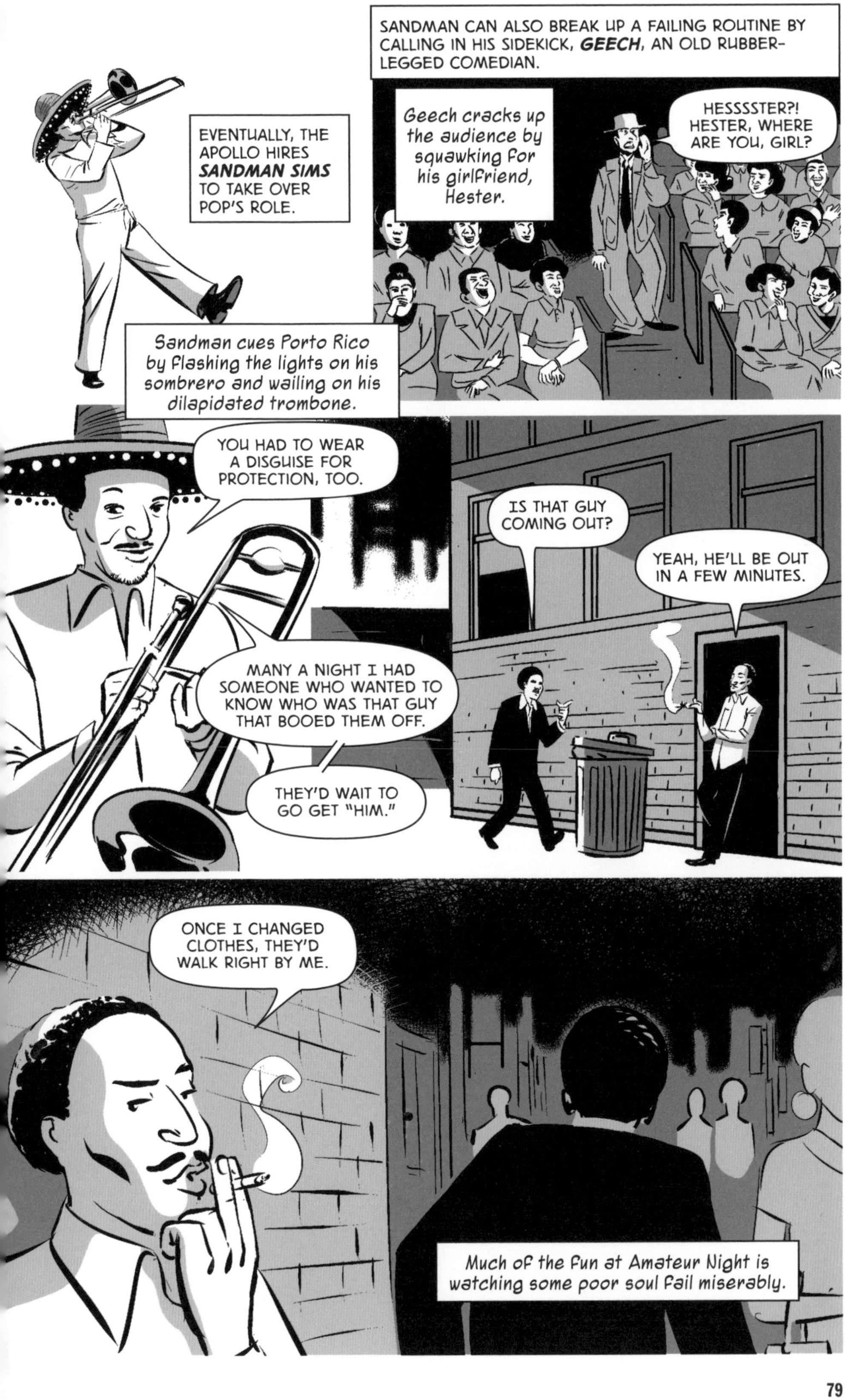
SANDMAN CAN ALSO BREAK UP A FAILING ROUTINE BY CALLING IN HIS SIDEKICK, GEECH, AN OLD RUBBER-LEGGED COMEDIAN.
EVENTUALLY, THE APOLLO HIRES SANDMAN SIMS TO TAKE OVER POP'S ROLE.
Geech cracks up the audience by squawking for his girlfriend, Hester.
HESSSSTER?! HESTER, WHERE ARE YOU, GIRL?
Sandman cues Porto Rico by flashing the lights on his sombrero and wailing on his dilapidated trombone.
YOU HAD TO WEAR A DISGUISE FOR PROTECTION, TOO.
MANY A NIGHT I HAD SOMEONE WHO WANTED TO KNOW WHO WAS THAT GUY THAT BOOED THEM OFF.
THEY'D WAIT TO GO GET "HIM."
IS THAT GUY COMING OUT?
YEAH, HE'LL BE OUT IN A FEW MINUTES.
ONCE I CHANGED CLOTHES, THEY'D WALK RIGHT BY ME.
Much of the fun at Amateur Night is watching some poor soul fail miserably.

IN THE OLD DAYS, ONE FAILED AMATEUR'S PATHOS PROVIDED HYSTERICAL FODDER FOR THE HARLEM GRAPEVINE FOR WEEKS. TODAY, IT RESULTS IN MILLIONS OF HITS ON YOUTUBE. JUST ASK *LAURYN HILL.*

WHAT SONG ARE YOU SINGING?

"WHO'S LOVING YOU?"

THIRTEEN-YEAR-OLD LAURYN HILL SEEMS FINE TALKING TO HOST *RICK AVILES.*

COME ON, LAURYN. WE'RE GOING TO LOVE YOU!

NOT SO FAST.

The youngster starts out off-key and nervous. And the boos rain down.

HOWEVER, SHE MAINTAINS HER COMPOSURE AND FINISHES.

And despite the rough start, she becomes one of the greatest stars of the '90s, winning multiple Grammy Awards including Album of the Year in 1999.

COMEDIAN *DAVE CHAPPELLE*, JUST SIXTEEN WHEN HE TAKES HIS SHOT, TELLS HIS TALE OF WOE ON *INSIDE THE ACTORS STUDIO*:

I SAID, I'M GOING TO GO TO THE APOLLO AND RIP THAT MOTHER!

SANDMAN! I WANTED TO CHOKE HIM!

THAT WAS THE *BEST* THING THAT EVER HAPPENED TO ME . . . AFTER THAT, I WAS FEARLESS. THAT NIGHT WAS *LIBERATING*.

I STILL REMEMBER THAT BOO. I HAD NEVER BEEN BOOED OFF STAGE BEFORE. I JUST REMEMBER LOOKING OUT AND SEEING EVERYBODY BOOING. EVERYBODY! EVEN OLD PEOPLE.

WHO BOOS A CHILD PURSUING HIS DREAMS? THIS IS THE *MEANEST* CROWD IN THE WORLD!

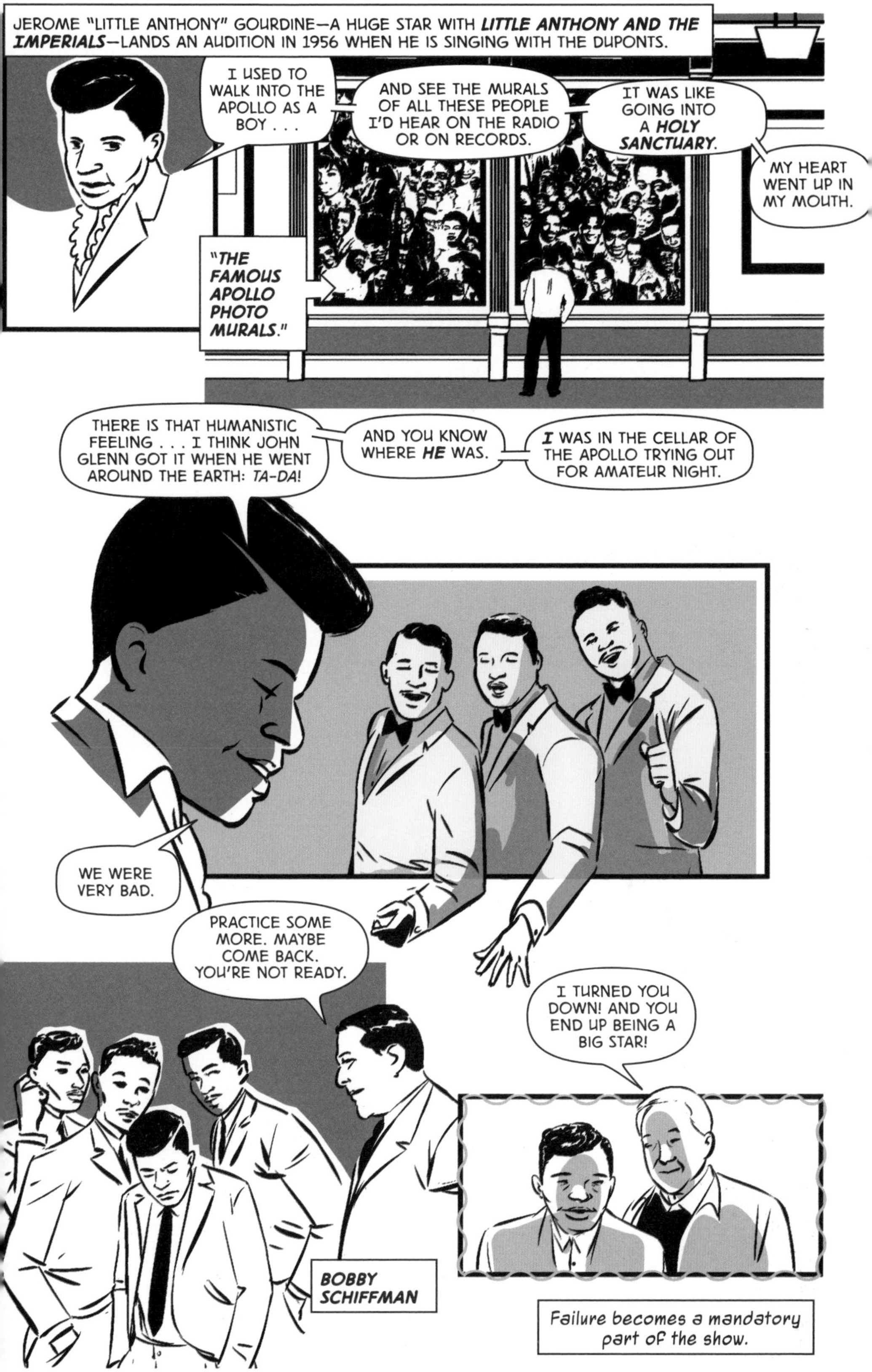
JEROME "LITTLE ANTHONY" GOURDINE—A HUGE STAR WITH LITTLE ANTHONY AND THE IMPERIALS—LANDS AN AUDITION IN 1956 WHEN HE IS SINGING WITH THE DUPONTS.
I USED TO WALK INTO THE APOLLO AS A BOY . . .
AND SEE THE MURALS OF ALL THESE PEOPLE I'D HEAR ON THE RADIO OR ON RECORDS.
IT WAS LIKE GOING INTO A HOLY SANCTUARY.
MY HEART WENT UP IN MY MOUTH.
"THE FAMOUS APOLLO PHOTO MURALS."
THERE IS THAT HUMANISTIC FEELING . . . I THINK JOHN GLENN GOT IT WHEN HE WENT AROUND THE EARTH: TA-DA!
AND YOU KNOW WHERE HE WAS.
I WAS IN THE CELLAR OF THE APOLLO TRYING OUT FOR AMATEUR NIGHT.
WE WERE VERY BAD.
PRACTICE SOME MORE. MAYBE COME BACK. YOU'RE NOT READY.
I TURNED YOU DOWN! AND YOU END UP BEING A BIG STAR!
BOBBY SCHIFFMAN
Failure becomes a mandatory part of the show.

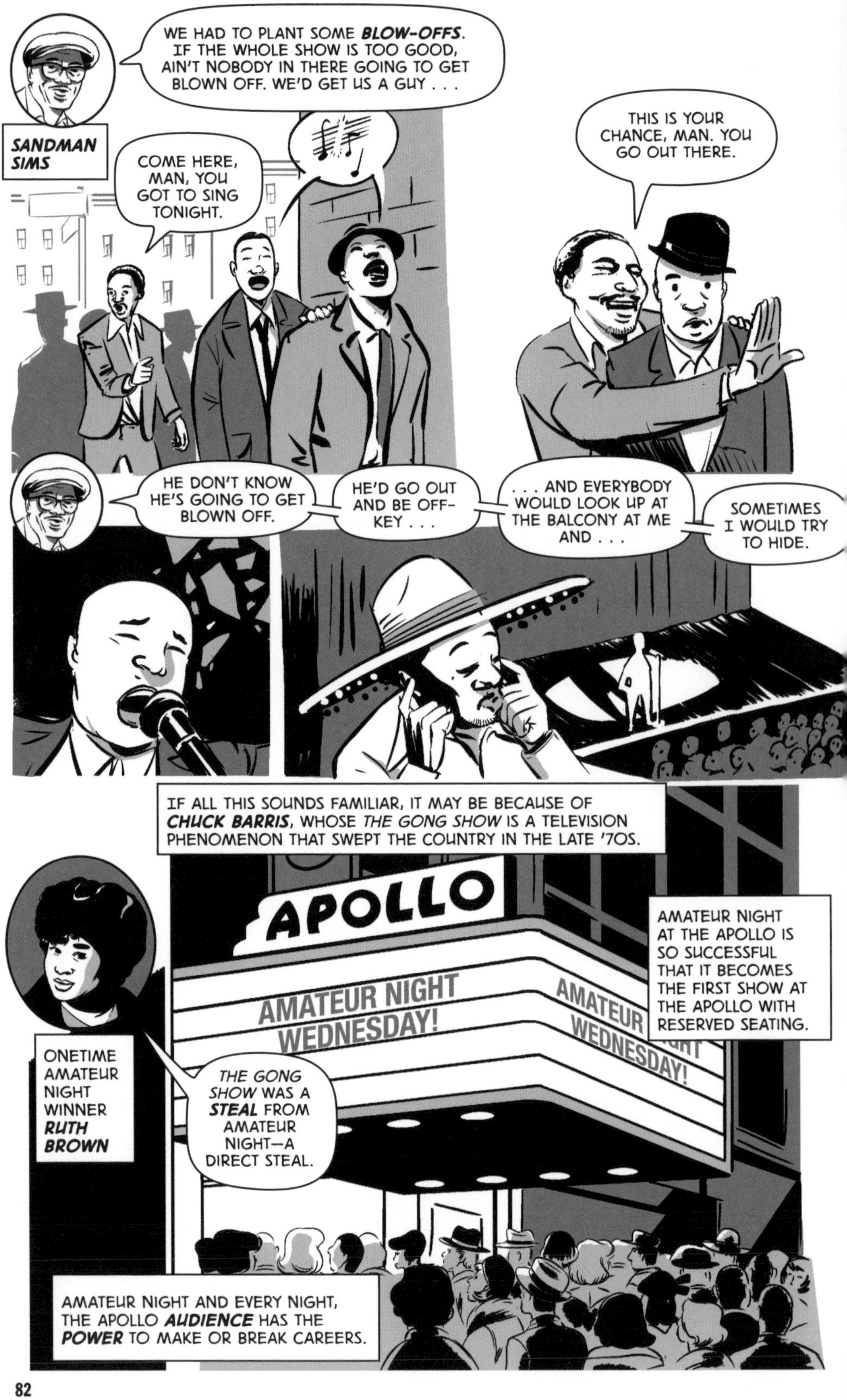
WE HAD TO PLANT SOME BLOW-OFFS. IF THE WHOLE SHOW IS TOO GOOD, AIN'T NOBODY IN THERE GOING TO GET BLOWN OFF. WE'D GET US A GUY . . .
SANDMAN SIMS
COME HERE, MAN, YOU GOT TO SING TONIGHT.
THIS IS YOUR CHANCE, MAN. YOU GO OUT THERE.
HE DON'T KNOW HE'S GOING TO GET BLOWN OFF.
HE'D GO OUT AND BE OFF-KEY . . .
. . . AND EVERYBODY WOULD LOOK UP AT THE BALCONY AT ME AND . . .
SOMETIMES I WOULD TRY TO HIDE.
IF ALL THIS SOUNDS FAMILIAR, IT MAY BE BECAUSE OF CHUCK BARRIS, WHOSE THE GONG SHOW IS A TELEVISION PHENOMENON THAT SWEPT THE COUNTRY IN THE LATE '70S.
APOLLO
AMATEUR NIGHT WEDNESDAY!
AMATEUR NIGHT AT THE APOLLO IS SO SUCCESSFUL THAT IT BECOMES THE FIRST SHOW AT THE APOLLO WITH RESERVED SEATING.
ONETIME AMATEUR NIGHT WINNER RUTH BROWN
THE GONG SHOW WAS A STEAL FROM AMATEUR NIGHT—A DIRECT STEAL.
AMATEUR NIGHT AND EVERY NIGHT, THE APOLLO AUDIENCE HAS THE POWER TO MAKE OR BREAK CAREERS.

BUT IT IS MUCH MORE THAN THAT.

The audience is the embodiment of the spirit of Harlem.

The *force* that truly makes the Apollo *great*.

Bereft of political power, housed in society's castoffs, and denied access to many cultural institutions, they take great pride in their fabled establishment.

The Apollo audience thus enforces a standard of excellence.

It is the *power* of the *powerless*.

THE SCHIFFMANS LOOK TO THE BLACK COMMUNITY TO LEARN WHAT THEY SHOULD BRING INTO THE APOLLO.

AND RECORD COMPANY EXECUTIVES, TALENT AND BOOKING AGENCIES, LOOK TO THE APOLLO AUDIENCE AS EARLY ADOPTERS WHO CAN GUIDE THEM TO WHAT MIGHT WORK IN THE WORLD AT LARGE.

ATLANTIC RECORDS' **AHMET ERTEGUN**

WE SAW EVERY SHOW FOR TWENTY YEARS. TWICE A WEEK.

OSCAR COHEN AND **JOE GLASER** OF ASSOCIATED BOOKING

AUDIENCES COME TO EXPECT THE **BEST**, AND GENERALLY THEIR WILD ENTHUSIASM INSPIRES THE BEST.

THEIR DISPLEASURE WITH THOSE WHO DON'T MEET THEIR EXPECTATIONS PRODUCES A REACTION FEW PERFORMERS WHO EXPERIENCE IT EVER FORGET.

THOSE WHO FAIL TO GIVE THE APOLLO CROWD THEIR ALL, OR ATTEMPT TO ELEVATE THEMSELVES AT THE AUDIENCE'S EXPENSE, ALWAYS REGRET IT.

NINA SIMONE WAS A VERY HOT COMMODITY WHO HAD A SUPER-BIG RECORD CALLED "PORGY."

BOBBY SCHIFFMAN

IT'S AMATEUR NIGHT. THE THEATER IS JAMMED WITH PEOPLE.

ABOUT THE FIFTH NUMBER IN THE SHOW, SHE STILL HADN'T DONE "PORGY." THE PEOPLE IN THE BACK STARTED TO YELL . . .

SHE CAME WITH A VERY HIGHFALUTIN' ATTITUDE TOWARD HER PEOPLE.

SING "PORGY"! COME ON, SING "PORGY"!

I'LL SING "PORGY" WHEN AND IF I GET READY TO SING "PORGY."

I KNEW THAT THIS WAS AMATEUR NIGHT. THE INTERESTING THING IS, THE AMATEURS ARE NOT BACKSTAGE. YOU'RE THE AMATEURS!

THE AUDIENCE GOT UP AND WALKED OUT EN MASSE.

THE NEXT TIME NINA SIMONE CAME TO THE THEATER, ON THE FIRST SHOW, THREE WOMEN GOT UP FROM THE AUDIENCE, WALKED DOWN THE AISLE, THREW HANDFULS OF PENNIES ON THE STAGE, AND WALKED OUT.

84

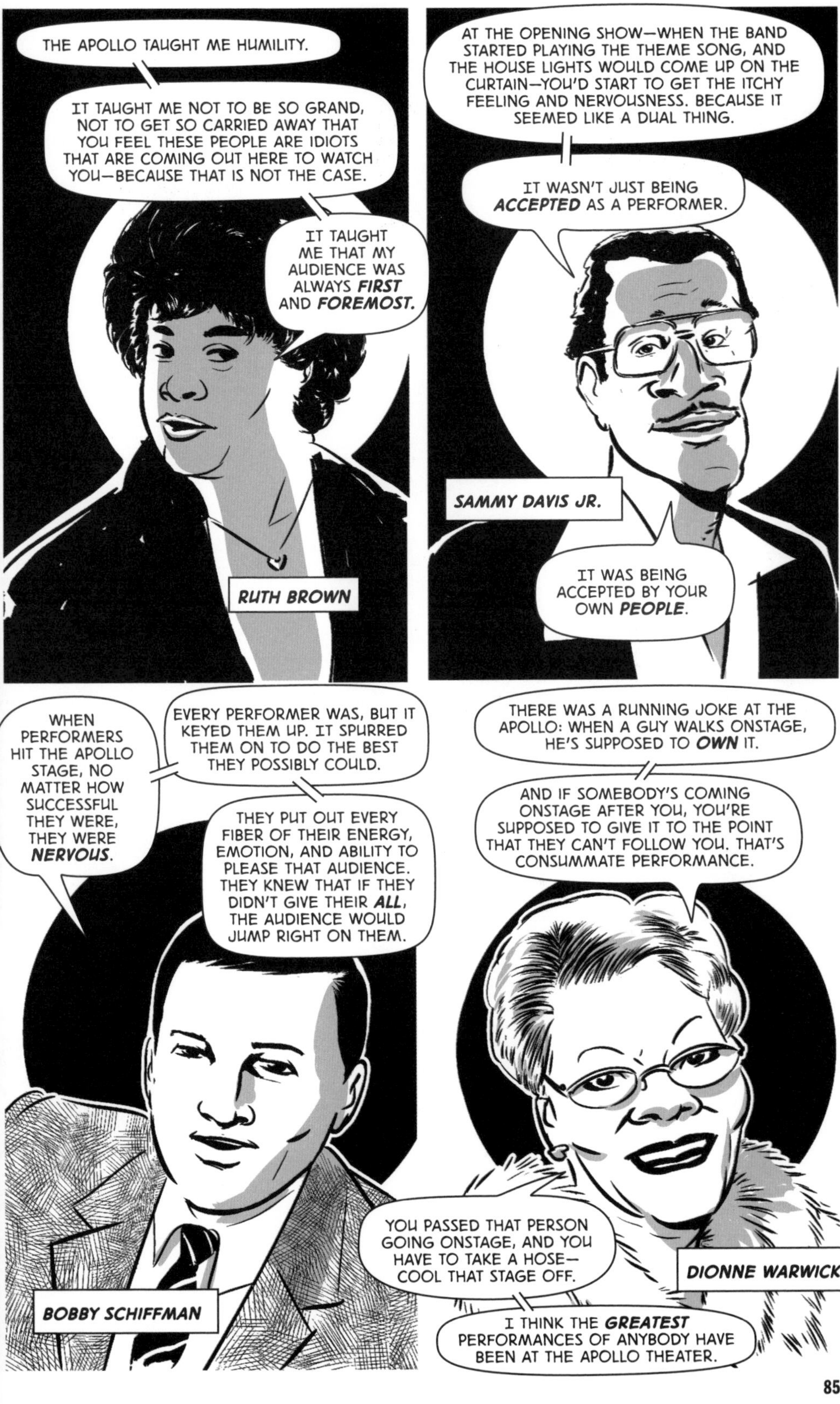
THE APOLLO TAUGHT ME HUMILITY.
IT TAUGHT ME NOT TO BE SO GRAND, NOT TO GET SO CARRIED AWAY THAT YOU FEEL THESE PEOPLE ARE IDIOTS THAT ARE COMING OUT HERE TO WATCH YOU—BECAUSE THAT IS NOT THE CASE.
IT TAUGHT ME THAT MY AUDIENCE WAS ALWAYS ***FIRST*** AND ***FOREMOST.***
RUTH BROWN
AT THE OPENING SHOW—WHEN THE BAND STARTED PLAYING THE THEME SONG, AND THE HOUSE LIGHTS WOULD COME UP ON THE CURTAIN—YOU'D START TO GET THE ITCHY FEELING AND NERVOUSNESS. BECAUSE IT SEEMED LIKE A DUAL THING.
IT WASN'T JUST BEING ***ACCEPTED*** AS A PERFORMER.
SAMMY DAVIS JR.
IT WAS BEING ACCEPTED BY YOUR OWN ***PEOPLE***.
WHEN PERFORMERS HIT THE APOLLO STAGE, NO MATTER HOW SUCCESSFUL THEY WERE, THEY WERE ***NERVOUS***.
EVERY PERFORMER WAS, BUT IT KEYED THEM UP. IT SPURRED THEM ON TO DO THE BEST THEY POSSIBLY COULD.
THEY PUT OUT EVERY FIBER OF THEIR ENERGY, EMOTION, AND ABILITY TO PLEASE THAT AUDIENCE. THEY KNEW THAT IF THEY DIDN'T GIVE THEIR ***ALL***, THE AUDIENCE WOULD JUMP RIGHT ON THEM.
BOBBY SCHIFFMAN
THERE WAS A RUNNING JOKE AT THE APOLLO: WHEN A GUY WALKS ONSTAGE, HE'S SUPPOSED TO ***OWN*** IT.
AND IF SOMEBODY'S COMING ONSTAGE AFTER YOU, YOU'RE SUPPOSED TO GIVE IT TO THE POINT THAT THEY CAN'T FOLLOW YOU. THAT'S CONSUMMATE PERFORMANCE.
YOU PASSED THAT PERSON GOING ONSTAGE, AND YOU HAVE TO TAKE A HOSE—COOL THAT STAGE OFF.
DIONNE WARWICK
I THINK THE ***GREATEST*** PERFORMANCES OF ANYBODY HAVE BEEN AT THE APOLLO THEATER.

IF AN ACT WOULD COME OFF, AND THEY GOT A STANDING OVATION, THEY'D WALK OFFSTAGE LIKE THIS . . .

LITTLE ANTHONY

YOU BETTER CALL THE FIRE DEPARTMENT. I FEEL *SORRY* FOR YOU COMING BEHIND ME.

THE FIRST ACT WOULD SET THE PACE FOR THE REST OF THE SHOW. THAT'S WHY OPENING ACTS WERE SO DARNED GOOD: THEY KNEW THEY HAD TO COME OUT *SMOKING*.

IF THE AUDIENCE LIKED THE OPENING ACT, BEFORE THE END OF THE WEEK, THAT ACT WAS NOT THE OPENER.

I REMEMBER SCHIFFMAN SENDING DOWN A NOTICE: "THE IMPERIALS CAN'T BE THIRD, MOVE THEM TO FIFTH."

WE WERE *KILLING* THE ACT THAT WAS COMING DOWN AFTER US, AND THEY COULDN'T HANDLE IT.

THERE WAS A COMPETITIVE HIGH AS PERFORMERS, BUT THEY WERE VERY LIBERAL AND NICE AFTER THE PERFORMANCE.

HEY, MAN, DON'T BE LOOKING STRAIGHT OUT LIKE THAT.

YOU SEE THEM GIRLS OVER THERE AT THE TOP? NOW, YOU GOT TO PLAY TO *THEM*.

THE *DELLS* OF "OH, WHAT A NIGHT" FAME.

KILL! GO OUT THERE AND WIPE 'EM OUT.

GLADYS KNIGHT

WE WERE *PROUD* WHEN WE CAME ONSTAGE.

OR WE COULD SAY TO EACH OTHER, "HEY, MAYBE IF YOU DO THIS LIKE THIS, IT MIGHT GO OVER BETTER."

IT WAS A SCHOOL, THAT'S WHAT IT WAS. MAYBE MORE THAN A THEATER, IT WAS A SCHOOL.

THE IMPLICIT LINK WITH THE PERFORMERS ONSTAGE CREATES A CHARGE LIKE THAT BETWEEN THE TWO POLES OF A BATTERY, AND IT *ELECTRIFIES* THE ATMOSPHERE AT THE APOLLO.

To be a part of the Apollo audience is to be a part of the show.

SOME ANTHROPOLOGISTS HAVE LINKED THIS SORT OF INTERACTION WITH THE AFRICAN PAST, WHEN ART WAS REGARDED AS AN INSEPARABLE PART OF LIFE THAT WAS NOT TO BE PURCHASED FOR A TWO-DOLLAR TICKET.

PROFESSOR *PHYL GARLAND*

IF THERE IS SOME TRUTH TO THIS, NOWHERE IN MODERN-DAY AMERICA IS IT MORE APPARENT THAN AT THE APOLLO.

SCREW THEM. I WOULDN'T WORK HERE IF THEY PAID ME A MILLION DOLLARS.

While the Schiffmans run the theater, even they acknowledge that the audience is the *real* boss . . .

OH, MAN, THEY CUT LOOSE ON THIS GUY. HE STRUGGLED THROUGH HIS ACT, AND HE ACTUALLY WAS *BAD*.

BOO!!

BOO!!

JOHNNY OTIS

YOU SEE, MR. OTIS, I HIRED HIM IN GOOD FAITH, BUT THE PEOPLE *OVERRULED* ME, AND THEY FIRED HIM.

WHEN SUPERSTARS LIKE JAMES BROWN APPEAR, EAGER FANS WAIT OUTSIDE, IN ANY WEATHER, FOR HOURS.

BECAUSE OF THE THEATER'S GENERAL ADMISSION, STAY-ALL-DAY POLICY IN THE EARLY DAYS, THE THEATER DOES NOT NORMALLY CLEAR AFTER EACH SHOW.

You might say standing in line toughens up the Apollo's patrons, sharpens their critical attitude, and tests their patience.

Ushers queue them up in two lines.

THE OTHER STRETCHES EAST AND AROUND THE CORNER ON SEVENTH AVENUE TO THE OLD ALHAMBRA THEATER.

ONE GOES WEST DOWN 125TH STREET, AROUND THE CORNER, AND UP EIGHTH AVENUE TO THE BRADDOCK HOTEL.

There are usually people waiting to take seats as they became available.

WE HAD A FILM CALLED *THE RIVER*—A DOCUMENTARY OF ALL THE MAIN RIVERS IN THE COUNTRY.

THE RIVER

TO MOVE PEOPLE OUT, THE APOLLO'S MANAGEMENT GETS CREATIVE.

DOLL THOMAS

LOOK AT TWENTY MINUTES OF ALL THAT WATER FALLING, AND THEY'RE GOING TO WANT GO TO THE BATHROOM.

THE MINUTE THEY GOT UP, WE PUT SOMEONE IN THEIR SEAT.

LADIES AND GENTLEMEN, IT'S SHOWTIME AT THE APOLLO!

A performer hitting the stage then is greeted by a frenzied scene as the film ends . . .

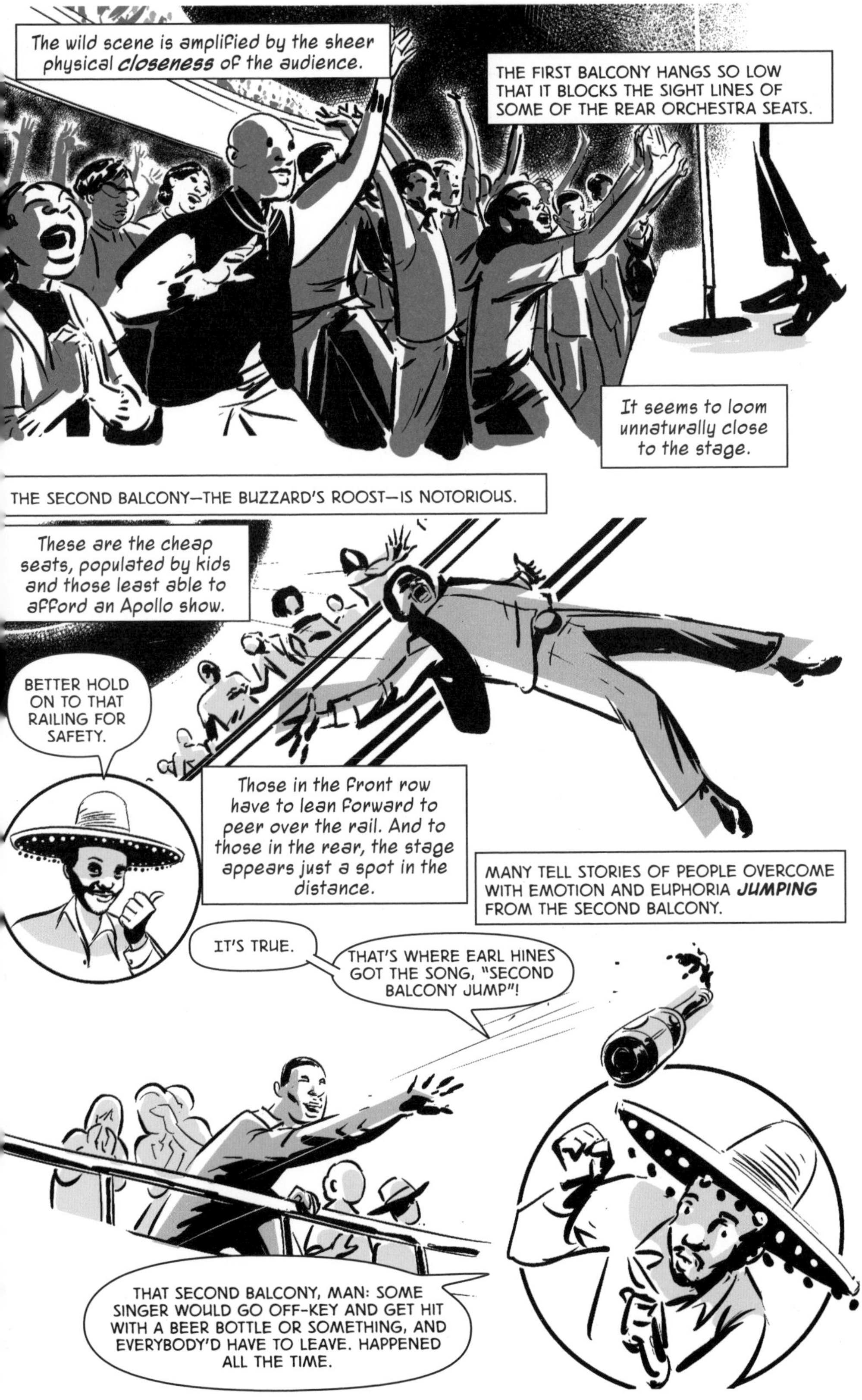

The wild scene is amplified by the sheer physical *closeness* of the audience.
THE FIRST BALCONY HANGS SO LOW THAT IT BLOCKS THE SIGHT LINES OF SOME OF THE REAR ORCHESTRA SEATS.
It seems to loom unnaturally close to the stage.
THE SECOND BALCONY—THE BUZZARD'S ROOST—IS NOTORIOUS.
These are the cheap seats, populated by kids and those least able to afford an Apollo show.
BETTER HOLD ON TO THAT RAILING FOR SAFETY.
Those in the front row have to lean forward to peer over the rail. And to those in the rear, the stage appears just a spot in the distance.
MANY TELL STORIES OF PEOPLE OVERCOME WITH EMOTION AND EUPHORIA ***JUMPING*** FROM THE SECOND BALCONY.
IT'S TRUE.
THAT'S WHERE EARL HINES GOT THE SONG, "SECOND BALCONY JUMP"!
THAT SECOND BALCONY, MAN: SOME SINGER WOULD GO OFF-KEY AND GET HIT WITH A BEER BOTTLE OR SOMETHING, AND EVERYBODY'D HAVE TO LEAVE. HAPPENED ALL THE TIME.

THE EARLY '60S

THE STAGE-SIDE BOXES, LIKE THE ONE FAVORED BY SANDMAN ON AMATEUR NIGHT, ARE OFTEN FILLED WITH CELEBRITIES.

OUR GAY FRIENDS WOULD FILL THAT BOX.

THERE WAS A GROUP OF DRAG QUEENS WHO USED TO BUY THE C BOX EVERY WEDNESDAY NIGHT. THEY HAD THOSE TICKETS PERMANENTLY RESERVED.

BOBBY SCHIFFMAN

GLADYS KNIGHT

THEY WOULD OOH AND AAH ABOUT OUR COSTUMES.

THEY USED TO CARRY ON!

IT BECAME AN ATTRACTION. PEOPLE USED TO COME TO SEE WHAT THEY WERE WEARING AND WHAT THEY WERE DOING UP THERE.

I WAS PROUD, BECAUSE THEY WERE PROUD OF US.

THERE'S OUR GIRL!

LOOK AT THOSE PIPS!

IT BECOMES MANDATORY FOR PERFORMERS TO GRASP AS MANY WILDLY WAVING HANDS AS POSSIBLE.

SOME FIND THE OPPORTUNITY FOR OPEN COMMUNION WITH THEIR FANS IRRESISTIBLE AND WADE INTO THE CROWD.

AS THE SCENE GETS WILDER OVER THE YEARS, HEFTY USHERS ARE ON HAND TO KEEP THE ACTION MANAGEABLE.

WHEN ACTS LIKE LIONEL HAMPTON AND JAMES BROWN BEGIN DEMANDING A PERCENTAGE OF THE HOUSE RECEIPTS, THE APOLLO STARTS CLEARING THE HOUSE AFTER EACH SHOW.

THE MOMENT THE LAST ACT WAS OVER, THEY'D TURN THE LIGHTS UP.

THE USHERS WOULD RUN UP AND DOWN THE AISLES GETTING EVERYBODY OUT.

THEY'D SEND THEM OUT THE SIDE DOOR ONTO 126TH STREET.

HAROLD CROMER

EVERYBODY PLEASE CLEAR THE THEATER!

THEY'D HAVE A FIGHT, BUT THEY'D GET THEM OUT.

HEY, MAN, I PAID MY MONEY. I CAN STAY IN THIS MOTHER ALL DAY.

THE MOST *VOCAL* SEGMENT OF THE AUDIENCE IS THE *KIDS*.

WE WERE ON LINE AT NINE IN THE MORNING ON SATURDAY WAITING FOR THE THEATER TO OPEN AT NOON, IN ORDER TO BE IN THE FRONT SEATS.

THOSE FIRST THREE ROWS, EVERYONE WANTED TO BE THERE, BECAUSE WHEN THE ARTIST CAME DOWN AND PUT THEIR HAND OUT, YOU COULD SAY, "OH, I TOUCHED HIM, WOW!"

As rhythm and blues, and then soul music, become dominant at the Apollo, the kids increasingly dominate the audience.

"LITTLE" LESLIE UGGAMS

COMEDIAN *SCOEY MITCHELL*

As long as it is at the Apollo, the audience accepts and encourages quality entertainment of any type.

PERHAPS BILLIE HOLIDAY EXPRESSED IT BEST IN HER AUTOBIOGRAPHY:

THERE'S NOTHING LIKE AN AUDIENCE AT THE APOLLO.

THAT'S ONE THING ABOUT THE APOLLO: YOU COULD BE AN OPERA SINGER AND COME IN THE APOLLO . . .

THEY DIDN'T ASK ME WHAT MY STYLE WAS, WHO I WAS, WHERE I'D COME FROM, WHO INFLUENCED ME, OR ANYTHING.

. . . AND THOUGH THEY MAY NOT REALLY UNDERSTAND THE FACT THAT YOU'RE SINGING IN ITALIAN, IF YOU WERE SINGING GOOD, THEY'D LET YOU KNOW IT.

THEY JUST BROKE THE HOUSE UP.

CHAPTER 5

The 1940s: Boppin'

THEY CALL HIM "BEAN." IN 1940, **COLEMAN HAWKINS** IS THE HOTTEST SAX MAN IN THE WORLD.

MUSICIANS WEAR OUT COPIES OF "BODY AND SOUL" TRYING TO FIGURE OUT BEAN'S PHENOMENAL SOLO.

WHAT THE? SPIN IT AGAIN, MAN.

Hawkins is onto something *new*. He's expanding the presumed capabilities of his instrument.

HAWKINS PLAYS THE APOLLO AND TOURS THE COUNTRY WITH HIS SIXTEEN-PIECE BAND, BUT HIS ARTISTIC JOURNEY FORESHADOWS A MAJOR SHAKE-UP OF THE BIG BAND SCENE.

His inventiveness rips apart the complacent world of swing.

AS WITH SO MANY KEY MOMENTS IN MUSIC AND POPULAR CULTURE, THE APOLLO IS THE SITE OF THIS REMARKABLE SCENE IN 1940.

Hawkins has just completed his week at the Apollo, headlining with Ralph Cooper and Pigmeat Markham.

HARRY JAMES

COLEMAN HAWKINS

TOMMY DORSEY

JACK JENNEY

BUNNY BERIGAN

On this very early Friday morning in late June, Bean celebrates by calling a few friends up onstage for a jam on Fats Waller's "Honeysuckle Rose."

JOHN KIRBY

COUNT BASIE

GENE KRUPA

JOE MARSALA

CARMEN MASTREN

WHAT A MARVELOUS **RELEASE** FOR THESE MUSICIANS: SWING MUSIC IS AT ITS PEAK POPULARITY, BUT IT IS BECOMING HIDEBOUND AND COMMERCIALIZED.

These Friday morning impromptu get-togethers have become quite popular at the Apollo.

SORRY, BOYS, YOU CAN'T BE PLAYING WITHOUT A CONTRACT. WE'VE GOT TO PROTECT THE UNION.

The Musician's Union begins handing out fines of $100 to $500 to musicians for playing without a contract.

THE APOLLO CONTINUES TO CONTRIBUTE TO THE NEW MUSIC SCENE EVEN AS THE INNOVATION MOVES UNDERGROUND TO SMALL CLUBS.

$100 FINE

WE'RE GOING TO **CLOSE** THESE SESSIONS DOWN.

TOO POPULAR.

Minton's, in particular, becomes the hip spot to jam, thanks to the club's new manager, ex-bandleader Teddy Hill.

MAN, WE'RE LUCKY TEDDY'S A UNION REP.

DIG, WE CAN GET BACK TO **JAMMIN'** WITHOUT WORRYIN' ABOUT THOSE FINES.

ON MONDAY NIGHTS, HILL HOSTS A "DOWN HOME" DINNER FOR EVERYONE IN THE FEATURED BAND AT THE APOLLO THAT WEEK.

BUT THE GREATEST ATTRACTION IS MINTON'S LITTLE HOUSE BAND.

These jam sessions produce a revolutionary new sound: *bebop*.

CHARLIE CHRISTIAN

JOE GUY

NICK FENTON

KENNY "KLOOK" CLARKE

FRANK SCHIFFMAN AND THE APOLLO ARE KEEPING A WATCHFUL EYE ON THESE NEW DEVELOPMENTS.

DIZZY GILLESPIE

THELONIOUS MONK

CHARLIE PARKER

In 1943, the Apollo becomes the first to book the experimental bebop band of *Earl Hines*—which showcases Dizzy Gillespie and *Charlie Parker*.

It is new music—aggressive, cynical, troubling, *modern*— for a new age.

A NEW AGE OF WAR.

NEARLY ONE MILLION AFRICAN AMERICANS SERVE IN WORLD WAR II.

The war effort affects everything.

Sometimes in ways that are coincidental but no less problematic for artists . . .

HOW'S OUR BAND GONNA GET TO GIGS WITH THIS *GAS RATIONING*?

THE BOSS CAN'T CHARTER BUSSES ANYMORE EITHER

MANY WHITE BANDS TURN TO THE RAILS BUT BLACK BANDS ARE HAMPERED BY RACIST JIM CROW RESTRICTIONS ON TRAINS IN THE SOUTH.

Finally, the NAACP prevails on the Office of Defense Transportation to ease its *charter bus ban* for black bands.

But only five buses are made available.

OTHER POLICIES MAKE IT HARDER FOR FANS TO GET OUT, TOO.

TICKETS GETTING HIGH WITH THIS 20 PERCENT *AMUSEMENT TAX* FOR THE WAR.

YEAH, AND GOTTA GET HOME BEFORE THAT BROWNOUT *CURFEW* AT MIDNIGHT!

NOT ENOUGH GAS IN THE TANK TO GET TO WORK AND A SHOW WITH THIS RATIONING.

THE APOLLO KEEPS BOPPIN'.

Paradoxically, swing becomes so popular that some top black bands break into formerly all-white territory, and play the Apollo less.

So the Apollo relies more on newer black bands like those of *Erskine Hawkins, Buddy Johnson, Cootie Williams,* and *Lucky Millinder.*

NO BAND CAN SURVIVE ON OCCASIONAL GIGS AT THE APOLLO, AND WORLD EVENTS ARE AFFECTING BANDS AROUND THE COUNTRY.

FEWER GIGS, AND CAN'T MAKE RECORDS SINCE THE UNION *RECORDING BAN* IN '42.

MAY

TWO YEARS LATER AND WE STILL AIN'T GETTING ROYALTIES.

WAR SERVICE CLAIMS MANY LEADERS AND SIDEMEN.

PAWN PAWN

THE APOLLO SUPPORTS MEN AND WOMEN IN UNIFORM. AT THE HARLEM DEFENSE RECREATION CENTER, THIRTY-FIVE TICKETS FOR APOLLO SHOWS ARE SET ASIDE FOR SOLDIERS EACH DAY.

TUESDAYS AT THE U.S.O. CENTER BECOME "APOLLO NIGHT."

LUCKY MILLINDER

EARL HINES

At the U.S.O., the headliners on each week's Apollo bill entertain and socialize with the servicemen.

MAY I HAVE THIS DANCE, MISS HORNE?

TRY IT LIKE THIS, SON.

HEY, CAB, CAN I GET YOUR AUTOGRAPH?

HI DE HO! YOU GOT IT, BRO!

LENA HORNE

BILL BOJANGLES ROBINSON

CAB CALLOWAY

WE LOVE OUR FIGHTING MEN. NOW SHOW US HOW MUCH YOU BOYS LOVE MISS BILLIE HOLIDAY!

WILLIE BRYANT

IN THE EARLY '40S, HARLEM IS NO LONGER THE MUST-GO DESTINATION FOR HIGH SOCIETY, BUT IT'S STILL A POPULAR HANGOUT FOR HIP WHITES.

MALCOLM X, THEN AN ITINERANT DISHWASHER AND HUSTLER KNOWN AS DETROIT RED, DESCRIBES THE SCENE IN HIS AUTOBIOGRAPHY:

ESPECIALLY AFTER THE NIGHTCLUBS DOWNTOWN CLOSED, THE TAXIS AND BLACK LIMOUSINES WOULD BE DRIVING UPTOWN, BRINGING THOSE WHITE PEOPLE WHO NEVER COULD GET ENOUGH OF NEGRO SOUL . . .

INSIDE EVERY AFTER-HOURS SPOT, THE SMOKE WOULD HURT YOUR EYES.

FOUR WHITE PEOPLE TO EVERY NEGRO WOULD BE IN THERE DRINKING WHISKEY FROM COFFEE CUPS AND EATING FRIED CHICKEN.

But frustration soon replaces optimism, and by the mid-'40s many African Americans are mired in disappointment.

During World War II, blacks fight in segregated units. When some finally are integrated, black soldiers usually serve in menial positions.

ON THE **HOME FRONT**, THOUSANDS OF AFRICAN AMERICANS FIND LUCRATIVE JOBS IN THE DEFENSE INDUSTRY.

For the first time their economic situation improves measurably.

STORIES OF BLACK SERVICEMEN BEATEN AND KILLED BY WHITE "CRACKERS" NEAR SOUTHERN MILITARY BASES TURN UP ALL TOO FREQUENTLY IN THE HARLEM NEWSPAPERS.

HARLEMITES ARE FURTHER UPSET WHEN MAYOR FIORELLO LA GUARDIA TEMPORARILY CLOSES THE SAVOY BALLROOM—HE SAYS TO PREVENT INCIDENTS ARISING OUT OF INTERRACIAL MINGLING.

EVENTS COME TO A HEAD ON THE NIGHT OF SUNDAY, AUGUST 1, 1943, IN THE **WORST** RIOT HARLEM HAS EVER EXPERIENCED.

A WHITE POLICEMAN ANSWERS A CALL FOR HELP AT THE **BRADDOCK HOTEL**.

It's a favorite hangout for Apollo entertainers at 126th Street near Eighth Avenue, just down from the theater's stage door.

A BLACK SOLDIER INTERVENES WHEN THE COP TRIES TO ARREST A WOMAN.

THE COP ARRESTS THE WOUNDED SOLDIER AND MARCHES HIM TO NEARBY SYDENHAM HOSPITAL.

A false rumor spreads.

HE'S DEAD! THEY KILLED HIM!

WAITING OUTSIDE THE HOSPITAL FOR WORD OF THE SOLDIER'S CONDITION, THE CROWD GROWS RESTLESS.

THE CROWD TURNS INTO A RAMPAGING MOB, GUTTING **HUNDREDS** OF WHITE-OWNED BUSINESSES ON AND AROUND 125TH STREET.

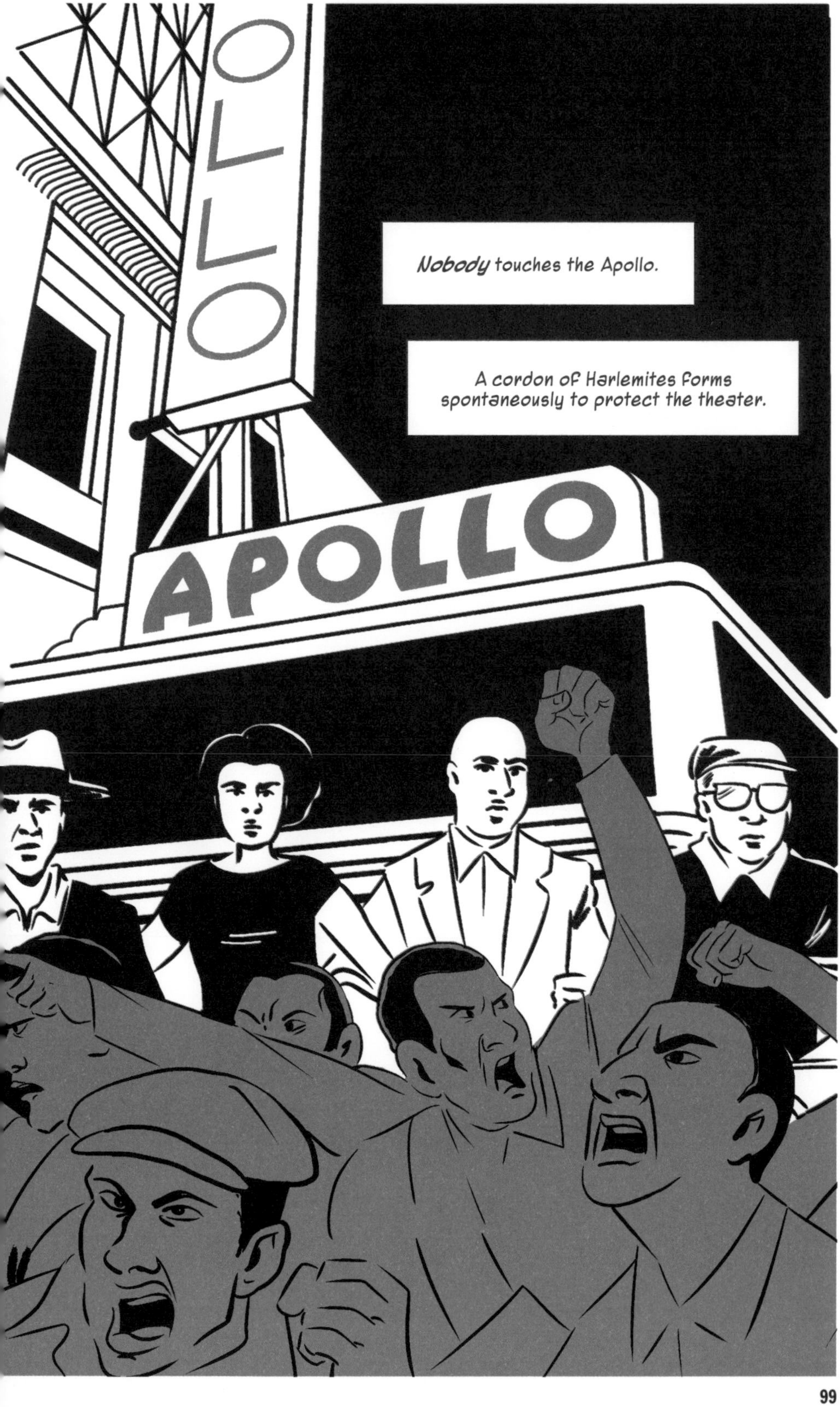
OLLO
Nobody touches the Apollo.
A cordon of Harlemites forms spontaneously to protect the theater.
APOLLO

The riot rages until dawn.

Hundreds are arrested, hundreds more are wounded, and at least six people die.

REV. ADAM CLAYTON POWELL SR., PASTOR OF HARLEM'S FAMOUS ABYSSINIAN BAPTIST CHURCH

IT WAS THE HOTTEST HELL EVER CREATED IN HARLEM.

MALCOLM X IN HIS AUTOBIOGRAPHY . . .

AFTER THE RIOT, THINGS GOT VERY TIGHT IN HARLEM.

IT WAS TERRIBLE FOR THE NIGHTLIFE PEOPLE, AND FOR THOSE HUSTLERS WHOSE MAIN INCOME HAD BEEN THE WHITE MAN'S MONEY.

THE 1935 RIOT HAD LEFT ONLY A RELATIVE TRICKLE OF THE MONEY WHICH HAD POURED INTO HARLEM DURING THE 1920S.

AND NOW THIS NEW RIOT ENDED EVEN THAT TRICKLE.

THE APOLLO GETS MORE THAN ITS SHARE OF THAT TRICKLE OF MONEY, HOWEVER.

WE'RE HANGIN' IN. DURING THE WEEK, THE AUDIENCE IS STILL ABOUT 40 PERCENT WHITE.

YES, AND AT THE AMATEUR NIGHT AND SATURDAY MIDNIGHT SHOWS, MAYBE 75 PERCENT.

MR. REED, WE WILL NEED TO INSTITUTE RESERVED SEATING FOR THOSE POPULAR SHOWS.

The Apollo is such a great deal that the crowds still come.

1945

APOLLO MANAGER LEONARD REED

FRANK SCHIFFMAN

Ticket prices top out at one dollar, and start at fifty cents before noon.

THE END OF THE WAR ALSO MARKS THE END FOR MANY OF THE BIG SWING BANDS—WHITE AND BLACK.

BENNY GOODMAN

ERSKINE HAWKINS

HARRY JAMES

BENNY CARTER

BUDDY JOHNSON

TOMMY DORSEY

IT WAS TOO EXPENSIVE TO KEEP THE BIG BANDS GOING.

DURING '47 IT STARTED PETERING OUT.

YOU HAD TELEVISION, AND PEOPLE WEREN'T GOING TO SHOWS AS MUCH. THAT KILLS A BIG BAND.

EDDIE "CLEANHEAD" VINSON

THERE WERE NO MORE JOBS. WE HAD TO STRUGGLE TOO HARD.

BILLY ECKSTINE AND I MET IN WASHINGTON, DC. HE HAD A BIG BAND AND I HAD A BIG BAND.

I'M BREAKING MY BAND DOWN. I'M SORRY.

BUT, IN THE END, OUR ART AND OUR ENTERTAINMENT IS A REFLECTION OF OUR WAY OF LIFE.

JOHNNY OTIS

BILLY ECKSTINE

WHEN I GOT HOME TO LOS ANGELES I WAS FORCED TO REDUCE THE SIZE OF MINE. I COULDN'T AFFORD FIFTEEN OR SIXTEEN GUYS.

IT WAS A CHANGE OF LIFESTYLE.

THE SEEDS OF THIS LIFESTYLE CHANGE ARE GROWING IN BILLY ECKSTINE'S NEW BAND.

GENE AMMONS

ART BLAKEY

FATS NAVARRO

Dizzy Gillespie

John Malachi

DEXTER GORDON

It boasts a *who's who* of modern jazz.

Charlie Parker

KENNY DORHAM

miles Davis

And makes its mark on the Apollo from 1944 to 1947, providing the indispensable *link* from the big band sound to bebop.

AND, OF COURSE, IT FEATURES ECKSTINE'S APOLLO AMATEUR NIGHT FIND: SARAH VAUGHAN.

DIZZY GILLESPIE AND CHARLIE PARKER ARE BEBOP'S BREAKOUT STARS AND GREATEST CHARACTERS.

Their Apollo appearances are major events for bop fans.

AS A PENNILESS, UNEMPLOYED MUSICIAN, DIZZY HANGS AROUND BACKSTAGE AT THE APOLLO.

HE MEETS HIS WIFE, LORRAINE WILLIS, AT THE THEATER, WHERE SHE IS A CHORUS GIRL.

He keeps his ears open for job opportunities and his eyes open for the chance to hustle a buck or two.

I GOT TO GET SERIOUS ABOUT MY BAND AND MAKE SOME DOUGH SO LORRAINE CAN *QUIT* THIS GIG.

BUT THAT IS AFTER THE LEGENDARY 1941 INCIDENT WITH BANDLEADER CAB CALLOWAY.

AFTER THE SHOW, DIZZY PROCLAIMS INNOCENCE AND IN THE ENSUING TUSSLE, HE STABS CALLOWAY IN THE BUTT WITH A PENKNIFE!

Calloway accuses Dizzy of being the spitball shooter.

The two later patch things up, become great friends, and frequently tell the story.

BACK IN 1939, BANDLEADER *LIONEL HAMPTON*, PREPARING FOR HIS LEGENDARY "HOT MALLETS" RECORDING SESSIONS, FIRST HEARS DIZ PLAYING WITH CALLOWAY AT THE APOLLO.

HE CAME OUT WITH A DIFFERENT STYLE THAN WE'D EVER HEARD BEFORE.

I ASKED HIM TO PLAY ON THIS SESSION I HAD.

The recordings are felt by many to be the *first* to feature the infant sounds of bebop.

DIZZY BECOMES A LEADER IN MORE WAYS THAN ONE.

His goatee, beret, and jive patter set the style for a generation that culminates with the Beats of the 1950s.

LIONEL HAMPTON

AS A BANDLEADER, HE IS RELAXED, YET ALWAYS IN CONTROL.

HEY, FELLAS, WHY YOU GUYS SO STIFF, MAN?

THIS IS A *SHOW*. DON'T BE SITTING UP THERE LIKE THAT.

DIZ KNOWS HE'S LICKED.

ALL RIGHT, FELLAS. THAT'S ENOUGH OF THE COMEDY.

WHEN CHARLIE PARKER LEAVES HIS HOMETOWN, KANSAS CITY, FOR NEW YORK WITH THE JAY MCSHANN BAND IN 1941, HE ATTRACTS RAPT ATTENTION FROM THE COGNOSCENTI.

LET'S GO BACK TO LIKE YOU WERE BEFORE. TIGHTEN UP AND TURN IT LOOSE!

If Dizzy Gillespie is the *light side* of the bebop revolution, Charlie "Bird" Parker is the *dark side*.

His is one of the most tragic stories in the cultural history of America, although the Apollo supports this genius even in his darkest hour.

Soon after leaving school, Charlie gets caught up in hard drugs, alcohol, and dissoluteness.

CHARLIE PARKER WAS A *GENIUS*.

BUT HE LIVES DAY TO DAY, HUSTLE TO HUSTLE, BED TO BED, FIX TO FIX.

Those who recognize Parker's greatness love him and forgive him his excesses.

He suffers devastating abuse from other musicians as he develops his revolutionary style at "cutting contests" all over Boss Pendergast's notoriously corrupt Kansas City.

Whenever his alto sax isn't in hock, he develops new musical ideas and modes of thought that continue to influence improvisational musicians today.

But his antics often get him into nonmusical jams.

ONE OF BIRD'S FAVORITE HANGOUTS IS THE BRADDOCK HOTEL BAR, WHERE APOLLO PERFORMERS OFTEN DROP IN BETWEEN SHOWS.

Bird takes advantage of its policy of two drinks for the price of one.

THERE HE GOES AGAIN.

Bird is so destitute thanks to his heroin habit that he can't even afford the price of the initial drink.

HIS FRIENDS DON'T MIND THE GAMBIT, BUT HE'S CAUGHT IN THE ACT BY A GROUP OF LOCAL HARD GUYS.

WHAT THE HELL?

YOU BUM, YOU OWE US A ROUND.

LUCKILY THE MCSHANN BAND IS PLAYING THE APOLLO, AND HIS FORMER BANDMATE, GENE RAMEY, BAILS HIM OUT.

MAN, I'M *BROKE*. BUT I'LL GET IT. WAIT, I'LL GET IT.

HIS WAY OF LIFE HELPS CREATE THE CHARLIE PARKER **LEGEND**, BUT HIS MUSIC MAKES HIM A **HERO**.

HIS APOLLO ENGAGEMENTS ARE EAGERLY AWAITED BY YOUNG ACOLYTES IN HARLEM LIKE **JACKIE MCLEAN**.

McLean, the great altoist deeply influenced by Bird's music—and unfortunately, Parker's drug habit as well—describes a 1948 Parker performance to A. B. Spellman in *Four Lives in the Bebop Business* . . .

WHEN BIRD WAS AT THE APOLLO, WE WOULD GO EARLY IN THE MORNING AND STAY AND WATCH THE SHOW ALL DAY LONG.

WE WOULD WATCH HIM FROM THE FIRST SHOW UNTIL AFTER THREE O'CLOCK, WHEN IT WAS TIME TO GO HOME FROM SCHOOL.

WE USED TO GO HOME AND PUT OUR BOOKS UP AND THEN TELL OUR PARENTS THAT WE WERE GOING TO THE APOLLO.

THEY'D LET US GO, AND WE'D SPLIT AND WATCH BIRD AGAIN UNTIL NINE, WHEN IT WAS TIME TO GO HOME AT NIGHT.

WE'D GET SOME HOT DOGS AT INTERMISSION, AND THAT WOULD BE ALL WE HAD TO EAT ALL DAY LONG.

A **CABARET CARD** IS REQUIRED TO PLAY IN NEW YORK ESTABLISHMENTS SERVING ALCOHOL. . .

THAT LEAVES THE APOLLO AS THE ONLY NEW YORK VENUE OPEN TO HIM. HE SEEMS TO HAVE **LOST HEART**.

Department of Public Works
Cabaret and Dance Hall Employees
Identification Card
Name: Charlie Parker
Title: Musician

His 1953 revue, "Charlie Parker and Strings," is a flop at the Apollo and elsewhere.

IN 1955 HE DIES, COUGHING UP BLOOD IN THE FIFTH AVENUE APARTMENT OF LEGENDARY BEBOP PATRON **BARONESS PANNONICA DE KOENIGSWARTER**.

Dizzy Gillespie pays for his funeral.

The attending doctor estimates him to be between fifty and sixty, based on his physical condition.

. . . But after years of problems, Charlie's is revoked. He can no longer play the bustling **52nd Street** jazz club scene.

Charlie Parker is thirty-four years old.

LIKE BIRD, WITH BILLIE HOLIDAY, GENIUS AND *HARD LIVING* GO HAND IN HAND.

A great blues singer, Billie also epitomizes the attractiveness of the pop singer in wartime America.

AND WHEN YOU SING IT, OTHER PEOPLE CAN FEEL SOMETHING, TOO.

GIVE ME A SONG I CAN FEEL, AND IT'S *NEVER* WORK.

After her early success at the Apollo in the '30s, Billie Holiday becomes one of the most critically acclaimed vocalists of the '40s.

IF YOU FIND A TUNE AND IT'S GOT SOMETHING TO DO WITH YOU, YOU FEEL IT.

THERE ARE A FEW SONGS I FEEL SO MUCH I CAN'T STAND TO SING THEM, BUT THAT'S SOMETHING ELSE AGAIN . . .

SHE IS TALKING ABOUT "STRANGE FRUIT," THE 1939 RECORDING THAT MAKES HER CAREER.

BILLIE, *PLEASE* DON'T SING IT. I SYMPATHIZE, BUT THIS SONG IS NOT APPROPRIATE.

This gripping song—*strange fruit* refers to lynched black bodies dangling from the limbs of trees—was written especially for Billie.

FRANK SCHIFFMAN

WHEN SHE FINISHES, THE ENTIRE THEATER FALLS SILENT, EXCEPT FOR THEIR COLLECTIVE SIGH.

Though vastly popular nationally, the troubled star is *busted* twice in the '40s for narcotics.

At the peak of her commercial success in 1947, a drug bust results, like Bird, in her Cabaret Card being pulled. Billie spirals into *chaos*.

BILLIE HOLIDAY   6/7/46   Armstrong Unit
Vocalist. Sings torch songs.
                                  10/15/48   3000.00
                                  8/28/49   3075.75
Unless a miraculous change takes 5/25/50   2500.00
place Billie's value to us is lost.
She has lost her public favor. She
seems unable to remain away from
stimulants.

BILLIE HOLIDAY

Terrible! She was sick, but she was also under the
effect of stimulants. Only a miracle can restore
this girl and make her worthwhile playing her again.

FRANK SCHIFFMAN'S INDEX CARD ON BILLIE TELLS THE END OF A SAD TALE OF DRUG ABUSE AND FAILING ABILITIES.

In 1959, Billie Holiday dies—cruelly arrested for drug possession and handcuffed even while laying terminally ill in her New York hospital bed.

IN HER PRIME, BILLIE IS AT THE FOREFRONT OF A WARTIME TREND THAT THE APOLLO EMBRACES AND ENCOURAGES.

THE POPULARITY OF THESE **"POP"** SONGS COINCIDES WITH THE LIFTING OF THE RECORDING BAN IN 1944.

Bars and restaurants stock their newfangled *jukeboxes*.

Inspired by the separations and sentimentality forced by World War II, Harlemites in the '40s want to hear *ballads*—love songs sung in intimate tones.

As home *record players* become more popular, consumers get in the habit of buying the latest top hits.

FOR AFRICAN AMERICANS, BILLY ECKSTINE IS PERHAPS THE GREATEST *SINGING IDOL* OF THE DECADE.

ECKSTINE'S SEAT-RUMBLING VIBRATO AND FACIAL CONTORTIONS REALLY GET TO THE APOLLO CROWD.

In 1945, Eckstine is also one of the few black singers to cross over from Billboard's *"Harlem Hit Parade"*— that became known as the black *"R&B"* chart—to the *"Honor Roll of Hits"* —the white "pop" chart.

Like Sinatra at the Paramount, Eckstine at the Apollo has a fanatical following of squealing adolescents who reverentially refer to him as "Mr. B."

HE KNOWS JUST HOW TO QUIET THE THRONGS AT THE APOLLO WHEN THEY GET CARRIED AWAY.

STEADY NOW . . .

My destiny...

BOYS WEAR "MR. B" SHIRTS

IN THE LATE '40S, ECKSTINE REALLY TAKES OFF, AND FROM 1949 INTO THE EARLY '50S THE "SEPIA SINATRA" IS THE HOTTEST THING AT THE APOLLO, FUELED BY HITS LIKE "MY DESTINY."

TWO OTHER APOLLO HEARTTHROBS ARE **NAT KING COLE** AND **BILL KENNY** OF THE INK SPOTS.

KENNY IS A 1935 APOLLO AMATEUR NIGHT WINNER.

If I didn't care...

Years later, Redd Foxx's TV character, Fred Sanford, loves to mimic Kenny's winsome high-pitched tenor.

THE NAT KING COLE TRIO SELL MILLIONS OF RECORDS IN THE MID-'40S.

When Cole goes solo in the late '40s, he is the top black act in show business.

125th APOLLO
NAT KING COLE
Held Over
for a Second Smash Week!
AND HIS TRIO

I DON'T CARE WHAT YOU HAVE TO DO, CLEAR NEXT WEEK.

YES, YES, I **KNOW** WE NEVER DO THAT.

PEARL BAILEY'S STAR IS ALSO ASCENDING BY THE LATE '40S, AFTER YEARS OF WORK WITH CAB CALLOWAY, COOTIE WILLIAMS, AND OTHERS SINCE HER 1934 AMATEUR NIGHT WIN.

BY 1953, HER SHOW WITH DUKE ELLINGTON GROSSES $40,000 AND SETS AN APOLLO **ATTENDANCE RECORD**.

"Pearly Mae" is a welcome tonic to war-weary Harlemites.

JOHN HAMMOND

PEARL BAILEY WAS THE APOLLO **IDEAL** OF A SINGER!

While her career later expands into nightclubs, Broadway, film, and television, Pearl always remains loyal to the Apollo.

HEY, BOBBY, WHEN CAN I COME **HOME**?

ANOTHER AMATEUR NIGHT WINNER, SARAH VAUGHAN, IS SIGNED BY ECKSTINE, ADORED BY BIRD, AND HAS HER FIRST SOLO RECORDING SESSION IN 1944, ARRANGED BY DIZZY GILLESPIE.

DIZ AND BIRD WERE THE BIGGEST AND MOST IMPORTANT CONTRIBUTORS TO MODERN JAZZ.

BUT, IN THE VOCAL FIELD, IT WOULD BE SARAH VAUGHAN.

I'll wait and pray...

BILLY ECKSTINE

HER **PERFECT PITCH** IS SOMETHING OF A PROBLEM AT THE APOLLO.

"Sassy" continually complains that the theater's piano is out of tune, even though Frank Schiffman has it tuned before every performance.

FORGET IT, POP, I'LL DO IT MYSELF.

Musicians love to play for the "Divine Sarah" because she uses her voice as an instrument, bending and coloring notes like a true improviser.

DINAH WASHINGTON COMBINES JAZZ STYLINGS WITH THE BLUES TO PRODUCE ONE OF THE GUTSIEST SOUNDS IN MUSIC.

But, she also has a great success with pop records like "Unforgettable" and "What a Difference a Day Makes."

LIONEL HAMPTON DISCOVERS HER IN THE WINDY CITY IN 1943.

MY MANAGER, JOE GLASER'S FRIEND, HAD A NIGHTCLUB IN THE LOOP.

LADIES

THEY HAD A YOUNG LADY WORKING IN THE LADIES' POWDER ROOM, AND EVERY TIME THE BAND WAS TO COME OUT TO PLAY, SHE WOULD POP HER HEAD OUT THE DOOR AND SING WITH THE BAND.

Like Sarah Vaughan, Dinah Washington had **roots** in gospel music, having begun as a singer with church choirs in Chicago.

WHAT'S YOUR NAME, GIRL?

RUTH JONES.

I DON'T LIKE THAT NAME— CAN I CALL YOU SOMETHING ELSE?

I DON'T CARE WHAT YOU CALL ME, AS LONG AS YOU GIVE ME A JOB!

FROM NOW ON, YOUR NAME WILL BE DINAH WASHINGTON . . .

LADIE

1940s. While vocalists *overshadow* most of the bands, those of Lionel Hampton and Louis Jordan become the hottest African American attractions of their time.

Hamp gains fame in 1936 when Benny Goodman taps him to play vibes in Goodman's integrated group.

LIONEL HAMPTON

LOUIS JORDAN

Hamp brings his great sixteen-piece band into the Apollo in December 1940—to the delight of the Apollo crowd.

With such an outstanding lineup, Hampton begins letting his men work out on longer and wilder solos that often whip audiences into a frenzy.

DEXTER GORDON
SAX

ILLINOIS JACQUET
SAX

JOE NEWMAN
TRUMPET

"Flying Home," a number he writes and originally records with Goodman, becomes Hamp's showstopper.

IN "FLYING HOME," THE LIGHTS WOULD GO OUT, AND YOU'D SEE THE AIRPLANES PROJECTED ON THE SCRIM BEHIND THE BANDSTAND. YOU'D HEAR THE MOTOR HUMMING, AND THAT'S WHEN THE SAXOPHONE PLAYER STARTED PLAYING HIS FAMOUS SOLO . . .

Hampton has a penchant for clearing the Apollo, even if it means leading the audience out with his own band!

"FLYING HOME" WOULD GO ON FOR TWENTY MINUTES.

IT WAS A FANTASTIC THING TO SEE HAMP PERFORM.

HAMP WOULD JUMP ON HIS DRUM, THE APOLLO'S ELECTRICIAN, BOB HALL, WOULD PUSH A BUTTON, AND A SMUDGEPOT WOULD COME UP LIKE THE STAGE WAS BLOWING UP.

Sammy Davis Jr. works with Hampton when young Sammy is still a member of the *Will Mastin Trio*.

YOU'D LOOK UP AND HEAR HIM, AND THEN SUDDENLY HE'D DISAPPEAR . . .

AND THE ONLY PEOPLE LEFT ON STAGE WOULD BE THE DRUMMER AND A BASS PLAYER.

MILITARY DRUMSTICKS ARE BIG—PARADE STICKS.

BUT THAT WASN'T *LOUD* ENOUGH.

HAMP HAD TO TURN THE STICKS AROUND TO THE OTHER END TO KEEP THAT BEAT GOING.

HE'D GO PARADING OUT IN THE AUDIENCE . . .

AND RIGHT OUT THE THEATER ONTO 125TH STREET . . .

TO ENTERTAIN THE PEOPLE WAITING ON LINE!

WE JUST BLEW UP THE COMMUNITY WITH HAPPINESS AND JOY AND EXCITEMENT. *FOURTH OF JULY* EVERY DAY!

APOLLO

TONIGHT LIONEL HAMPTON

TONIGHT LIONEL HAMPTON

HAMP!

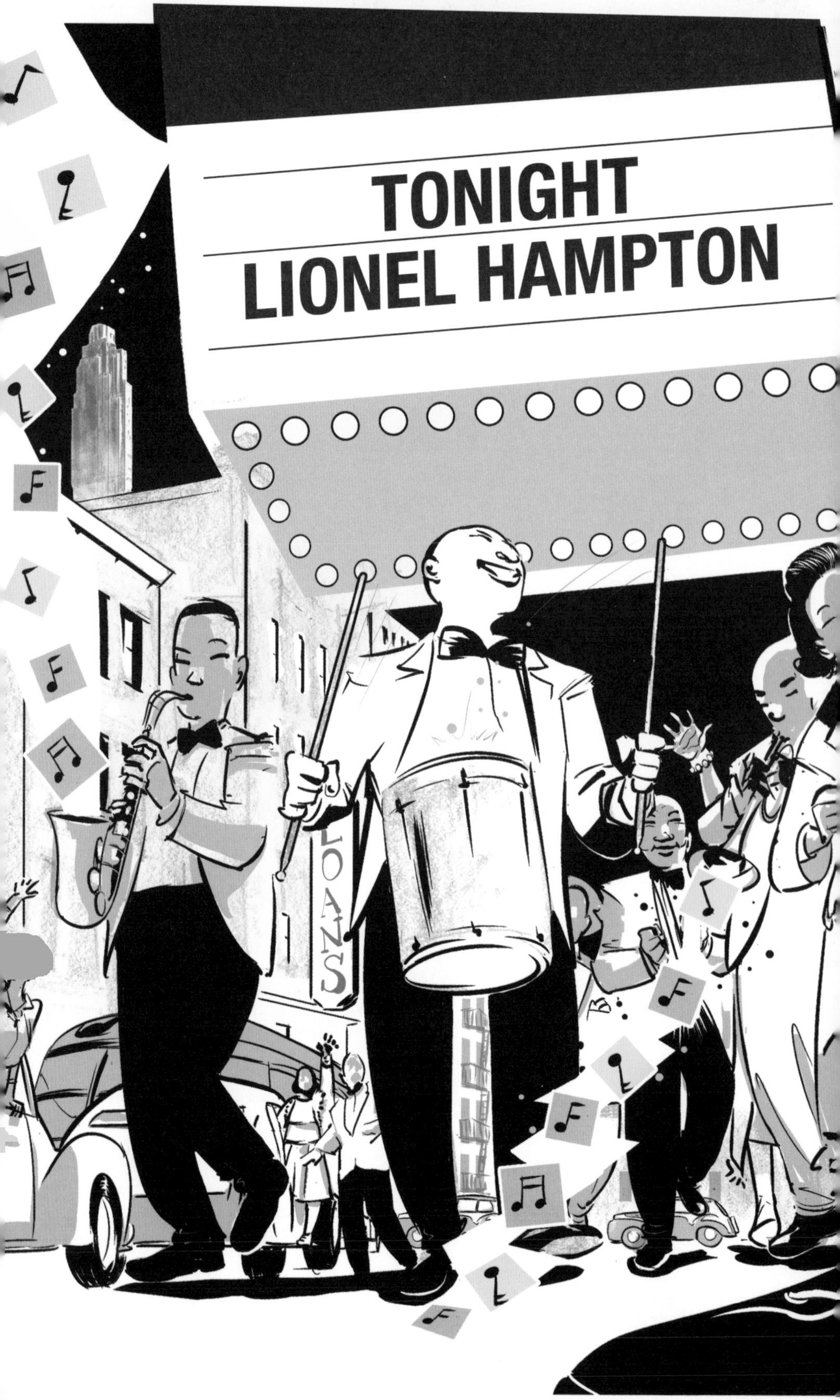
TONIGHT
LIONEL HAMPTON
LOANS

Hampton, with deep jazz roots, and Louis Jordan, who started with Chick Webb, would become great influences on the rhythm-and-blues and rock-and-roll revolutions to come.

LOUIS JORDAN

LIONEL HAMPTON

JAZZMEN PLAY MOSTLY FOR THEMSELVES. I WANT TO PLAY FOR THE **PEOPLE**!

ALL THAT ROCK-AND-ROLL STUFF. IT **ALL** STARTED WITH US. ALL THAT DANCING AND THINGS ONSTAGE. IT WAS ALL MY IDEAS.

JORDAN ALSO **SPEAKS** FOR THE PEOPLE AS AN INTERPRETER OF BLACK STREET LINGO TO THE WHITE WORLD.

Jack, You're Dead

Reet, Petite, and Gone

Knock Me a Kiss

Gonna Move to the Outskirts of Town

Is You Is or Is You Ain't My Baby

Starting in 1942, Jordan is a regular on the "Harlem Hit Parade."

In 1946 alone, he scores eleven hits.

JORDAN MODELS HIMSELF AFTER CAB CALLOWAY, AND, LIKE HIS MENTOR, JORDAN ALSO CLOWNS IN FILMS.

His early two-reeler films have been called the first rock-and-roll films, and precursors to music videos.

JORDAN'S RELATIONSHIP WITH THE APOLLO AUDIENCE IS BLISSFUL. IN 1948, HE JOINS NAT COLE AS ONE OF FEW ARTISTS **HELD OVER** FOR A SECOND WEEK.

LOUIS JORDAN FOR PRESIDENT

RDAN FOR SIDENT

JORDAN FOR PRESIDENT

AS LATE AS 1960, JORDAN CAN STILL PACK THEM IN, AND RUNS A "LOUIS JORDAN FOR PRESIDENT" CAMPAIGN FROM THE APOLLO.

SAMMY DAVIS JR. GROWS UP IN A FAMILY OF VAUDEVILLIANS WHO CONSTANTLY TOUR THE COUNTRY AS PART OF THE ACT OF HIS FATHER AND HIS ADOPTED UNCLE, **WILL MASTIN**.

BILL "BOJANGLES" ROBINSON IS SO IMPRESSED WITH SAMMY THAT HE VOLUNTEERS TO TUTOR THE BOY.

HE'S A PERFECTIONIST.

EVERYONE KNEW MY MOTHER. SHE WAS A CHORUS GIRL AT THE APOLLO.

WHEN I FIRST CAME IN WITH THE WILL MASTIN TRIO, I WAS BABY SANCHEZ'S SON: *BE NICE TO HIM.*

When Sammy Davis Jr. first appears at the Apollo in 1947 with his father and uncle, they split $650 for the week.

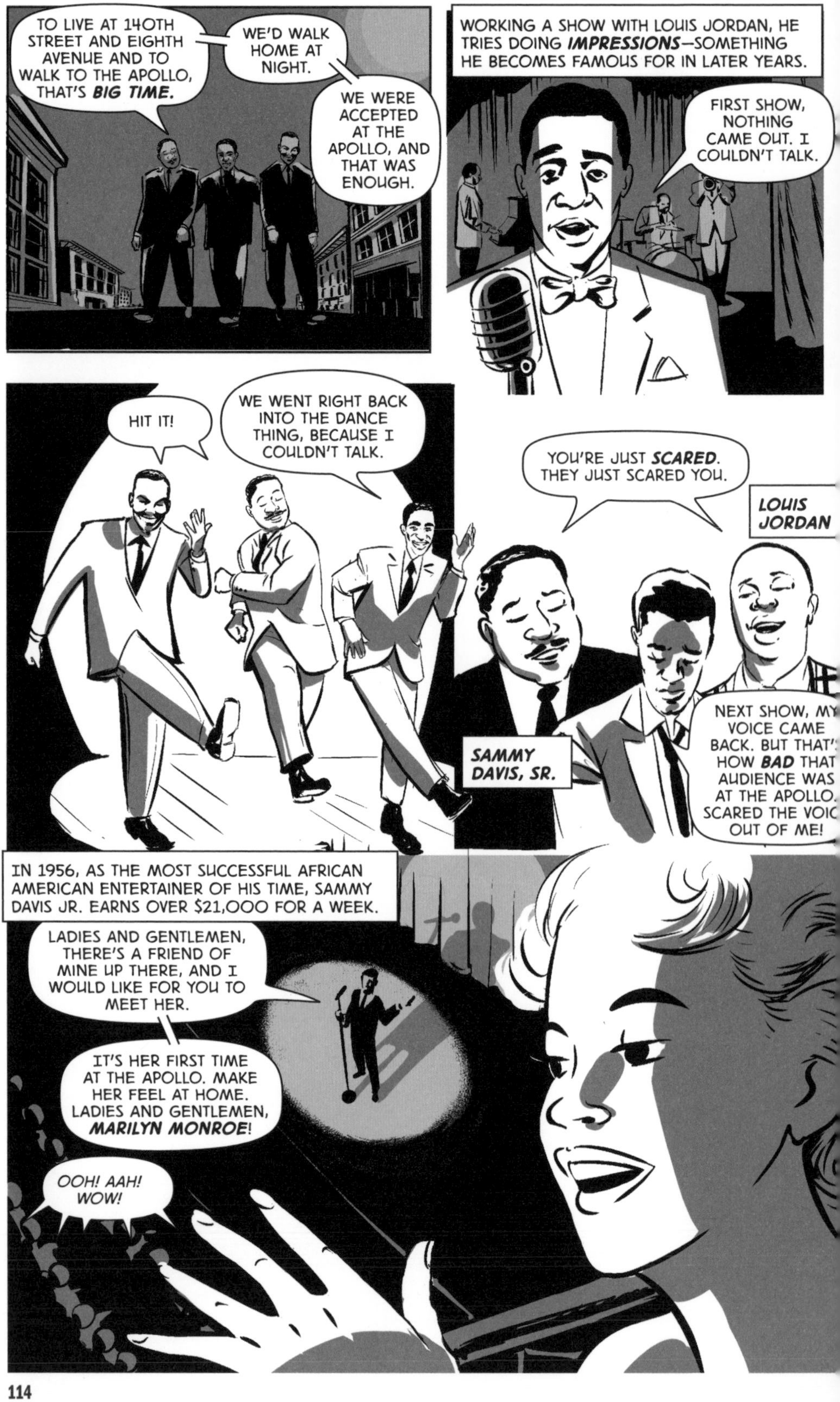

TO LIVE AT 140TH STREET AND EIGHTH AVENUE AND TO WALK TO THE APOLLO, THAT'S **BIG TIME.**
WE'D WALK HOME AT NIGHT.
WE WERE ACCEPTED AT THE APOLLO, AND THAT WAS ENOUGH.
WORKING A SHOW WITH LOUIS JORDAN, HE TRIES DOING **IMPRESSIONS**—SOMETHING HE BECOMES FAMOUS FOR IN LATER YEARS.
FIRST SHOW, NOTHING CAME OUT. I COULDN'T TALK.
HIT IT!
WE WENT RIGHT BACK INTO THE DANCE THING, BECAUSE I COULDN'T TALK.
YOU'RE JUST **SCARED**. THEY JUST SCARED YOU.
LOUIS JORDAN
SAMMY DAVIS, SR.
NEXT SHOW, MY VOICE CAME BACK. BUT THAT'S HOW **BAD** THAT AUDIENCE WAS AT THE APOLLO. SCARED THE VOIC OUT OF ME!
IN 1956, AS THE MOST SUCCESSFUL AFRICAN AMERICAN ENTERTAINER OF HIS TIME, SAMMY DAVIS JR. EARNS OVER $21,000 FOR A WEEK.
LADIES AND GENTLEMEN, THERE'S A FRIEND OF MINE UP THERE, AND I WOULD LIKE FOR YOU TO MEET HER.
IT'S HER FIRST TIME AT THE APOLLO. MAKE HER FEEL AT HOME. LADIES AND GENTLEMEN, **MARILYN MONROE**!
OOH! AAH! WOW!

SAMMY SUCCESSFULLY DANCES HIS WAY INTO THE FUTURE. BUT SOME OF THE GREATEST DANCERS OF THE '40S—**BUNNY BRIGGS**, **BABY LAURENCE**, AND **TEDDY HALE**—HAVE BEEN CALLED THE DYING BREED.

As bop gains dominance in the '40s, even the greatest dancers find themselves *subordinate* to music that is more complex and less danceable.

BUNNY BRIGGS

BABY LAURENCE

TEDDY HALE

TRAGICALLY, TEDDY HALE AND BABY LAURENCE ALSO FALL VICTIM TO BOP'S GREATEST **SCOURGE**—HEROIN.

GREGORY HINES

BUNNY BRIGGS

SAVION GLOVER

BUNNY BRIGGS ADAPTS, BECOMES A MENTOR TO NEW DANCERS, AND LONG WORKS SUCCESSFULLY, APPEARING ON BROADWAY IN *BLACK AND BLUE* IN 1989, RECEIVING A TONY AWARD NOMINATION.

But for dancers—once the *backbone* of the Apollo's vaudeville-variety format—and for other acts dependent on that format, the 1940s are a transitional time.

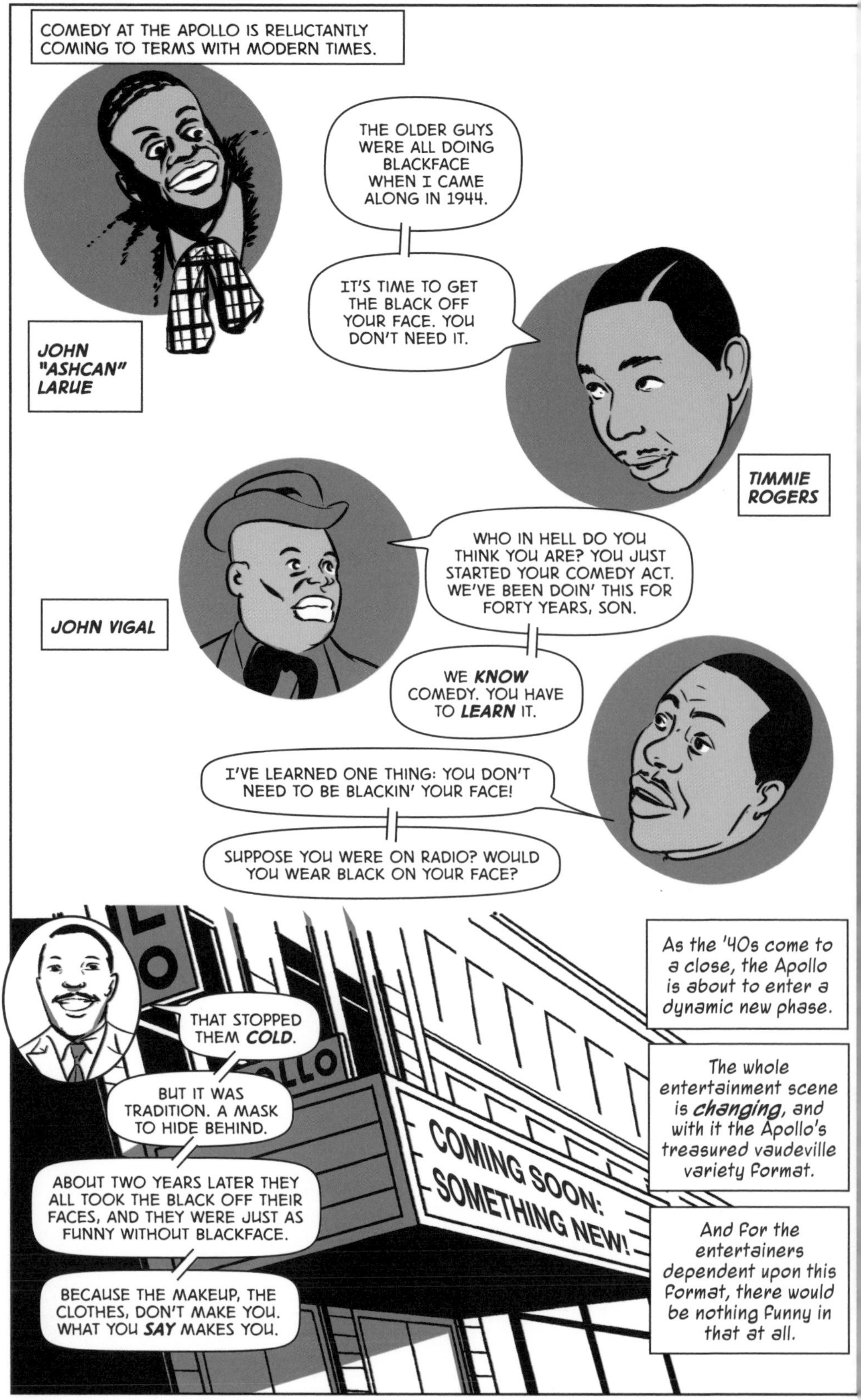
COMEDY AT THE APOLLO IS RELUCTANTLY COMING TO TERMS WITH MODERN TIMES.
JOHN "ASHCAN" LARUE
THE OLDER GUYS WERE ALL DOING BLACKFACE WHEN I CAME ALONG IN 1944.
IT'S TIME TO GET THE BLACK OFF YOUR FACE. YOU DON'T NEED IT.
TIMMIE ROGERS
JOHN VIGAL
WHO IN HELL DO YOU THINK YOU ARE? YOU JUST STARTED YOUR COMEDY ACT. WE'VE BEEN DOIN' THIS FOR FORTY YEARS, SON.
WE **KNOW** COMEDY. YOU HAVE TO **LEARN** IT.
I'VE LEARNED ONE THING: YOU DON'T NEED TO BE BLACKIN' YOUR FACE!
SUPPOSE YOU WERE ON RADIO? WOULD YOU WEAR BLACK ON YOUR FACE?
THAT STOPPED THEM **COLD**.
BUT IT WAS TRADITION. A MASK TO HIDE BEHIND.
ABOUT TWO YEARS LATER THEY ALL TOOK THE BLACK OFF THEIR FACES, AND THEY WERE JUST AS FUNNY WITHOUT BLACKFACE.
BECAUSE THE MAKEUP, THE CLOTHES, DON'T MAKE YOU. WHAT YOU **SAY** MAKES YOU.
COMING SOON: SOMETHING NEW!
As the '40s come to a close, the Apollo is about to enter a dynamic new phase.
The whole entertainment scene is ***changing***, and with it the Apollo's treasured vaudeville variety format.
And for the entertainers dependent upon this format, there would be nothing funny in that at all.

CHAPTER 6

The 1950s: Rockin'

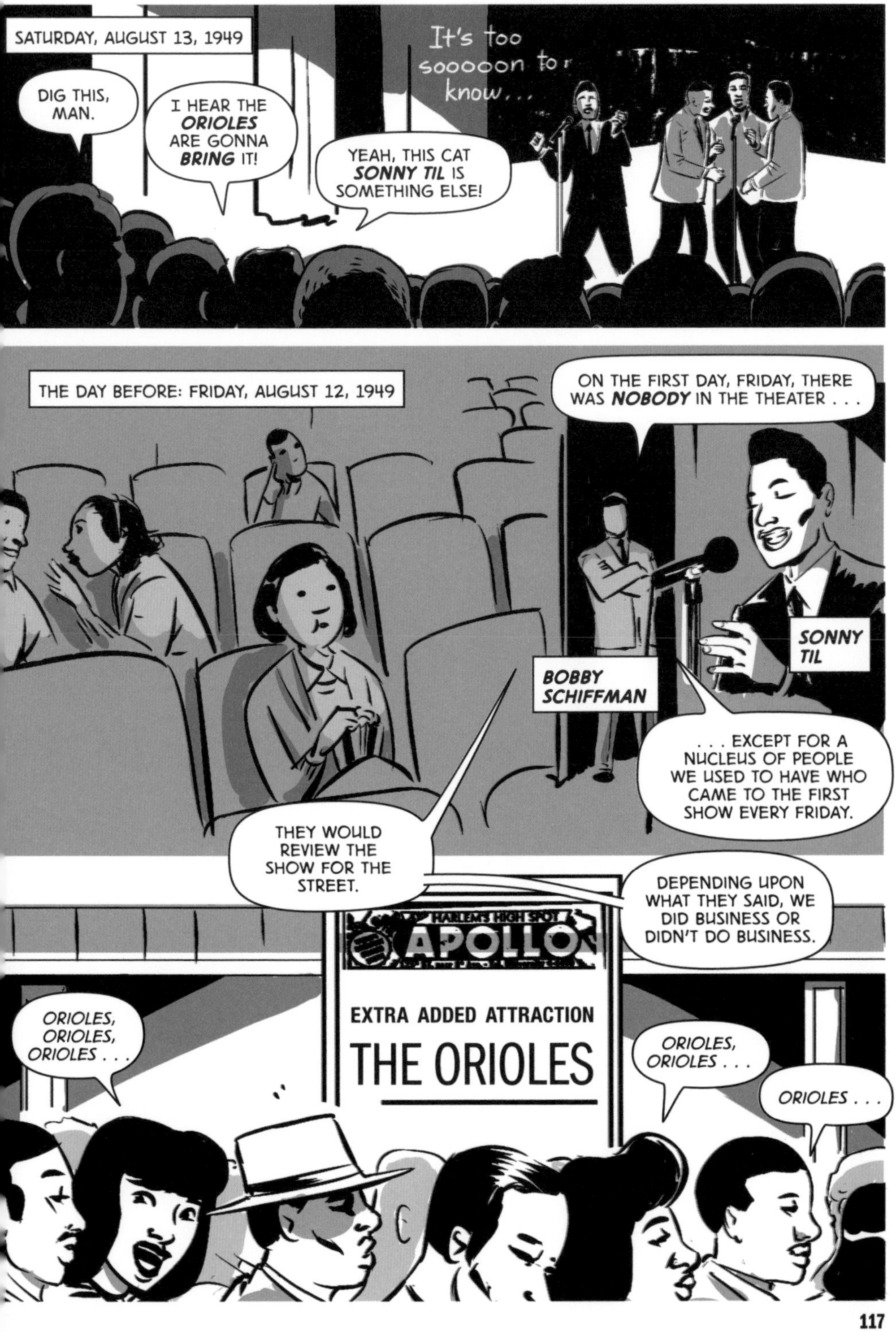
SATURDAY, AUGUST 13, 1949
DIG THIS, MAN.
I HEAR THE ORIOLES ARE GONNA BRING IT!
YEAH, THIS CAT SONNY TIL IS SOMETHING ELSE!
It's too sooooon to know...
THE DAY BEFORE: FRIDAY, AUGUST 12, 1949
ON THE FIRST DAY, FRIDAY, THERE WAS NOBODY IN THE THEATER . . .
SONNY TIL
BOBBY SCHIFFMAN
. . . EXCEPT FOR A NUCLEUS OF PEOPLE WE USED TO HAVE WHO CAME TO THE FIRST SHOW EVERY FRIDAY.
THEY WOULD REVIEW THE SHOW FOR THE STREET.
DEPENDING UPON WHAT THEY SAID, WE DID BUSINESS OR DIDN'T DO BUSINESS.
HARLEM'S HIGH SPOT
APOLLO
EXTRA ADDED ATTRACTION
THE ORIOLES
ORIOLES, ORIOLES, ORIOLES . . .
ORIOLES, ORIOLES . . .
ORIOLES . . .

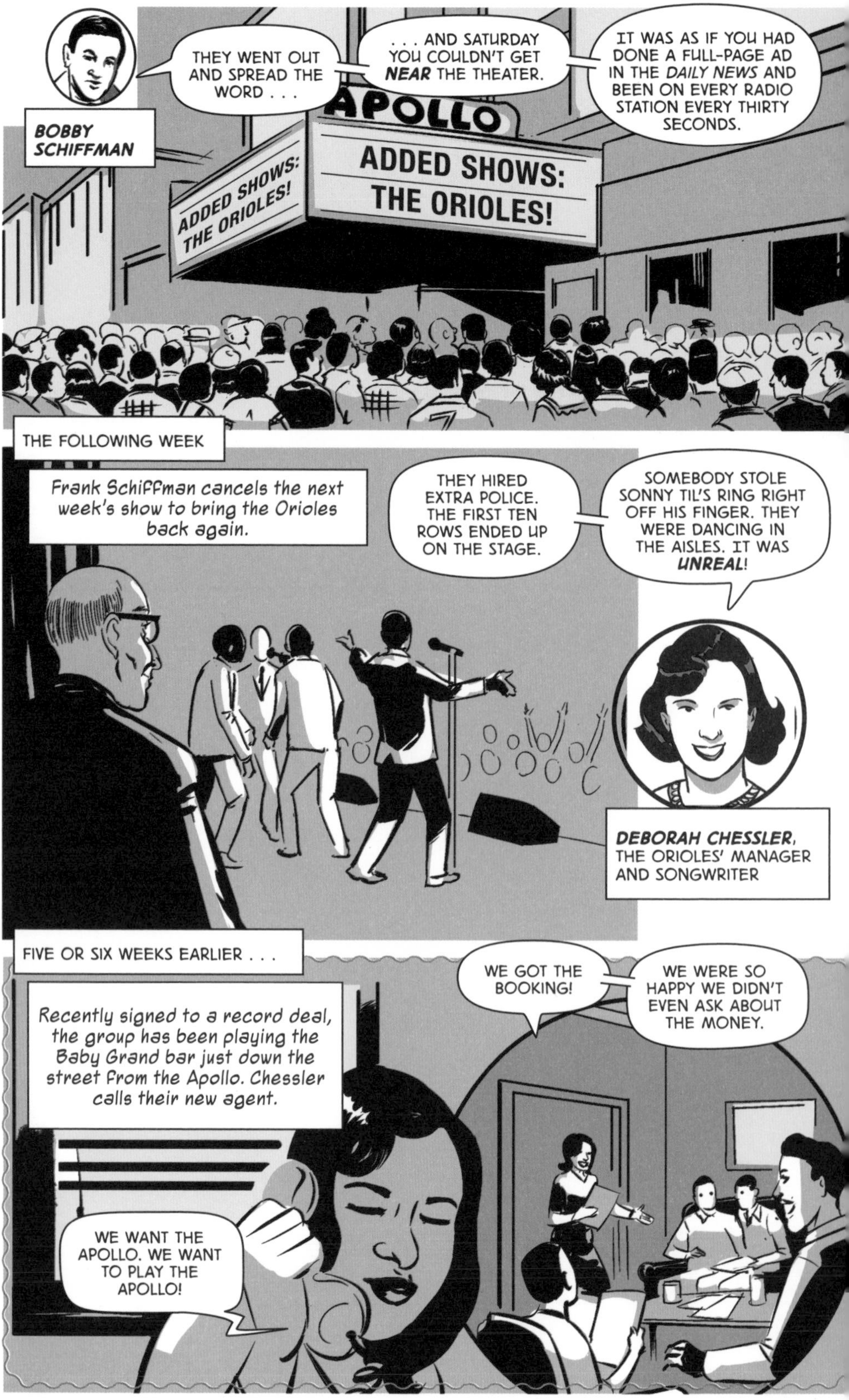
BOBBY SCHIFFMAN
THEY WENT OUT AND SPREAD THE WORD . . .
. . . AND SATURDAY YOU COULDN'T GET NEAR THE THEATER.
IT WAS AS IF YOU HAD DONE A FULL-PAGE AD IN THE DAILY NEWS AND BEEN ON EVERY RADIO STATION EVERY THIRTY SECONDS.
APOLLO
ADDED SHOWS: THE ORIOLES!
ADDED SHOWS: THE ORIOLES!
THE FOLLOWING WEEK
Frank Schiffman cancels the next week's show to bring the Orioles back again.
THEY HIRED EXTRA POLICE. THE FIRST TEN ROWS ENDED UP ON THE STAGE.
SOMEBODY STOLE SONNY TIL'S RING RIGHT OFF HIS FINGER. THEY WERE DANCING IN THE AISLES. IT WAS UNREAL!
DEBORAH CHESSLER, THE ORIOLES' MANAGER AND SONGWRITER
FIVE OR SIX WEEKS EARLIER . . .
Recently signed to a record deal, the group has been playing the Baby Grand bar just down the street from the Apollo. Chessler calls their new agent.
WE GOT THE BOOKING!
WE WERE SO HAPPY WE DIDN'T EVEN ASK ABOUT THE MONEY.
WE WANT THE APOLLO. WE WANT TO PLAY THE APOLLO!

THE ORIOLES KNOCK OUT THE APOLLO CROWD WITH A NEW SMALL-GROUP LOOK AND A FRESH SOUND: *RHYTHM AND BLUES*.

Cryin' in the Chaaaapel...

The group has a string of hits.

SONG PLUGGERS FREQUENTLY SEND THEM **DEMO RECORDS** OF SONGS, INCLUDING A TUNE INTENDED AS A COUNTRY-AND-WESTERN TEARJERKER.

IN BETWEEN SHOWS AT THE APOLLO, WE LISTENED IN THE DRESSING ROOM.

WE LEARNED "CRYIN' IN THE CHAPEL" IN ONE NIGHT.

THE NEXT NIGHT THEY DID IT IN THE THEATER.

THE FOLLOWING MORNING WE WERE DOWN AT THE RECORDING STUDIO.

IT HIT **OVERNIGHT**.

In the fall of 1953, "Cryin' in the Chapel" becomes the first R&B song to make the pop charts.

THE ORIOLES PROBABLY STARTED THE WHOLE RHYTHM-AND-BLUES SCENE. THEY WERE THE INNOVATORS.

ANYBODY LISTENING COULD REMEMBER THE MELODY, AND WENT AWAY SINGING ORIOLES SONGS.

Billboar

Yes, but there is more to rhythm and blues.

WE WERE WORKING UNDER ALL KINDS OF ADVERSE SITUATIONS. THERE WAS A LOT OF *HURT* THAT WENT ALONG WITH IT.

RUTH BROWN

After World War II, and the promise of the war years, disappointments and discrimination are an increasing burden for black America.

WHAT REALLY *SUSTAINED* US WAS THE MUSIC.

ALL OF THE THINGS THAT WENT WRONG DURING THE TRAVELS, OR THE HARASSMENT, YOU TOOK THAT OUT ONSTAGE.

THAT'S WHERE THE *FEELING* COMES FROM.

IT WAS A TOTAL EXPERIENCE. THE RHYTHM COVERED UP FOR THE BLUES.

THAT'S WHAT RHYTHM AND BLUES WAS.

JOHNNY OTIS STARTS USING THE TERM IN 1948 AFTER HE BREAKS UP HIS BIG BAND.

A BOOGIE-WOOGIE PIANO PLAYER, A GUITAR PLAYER, A COUPLE OF HORNS, AND A DRUMMER WOULD PROBABLY PLEASE PEOPLE MORE THAN A BIG FULL-BLOWN JAZZ BAND.

I *SAW* RHYTHM AND BLUES COMING.

THE JOHNNY OTIS RHYTHM AND BLUES CARAVAN.

JOHNNY OTIS BAND

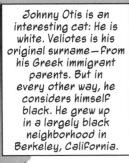

Johnny Otis is an interesting cat: He is white. Veliotes is his original surname—from his Greek immigrant parents. But in every other way, he considers himself black. He grew up in a largely black neighborhood in Berkeley, California.

I DID NOT BECOME BLACK BECAUSE I WAS ATTRACTED TO NEGRO MUSIC . . .

I BECAME WHAT I AM BECAUSE AS A CHILD, I REACTED TO THE WAY OF LIFE, THE SPECIAL VITALITY, THE ATMOSPHERE OF THE BLACK COMMUNITY. I CANNOT THINK OF MYSELF AS WHITE.

Harlemites—especially the young folks—feel the music's vitality, shake under its power, and are liberated by the emotional expressiveness of rhythm and blues.

But the music meets with open derision in some circles who see it as vulgar, primitive, or trifling.

I WAS LIKE A *TRAITOR* TO SOME OF THE BROTHERS. I FELT UNEASY AROUND SOME OF THE JAZZ ESTABLISHMENT—LIKE I WAS BREAKING A SACRED TRUST.

The Apollo has to appeal to everyone, so the new sound emerges out of a *mix* of new and old in the early 1950s.

EARLY 50'S APOLLO HEADLINERS

MAY 5, 1950
THE ORIOLES AND BUDDY RICH

 JANUARY 4, 1951, ELLA FITZGERALD

APRIL 27, 1951, NAT KING COLE

 APRIL 25, 1952, JOHNNY OTIS

AUGUST 22, 1952, DINAH WASHINGTON

JULY 3, 1953, RUTH BROWN

AUGUST 14, 1953, DUKE ELLINGTON

ONE OF THE GREATEST-EVER R&B STARS IS PLUCKED FROM COUNT BASIE'S CLASSIC BIG BAND—IF YOU CAN PLUCK A GUY WHO IS SIX-FOOT-TWO AND 250 POUNDS.

AT ATLANTIC RECORDS, WE THOUGHT *JOE TURNER* WAS ONE OF THE GREAT BLUES SINGERS OF ALL TIME. BUT WE DIDN'T KNOW WHERE HE WAS.

AHMET ERTEGUN, ATLANTIC RECORDS CO-FOUNDER

WE HEARD HE WAS OUT IN CALIFORNIA, TEXAS, OR CHICAGO . . .

I READ THAT JIMMIE RUSHING HAD QUIT THE BASIE BAND AND THAT JOE TURNER HAD TAKEN HIS PLACE.

THE FOLLOWING WEEK I SAW THAT COUNT BASIE WAS PLAYING AT THE APOLLO.

JOE TURNER SINGS STRICTLY TRADITIONAL EIGHT- OR TWELVE-BAR BLUES. BUT THE ARRANGEMENTS FOR THE STAGE HAD BECOME MUCH MORE SOPHISTICATED.

THEY PROBABLY HADN'T HAD MANY REHEARSALS, IF ANY.

JOE CAME BACK RIGHT ON THE BEAT WHERE HE WAS *SUPPOSED* TO, BUT THE ARRANGEMENT WENT ANOTHER WAY.

SO HALFWAY INTO THE SONG THEY WERE *COMPLETELY OFF*, WHICH SENT THE CROWD INTO HYSTERICAL LAUGHTER.

I FELT VERY BAD FOR JOE TURNER. I WENT BACKSTAGE DURING THE BREAK, BUT HE'D ALREADY LEFT.

EXIT →

HEAD STAGEHAND **WILLIAM SPAYNE**

AHMET ERTEGUN

BRADDOCK HOTEL

MAN, **FORGET** ABOUT ALL THIS. I KNOW I CAN MAKE HIT RECORDS WITH YOU. WE'RE GOING TO DO A WHOLE **NEW THING**!

♪ Chains of ♪
Looooove....

I WROTE, WITH HIS HELP, A SONG CALLED "CHAINS OF LOVE," AND JESSE STONE WROTE A BEAUTIFUL ARRANGEMENT. THAT BECAME A BIG HIT!

YOU MAY HAVE HEARD OF ANOTHER SONG BIG JOE TURNER AND THIS TEAM MADE FAMOUS.

...SHAKE, RATTLE AND ROLL!

ERTEGUN IS ALSO BEHIND THE MAKING OF PERHAPS THE MOST IMPORTANT GROUP OF THE R&B ERA: **THE DRIFTERS**.

And, as so many of these tales do, the story starts at the Apollo.

APOLL

SEVENTEEN-YEAR-OLD *CLYDE MCPHATTER* WINS AMATEUR NIGHT IN 1950.

BILLY WARD HIRES CLYDE FOR HIS NEW GROUP, THE *DOMINOES*. THEY DEBUT AT THE APOLLO WITH THE ORIOLES.

OH MY GOD, THAT VOICE IS SO ANGELIC. SO MUCH GOSPEL FEELING!

AHMET ERTEGUN

A YEAR OR SO LATER, ERTEGUN HEARS THAT MCPHATTER IS NO LONGER WITH THE DOMINOES.

ARE YOU FREE?

YEAH, MAN, THEY FIRED ME!

I COULDN'T BELIEVE IT.

THAT WAS THE BEGINNING OF THE DRIFTERS.

AHMET ERTEGUN

CLYDE MCPHATTER

IT'S BEEN SAID THAT THE GROUP TAKES ITS NAME FROM THE FACT THAT THE MEMBERS HAD DRIFTED IN AND OUT OF MANY DIFFERENT GROUPS.

The Drifters hit immediately with "Money Honey," but McPhatter goes into the army in 1955, and they carry on without him.

Clyde goes solo when he gets out. The group continues until 1958, then breaks up.

HEY, MAN, WHAT ABOUT OUR GODDAMNED CONTRACT?!

BOBBY SCHIFFMAN

The group's manager had signed a multiyear contract with the Apollo. To avoid default, he asks *Ben E. King*'s group, the Five Crowns, to become the Drifters.

ATLANTIC RECORDS ASSIGNS TWO ACE SONGWRITING TEAMS TO CREATE NEW SONGS FOR THE GROUP.

Save The Last Dance For Me

There Goes My Baby

This Magic Moment

They write the biggest hits of any of the Drifters' lineups.

JERRY LEIBER AND MIKE STOLLER, AND DOC POMUS AND MORT SHUMAN

AFTER BEN E. KING LEAVES IN 1960, THE GROUP REORGANIZES YET AGAIN, AND CONTINUES TO PRODUCE HITS INTO THE MID-'60S.

Under The Boardwalk

Up On The Roof

On Broadway

KING AND THE DRIFTERS HAVE A RUN-IN AT THE APOLLO WITH A WILD MAN NAMED *SCREAMIN' JAY HAWKINS*, WHO HIT IN 1956 WITH "I PUT A SPELL ON YOU."

ALAN FREED TOLD ME, WITH A SONG LIKE THAT YOU NEED SOMETHING *WEIRD*.

HENRY

Freed, the DJ who coined the term "rock and roll," helps Hawkins to devise a routine where a closed coffin is wheeled onstage . . . out of which Screamin' Jay would suddenly emerge.

Hawkins carries the coffin wherever he goes in a zebra-striped hearse. Some creeped-out stagehands *refuse* to handle it.

A matchbook would be inserted in the latch to keep the lid from locking.

SCREAMIN' JAY HAD ASKED THE DRIFTERS TO PERFORM THAT TASK FOR HIM . . .

OH DAMN!

BUT THEY NEVER DID IT.

@#$%&!!

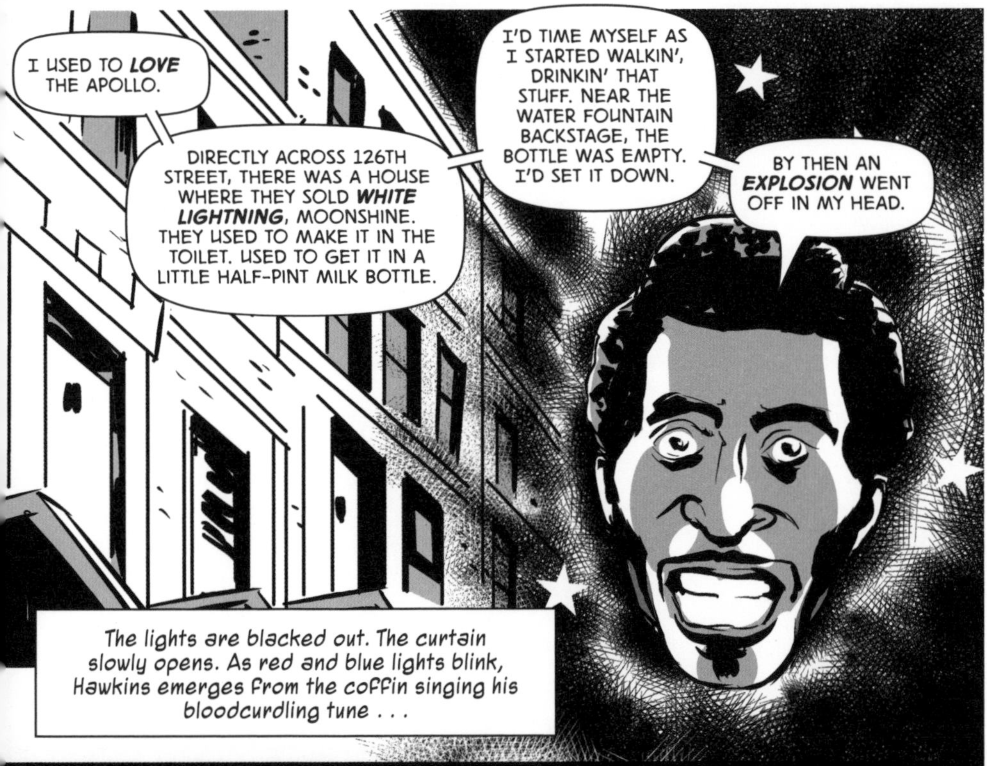
I USED TO LOVE THE APOLLO.
DIRECTLY ACROSS 126TH STREET, THERE WAS A HOUSE WHERE THEY SOLD WHITE LIGHTNING, MOONSHINE. THEY USED TO MAKE IT IN THE TOILET. USED TO GET IT IN A LITTLE HALF-PINT MILK BOTTLE.
I'D TIME MYSELF AS I STARTED WALKIN', DRINKIN' THAT STUFF. NEAR THE WATER FOUNTAIN BACKSTAGE, THE BOTTLE WAS EMPTY. I'D SET IT DOWN.
BY THEN AN EXPLOSION WENT OFF IN MY HEAD.
The lights are blacked out. The curtain slowly opens. As red and blue lights blink, Hawkins emerges from the coffin singing his bloodcurdling tune . . .

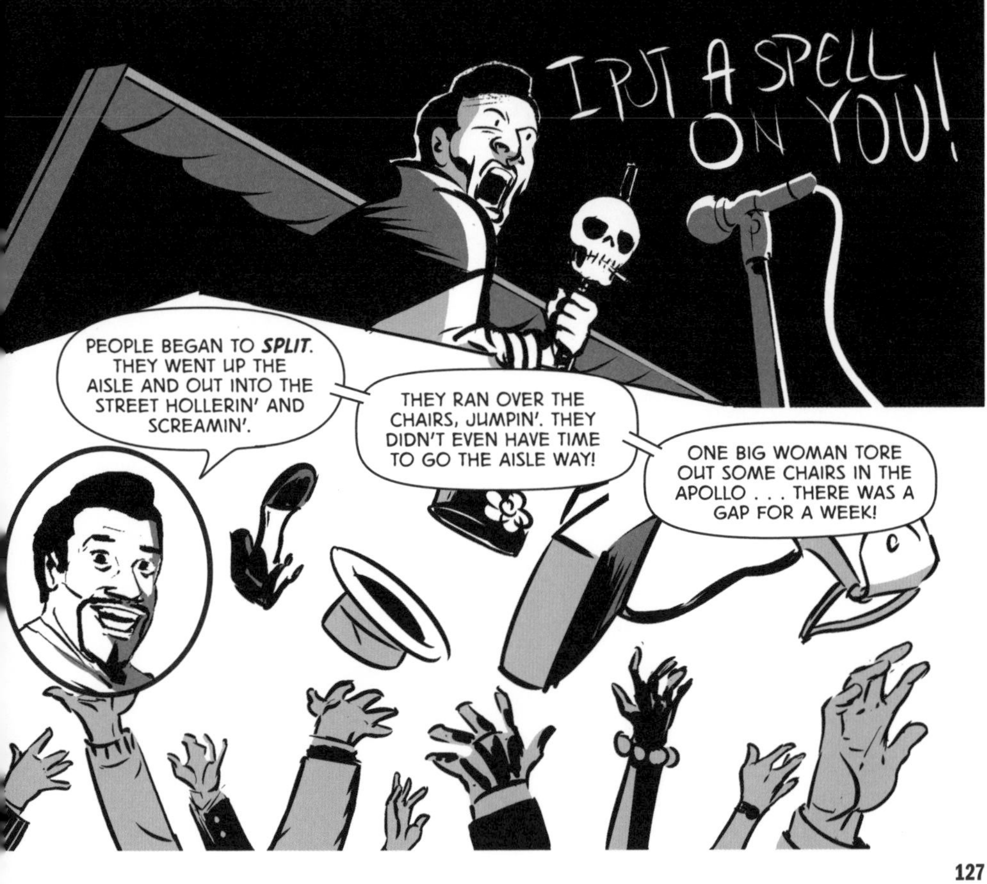
I PUT A SPELL ON YOU!
PEOPLE BEGAN TO SPLIT. THEY WENT UP THE AISLE AND OUT INTO THE STREET HOLLERIN' AND SCREAMIN'.
THEY RAN OVER THE CHAIRS, JUMPIN'. THEY DIDN'T EVEN HAVE TIME TO GO THE AISLE WAY!
ONE BIG WOMAN TORE OUT SOME CHAIRS IN THE APOLLO . . . THERE WAS A GAP FOR A WEEK!

BO DIDDLEY IS CAUSING RIOTS IN THE APOLLO, TOO, AND HE CLAIMS A **NEW** APOLLO HOUSE ATTENDANCE RECORD IN 1956.

His self-titled first hit for Chess Records lays down a thundering beat unlike anything ever heard before.

It's a fundamental element of what will become rock and roll—as Elvis realizes on his first visit to New York when he catches Bo at the Apollo.

THE FIRST TIME WE HAD BO DIDDLEY, I THOUGHT WE WERE GONNA HAVE AN UPRISING.

THE MUSIC WAS SO STIMULATING TO EVERYBODY, INCLUDING ME, THAT IT WAS WHIPPING THE CROWD INTO A **FRENZY**.

IT WAS JUST A COMPLETELY NEW, DIFFERENT STYLE.

BOBBY SCHIFFMAN

ROCK AND ROLL'S MAIN INGREDIENT WAS THE **BEAT**, AND BO DIDDLEY WAS THE LEADING EXPONENT OF THAT. TO HIM, MELODY MEANT NOTHING. LYRICS MEANT NOTHING. IT WAS THE BEAT THAT WAS INFECTIOUS.

IT WOULD DRIVE YOU **CRAZY**. HE REALLY SET THE PLACE ON FIRE.

WHEN **BUDDY HOLLY AND THE CRICKETS** DEBUT AT THE APOLLO IN 1957, CHANNELING BO DIDDLEY BAILS THEM OUT OF TROUBLE.

Cricket's guitarist *Niki Sullivan* tells Holly's biographer, John Goldrosen, about it.

THE FIRST TIME WE WENT ON WAS A WEEKDAY MATINEE.

THEY OPENED THE CURTAINS AND BUDDY STEPPED TOWARD THE MIKE.

IT'D BETTER SOUND LIKE THE RECORD!

YOU COULD HAVE HEARD A PIN DROP.

THE SAME THING ON THE EVENING SHOW, AND THE NEXT DAY—**NOTHING**.

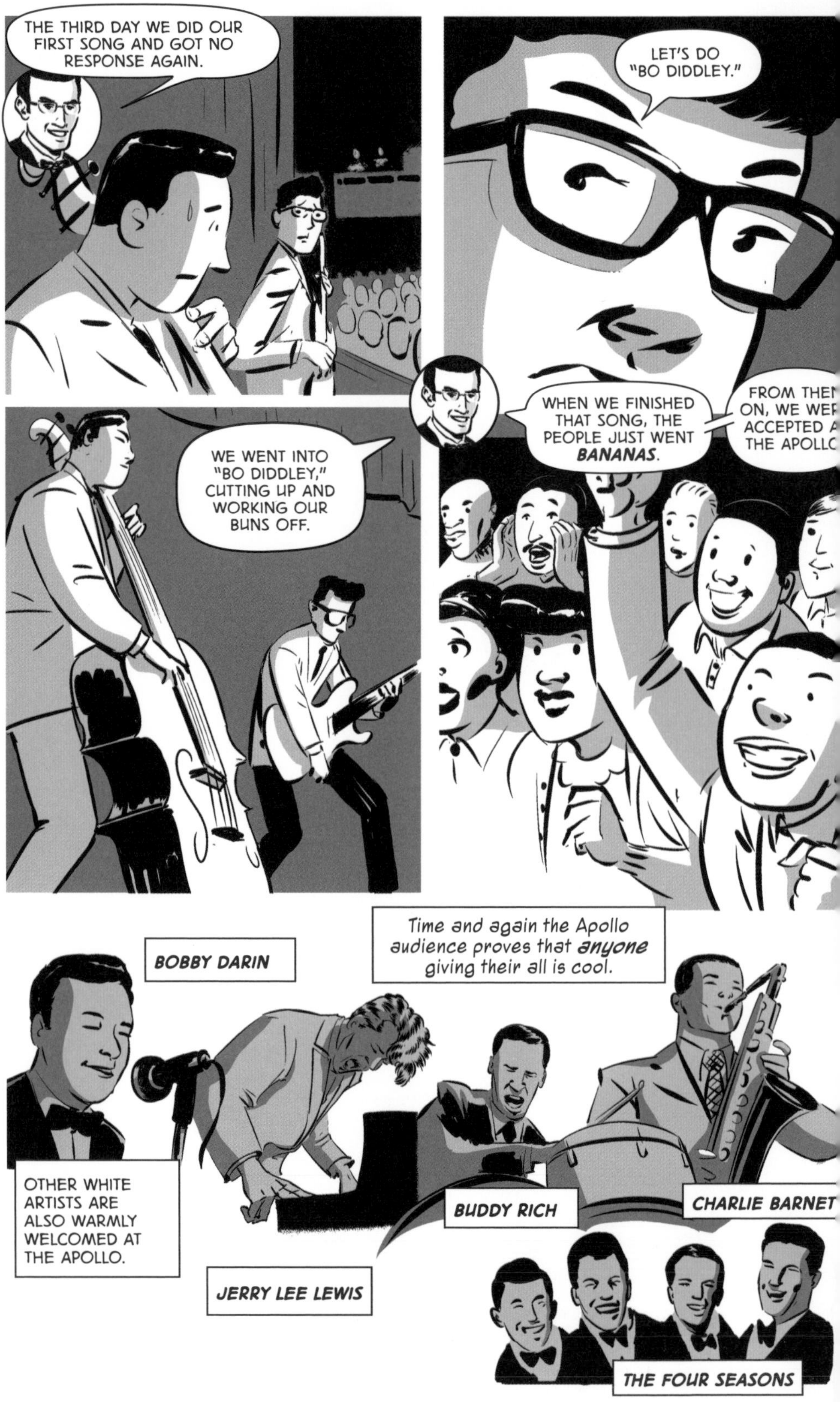

THE THIRD DAY WE DID OUR FIRST SONG AND GOT NO RESPONSE AGAIN.
LET'S DO "BO DIDDLEY."
WE WENT INTO "BO DIDDLEY," CUTTING UP AND WORKING OUR BUNS OFF.
WHEN WE FINISHED THAT SONG, THE PEOPLE JUST WENT ***BANANAS***.
FROM THEN ON, WE WER ACCEPTED A THE APOLLO
Time and again the Apollo audience proves that ***anyone*** giving their all is cool.
BOBBY DARIN
OTHER WHITE ARTISTS ARE ALSO WARMLY WELCOMED AT THE APOLLO.
JERRY LEE LEWIS
BUDDY RICH
CHARLIE BARNET
THE FOUR SEASONS

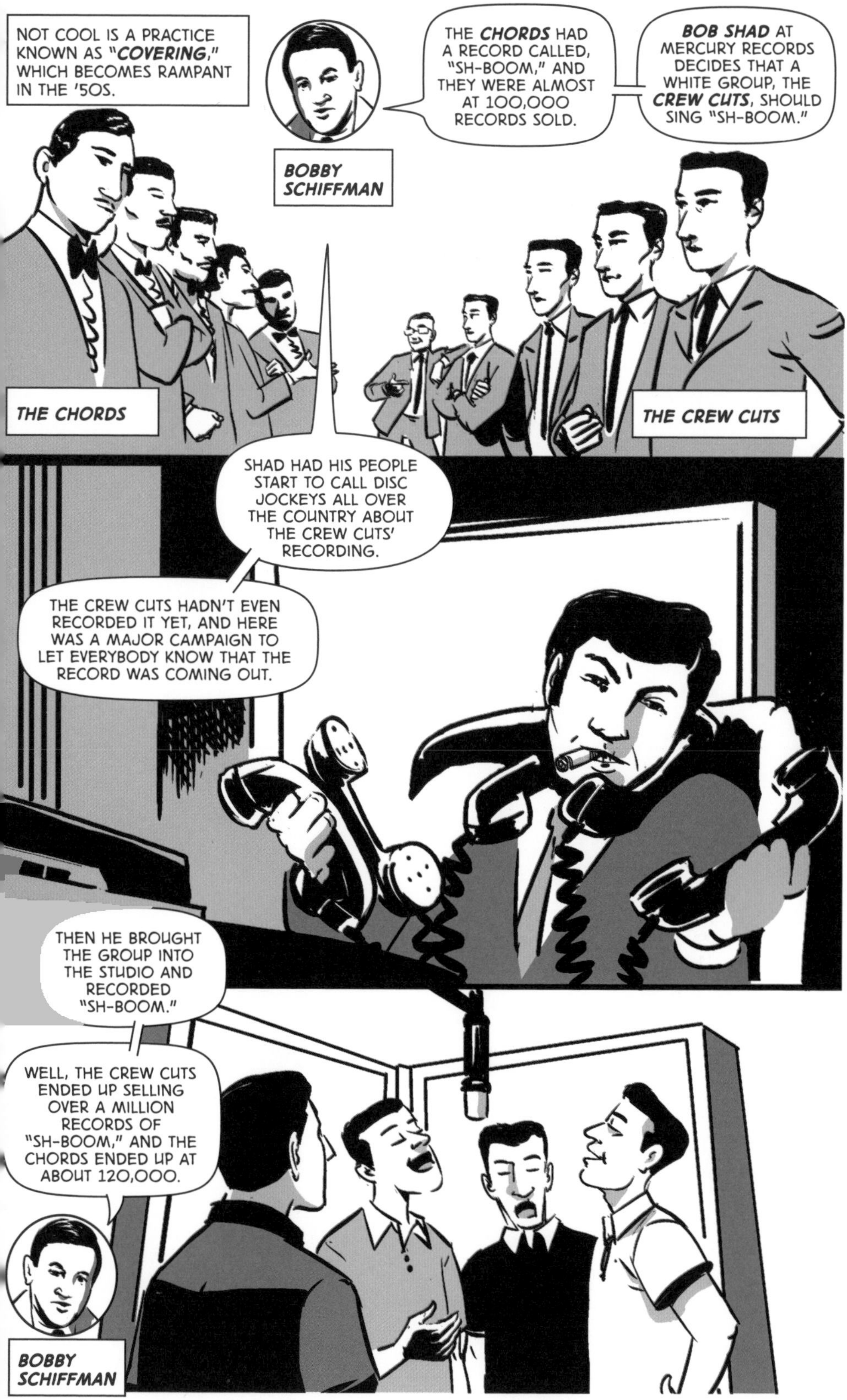
NOT COOL IS A PRACTICE KNOWN AS "COVERING," WHICH BECOMES RAMPANT IN THE '50S.
BOBBY SCHIFFMAN
THE CHORDS HAD A RECORD CALLED, "SH-BOOM," AND THEY WERE ALMOST AT 100,000 RECORDS SOLD.
BOB SHAD AT MERCURY RECORDS DECIDES THAT A WHITE GROUP, THE CREW CUTS, SHOULD SING "SH-BOOM."
THE CHORDS
THE CREW CUTS
SHAD HAD HIS PEOPLE START TO CALL DISC JOCKEYS ALL OVER THE COUNTRY ABOUT THE CREW CUTS' RECORDING.
THE CREW CUTS HADN'T EVEN RECORDED IT YET, AND HERE WAS A MAJOR CAMPAIGN TO LET EVERYBODY KNOW THAT THE RECORD WAS COMING OUT.
THEN HE BROUGHT THE GROUP INTO THE STUDIO AND RECORDED "SH-BOOM."
WELL, THE CREW CUTS ENDED UP SELLING OVER A MILLION RECORDS OF "SH-BOOM," AND THE CHORDS ENDED UP AT ABOUT 120,000.
BOBBY SCHIFFMAN

THAT KIND OF *HURTS* WHEN I LOOK BACK ON IT. A LOT OF THE TUNES I DID WERE COVERED.

AT THAT TIME MUSIC RECORDED BY BLACK ARTISTS WAS CALLED "*RACE MUSIC*" AND ONLY PLAYED ON CERTAIN STATIONS.

I HAD A TUNE, "MAMBO BABY." GEORGIA GIBBS COVERED IT. NOTE FOR NOTE.

THEY WENT ON NATIONAL TV AND SANG MY SONGS. JOHNNY CARSON, ED SULLIVAN. I WAS NEVER EVEN INVITED.

RUTH BROWN

GEORGIA GIBBS

IT DIMINISHED MY ELIGIBILITY TO EXPAND MYSELF. I WASN'T *VISIBLE*.

PERHAPS THE CLASSIC EXAMPLE OF A CLEANED-UP VERSION OF A HIT R&B TUNE IS BILL HALEY'S COVER OF BIG JOE TURNER'S "SHAKE, RATTLE AND ROLL."

White cover artists often *bowdlerize* the original lyrics to make them more palatable to the white market.

THE BLACK COMMUNITY ALWAYS HAD AN HONEST, WHOLESOME APPROACH TO SEXUALITY.

"YOU'RE WEARIN' THOSE DRESSES. THE SUN COME SHININ' THROUGH."

"I CAN'T BELIEVE MY EYES, ALL THAT MESS BELONGS TO YOU."

ISN'T THAT NICE? I THINK IT'S *BEAUTIFUL*.

IT'S A POETIC GHETTO VERSION OF "YOU'RE BEAUTIFUL."

JOHNNY OTIS

Bill Haley's version substitutes "hair done up so nice" for the sun shining through, and the second line becomes: "You look so warm, but your heart is cold as ice."

SOME SEE A CONNECTION BETWEEN THE WAY AFRICAN AMERICAN ARTISTS ARE ABUSED BY THE SYSTEM AND THE DRUG ABUSE THAT AFFECTS THEIR COMMUNITY.

Although the Apollo itself is relatively drug-free, there are often dealers lurking around the stage door. The temptation seems especially great for the new young stars of the rhythm-and-blues era.

THIS SYSTEM HAD PRESSURED SO MANY MARVELOUS PEOPLE, WHO DIDN'T DESERVE THAT. THEY DESERVED *REWARDS*, NOT *PUNISHMENT*.

THAT IS NOT TO SAY THAT SOME PEOPLE AREN'T JUST FOOLS. EVERYBODY ISN'T MOVED INTO A NEGATIVE LIFESTYLE BECAUSE THEY'RE BLACK. THAT'S A LOT OF CRAP.

I DON'T MEAN TO IDEALIZE PEOPLE UNNECESSARILY, BUT THAT HAS A LOT TO DO WITH IT. THAT'S WHY THERE IS MORE DOPE IN THE BLACK COMMUNITY.

THEY'RE SITTING DUCKS. THE *PRESSURE* MAKES FOR MORE *SUSCEPTIBILITY*.

133

LESLIE UGGAMS LITERALLY GROWS UP IN THE MIDDLE OF THE SCENE.

She wins Amateur Night at age seven, and the Schiffmans have Lucky Millinder create an act for her. Her first Apollo show is with Louis Armstrong.

COMING FROM THE KIND OF NEIGHBORHOOD I CAME FROM, HALF THE TIME THERE WASN'T A FATHER, OR IF THERE WAS A FATHER, THERE WERE NINE OTHER SISTERS AND BROTHERS, AND NOBODY PAID ANY ATTENTION TO YOU.

SO, WITH SOME PEOPLE IN THE BUSINESS, THEY FINALLY GOT THE ATTENTION THEY DIDN'T GET AT HOME.

NOW ALL OF A SUDDEN YOU BECOME A BIG STAR, AND PEOPLE WHO DIDN'T **RESPECT** YOU, ALL OF A SUDDEN, IT'S "WOULD YOU SIGN AN AUTOGRAPH?"

Leslie Uggams avoids the pitfalls and goes on to a successful singing and acting career.

THE POWER WAS LIKE, "OH, HEY, NOW I AM SOMEBODY! I WANT TO BE COOL . . . OH, WHAT IS THAT YOU'RE DOING? I'D LIKE TO TRY THAT."

Others are not so lucky. . .

ESTHER PHILLIPS MAKES REMARKABLE COMEBACKS FROM A TOUGH LIFE. FIRST IN THE '60S, AND THEN IN 1975, ON AN EARLY EPISODE OF *SATURDAY NIGHT LIVE*, SHE PERFORMS HER HIT DISCO REMAKE OF DINAH WASHINGTON'S "WHAT A DIFFERENCE A DAY MAKES"—A SONG THAT GOES BACK TO LITTLE ESTHER PHILLIPS'S EARLY DAYS AT THE APOLLO.

BETWEEN SHOWS I WOULD GET KIND OF **FIDGETY** BECAUSE I HAD NOBODY TO PLAY WITH. SO I'D GO DOWN AND PLAY WITH THE LIGHTS AND MESS UP THE MOVIE.

ESTHER PHILLIPS

I WAS KIND OF A LITTLE BRAT, I GUESS, BUT I WAS **BORED**.

Johnny Otis discovers the irrepressible thirteen-year-old in L.A. and records "Double Crossing Blues" with her. It becomes one of the biggest rhythm-and-blues hits of 1950, and she goes on the road with Otis.

"ARE YOU OUT OF YOUR @#$%&! MIND . . ."

LESLIE UGGAMS

DINAH WASHINGTON COULD CUSS BETTER THAN **ANYBODY** I EVER HEARD IN MY LIFE, BUT SHE HAD A HEART OF GOLD.

WE HAD HER DRESSED LIKE A LITTLE SOUTHERN GIRL. THAT'S WHAT ESTHER WAS.

SOME PEOPLE CRITICIZED US FOR THAT.

JOHNNY OTIS

#$%
@#%#

DINAH WASHINGTON

SO DINAH WASHINGTON BRINGS LITTLE ESTHER BACK WITH HER HAIR DONE, HIGH-HEEL SHOES ON, NYLON STOCKINGS, AND A FORM-FITTING DRESS. SHE LOOKED LIKE SHE WAS THIRTY.

SHE'D TELL MY MOTHER, "OK, JUANITA, TAKE BABY INTO THE DRESSING ROOM. I GOT SOME STRONG CUSS WORDS I GOTTA USE HERE."

THAT'S **DISGRACEFUL**, HAVING HER LOOK LIKE SHE'S IN THE COTTON FIELDS!

BUT DINAH'S VOICE CARRIED **EVERYWHERE**, IT WASN'T LIKE YOU COULDN'T HEAR IT.

I COULDN'T TELL ESTHER ANYTHING, BECAUSE ESTHER WAS A VERY PRECOCIOUS CHILD, LIKE A WOMAN AT THIRTEEN, AND SHE LIKED IT.

Soon after she leaves Otis in 1952, Little Esther is a fifteen-year-old heroin addict.

ESTHER PHILLIPS

Despite her comebacks, she *succumbs* to the long-term effects of her drug abuse. She dies in 1984 at the age of forty-eight.

HER MALE COUNTERPART IS, PERHAPS, *LITTLE WILLIE JOHN.*

He was active in promoting the nascent career of his friend James Brown, who used to open for Willie John at the Apollo in the early days.

IF HE WANTED TO DO SOMETHING, HE DID IT WITHOUT EVEN A MOMENT'S HESITATION. *CAREFREE.*

LITTLE WILLIE JOHN

JAMES BROWN

ST. CLAIR PINCKNEY— JB'S MUSICAL DIRECTOR.

Another Johnny Otis discovery, the seventeen-year-old Little Willie John hits in 1955 with "All Around the World." His biggest success is "Fever" in 1956—later rearranged and covered by *Peggy Lee.*

DANNY RAY— JB'S EMCEE

HE WAS A CONSTANT RIOT ALL DAY LONG.

PEGGY LEE FEVER

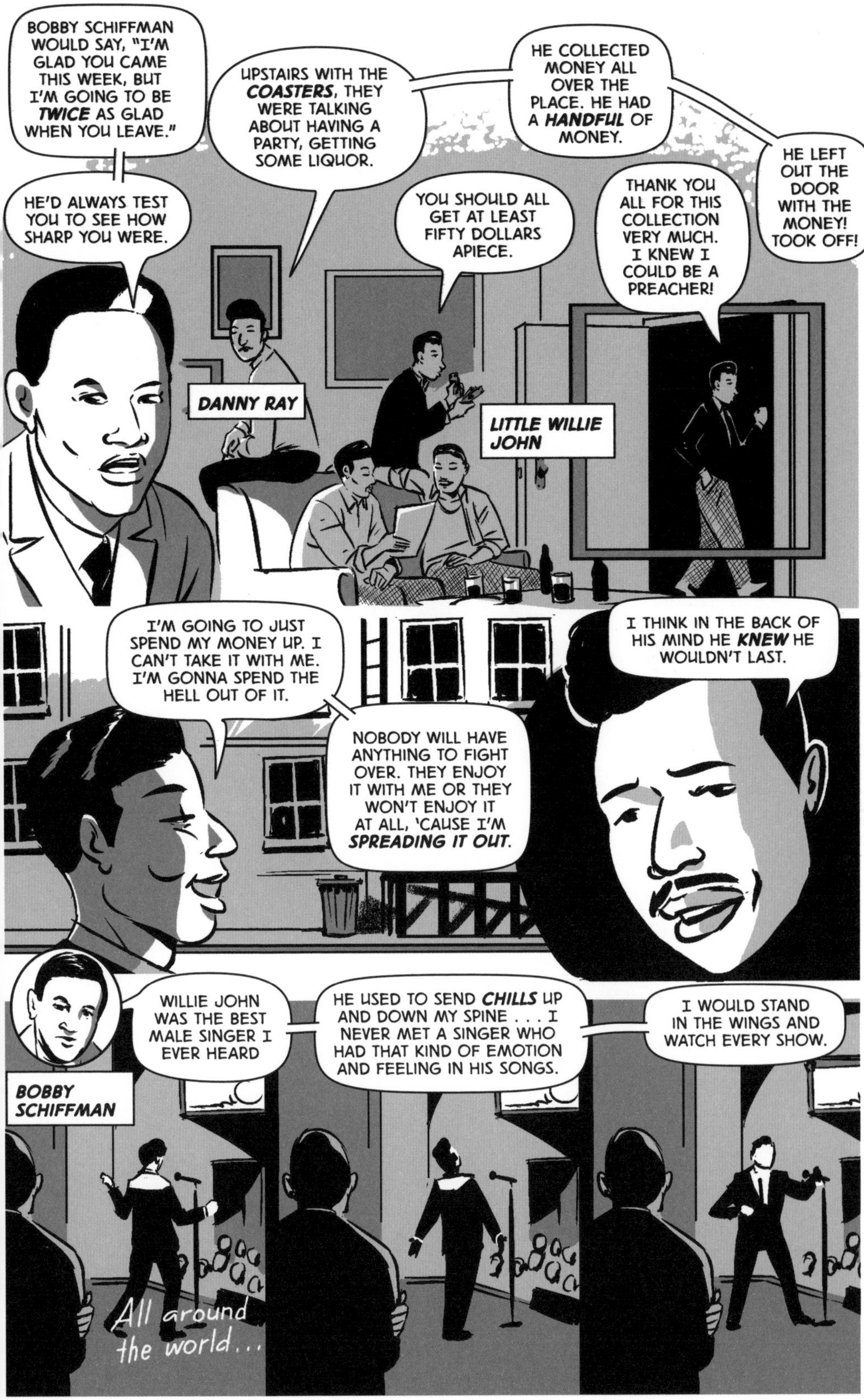
BOBBY SCHIFFMAN WOULD SAY, "I'M GLAD YOU CAME THIS WEEK, BUT I'M GOING TO BE *TWICE* AS GLAD WHEN YOU LEAVE."
HE'D ALWAYS TEST YOU TO SEE HOW SHARP YOU WERE.
UPSTAIRS WITH THE *COASTERS*, THEY WERE TALKING ABOUT HAVING A PARTY, GETTING SOME LIQUOR.
HE COLLECTED MONEY ALL OVER THE PLACE. HE HAD A *HANDFUL* OF MONEY.
HE LEFT OUT THE DOOR WITH THE MONEY! TOOK OFF!
YOU SHOULD ALL GET AT LEAST FIFTY DOLLARS APIECE.
THANK YOU ALL FOR THIS COLLECTION VERY MUCH. I KNEW I COULD BE A PREACHER!
DANNY RAY
LITTLE WILLIE JOHN
I'M GOING TO JUST SPEND MY MONEY UP. I CAN'T TAKE IT WITH ME. I'M GONNA SPEND THE HELL OUT OF IT.
NOBODY WILL HAVE ANYTHING TO FIGHT OVER. THEY ENJOY IT WITH ME OR THEY WON'T ENJOY IT AT ALL, 'CAUSE I'M *SPREADING IT OUT*.
I THINK IN THE BACK OF HIS MIND HE *KNEW* HE WOULDN'T LAST.
BOBBY SCHIFFMAN
WILLIE JOHN WAS THE BEST MALE SINGER I EVER HEARD
HE USED TO SEND *CHILLS* UP AND DOWN MY SPINE . . . I NEVER MET A SINGER WHO HAD THAT KIND OF EMOTION AND FEELING IN HIS SONGS.
I WOULD STAND IN THE WINGS AND WATCH EVERY SHOW.
All around the world . . .

Willie John's substance of choice is booze. His reckless lifestyle causes his career to falter.

He kills a man in a bar fight, and is sent to the Washington State Penitentiary for manslaughter in 1966.

James Brown and Bobby Schiffman spearhead an unsuccessful effort to gain his release.

I DON'T THINK I'M GOING TO GET OUT OF HERE.

DON'T *EVER* LET IT WORRY YOU. IF I GET OUT, I GET OUT. IF I STAY, I STAY . . . STILL GONNA BE THE SAME MAN IN OR OUT OF HERE.

In 1968, Little Willie John dies in prison of pneumonia. He is thirty years old.

LITTLE WILLIE JOHN

HUSBAND-DAD-BROTHER
WILLIAM E JOHN
NOV. 15, 1937 - MAY 26, 1968
ALWAYS IN OUR MEMORY

FRANKIE LYMON HAS TO DEAL WITH THE PITFALLS OF STARDOM AT AN EVEN EARLIER AGE.

Discovered at the Apollo, Frankie and his group, the Teenagers, hit it big with their first record, "Why Do Fools Fall in Love?" a song written by the precocious thirteen-year-old.

FRANKIE LYMON TAKES ANOTHER TEENAGED STAR UNDER HIS WING.

HE WAS *YOUNGER*, BUT HE WAS *SMARTER* THAN I WAS. HE WAS A MAN. I WAS A KID.

FRANKIE WAS A *TRAGEDY*.

LITTLE ANTHONY

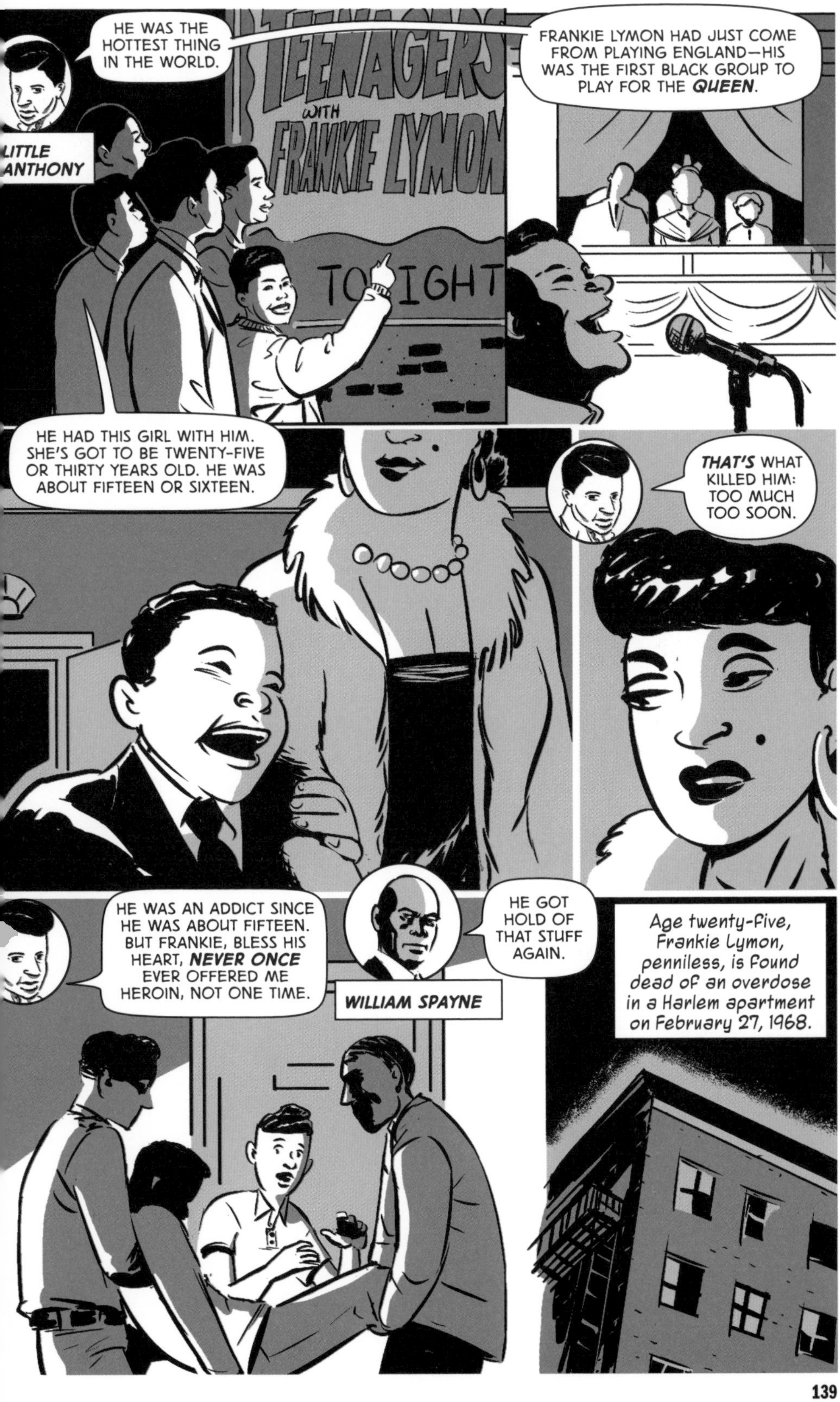
LITTLE ANTHONY
HE WAS THE HOTTEST THING IN THE WORLD.
TEENAGERS WITH FRANKIE LYMON
TO IGHT
FRANKIE LYMON HAD JUST COME FROM PLAYING ENGLAND—HIS WAS THE FIRST BLACK GROUP TO PLAY FOR THE QUEEN.
HE HAD THIS GIRL WITH HIM. SHE'S GOT TO BE TWENTY-FIVE OR THIRTY YEARS OLD. HE WAS ABOUT FIFTEEN OR SIXTEEN.
THAT'S WHAT KILLED HIM: TOO MUCH TOO SOON.
HE WAS AN ADDICT SINCE HE WAS ABOUT FIFTEEN. BUT FRANKIE, BLESS HIS HEART, NEVER ONCE EVER OFFERED ME HEROIN, NOT ONE TIME.
WILLIAM SPAYNE
HE GOT HOLD OF THAT STUFF AGAIN.
Age twenty-five, Frankie Lymon, penniless, is found dead of an overdose in a Harlem apartment on February 27, 1968.

ALL THIS SUCCESS, ALL THIS MONEY, ALL THIS ADULATION IS COMING FROM RECORD SALES AND THE VAST, UNENDING RADIO POUNDING OF HIT SONGS CREATED BY NEW YOUNG ARTISTS IN THE '50S.

Before the war, record companies *resist* the playing of their discs on the air. They think airplay will dissipate retail sales. Some companies even *ban* radio play outright.

At first, jukeboxes are the way the recording industry merchandises and publicizes its product.

After World War II, however, a *synergy* develops among . . .

1) the record companies that multiply throughout the R&B era

2) the artists and groups who are suddenly in great demand

3) the *disc jockeys* who purvey the sound to eager youngsters around the country.

THE RISE OF THE DISC JOCKEY MAY BE ONE OF THE FEW TIMES IN THE HISTORY OF INDUSTRY WHERE **MEN** REPLACE **MACHINES**.

?

Frank Schiffman has temporarily **broken stride** with the black community, which always led him to new sounds and styles.

THE APOLLO PRESENTS THE PIONEERS OF RHYTHM AND BLUES, BUT THEY ARE STILL PROGRAMMED INTO THE OLD-STYLE VARIETY SHOWS.

It isn't really working anymore. The Apollo is going through hard times.

BOBBY SCHIFFMAN, WHO IS ASSUMING MORE AND MORE **CONTROL** OVER THE APOLLO, REALIZES THAT NOT ONLY HAS A NEW SOUND ARRIVED, BUT WITH IT A WHOLE **NEW WAY** OF LISTENING TO MUSIC.

A DISC JOCKEY ON WWRL NAMED **DR. JIVE**—TOMMY SMALLS—AND I FIGURED OUT THAT PEOPLE WEREN'T COMING TO SEE THE TAP DANCER AND THE OTHER ACTS.

THEY WERE COMING TO SEE THE VOCAL ACT THAT HAD THE HIT RECORD BEING PLAYED ON THE RADIO.

WE SPAWNED THE IDEA OF **ELIMINATING** THE OTHER ACTS AND PUTTING IN THOSE ACTS THAT HAD HIT RECORDS. THAT BECAME KNOWN AS THE **R&B REVUE**.

BOBBY SCHIFFMAN

DR. JIVE (A.K.A. TOMMY SMALLS)

HARLEM'S HIGH SPOT
APOLLO
ONE WEEK ONLY BEG. FRI., MAR. 30th 1956
DR. JIVE'S
NEWEST AND GREATEST
RHYTHM AND BLUES
REVUE
BO DIDDLEY — THE MOONGLOWS
TEEN QUEENS — THE SOLITAIRES
CHARLIE and RAY — DEAN BARLOW
FI-TONES · SUGAR & SPICE · CLAUDIA SWANN
Brooks Benton · Schoolboys · Buddy Griffin

THE APOLLO WAS THE PIONEER IN THAT TYPE OF PRESENTATION.

THE GUYS THAT FOLLOWED US INTO THE WHITE MARKETPLACE, LIKE ALAN FREED WITH HIS *ROCK AND ROLL REVUE*, TOOK HIS IDEA RIGHT FROM THE APOLLO THEATER.

By the mid-'50s, these revues, featuring as many as a dozen singing acts, become the dominant form of entertainment at the theater.

BOBBY SCHIFFMAN

The R&B revues capitalize on the popularity of the DJs. *They*, not the performers, are the headliners.

DR. JIVE BRINGS HIS FIRST RHYTHM-AND-BLUES REVUE TO THE APOLLO IN 1955. MANY OTHER DJS SOON JOIN HIM.

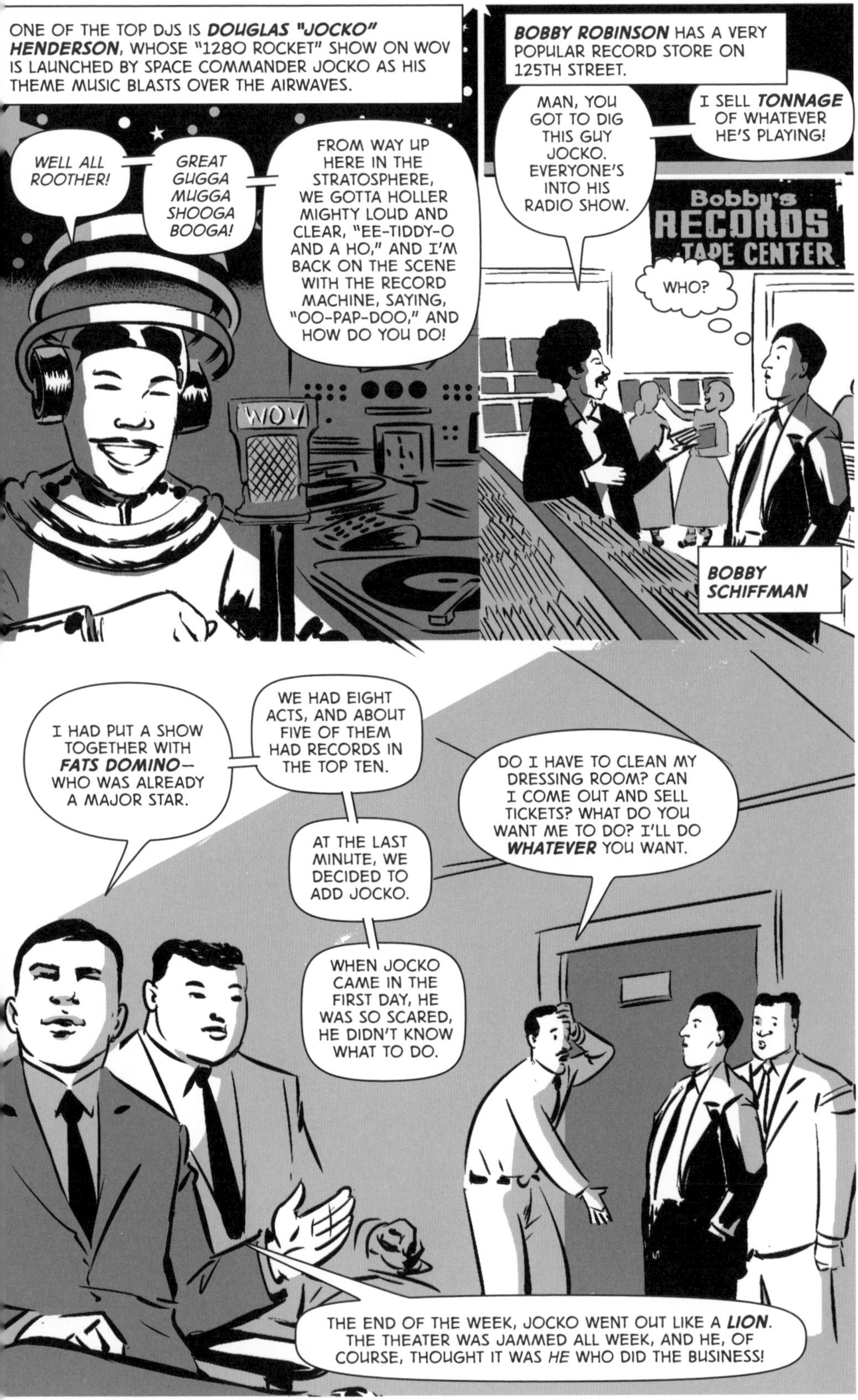
ONE OF THE TOP DJS IS DOUGLAS "JOCKO" HENDERSON, WHOSE "1280 ROCKET" SHOW ON WOV IS LAUNCHED BY SPACE COMMANDER JOCKO AS HIS THEME MUSIC BLASTS OVER THE AIRWAVES.
WELL ALL ROOTHER!
GREAT GUGGA MUGGA SHOOGA BOOGA!
FROM WAY UP HERE IN THE STRATOSPHERE, WE GOTTA HOLLER MIGHTY LOUD AND CLEAR, "EE-TIDDY-O AND A HO," AND I'M BACK ON THE SCENE WITH THE RECORD MACHINE, SAYING, "OO-PAP-DOO," AND HOW DO YOU DO!
WOV
BOBBY ROBINSON HAS A VERY POPULAR RECORD STORE ON 125TH STREET.
MAN, YOU GOT TO DIG THIS GUY JOCKO. EVERYONE'S INTO HIS RADIO SHOW.
I SELL TONNAGE OF WHATEVER HE'S PLAYING!
Bobby's RECORDS TAPE CENTER
WHO?
BOBBY SCHIFFMAN
I HAD PUT A SHOW TOGETHER WITH FATS DOMINO— WHO WAS ALREADY A MAJOR STAR.
WE HAD EIGHT ACTS, AND ABOUT FIVE OF THEM HAD RECORDS IN THE TOP TEN.
AT THE LAST MINUTE, WE DECIDED TO ADD JOCKO.
WHEN JOCKO CAME IN THE FIRST DAY, HE WAS SO SCARED, HE DIDN'T KNOW WHAT TO DO.
DO I HAVE TO CLEAN MY DRESSING ROOM? CAN I COME OUT AND SELL TICKETS? WHAT DO YOU WANT ME TO DO? I'LL DO WHATEVER YOU WANT.
THE END OF THE WEEK, JOCKO WENT OUT LIKE A LION. THE THEATER WAS JAMMED ALL WEEK, AND HE, OF COURSE, THOUGHT IT WAS HE WHO DID THE BUSINESS!

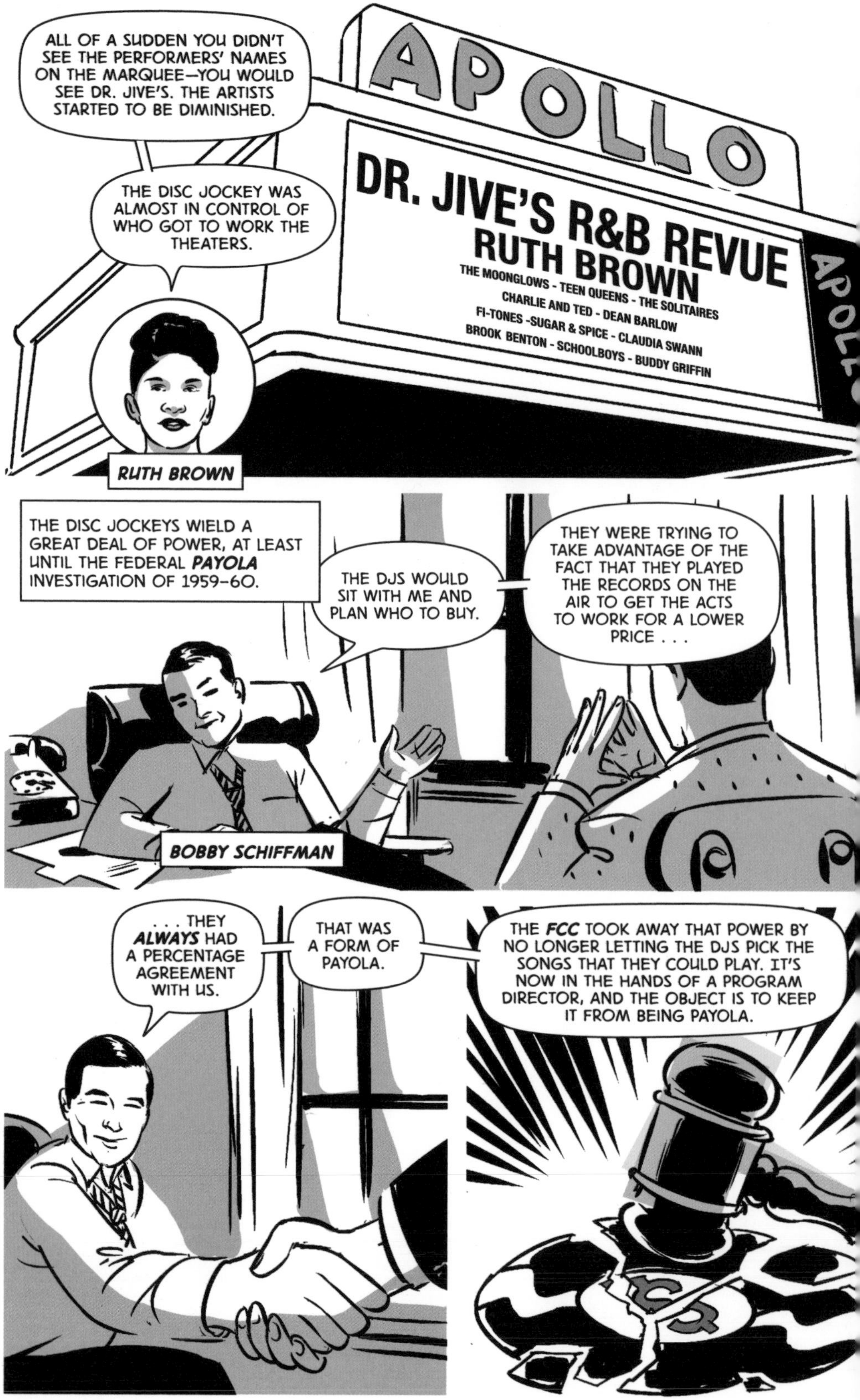
ALL OF A SUDDEN YOU DIDN'T SEE THE PERFORMERS' NAMES ON THE MARQUEE—YOU WOULD SEE DR. JIVE'S. THE ARTISTS STARTED TO BE DIMINISHED.
THE DISC JOCKEY WAS ALMOST IN CONTROL OF WHO GOT TO WORK THE THEATERS.
APOLLO
DR. JIVE'S R&B REVUE
RUTH BROWN
THE MOONGLOWS - TEEN QUEENS - THE SOLITAIRES
CHARLIE AND TED - DEAN BARLOW
FI-TONES -SUGAR & SPICE - CLAUDIA SWANN
BROOK BENTON - SCHOOLBOYS - BUDDY GRIFFIN
RUTH BROWN
THE DISC JOCKEYS WIELD A GREAT DEAL OF POWER, AT LEAST UNTIL THE FEDERAL *PAYOLA* INVESTIGATION OF 1959–60.
THE DJS WOULD SIT WITH ME AND PLAN WHO TO BUY.
THEY WERE TRYING TO TAKE ADVANTAGE OF THE FACT THAT THEY PLAYED THE RECORDS ON THE AIR TO GET THE ACTS TO WORK FOR A LOWER PRICE . . .
BOBBY SCHIFFMAN
. . . THEY *ALWAYS* HAD A PERCENTAGE AGREEMENT WITH US.
THAT WAS A FORM OF PAYOLA.
THE *FCC* TOOK AWAY THAT POWER BY NO LONGER LETTING THE DJS PICK THE SONGS THAT THEY COULD PLAY. IT'S NOW IN THE HANDS OF A PROGRAM DIRECTOR, AND THE OBJECT IS TO KEEP IT FROM BEING PAYOLA.

WE HAD DONE SHOWS WITH VARIETY ENTERTAINMENT, AND WHEN YOU COME UP WITH A FORMAT OF ALL THESE SINGING ACTS IN A ROW YOU SAY, "WHAT THE HELL IS *THIS*?"

I GOT SICK OF THIS BECAUSE I HAD NOTHING TO DO. ALL I HAD TO DO WAS GO DOWNSTAIRS, SEE THE BAND REHEARSE, AND SAY, "YOU GO FIRST, YOU GO SECOND, YOU THIRD, YOU FOURTH."

APOLLO MANAGER LEONARD REED

WHEN FRANK SCHIFFMAN SAW HIS FIRST R&B REVUE, HE COULDN'T *BELIEVE* IT.

MR. SCHIFFMAN, WHEN ARE WE GONNA GO BACK TO A *GOOD* SHOW?

I WANT TO SHOW YOU SOMETHING.

LEONARD REED

WHAT DO YOU CALL A GOOD SHOW? ONE THAT DOESN'T DO US ANY BUSINESS?

I DON'T LIKE IT EITHER, LEONARD, BUT YOU MUST LEARN THAT *MONEY* COMING THROUGH THAT GATE *IS* OUR BUSINESS.

WHEN A *"MAMBO CRAZE"* HITS IN THE '50S, THE SCHIFFMANS SEE ANOTHER POTENTIAL MONEYMAKER.

Latin music has *always* flowed at the Apollo. Dizzy Gillespie brought Cuban greats like *Chano Pozo* to the theater starting in the late '40s.

MIGUELITO VALDÉS

TITO PUENTE

JOE LOCO

MERCEDITA VALDÉS

GILBERTO VALDÉS

LUCY FABERY

MONGO SANTAMARÍA

Legendary Jazz DJ *Symphony Sid Torin* has been promoting shows at the Apollo since the late '40s. He tries a Mambo Rhumba Festival of all Latin acts at the Apollo in 1954.

MAMBO ACE ANIBAL VÁZQUEZ.

Although critically popular, the Latin shows underperform at the box office.

STILL, TOP LATIN ARTISTS SUCH AS *TITO PUENTE* AND *MACHITO* CONTINUE TO HEADLINE APOLLO SHOWS, APPEALING TO *SPANISH HARLEM* AND LATIN MUSIC BUFFS FROM ALL OVER TOWN.

BUT IT IS THE RHYTHM-AND-BLUES REVUES THAT TURN THE THEATER AROUND FINANCIALLY

BOBBY SCHIFFMAN

DURING THAT ERA, THE THEATER WAS OPERATING AT CAPACITY MORE THAN ANYTIME ELSE.

THERE WERE SITUATIONS WHERE WE WERE DOING AS MANY AS *SEVEN* SHOWS A DAY. THAT'S UNHEARD OF.

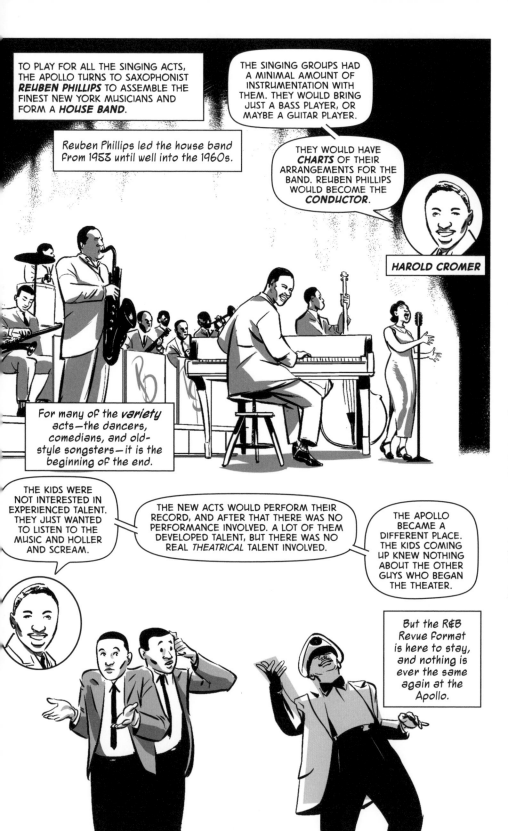

TO PLAY FOR ALL THE SINGING ACTS, THE APOLLO TURNS TO SAXOPHONIST **REUBEN PHILLIPS** TO ASSEMBLE THE FINEST NEW YORK MUSICIANS AND FORM A **HOUSE BAND**.

THE SINGING GROUPS HAD A MINIMAL AMOUNT OF INSTRUMENTATION WITH THEM. THEY WOULD BRING JUST A BASS PLAYER, OR MAYBE A GUITAR PLAYER.

Reuben Phillips led the house band from 1953 until well into the 1960s.

THEY WOULD HAVE **CHARTS** OF THEIR ARRANGEMENTS FOR THE BAND. REUBEN PHILLIPS WOULD BECOME THE **CONDUCTOR**.

HAROLD CROMER

For many of the **variety** acts—the dancers, comedians, and old-style songsters—it is the beginning of the end.

THE KIDS WERE NOT INTERESTED IN EXPERIENCED TALENT. THEY JUST WANTED TO LISTEN TO THE MUSIC AND HOLLER AND SCREAM.

THE NEW ACTS WOULD PERFORM THEIR RECORD, AND AFTER THAT THERE WAS NO PERFORMANCE INVOLVED. A LOT OF THEM DEVELOPED TALENT, BUT THERE WAS NO REAL *THEATRICAL* TALENT INVOLVED.

THE APOLLO BECAME A DIFFERENT PLACE. THE KIDS COMING UP KNEW NOTHING ABOUT THE OTHER GUYS WHO BEGAN THE THEATER.

But the R&B Revue format is here to stay, and nothing is ever the same again at the Apollo.

CHAPTER 7

Roots: Blues and Gospel at the Apollo

SCHIFFMAN TRIES TO MAKE IT WORK, IN HIS WAY. HE FIRST PRESENTS BLUES LEGEND **LEAD BELLY** IN A SKIT AT THE LAFAYETTE IN 1934.

OH GOVERNOR, SIR, I JUST WANTS TO SING FOR THE PEOPLE.

His interest in Lead Belly (a.k.a. Huddie William Ledbetter) derives from Lead Belly's notorious reputation as a killer.

YOUR SONGS HAVE MOVED ME TO TEARS. AS GOVERNOR OF THE GREAT STATE OF LOUISIANA, I HEREBY PARDON YOU.

The "governor" "pardons" Lead Belly thirty-one times a week. People love it.

A RETURN ENGAGEMENT TWO YEARS LATER, WITHOUT THE PRISON SHTICK OR HYPE, IS A FLOP.

IN THE LATE '40S, A NEW BREED OF BLUES **SHOUTERS** AND GUTSY SINGERS GAINS PROMINENCE.

The Midnight Speeeecial...

WYNONIE HARRIS

EDDIE "CLEANHEAD" VINSON

DINAH WASHINGTON "QUEEN OF THE BLUES"

Not blues performers in the traditional sense, their rougher, bluesy style—often backed by rockin' saxes and guitars—was a key *link* to rhythm and blues.

JOHNNY OTIS RUNS INTO RESISTANCE WHEN HE WANTS TO BRING HIS LATEST DISCOVERY, **WILLIE MAE "BIG MAMA" THORNTON,** INTO THE APOLLO.

I JUST FOUND HER IN TEXAS. SHE KNOCKED ME OUT!

YOU CAN USE HER IN THE SOUTH, BUT A BIG ROUGH CHICK—THE AUDIENCE IS NOT GOING TO DIG THAT.

BOBBY SCHIFFMAN

FRANK SCHIFFMAN

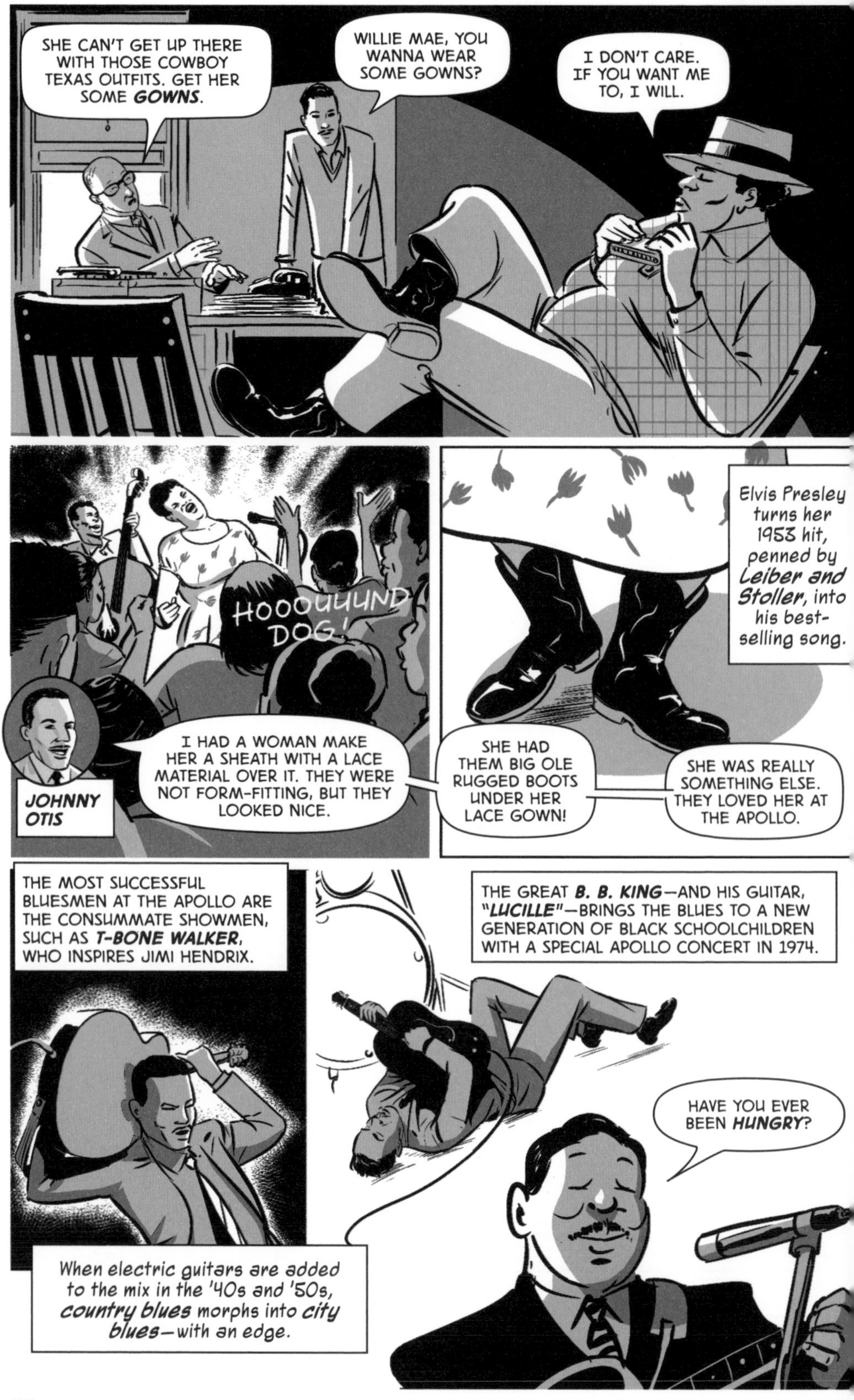
SHE CAN'T GET UP THERE WITH THOSE COWBOY TEXAS OUTFITS. GET HER SOME **GOWNS**.
WILLIE MAE, YOU WANNA WEAR SOME GOWNS?
I DON'T CARE. IF YOU WANT ME TO, I WILL.
HOOOUUUND DOG!
JOHNNY OTIS
I HAD A WOMAN MAKE HER A SHEATH WITH A LACE MATERIAL OVER IT. THEY WERE NOT FORM-FITTING, BUT THEY LOOKED NICE.
Elvis Presley turns her 1953 hit, penned by **Leiber and Stoller**, into his best-selling song.
SHE HAD THEM BIG OLE RUGGED BOOTS UNDER HER LACE GOWN!
SHE WAS REALLY SOMETHING ELSE. THEY LOVED HER AT THE APOLLO.
THE MOST SUCCESSFUL BLUESMEN AT THE APOLLO ARE THE CONSUMMATE SHOWMEN, SUCH AS **T-BONE WALKER**, WHO INSPIRES JIMI HENDRIX.
THE GREAT **B. B. KING**—AND HIS GUITAR, **"LUCILLE"**—BRINGS THE BLUES TO A NEW GENERATION OF BLACK SCHOOLCHILDREN WITH A SPECIAL APOLLO CONCERT IN 1974.
When electric guitars are added to the mix in the '40s and '50s, **country blues** morphs into **city blues**—with an edge.
HAVE YOU EVER BEEN **HUNGRY**?

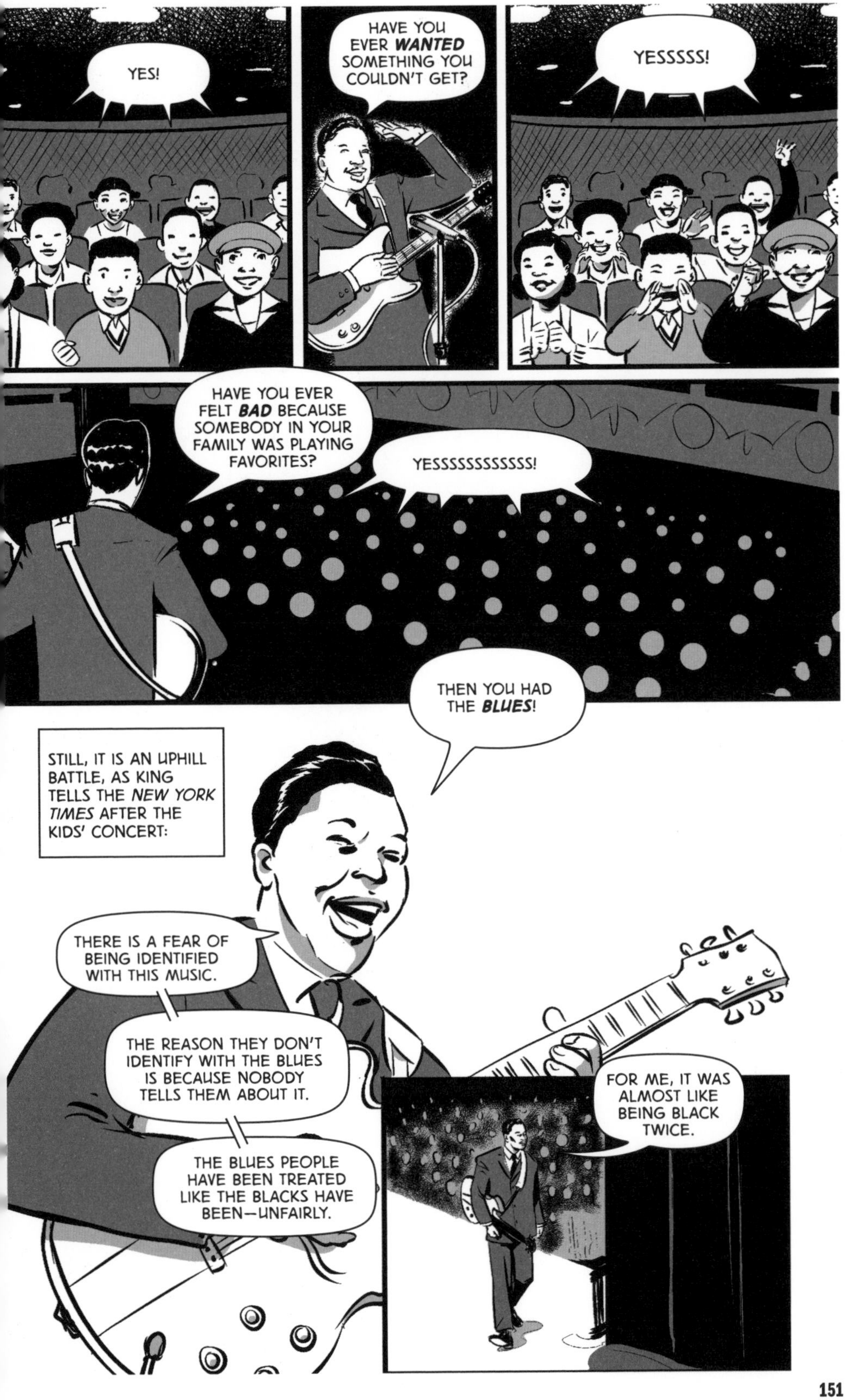
YES!
HAVE YOU EVER *WANTED* SOMETHING YOU COULDN'T GET?
YESSSSS!
HAVE YOU EVER FELT *BAD* BECAUSE SOMEBODY IN YOUR FAMILY WAS PLAYING FAVORITES?
YESSSSSSSSSSSSS!
THEN YOU HAD THE *BLUES*!
STILL, IT IS AN UPHILL BATTLE, AS KING TELLS THE *NEW YORK TIMES* AFTER THE KIDS' CONCERT:
THERE IS A FEAR OF BEING IDENTIFIED WITH THIS MUSIC.
THE REASON THEY DON'T IDENTIFY WITH THE BLUES IS BECAUSE NOBODY TELLS THEM ABOUT IT.
THE BLUES PEOPLE HAVE BEEN TREATED LIKE THE BLACKS HAVE BEEN—UNFAIRLY.
FOR ME, IT WAS ALMOST LIKE BEING BLACK TWICE.

MAXINE BROWN, WHO HAD A NUMBER OF SOUL HITS IN THE '60S, IS FIRST A **GOSPEL** SINGER.

Unlike traditional blues, gospel is a powerful attraction at the Apollo.

Religious folks, though, consider the Apollo the "*devil's house.*"

MY MOTHER HAD PASSED AWAY BY THE TIME I SANG AT THE APOLLO. SHE WOULD NEVER HAVE COME TO SEE ME THERE.

I THOUGHT I WAS COMMITTING A **SIN**.

SISTER ROSETTA THARPE IS AN ARTIST EQUALLY COMFORTABLE WITH RELIGIOUS AND SECULAR MUSIC.

Down by the riverside . . .

She is virtually the only gospel singer to play the Apollo in the '30s and '40s.

The first big gospel recording star, Tharpe influences later rockers from *Little Richard* to *Jerry Lee Lewis.*

Music that begins as an amateur church endeavor turns professional, as gospel recordings become successful and gospel performers tour large churches and religious conventions.

THURMAN RUTH IS LEADER OF THE **SELAH JUBILEE SINGERS** AND A GOSPEL DJ ON WOV.

THURMAN RUTH

WE WERE BROADCAST ON ALL FOUR RADIO STATIONS IN BROOKLYN.

WHEN WE'D SING, THE CHURCH WOULD BE **JAMMED**.

IN THE '50S, GOSPEL MUSIC IS BECOMING MORE POPULAR THAN PREACHERS.

WE STARTED SINGING IN CHURCHES EVERY SUNDAY NIGHT BEFORE OUR MINISTERS WOULD PREACH.

AFTER WE'D SING, MOST OF THE FOLKS WOULD GET UP AND GO OUT BEFORE THE PREACHING.

It is inevitable that someone will think of **combining** the power and popularity of gospel with the successful rhythm-and-blues revue format.

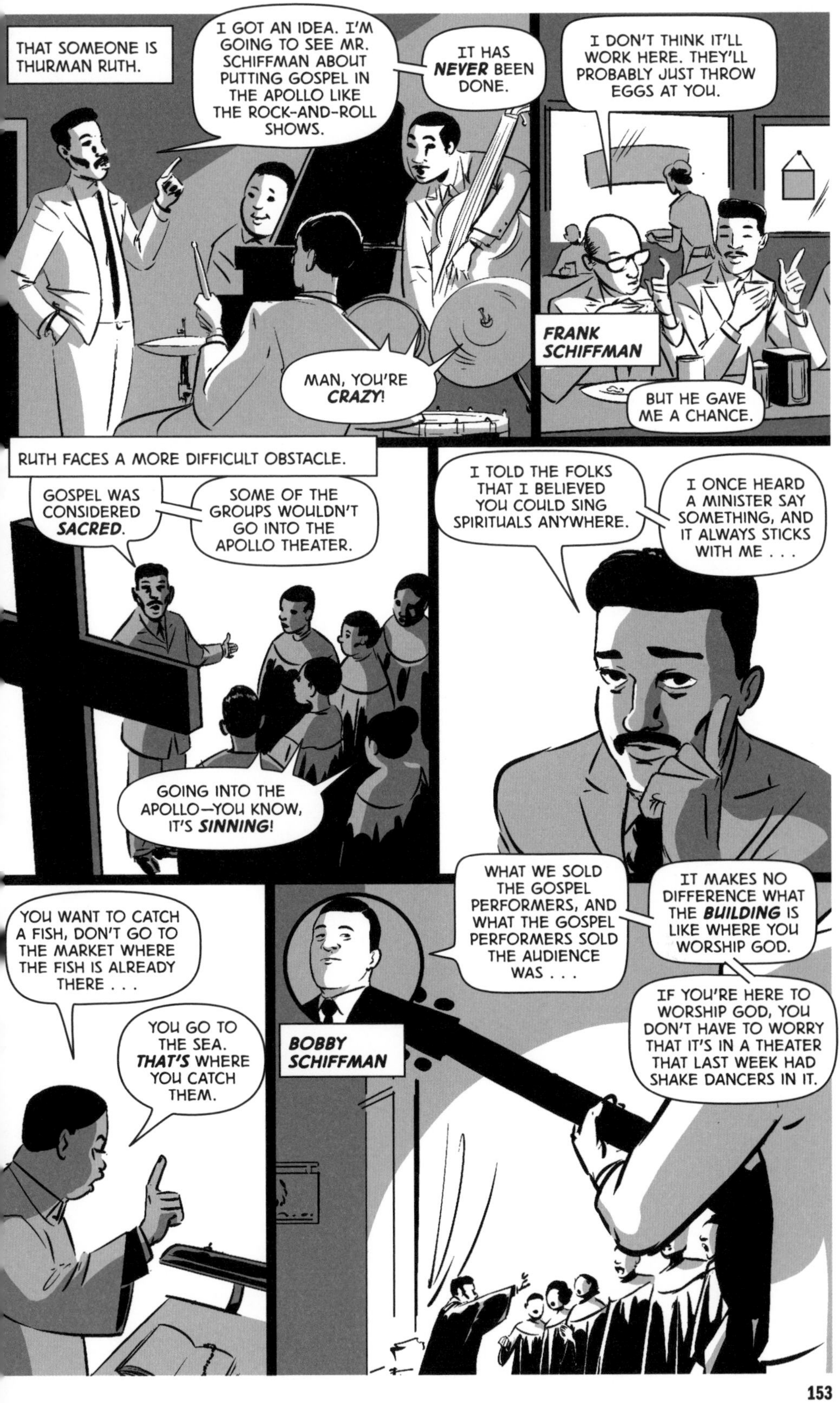
THAT SOMEONE IS THURMAN RUTH.
I GOT AN IDEA. I'M GOING TO SEE MR. SCHIFFMAN ABOUT PUTTING GOSPEL IN THE APOLLO LIKE THE ROCK-AND-ROLL SHOWS.
IT HAS **NEVER** BEEN DONE.
MAN, YOU'RE ***CRAZY***!
I DON'T THINK IT'LL WORK HERE. THEY'LL PROBABLY JUST THROW EGGS AT YOU.
FRANK SCHIFFMAN
BUT HE GAVE ME A CHANCE.
RUTH FACES A MORE DIFFICULT OBSTACLE.
GOSPEL WAS CONSIDERED ***SACRED***.
SOME OF THE GROUPS WOULDN'T GO INTO THE APOLLO THEATER.
GOING INTO THE APOLLO—YOU KNOW, IT'S ***SINNING***!
I TOLD THE FOLKS THAT I BELIEVED YOU COULD SING SPIRITUALS ANYWHERE.
I ONCE HEARD A MINISTER SAY SOMETHING, AND IT ALWAYS STICKS WITH ME . . .
YOU WANT TO CATCH A FISH, DON'T GO TO THE MARKET WHERE THE FISH IS ALREADY THERE . . .
YOU GO TO THE SEA. ***THAT'S*** WHERE YOU CATCH THEM.
BOBBY SCHIFFMAN
WHAT WE SOLD THE GOSPEL PERFORMERS, AND WHAT THE GOSPEL PERFORMERS SOLD THE AUDIENCE WAS . . .
IT MAKES NO DIFFERENCE WHAT THE ***BUILDING*** IS LIKE WHERE YOU WORSHIP GOD.
IF YOU'RE HERE TO WORSHIP GOD, YOU DON'T HAVE TO WORRY THAT IT'S IN A THEATER THAT LAST WEEK HAD SHAKE DANCERS IN IT.

I TOLD THEM THAT THIS WOULD BE THE FIRST TIME THEY WOULD EVER BE PRESENTED IN A GREAT WAY.

BEAUTIFUL STAGE, GREAT LIGHTING, AND ACOUSTICS.

ABOVE ALL, THIS WAS THE FIRST TIME THEY WERE GUARANTEED TO HAVE *MONEY* . . .

AND THEY WERE GOING TO GET IT WHETHER THE SHOW WAS A FLOP OR NOT.

IF YOU PLAYED A CHURCH OR AUDITORIUM AND THE PEOPLE WERE NOT THERE, YOU DIDN'T GET THE MONEY.

MR. SCHIFFMAN *GUARANTEED* THE MONEY.

ONE GROUP IN THOSE DAYS COULD MAKE $3,000 FOR A WEEK'S ENGAGEMENT.

THURMAN RUTH'S GOSPEL CARAVAN DEBUTS AT THE APOLLO ON DECEMBER 15, 1955.

SINCE i LAID MY BURDEN DOWN...

Ruth maintains a *joyous* churchlike atmosphere for the Apollo gospel shows.

To insure the broadest appeal to different denominations, he features all types of religious singing . . .

THURMAN UTH

JUBILEE SINGING IS JUST THAT: JUBILATION THAT'S FAST, A JOYOUS MEDIUM.

GOSPEL IS KIND OF SLOW WITH LOTS OF PREACHING. THEY ALMOST TALK IT MORE THAN SING IT.

SPIRITUALS IS THE OLD TRADITIONAL SONGS THAT STARTED OFF EVERYTHING: "SWING LOW, SWEET CHARIOT."

WITNESSES TESTIFY THE GOSPEL SHOWS ARE THE MOST STIMULATING AND EXCITING EVER SEEN AT THE APOLLO.

PEOPLE WOULD GET OVERWHELMED.

THEY'D FALL OUT OF THE BALCONIES. IT'S TRUE.

IT'S NOT LIKE A ROCK SHOW. THIS GOES A STEP FURTHER BECAUSE YOU'RE EMOTIONALLY INVOLVED IN THE SPIRIT OF GOD.

IT JUST FELT LIKE THE CEILING WAS GONNA BURST OPEN. PEOPLE WOULD FAINT.

YOU'D GET OVEREXCITED, HAPPY, AND SHOUT.

THE GOSPEL ACTS SANG FROM THE BOTTOM OF THEIR TOES OR SOMETHING.

IT WAS VERY, VERY MOVING.

YOUNG DIONNE WARWICK

BEVERLY LEE OF THE SHIRELLES

155

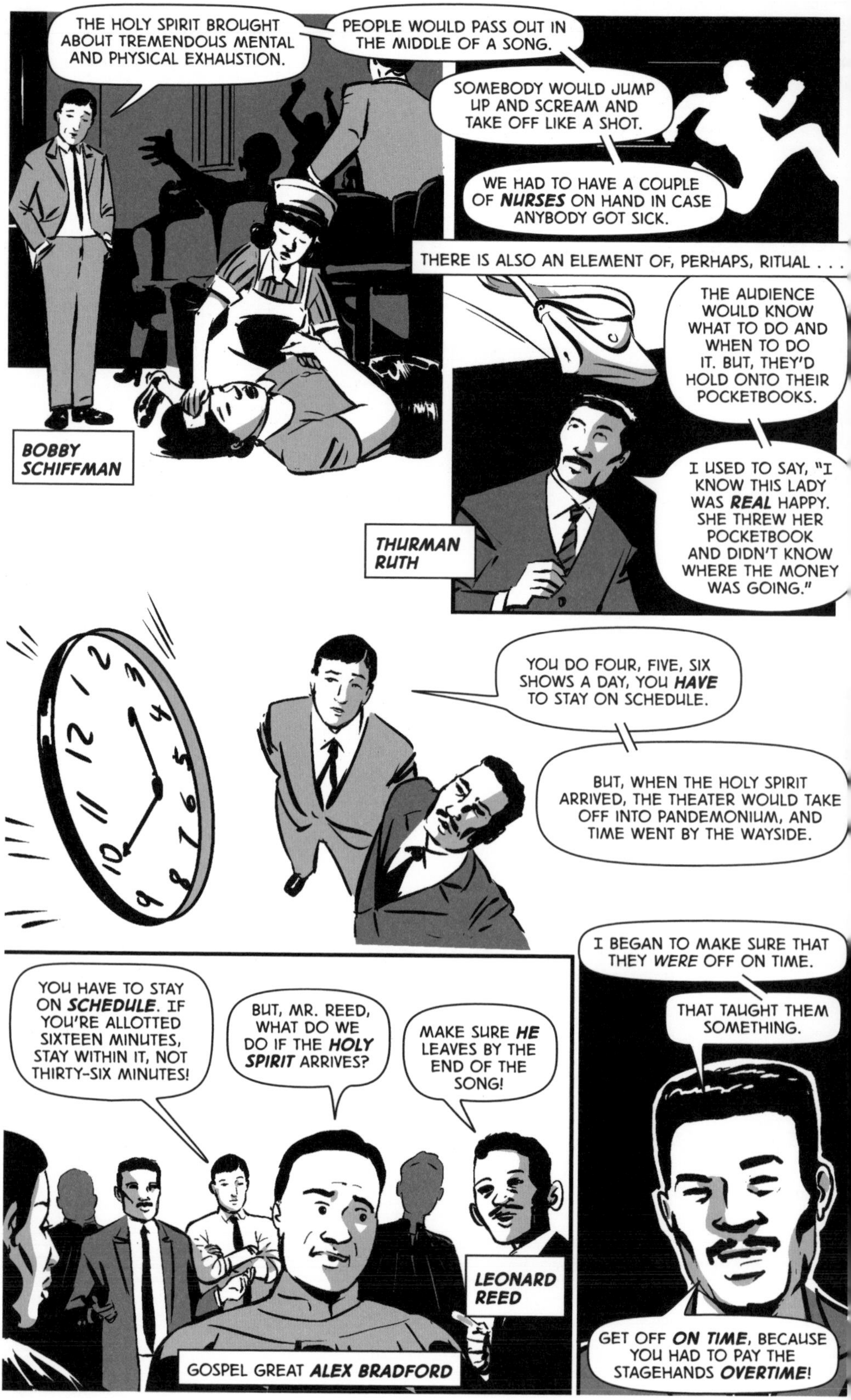
THE HOLY SPIRIT BROUGHT ABOUT TREMENDOUS MENTAL AND PHYSICAL EXHAUSTION.
PEOPLE WOULD PASS OUT IN THE MIDDLE OF A SONG.
SOMEBODY WOULD JUMP UP AND SCREAM AND TAKE OFF LIKE A SHOT.
WE HAD TO HAVE A COUPLE OF NURSES ON HAND IN CASE ANYBODY GOT SICK.
BOBBY SCHIFFMAN
THERE IS ALSO AN ELEMENT OF, PERHAPS, RITUAL . . .
THE AUDIENCE WOULD KNOW WHAT TO DO AND WHEN TO DO IT. BUT, THEY'D HOLD ONTO THEIR POCKETBOOKS.
I USED TO SAY, "I KNOW THIS LADY WAS REAL HAPPY. SHE THREW HER POCKETBOOK AND DIDN'T KNOW WHERE THE MONEY WAS GOING."
THURMAN RUTH
YOU DO FOUR, FIVE, SIX SHOWS A DAY, YOU HAVE TO STAY ON SCHEDULE.
BUT, WHEN THE HOLY SPIRIT ARRIVED, THE THEATER WOULD TAKE OFF INTO PANDEMONIUM, AND TIME WENT BY THE WAYSIDE.
YOU HAVE TO STAY ON SCHEDULE. IF YOU'RE ALLOTTED SIXTEEN MINUTES, STAY WITHIN IT, NOT THIRTY-SIX MINUTES!
BUT, MR. REED, WHAT DO WE DO IF THE HOLY SPIRIT ARRIVES?
MAKE SURE HE LEAVES BY THE END OF THE SONG!
LEONARD REED
GOSPEL GREAT ALEX BRADFORD
I BEGAN TO MAKE SURE THAT THEY WERE OFF ON TIME.
THAT TAUGHT THEM SOMETHING.
GET OFF ON TIME, BECAUSE YOU HAD TO PAY THE STAGEHANDS OVERTIME!

Nearly *everybody* who is *anybody* in the world of gospel plays the Apollo gospel shows.

ALEX BRADFORD BECOMES A GREAT INFLUENCE ON SINGERS FROM LITTLE RICHARD TO RAY CHARLES.

Too close to heaven...

THE *GREATEST* SINGING GROUP THAT I HAD AT THE APOLLO.

I HAD ANOTHER BIG-NAME GROUP CLOSING ONCE . . .

BRADFORD WAS ALWAYS A WINNER: A *SHOWMAN.*

HE WENT OVER VERY BIG AT OUR FIRST SHOW.

THE SWANEE QUINTET

. . . BUT THE SWANEE QUINTET WAS SO TOUGH THAT I HAD TO LET THEM CLOSE THE SHOW.

THE OTHER GROUP WAS COMPLAINING ALL THE TIME.

CLARA WARD AND THE WARD SINGERS

THE FOLKS USED TO COME OUT TO THE APOLLO TO SEE THE WARD SINGERS DRESS.

ALBERTINA WALKER AND THE CARAVANS

THEY WERE *REAL* BIG.

SO MANY FINE LADIES CAME OUT OF HER GROUP: *SHIRLEY CAESAR, INEZ ANDREWS, DOROTHY NORWOOD, CASSIETTA GEORGE* . . .

THEY WERE GREAT SINGERS, AND THEIR HAIRPIECES WERE SO NICE.

A GROUP MIGHT OUT-SING THEM, BUT THEY COULDN'T *OUT-DRESS* THEM.

THE DIXIE HUMMINGBIRDS

IRA TUCKER WAS ONE OF THE GREATEST LEAD SINGERS. THEY WERE MY *FAVORITE* SINGERS.

THE SWAN SILVERTONES

THE *SWAN SILVERTONES*, WITH *REVEREND CLAUDE JETER*, DID SOMETHING AT THE APOLLO THAT I'VE NEVER SEEN ANY OTHER GROUP DO.

TO ME, THEY WEREN'T REAL GOSPEL OR PURE GOSPEL.

THEY DID THAT THING WITH *PAUL SIMON*, "LOVE ME LIKE A ROCK."

THAT GROUP ALWAYS WANTED TO DO ROCK AND ROLL.

THEY HAD SO MANY FOLKS SHOUTING AND GETTING HAPPY THAT THE CARAVANS COULDN'T EVEN GO ON. CURTAIN TIME. CUT THE LAST ACT OFF.

THE CARAVANS WERE OUT THERE WITH THE SWAN SILVERTONES, SHOUTING AND HAPPY THEMSELVES.

157

THURMAN RUTH INTRODUCES THE **STAPLE SINGERS** TO NEW YORK AT THE APOLLO.

WHEN I WAS A DJ IN NEW YORK, I WOULDN'T EVEN PLAY THEIR SONGS BECAUSE THEY SOUNDED SO COUNTRYLIKE, SO **DOWN HOME**.

I BOOKED THEM AS A HEADLINE ACT SIX OR EIGHT WEEKS LATER.

THE STAPLE SINGERS

THAT'S WHEN THEY REALLY GOT STARTED.

I WAS ON VACATION IN CHICAGO AND I WENT DOWN TO SOME CHURCH WITH IRA TUCKER AND HEARD **MAVIS STAPLES**.

MAN, I NEVER HEARD **ANYTHING** LIKE THAT IN MY LIFE. SHE TORE THE CHURCH UP.

BROTHER RUTH, *PLEASE* LET ME PLAY YOUR APOLLO CARAVAN.

BUT BEFORE I GOT A CHANCE, SHE LEFT GOSPEL AND GOT ON TO OTHER THINGS. NEVER PLAYED THE APOLLO FOR ME.

I BROUGHT **ARETHA FRANKLIN** TO NEW YORK FOR THE FIRST TIME— SHE AND HER FATHER, **REVEREND C. L. FRANKLIN**—FROM DETROIT.

HE WAS ONE OF OUR GREATEST BAPTIST PREACHERS, ONE OF THE GREATEST **REVIVAL** MINISTERS.

ARETHA FRANKLIN

HIS RECORDS WERE MORE SUCCESSFUL THAN ANYONE ELSE.

A CHANGE IS COMING—THE **SOUL STIRRERS** WITH **SAM COOKE**.

Touch the hem of his garment...

The handsome nineteen-year-old has a dramatic impact on gospel and, ultimately, pop and soul music.

By the time of the Apollo gospel shows, the Soul Stirrers has lost its founder, *R. H. Harris*, and Sam Cooke takes over.

IN 1956, AGAINST THE WISHES OF THE OTHER SOUL STIRRERS, SAM COOKE RECORDS A POP SONG, "LOVEABLE."

SAM, *LISTEN* TO ME, WE'VE BEEN FRIENDS A LONG TIME.

YOU COULD MAKE SO MUCH MORE MONEY IF YOU SING FOR THE POP MARKET.

BOBBY SCHIFFMAN

THE APOLLO IS A *CATALYST* IN THE CROSSOVER FROM GOSPEL TO SOUL MUSIC.

BROTHERS AND SISTERS, WE HAVE A VERY SPECIAL GUEST WHO'D LIKE TO SING A SONG FOR YOU TONIGHT: *MR. JAMES BROWN!*

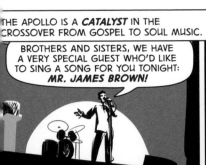

The Apollo is virtually the *only* place where gospel people and soul people meet on *common ground.*

Our Father who art in heaven...

LITTLE ANTHONY AND THE IMPERIALS

I WAS INFLUENCED BY THE GOSPEL SINGERS AT THE APOLLO.

THE IMPERIALS NEEDED SOMETHING TO MAKE THAT AUDIENCE COME UP OUT OF THEIR SEATS.

I TOLD MY GUITAR PLAYER, "GIVE ME THAT THING THAT WE DO IN CHURCH, THAT RUN THAT EVERYBODY GETS UP ON."

AT FIRST THE SONG WAS PURE GOSPEL WITH FEW SET WORDS.

THE OLD MAN LOVED IT.

I'm Alright!

I WANT YOU TO GO DOWN TO THE BASEMENT AND PRACTICE WITH SAM. HE'S GOING TO PUT SOME **WORDS** TO IT.

FRANK SCHIFFMAN

YOU CAN TAKE AN **EMOTIONAL** THING AND TURN IT FROM A **SPIRITUAL** THING TO A **SENSUAL** THING.

Sam, working with Anthony, comes up with lyrics that make "I'm Alright" a rousing, sexy love song.

LITTLE ANTHONY

WE OPENED UP A CAN OF WORMS THAT I REGRET TO THIS DAY.

Thurman Ruth soon attracts competitors, like **Doc Wheeler** and **Fred Barr** from WWRL, who bring in their own gospel packages.

I'D COME BY WHEN THEY WERE THERE, AND THEY'D COME BY WHEN I HAD MY SHOW. IT WAS A **FRIENDLY** THING.

THURMAN RUTH

DIONNE WARWICK HAS HER OWN AMATEUR GOSPEL GROUP, AND HER MOTHER SINGS GOSPEL IN THE **DRINKARD SISTERS**.

WEDNESDAY NIGHT WAS AMATEUR NIGHT, AND IT WAS NO DIFFERENT WHEN THEY HAD GOSPEL SHOWS THERE.

BUT IT WAS FOR GOSPEL SINGERS.

OUR GROUP DECIDED TO GO UP THERE. WE WON **FIRST PRIZE**.

BUT WE NEVER WENT BACK TO SING GOSPEL AGAIN.

Despite the conflict of conscience, more and more singers make the move from gospel to **commercial** soul music.

By the early '60s, the gospel shows have lost their unique allure and fade out.

Soul music takes the gospel rhythm and feeling and secularizes its message—creating a broader appeal and attracting a **far larger** audience—both black and white.

CHAPTER 8

The 1960s: Soulful

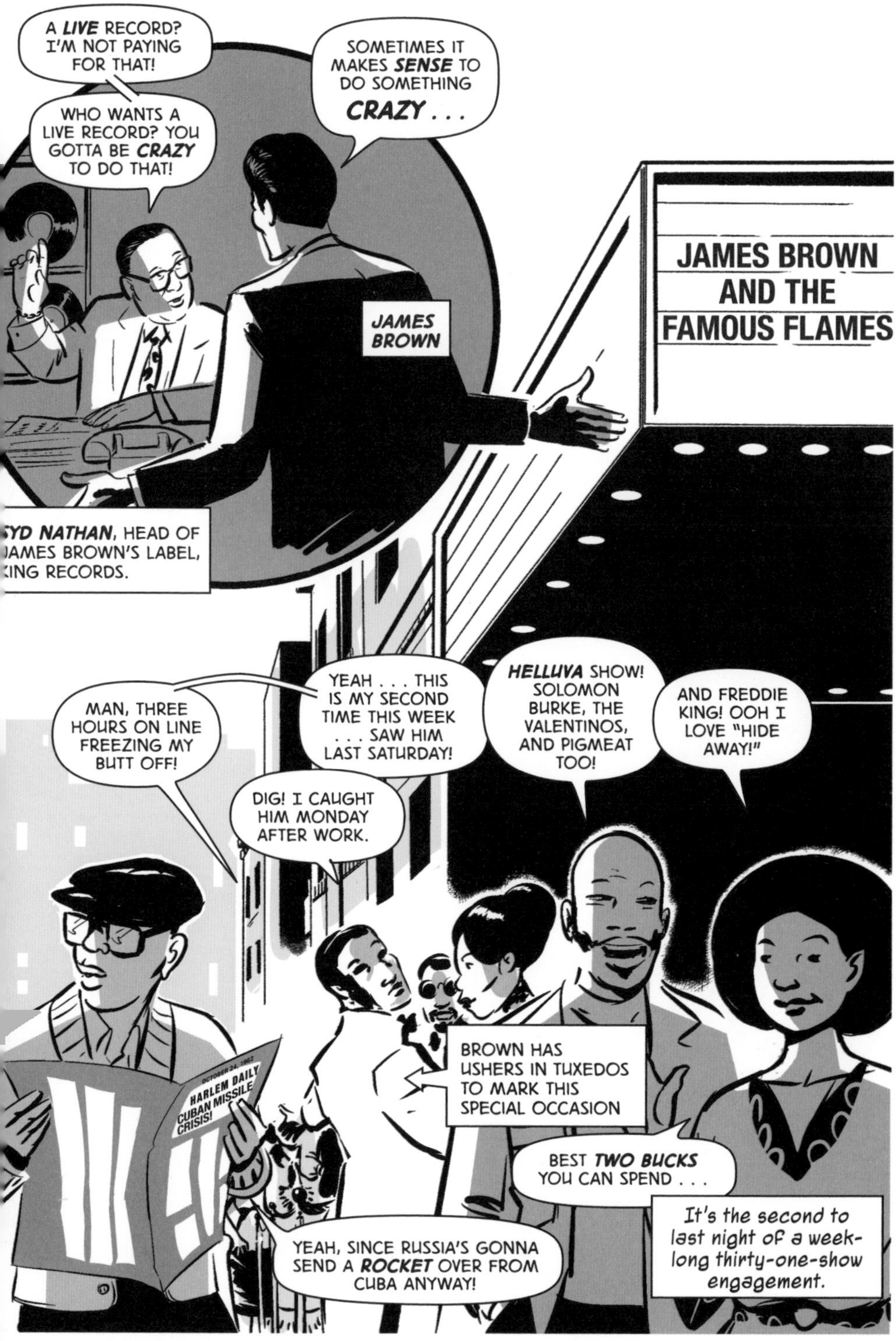
A LIVE RECORD? I'M NOT PAYING FOR THAT!
WHO WANTS A LIVE RECORD? YOU GOTTA BE CRAZY TO DO THAT!
SOMETIMES IT MAKES SENSE TO DO SOMETHING CRAZY . . .
JAMES BROWN
JAMES BROWN AND THE FAMOUS FLAMES
SYD NATHAN, HEAD OF JAMES BROWN'S LABEL, KING RECORDS.
MAN, THREE HOURS ON LINE FREEZING MY BUTT OFF!
YEAH . . . THIS IS MY SECOND TIME THIS WEEK . . . SAW HIM LAST SATURDAY!
DIG! I CAUGHT HIM MONDAY AFTER WORK.
HELLUVA SHOW! SOLOMON BURKE, THE VALENTINOS, AND PIGMEAT TOO!
AND FREDDIE KING! OOH I LOVE "HIDE AWAY!"
HARLEM DAILY
CUBAN MISSILE CRISIS!
BROWN HAS USHERS IN TUXEDOS TO MARK THIS SPECIAL OCCASION
BEST TWO BUCKS YOU CAN SPEND . . .
YEAH, SINCE RUSSIA'S GONNA SEND A ROCKET OVER FROM CUBA ANYWAY!
It's the second to last night of a week-long thirty-one-show engagement.

MR. DYNAMITE, THE AMAZING MR. "PLEASE, PLEASE" HIMSELF—THE STAR OF THE SHOW, *JAMES BROWN AND THE FAMOUS FLAMES!*

LUCAS "FATS" GONDER

EIGHT MICS FEEDING INTO A BIG AMPEX STEREO TAPE MACHINE ARE CAPTURING EVERYTHING.

Brown puts up $5,700 of his own money to make this recording possible.

SING IT, @#$%&!

The fans are not notified in advance that the event is being recorded, so the response is *spontaneous*.

The audience response is so raw and overwhelming that the engineer actually has to minimize certain reactions for the record . . .

¡FEEL ALL RIGHT

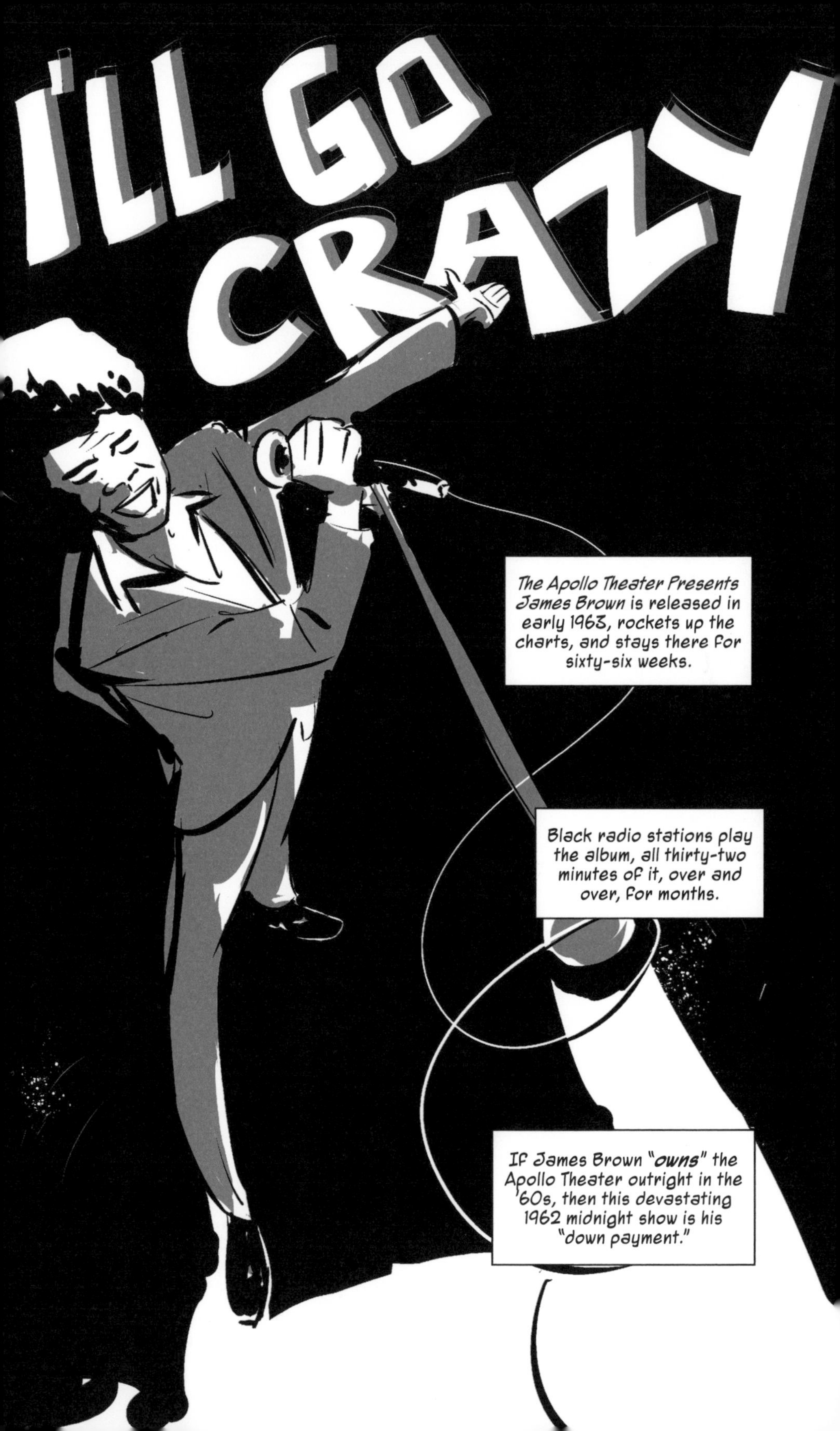
I'LL GO CRAZY
The Apollo Theater Presents James Brown is released in early 1963, rockets up the charts, and stays there for sixty-six weeks.
Black radio stations play the album, all thirty-two minutes of it, over and over, for months.
If James Brown "owns" the Apollo Theater outright in the '60s, then this devastating 1962 midnight show is his "down payment."

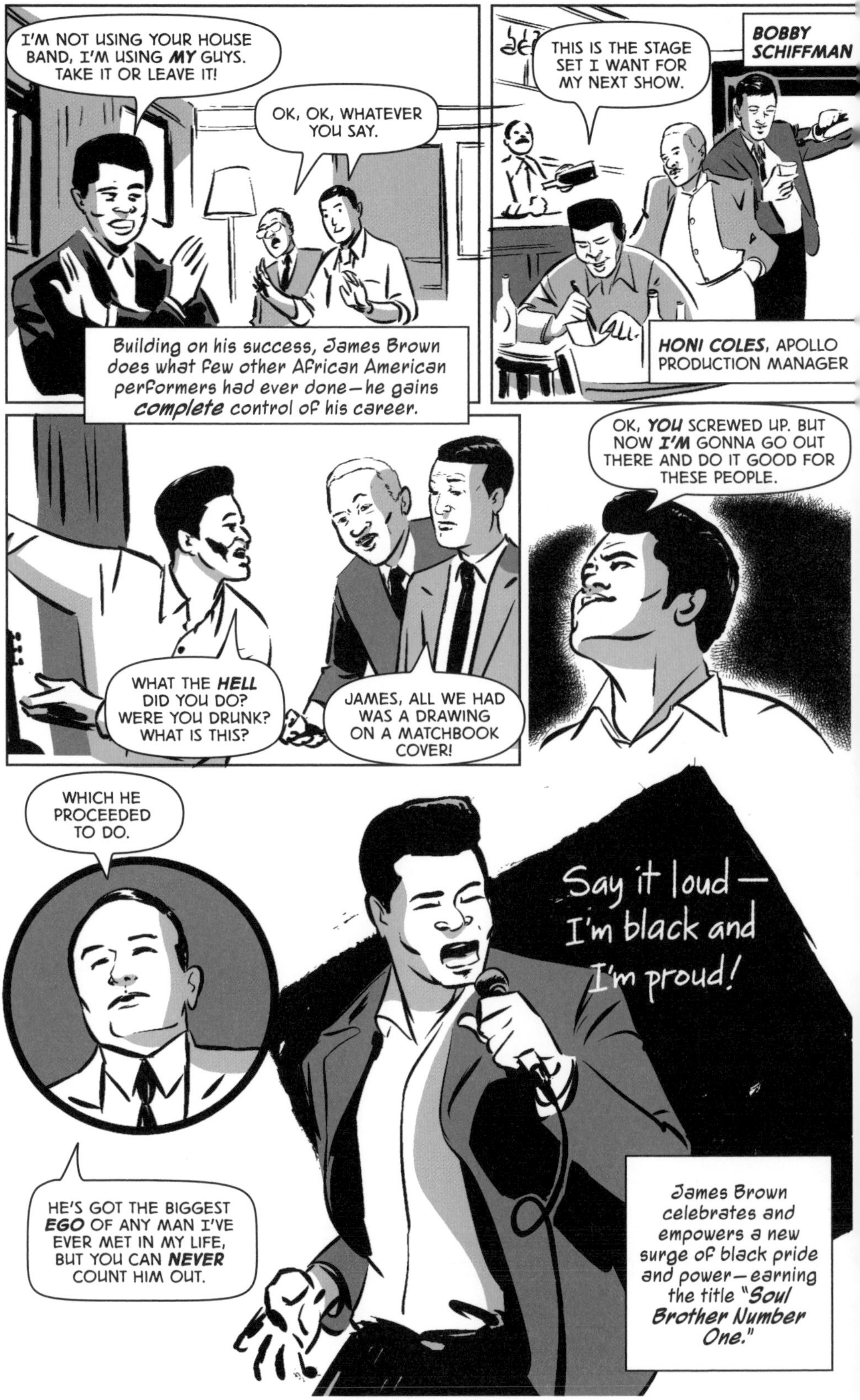
I'M NOT USING YOUR HOUSE BAND, I'M USING MY GUYS. TAKE IT OR LEAVE IT!
OK, OK, WHATEVER YOU SAY.
Building on his success, James Brown does what few other African American performers had ever done—he gains complete control of his career.
THIS IS THE STAGE SET I WANT FOR MY NEXT SHOW.
BOBBY SCHIFFMAN
HONI COLES, APOLLO PRODUCTION MANAGER
WHAT THE HELL DID YOU DO? WERE YOU DRUNK? WHAT IS THIS?
JAMES, ALL WE HAD WAS A DRAWING ON A MATCHBOOK COVER!
OK, YOU SCREWED UP. BUT NOW I'M GONNA GO OUT THERE AND DO IT GOOD FOR THESE PEOPLE.
WHICH HE PROCEEDED TO DO.
HE'S GOT THE BIGGEST EGO OF ANY MAN I'VE EVER MET IN MY LIFE, BUT YOU CAN NEVER COUNT HIM OUT.
Say it loud— I'm black and I'm proud!
James Brown celebrates and empowers a new surge of black pride and power—earning the title "Soul Brother Number One."

In the midst of historic social upheaval, its **fourth decade** as a black theater becomes the Apollo's most celebrated and successful yet.

STOP THE WAR!

Civil Rights Now!

The Apollo is selling 800,000 to one million tickets a year. A so-so week might draw 16,000 customers. An especially hot attraction can *triple* that number.

THINGS ARE CHANGING. ONLY 15 PERCENT OF OUR WEEKDAY AND 25 PERCENT OF OUR WEEKEND AUDIENCE IS WHITE NOW.

WHITES AREN'T THAT COMFORTABLE COMING UP HERE ANYMORE.

FRANK SCHIFFMAN

BOBBY SCHIFFMAN

THIS SOMEWHAT WISTFUL MOTTO APPEARS DURING A ONE-MONTH PERIOD EARLY IN 1964, WHEN FOUR WHITE PEOPLE ARE MURDERED IN HARLEM.

★ WORLD-FAMOUS ★
AIR COND
APOLLO
AMERICA'S GREATEST STAGE SHOWS
IN THE HEART OF FRIENDLY HARLEM!
125th ST. near 8th Ave. · Tele. UNiversity 4-4470

... EVEN WHEN THE REST OF THE CITY WON'T.

HARLEM NEEDS THE APOLLO.

WE WILL ALWAYS REACH OUT TO THE PEOPLE OF HARLEM WHO LOVE THIS PLACE.

HONI COLES

PERCY SUTTON, THE MANHATTAN BOROUGH PRESIDENT WHO WILL ONE DAY TAKE OVER THE APOLLO

THE SCHIFFMANS HAVE TRADITIONALLY INVOLVED THEMSELVES IN HARLEM COMMUNITY AFFAIRS.

IF ALL BUSINESSMEN HAD DONE AS MUCH, COMMUNITY TENSION WOULD BE CONSIDERABLY LESSENED.

A LETTER OF APPRECIATION TO FRANK SCHIFFMAN FROM MARTIN LUTHER KING, JR. PROUDLY HUNG IN THE APOLLO OFFICE. IN PART, IT READ:

WHEN THE BRIGHT DAY OF FREEDOM EMERGES, AND THE TRAGIC EXPRESSION OF MAN'S INHUMANITY TO MAN IS CAST INTO UNENDING LIMBO, YOUR NAME WILL CERTAINLY SHINE AS ONE OF THOSE INDIVIDUALS WHO HAD THE VISION, COURAGE AND DEDICATION TO WORK FOR A REIGN OF JUSTICE AND A RULE OF LOVE.

THE APOLLO BECOMES MORE ACTIVE IN THE COMMUNITY AND IN BLACK CAUSES.

SEE, WE CAN GET TV CAMERAS *HERE* WHEN WE CAN'T GET THEM ANYWHERE ELSE IN HARLEM.

The theater hosts *dozens* of fundraisers and educational programs.

Cries for *freedom* in the streets echo the cries of freedom in the new black music.

CRIES OF A DIFFERENT SORT ARE COMING FROM WITHIN THE THEATER AS THE APOLLO, IN 1960, FIRST USES THE WORD "SOUL" TO DESCRIBE RAY CHARLES AS THE "SOUL GENIUS."

WHAT'd I SAY

Uuh
Uuh
ooh
ooh

THE SWEET SOUNDS OF *LOVE*, MAN!

THAT'S SOUL MUSIC, BABY!

Many radio stations ban "What'd I Say" as too sexy, but it's a giant crossover hit anyway.

THE SWEET SOUNDS OF **JACKIE WILSON** MAKE HIM THE APOLLO'S **ALL-TIME** BOX OFFICE CHAMP IN MAY 1963—UNTIL JAMES BROWN SETS **ANOTHER** RECORD THE FOLLOWING YEAR.

Lonely teardrops...

Higher and higher!

JACKIE WILSON DROVE THE WOMEN CRAZY. WE WERE FRIENDS WITH HIM AND *WE* WERE **DROOLING**.

HE WAS LIKE A VERY SLINKY, POWERFUL **LEOPARD** ONSTAGE.

Earnings from Wilson's smash hit help songwriter *Berry Gordy* to start a little record company called *Motown*.

SOUL STAR **SAM COOKE** ALSO STARTS HIS OWN RECORD LABEL, **SAR**, TWO YEARS BEFORE BROWN MAKES HIS LIVE ALBUM.

BEVERLY LEE OF THE SHIRELLES

COOKE'S SLEEK GOOD LOOKS AND **SEXY** VOICE PUSH HIS GOSPEL ROOTS TO THE LIMITS OF PROPRIETY AS HE RACKS UP HIT AFTER HIT.

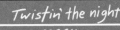
Twistin' the night awaaay...

Among his artists are Bobby Womack's group, the *Valentinos*, who appear with James Brown at the Apollo the week Brown records the live album.

Like Ray Charles and Jackie Wilson, Sam Cooke is a vital link between gospel and soul.

HOWEVER, HE STRUGGLES WITH HIS CHOICE TO "GO POP." THE SUPERSTAR EVEN TRIES A RETURN TO GOSPEL, BUT IS RUDELY REJECTED AT A SOUL STIRRERS SHOW IN CHICAGO, ACCORDING TO AUTHOR ANTHONY HEILBUT.

COOKE IS ALSO A **GROUNDBREAKER** IN THE WHITE MARKET, THANKS TO HIS CLEAN-CUT IMAGE, GOOD LOOKS, AND SMOOTH SOUND.

GET THAT NO-GOOD BLUES SINGER DOWN!

THIS IS A **CHRISTIAN** PROGRAM.

HE DIES UNDER DISPUTED CIRCUMSTANCES ON DECEMBER 10, 1964, SHOT BY THE OWNER OF THE HACIENDA MOTEL OUTSIDE HER OFFICE DOOR.

IN CHICAGO, **200,000** FANS LINE UP TO VIEW HIS BODY.

DAILY DEFENDER
America's Most Exciting Daily
FINAL

SAM COOKE KILLED IN L.A. MOTEL

YEARS LATER, STREET VENDORS OUTSIDE THE APOLLO SELL MEMORIAL PHOTOGRAPHS OF MARTYRS MARTIN LUTHER KING JR., JOHN F. KENNEDY, ROBERT F. KENNEDY . . . AND SAM COOKE.

THE SHIRELLES

the SHIRELLES
BABY IT'S

His posthumous anthem, "A Change Is Going to Come," becomes a *quintessential* protest song for the Civil Rights movement.

WHOLESOME AND UNTHREATENING, THE *GIRL GROUPS* OF THE LATE '50S AND EARLY '60S, LIKE THE SHIRELLES, ARE ADORED BY BLACKS AND WHITES ALIKE.

JOCKO'S ROCKET SHIP REVUE, 1958

WELL, ALL *ROOOTHER* FOLKS . . . FOR THE FIRST TIME EVER AT THE APOLLO, OR ANYWHERE—THE SHIRELLES!

MR. PHILLIPS, WE DIDN'T KNOW WE WERE SUPPOSED TO HAVE *ARRANGEMENTS*.

NEXT TIME, HONEY. WE GOT YOU COVERED NOW.

WLIV

I Met Him On A Sunday

BEVERLY LEE AND THE *SHIRELLES* WITH REUBEN PHILLIPS, APOLLO HOUSE BAND LEADER

AS WE WENT BACK TO THE APOLLO THROUGH THE YEARS, WE DEVELOPED A *FOLLOWING*.

SOME YOUNG KIDS WOULD HANG BACKSTAGE, AND WE WOULD *BABYSIT* FOR THEM BETWEEN SHOWS.

I ALWAYS THOUGHT OF OUR SONGS AS VERY CORNY AND LOLLIPOP-ISH.

THEIR FIRST GOLD RECORD, FOR "SOLDIER BOY," IS PRESENTED TO THEM AT THE APOLLO.

BUT THE PEOPLE AT THE APOLLO ACCEPTED AND LIKED THEM.

BEVERLY LEE

WE *THOUGHT* THEY WOULD WANT MORE RHYTHM AND BLUES AND SOUL.

NANCY WILSON BRINGS A *SOPHISTICATED* SOUND TO THE APOLLO THAT IS HARD TO CATEGORIZE.

MOST JAZZ BUFFS WILL SAY I'M NOT A JAZZ SINGER.

MOST RHYTHM-AND-BLUES BUFFS WILL SAY I'M NOT AN R&B SINGER.

MOST POP BUFFS WILL SAY I'M NOT A POP SINGER.

Guess who I saw today...

CANNONBALL ADDERLEY, THE STAR ALTO SAX PLAYER, SEES HER AND HELPS HER GET A RECORDING CONTRACT.

AT FIRST I WAS ON THE *BOTTOM* OF THE BILL AND HAD THE DRESSING ROOM ON THE TOP FLOOR.

BY THE TIME I GOT TO THE APOLLO, I WAS VERY WELL SEASONED. I HAD HAD A TELEVISION SHOW AT FIFTEEN.

THE APOLLO WAS A DIFFERENT THING. MOST PEOPLE WHO WERE IN FRONT OF ME ON THE SHOW DESERVED TO BE.

DRESSING Room 11

I WAS NOT AFRAID OF THE APOLLO, AND IT WAS WONDERFUL TO GET THE KIND OF RECEPTION I GOT THERE.

THE NEXT TIME I WENT BACK I WAS THE *HEADLINER*. IT HAPPENED THAT FAST.

169

THE FIRST TIME I HAD A PERFORMANCE AT THE APOLLO, I OPENED THE SHOW. I WAS THE *BABY* IN THE BUSINESS.

DIONNE WARWICK

SHE IS A YOUNG, CLASSICALLY TRAINED MUSICIAN SINGING BACKUP FOR THE DRIFTERS WHEN SHE MEETS *BURT BACHARACH* AND *HAL DAVID*. THEY WRITE A STRING OF HITS FOR HER.

IT'S NOT THE REGULAR I–IV–V–IV CHANGES.

THIS SONG CAN'T BE PLAYED.

HERE IS THIS KID FROM NEW JERSEY WITH THIS GODDAMNED MUSIC THAT NOBODY UNDERSTANDS. WHAT IS SHE *DOING* TO US?

I WILL SIT AND PLAY IT FOR YOU, AND THEN YOUR BAND WILL PLAY IT.

REUBEN PHILLIPS

MY MUSIC WAS PROBABLY THE *HARDEST* IN THE INDUSTRY.

ANYONE WHO HAD A HEART

THEY DON'T *UNDERSTAND* YOUR MUSIC. THEY'LL BOO YOU OFF THE STAGE.

I NEVER HAD ANY PROBLEM RELATING TO THE PEOPLE AT THE APOLLO, BECAUSE THAT WAS MY *HERITAGE*.

HAL DAVID WROTE LYRICS THAT SPOKE TO YOUR *HEART*.

EVERYBODY'S GOT ONE OF *THOSE*, REGARDLESS OF HOW RICH OR POOR YOU ARE, OR THE COLOR OF YOUR SKIN.

BOBBY SCHIFFMAN

Peeeeople...

THE MAN WHO RUNS THIS THEATER TOLD ME I CAN'T SING THIS SONG HERE. I'LL SING IT *ANYWHERE*.

I'M BRINGING DOWNTOWN *UPTOWN*!

DOWNTOWN, UPTOWN, ALL OVER THE COUNTRY—RADIO WAVES ARE BREACHING RACIAL BARRIERS.

...HEAT WAVE!

Hundreds of hits-oriented stations play soul records in *heavy rotation*, along with white rock and roll and pop.

POWERFUL *RECORD COMPANIES* USURP DJS—HOBBLED BY THE PAYOLA SCANDAL—AND ORGANIZE SHOW PACKAGES FOR THE APOLLO CONSISTING *ENTIRELY* OF THEIR OWN RECORDING ARTISTS.

APOLLO

THIS WEEK
THE ATLANTIC CARAVAN OF STARS

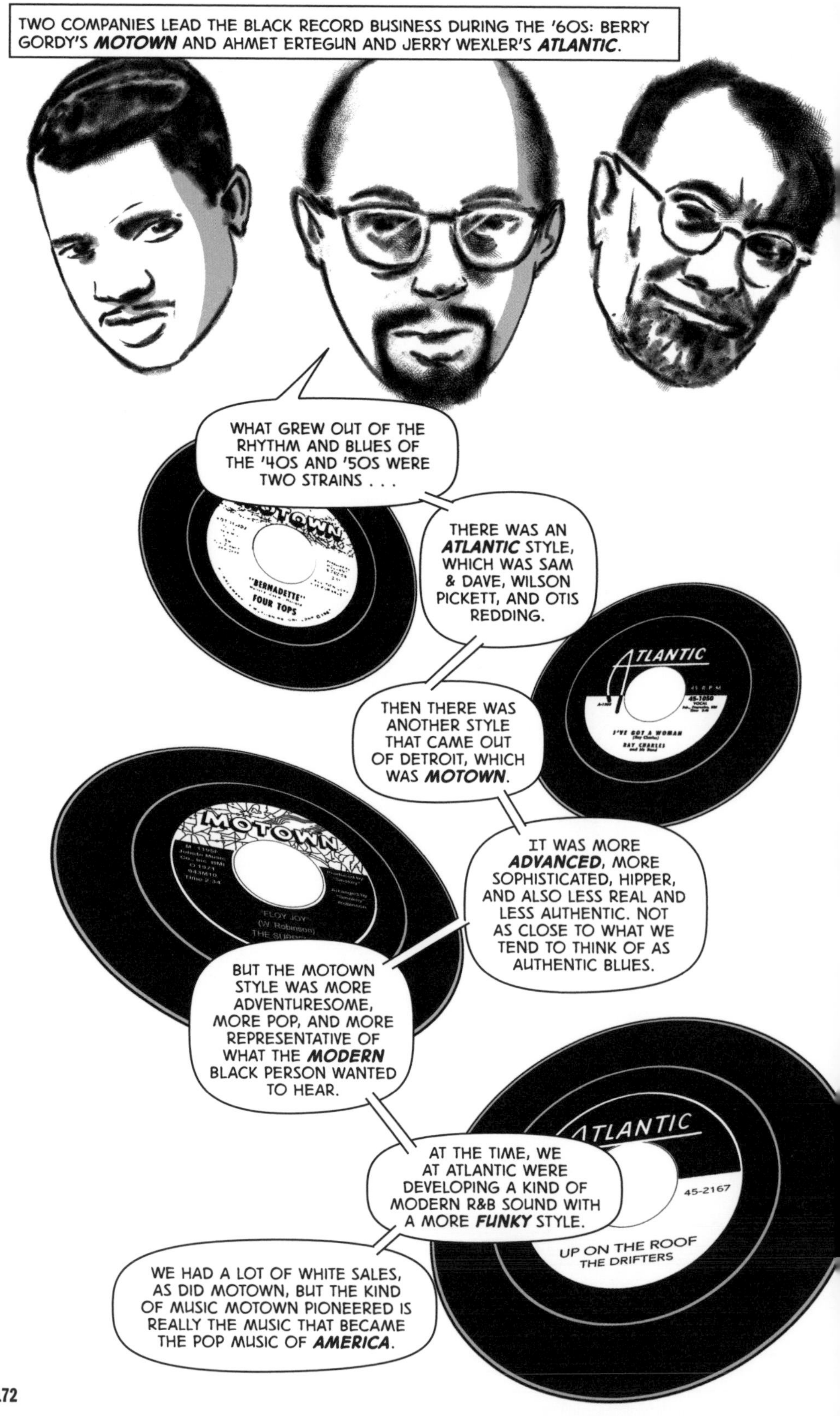
TWO COMPANIES LEAD THE BLACK RECORD BUSINESS DURING THE '60S: BERRY GORDY'S ***MOTOWN*** AND AHMET ERTEGUN AND JERRY WEXLER'S ***ATLANTIC***.
WHAT GREW OUT OF THE RHYTHM AND BLUES OF THE '40S AND '50S WERE TWO STRAINS . . .
"BERNADETTE"
FOUR TOPS
THERE WAS AN ***ATLANTIC*** STYLE, WHICH WAS SAM & DAVE, WILSON PICKETT, AND OTIS REDDING.
ATLANTIC
THEN THERE WAS ANOTHER STYLE THAT CAME OUT OF DETROIT, WHICH WAS ***MOTOWN***.
MOTOWN
IT WAS MORE ***ADVANCED***, MORE SOPHISTICATED, HIPPER, AND ALSO LESS REAL AND LESS AUTHENTIC. NOT AS CLOSE TO WHAT WE TEND TO THINK OF AS AUTHENTIC BLUES.
BUT THE MOTOWN STYLE WAS MORE ADVENTURESOME, MORE POP, AND MORE REPRESENTATIVE OF WHAT THE ***MODERN*** BLACK PERSON WANTED TO HEAR.
ATLANTIC
45-2167
UP ON THE ROOF
THE DRIFTERS
AT THE TIME, WE AT ATLANTIC WERE DEVELOPING A KIND OF MODERN R&B SOUND WITH A MORE ***FUNKY*** STYLE.
WE HAD A LOT OF WHITE SALES, AS DID MOTOWN, BUT THE KIND OF MUSIC MOTOWN PIONEERED IS REALLY THE MUSIC THAT BECAME THE POP MUSIC OF ***AMERICA***.

BERRY GORDY AND HIS SISTER, ESTHER, CAME TO SEE ME IN '62.

MR. SCHIFFMAN, WE ARE HAVING **GREAT** SUCCESS IN DETROIT WITH MANY OF OUR ARTISTS.

BOBBY SCHIFFMAN

WE'D LIKE TO DO A MOTOWN PACKAGE— YOU'D GET AN AMAZING DEAL.

I'VE NEVER HEARD OF **ANY** OF THEM!

AT FIRST, I THOUGHT IT WAS *MOTORTOWN*.

AS A MATTER OF FACT, I HAD A SIGN MADE THAT SAID MOTORTOWN, AND HAD TO CHANGE IT.

MOTORTOWN REVUE
• THE SUPREMES • SMOKEY ROBINSON AND THE MIRACLES • MARTHA AND THE VANDELLAS • EARL VAN DYKE SEXTET

WE DID THIRTY-ONE SHOWS OVER SEVEN DAYS.

SMOKEY ROBINSON AND THE MIRACLES, DIANA ROSS AND THE SUPREMES, THE TEMPTATIONS, MARTHA AND THE VANDELLAS, MARVIN GAYE, STEVIE WONDER, THE CONTOURS, AND MARV JOHNSON.

THE **PACKAGE** COST THE APOLLO $7,000 FOR THE **WEEK**, AND SOON MOST OF THOSE PEOPLE WERE GETTING $40,000 TO $50,000 A **NIGHT, EACH**.

RECORDED **LIVE** at the **APOLLO** IN NEW YORK VOL. 1

MIRACLES MARY WELLS
MARVELETTES ∗ MARV GAYE
"THE MOTOR-TOWN REVUE" ∗ CONTOURS
STEVIE WONDER - SUPREMES

BOBBY ISN'T THE ONLY ONE AT THE APOLLO WHO DOESN'T KNOW WHO HE IS DEALING WITH AT FIRST.

I WAS THE *COMIC*, AND THE SUPREMES WERE ON IN FRONT OF ME.

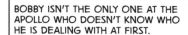

THE DISC JOCKEY WHO WAS SUPPOSED TO *MC* WENT TO PLAY TONK, AND HE WASN'T THERE TO TAKE THE SUPREMES OFF THE STAGE.

SO I WENT OUT AND SAID, "LADIES AND GENTLEMEN, THE SUPREMES," AND THEN I WENT ON AND DID MY ACT.

THE NEXT SHOW, THE SAME THING HAPPENED.

I DIDN'T WANT TO MC, AND JUST TO KEEP A BAD HABIT FROM STARTING, I DIDN'T TAKE THEM OFF.

SCOEY MITCHEI

SO THEY HAD TO WALK OFF ON THEIR *OWN*, AND THEN I WALKED ON AND INTRODUCED MYSELF AND DID MY ACT.

LATER . . .

MISS ROSS WANTS TO SEE YOU UPSTAIRS.

A STAGEHAND

WHERE WERE *YOU*?

BEG PARDON?

WHY WEREN'T YOU THERE TO TAKE US *OFF*?

OH, I SEE. NO, I'M NOT THE MC I'M THE COMIC ON THE SHOW.

COMIC, MC, WHAT *DIFFERENCE* DOES IT MAKE?

I TELL YOU WHAT, LITTLE GIRL. YOU BETTER STOP *FUSSING* WITH ME AND GO AND TRY AND GET YOURSELF A HIT RECORD!

THEY ROLLED OFF ABOUT TWENTY-EIGHT OF THEM RIGHT AFTER.

YOU LISTEN *GOOD*!

After "Where Did Our Love Go?", the Supremes *break* James Brown's Apollo attendance record.

The Supremes take the Apollo and America by *storm*. By the early '70s, two other Motown stars, the *Temptations* and *Gladys Knight and the Pips*, also set *new* Apollo house records.

GORDY'S SHOP HAS SOME OF THE ASSEMBLY-LINE TRAITS OF HIS POWERFUL INDUSTRIAL NEIGHBORS IN DETROIT.

EDDIE HOLLAND

LAMONT DOZIER

BRIAN HOLLAND

BOBBY AND FRANK SCHIFFMAN

HONI COLES

CHOLLY ATKINS

BERRY GORDY

SMOKEY ROBINSON

BUT IN MANY WAYS, BERRY GORDY AND MOTOWN DO WHAT FRANK SCHIFFMAN AND THE APOLLO HAVE **ALWAYS** DONE.

GORDY AND HIS TEAM WORK CLOSELY WITH HIS ARTISTS, **NURTURING** THEM, **TRAINING** THEM, SOMETIMES **HONING** ACTS FOR MONTHS BEFORE RELEASING A RECORD OR SENDING THEM ON THE ROAD.

NO AMOUNT OF COACHING OR HIT RECORDS CAN INSTILL ENOUGH CONFIDENCE IN THE PRINCE OF MOTOWN AT THE APOLLO.

MARVIN GAYE WAS VERY MUCH AFFECTED BY HIS FEELING THAT HE WAS LOUSY ONSTAGE.

IN TRUTH, THERE WAS A LOT TO BE DESIRED IN HIS OFFERING, IN THE BEGINNING.

MARVIN GAYE

BERRY GORDY

BOBBY SCHIFFMAN

STILL, HE WAS EXTREMELY POPULAR. THE GIRLS AND GUYS ABSOLUTELY **ADORED** HIM.

STILL, HE WAS ALWAYS VERY **NERVOUS** ABOUT GOING ON THE STAGE.

HI PAL, WHAT TIME DO YOU WANT ME TO PICK YOU UP AT LA GUARDIA?

MY FLIGHT GETS IN AT ELEVEN FRIDAY MORNING.

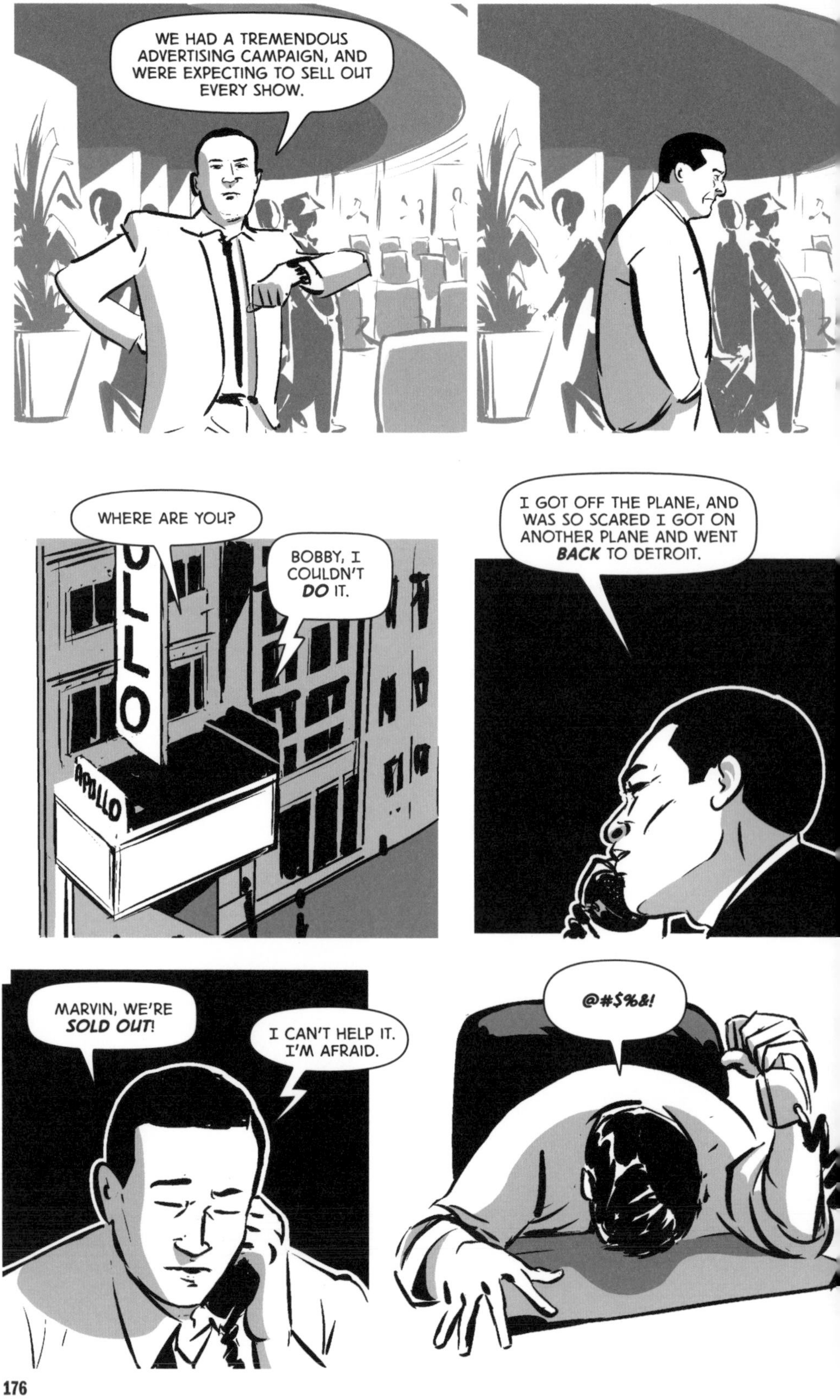
WE HAD A TREMENDOUS ADVERTISING CAMPAIGN, AND WERE EXPECTING TO SELL OUT EVERY SHOW.
WHERE ARE YOU?
BOBBY, I COULDN'T ***DO*** IT.
OLLO
APOLLO
I GOT OFF THE PLANE, AND WAS SO SCARED I GOT ON ANOTHER PLANE AND WENT ***BACK*** TO DETROIT.
MARVIN, WE'RE ***SOLD OUT***!
I CAN'T HELP IT. I'M AFRAID.
@#$%&!

WHAT REALLY *IGNITES* THE APOLLO MOTOWN REVUES IS THE SLICK, SOPHISTICATED CHOREOGRAPHY OF GROUPS LIKE THE *FOUR TOPS* AND THE *TEMPTATIONS*.

THE APOLLO PERPETUATED THAT STYLE, AND THE AUDIENCE JUST ATE IT UP.

THE PIPS WERE DOING THEIR CHOREOGRAPHY *BEFORE* THE TEMPTS AND ALL THE OTHER FAST-STEPPING GROUPS GOT TO BE POPULAR.

THE TEMPTS USED TO STAND IN THE WINGS AND WATCH EVERY MOVE THE PIPS MADE.

THAT'S HOW BERRY GORDY FOUND OUT ABOUT US: HIS *ACT* WAS GOING BACK AND TELLING HIM ABOUT US.

GLADYS KNIGHT

NATURALLY, THEY WANTED TO BE AS GOOD OR MAYBE BETTER THAN THE PIPS—BUT WE HAD A CERTAIN CAMARADERIE IN THOSE DAYS THAT KEPT THE COMPETITION *HEALTHY*.

LOOK, *HERE'S* HOW YOU WALK OFFSTAGE . . .

GLADYS, HONEY, YOU JUST BE *FEMININE*— NO DANCING.

CHOLLY ATKINS WAS OUR *EVERYTHING*.

THE APOLLO'S CHOLLY ATKINS WORKS WITH THE FOUR TOPS AND OTHERS IN THE BASEMENT REHEARSAL HALL.

WE USED TO WORK FROM NINE IN THE MORNING UNTIL NINE IN THE EVENING, REHEARSING.

HE WOULD COME RIGHT DOWN THE AISLE AT THE APOLLO IF WE WEREN'T DOING SOMETHING CORRECTLY.

ATKINS WORKS CLOSELY WITH HIS FORMER DANCE PARTNER, HONI COLES, THE APOLLO'S PRODUCTION MANAGER.

HEY, MAN, THEY'RE DOING ALL RIGHT.

GET OVER *HERE*—YOU'RE NOT SUPPOSED TO BE OVER *THERE!*

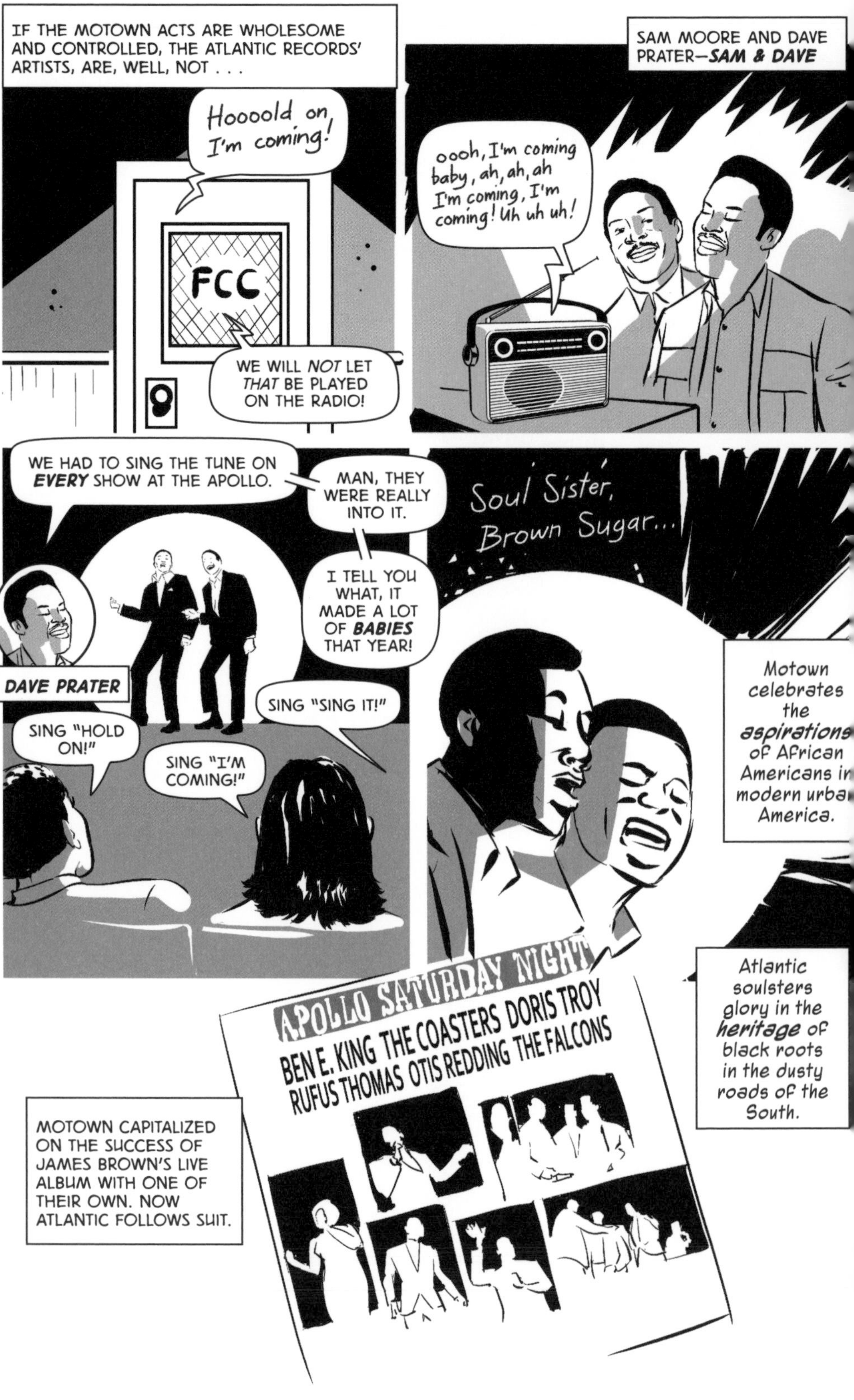

IF THE MOTOWN ACTS ARE WHOLESOME AND CONTROLLED, THE ATLANTIC RECORDS' ARTISTS, ARE, WELL, NOT . . .
Hooooold on, I'm coming!
FCC
WE WILL NOT LET THAT BE PLAYED ON THE RADIO!
SAM MOORE AND DAVE PRATER—SAM & DAVE
oooh, I'm coming baby, ah, ah, ah I'm coming, I'm coming! Uh uh uh!
WE HAD TO SING THE TUNE ON EVERY SHOW AT THE APOLLO.
MAN, THEY WERE REALLY INTO IT.
I TELL YOU WHAT, IT MADE A LOT OF BABIES THAT YEAR!
DAVE PRATER
SING "SING IT!"
SING "HOLD ON!"
SING "I'M COMING!"
Soul Sister, Brown Sugar...
Motown celebrates the aspirations of African Americans in modern urban America.
APOLLO SATURDAY NIGHT
BEN E. KING THE COASTERS DORIS TROY
RUFUS THOMAS OTIS REDDING THE FALCONS
Atlantic soulsters glory in the heritage of black roots in the dusty roads of the South.
MOTOWN CAPITALIZED ON THE SUCCESS OF JAMES BROWN'S LIVE ALBUM WITH ONE OF THEIR OWN. NOW ATLANTIC FOLLOWS SUIT.

FIDEL CASTRO MAKES A POINT OF STAYING HERE ON 125TH STREET IN 1960.

HOTEL THERESA

OTIS REDDING

MAN, I DON'T KNOW ABOUT THIS. I THINK WE'RE TOO *COUNTRY*.

YOU REALLY THINK THEY'RE GOING TO GO FOR WHAT I DO, WHAT *WE* DO DOWN HOME?

ATLANTIC CARAVAN OF STARS

OTIS REDDING

BEN E. KING

Like many other Apollo first-timers, *Otis Redding* doesn't realize he needs charts for the *King Curtis* band, who will back him.

DAMN, ONLY 400 BUCKS FOR THIS GIG, AND NOW I GOTTA PAY FOR CHARTS?!

Otis, like his Motown counterpart, Marvin Gaye, is not confident in his stage presence.

These arms of miiiiinnnne....

HE WAS *INEPT* ONSTAGE.

ATLANTIC CO-FOUNDER JERRY WEXLER

DESPITE HIS INERTIA, THE WOMEN AT THE APOLLO *LOVED* HIM.

OTIS, REMEMBER WHAT RUFUS THOMAS SAID: "FIND ONE WOMAN IN THE CROWD, AND SING TO HER."

ATLANTIC STAR *SOLOMON BURKE* DID NOT LACK CONFIDENCE IN ANYTHING.

His gospel-imbued sound was *fundamental* to the emergence of soul music and influenced many, including Mick Jagger.

GET YOUR POPCORN HERE!

SING IT PRETTY NOW!

OOH! AHH! OOH!

179

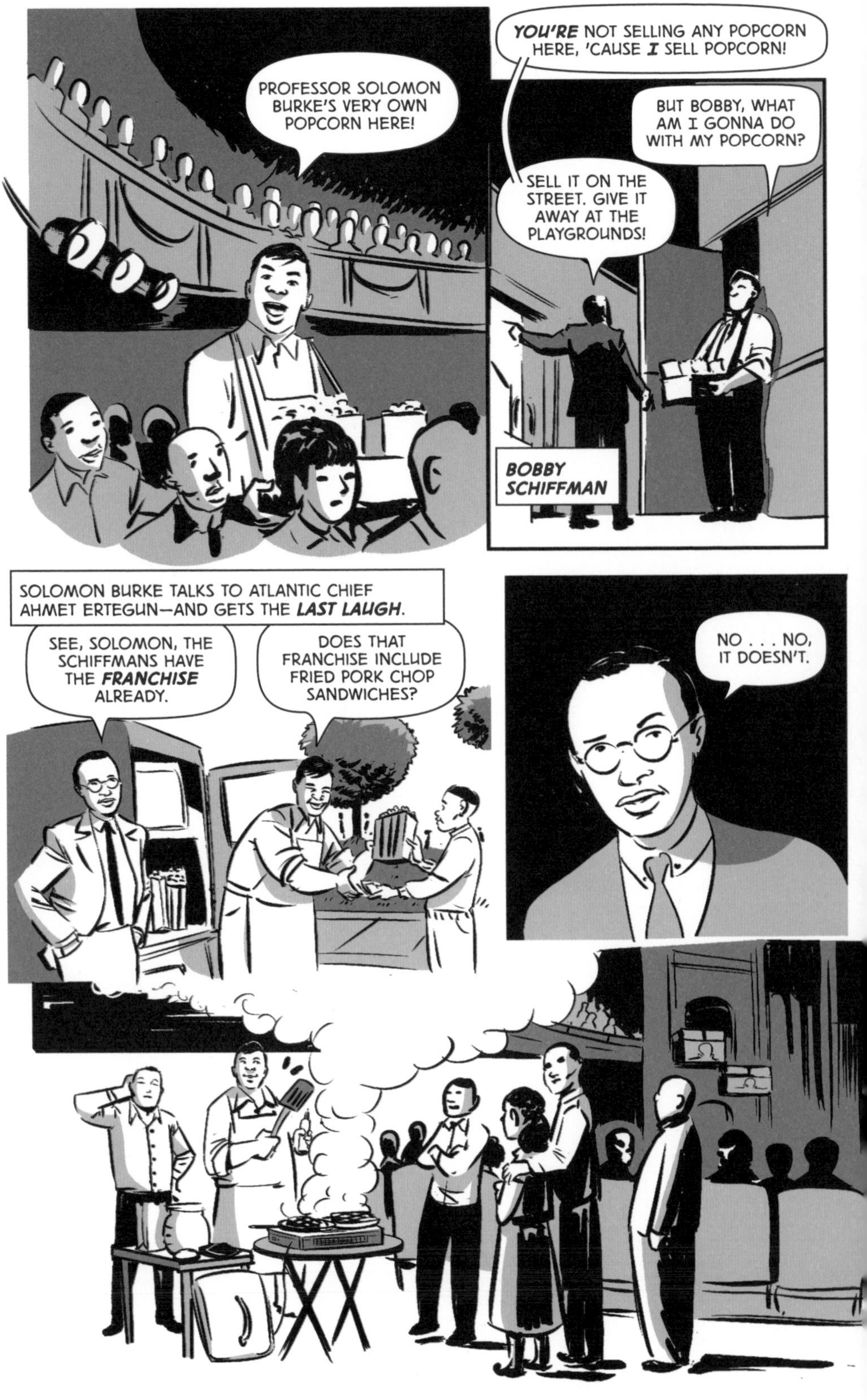
PROFESSOR SOLOMON BURKE'S VERY OWN POPCORN HERE!
YOU'RE NOT SELLING ANY POPCORN HERE, 'CAUSE I SELL POPCORN!
BUT BOBBY, WHAT AM I GONNA DO WITH MY POPCORN?
SELL IT ON THE STREET. GIVE IT AWAY AT THE PLAYGROUNDS!
BOBBY SCHIFFMAN
SOLOMON BURKE TALKS TO ATLANTIC CHIEF AHMET ERTEGUN—AND GETS THE LAST LAUGH.
SEE, SOLOMON, THE SCHIFFMANS HAVE THE FRANCHISE ALREADY.
DOES THAT FRANCHISE INCLUDE FRIED PORK CHOP SANDWICHES?
NO . . . NO, IT DOESN'T.

1961. BEFORE SHE MAKES HER CLASSICS FOR ATLANTIC RECORDS, JOHN HAMMOND RECORDS **ARETHA FRANKLIN** FOR COLUMBIA.

COME ON, FRANK, GIVE HER A SHOT. SHE'S **MARVELOUS**.

I DON'T KNOW, JOHN, SHE HAS NO TRACK RECORD SINGING POP. SHE'S A **GOSPEL** SINGER.

TRUST ME.

FRANK SCHIFFMAN

JOHN HAMMOND

I BOOK HER WITH SAM COOKE AND LITTLE ANTHONY AND SHE **NEVER** SHOWS UP!

NOW SHE COMES . . . THREE DAYS **LATE**?!

I'M HOLDING YOU PERSONALLY RESPONSIBLE!

Rock a bye your baby with a dixie melody . .

THE APOLLO HELPS TRAIN HER AND NURTURE HER IMMENSE TALENT.

1971. ARETHA FRANKLIN'S APOLLO APPEARANCE IS A NOW MAJOR **CULTURAL EVENT**.

i ain't never loved a man

THE TWO OPENING-NIGHT SHOWS CANNOT ACCOMMODATE THE THRONGS.

SHE'S HOME— ARETHA FRANKLIN

LOTS OF CELEBRITIES FOR THE **QUEEN OF SOUL** TONIGHT . . .

THERE'S **REVEREND JESSE JACKSON**, AND THERE, **ZULU CHIEF MANGOSUTHU GATSHA BUTHELEZI**.

THIS IS THE MOST **OVERWHELMING** THING WE'VE EVER HAD IN THE THEATER.

PETER LONG, APOLLO'S P.R. DIRECTOR

REVIEW:

The thousands of black people who saw and heard Miss Franklin were more than an audience. They were part of a black interaction. They came not only to see and hear "Lady Soul" . . . but also to participate with her in an **exultation** of her blackness.

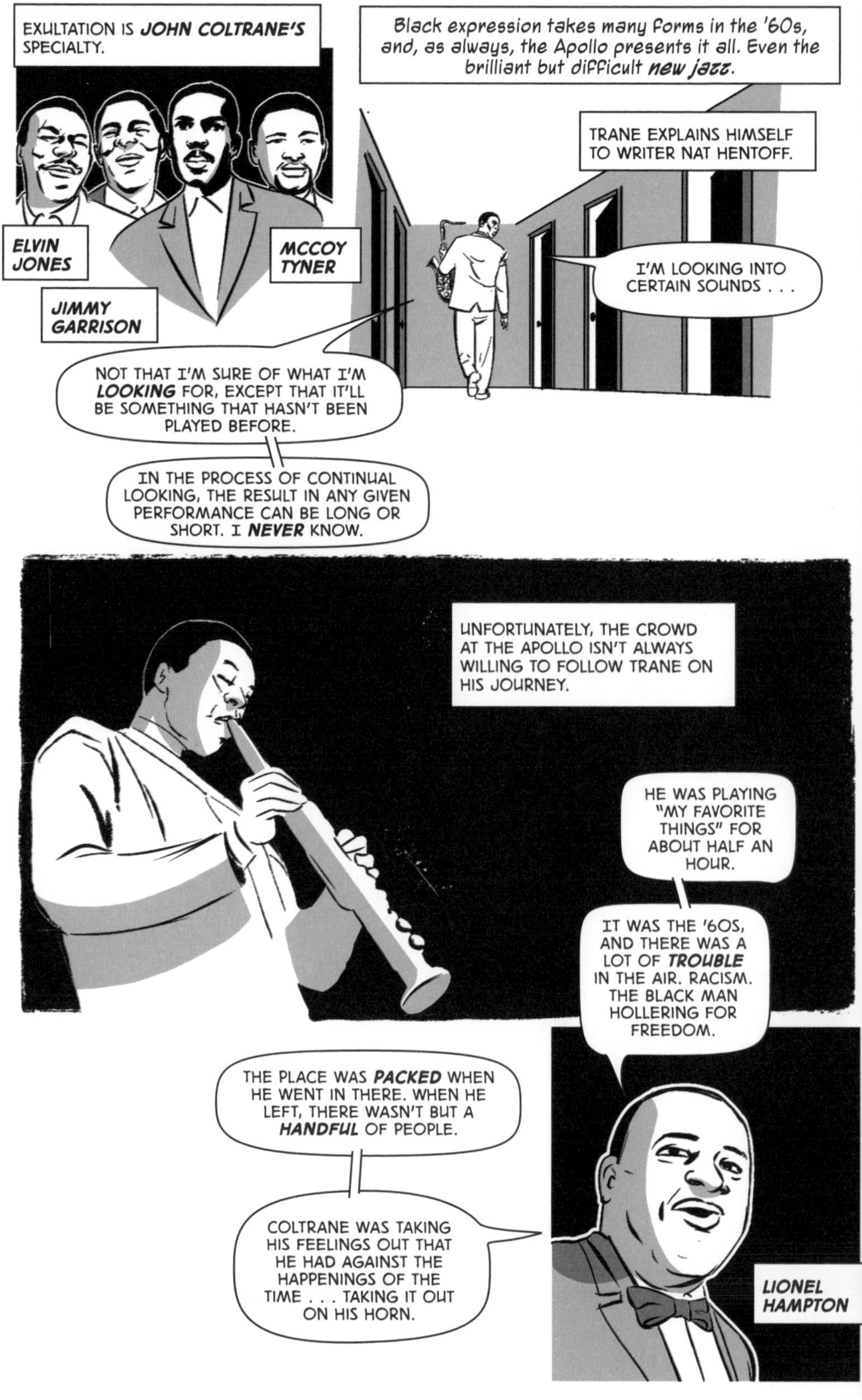
EXULTATION IS ***JOHN COLTRANE'S*** SPECIALTY.
ELVIN JONES
JIMMY GARRISON
MCCOY TYNER
Black expression takes many forms in the '60s, and, as always, the Apollo presents it all. Even the brilliant but difficult ***new jazz***.
TRANE EXPLAINS HIMSELF TO WRITER NAT HENTOFF.
I'M LOOKING INTO CERTAIN SOUNDS . . .
NOT THAT I'M SURE OF WHAT I'M ***LOOKING*** FOR, EXCEPT THAT IT'LL BE SOMETHING THAT HASN'T BEEN PLAYED BEFORE.
IN THE PROCESS OF CONTINUAL LOOKING, THE RESULT IN ANY GIVEN PERFORMANCE CAN BE LONG OR SHORT. I ***NEVER*** KNOW.
UNFORTUNATELY, THE CROWD AT THE APOLLO ISN'T ALWAYS WILLING TO FOLLOW TRANE ON HIS JOURNEY.
HE WAS PLAYING "MY FAVORITE THINGS" FOR ABOUT HALF AN HOUR.
IT WAS THE '60S, AND THERE WAS A LOT OF ***TROUBLE*** IN THE AIR. RACISM. THE BLACK MAN HOLLERING FOR FREEDOM.
THE PLACE WAS ***PACKED*** WHEN HE WENT IN THERE. WHEN HE LEFT, THERE WASN'T BUT A ***HANDFUL*** OF PEOPLE.
COLTRANE WAS TAKING HIS FEELINGS OUT THAT HE HAD AGAINST THE HAPPENINGS OF THE TIME . . . TAKING IT OUT ON HIS HORN.
LIONEL HAMPTON

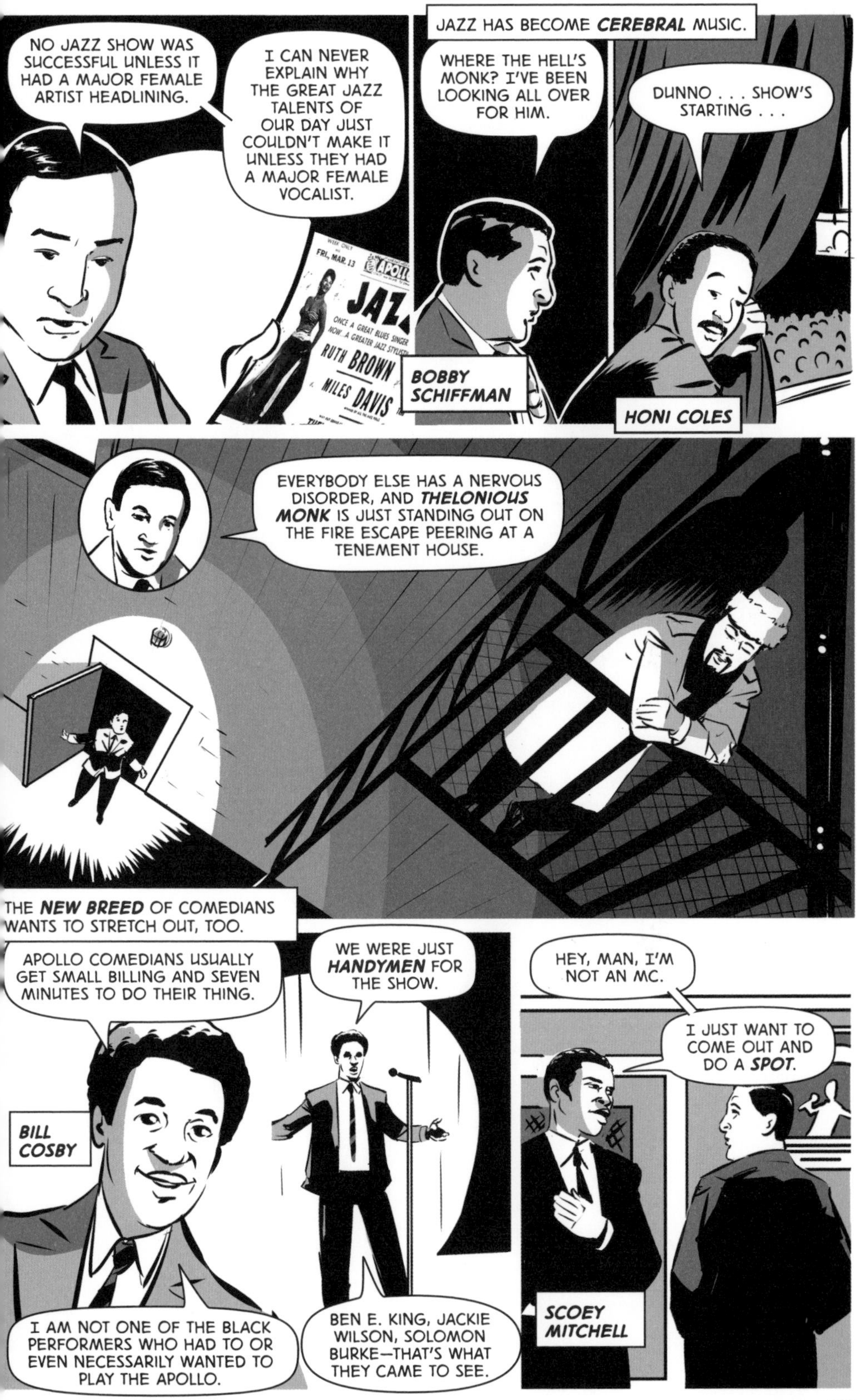
NO JAZZ SHOW WAS SUCCESSFUL UNLESS IT HAD A MAJOR FEMALE ARTIST HEADLINING.
I CAN NEVER EXPLAIN WHY THE GREAT JAZZ TALENTS OF OUR DAY JUST COULDN'T MAKE IT UNLESS THEY HAD A MAJOR FEMALE VOCALIST.
FRI., MAR. 13
JAZZ
ONCE A GREAT BLUES SINGER NOW A GREATER JAZZ STYLIST
RUTH BROWN
MILES DAVIS
JAZZ HAS BECOME ***CEREBRAL*** MUSIC.
WHERE THE HELL'S MONK? I'VE BEEN LOOKING ALL OVER FOR HIM.
BOBBY SCHIFFMAN
DUNNO . . . SHOW'S STARTING . . .
HONI COLES
EVERYBODY ELSE HAS A NERVOUS DISORDER, AND ***THELONIOUS MONK*** IS JUST STANDING OUT ON THE FIRE ESCAPE PEERING AT A TENEMENT HOUSE.
THE ***NEW BREED*** OF COMEDIANS WANTS TO STRETCH OUT, TOO.
APOLLO COMEDIANS USUALLY GET SMALL BILLING AND SEVEN MINUTES TO DO THEIR THING.
BILL COSBY
I AM NOT ONE OF THE BLACK PERFORMERS WHO HAD TO OR EVEN NECESSARILY WANTED TO PLAY THE APOLLO.
WE WERE JUST ***HANDYMEN*** FOR THE SHOW.
BEN E. KING, JACKIE WILSON, SOLOMON BURKE—THAT'S WHAT THEY CAME TO SEE.
HEY, MAN, I'M NOT AN MC.
I JUST WANT TO COME OUT AND DO A ***SPOT***.
SCOEY MITCHELL

THE FIRST TIME **RICHARD PRYOR** PLAYED THE APOLLO WE PAID HIM $350 AND HE WAS OUTRAGEOUS!

YOU KNOW THE OLD ADAGE ABOUT BLACK FOLKS HAVING RHYTHM?

WELL, ON THE FINALE, EVERYTHING RICHARD DID WAS INTENTIONALLY **OUT OF SYNC**.

HE WAS IN THE WRONG KEY. HE WAS TAPPING HIS FOOT AT THE WRONG BEAT.

THE REST ONSTAGE KEPT MUGGING WITH HIM. HE WAS A BRILLIANT COMIC!

BOBBY SCHIFFMAN

COUNT BASIE, BILLY ECKSTINE, COLES AND ATKINS, AND **FREDA PAYNE**

HE WAS **DIRTY**, AND THERE WERE PEOPLE WHO WALKED.

BUT RICHIE WAS BEFORE HIS TIME. HIS COMEDY ROUTINES WERE VERY STREET-ORIENTED AND **FRESH**. THE PEOPLE JUST LOVED HIM.

OFFSTAGE, RICHIE'S A VERY SOFT-SPOKEN, EASY TO TALK TO, UNASSUMING PERSON.

AS OPPOSED TO **REDD FOXX**, WHO IS ONSTAGE ALL THE TIME. FOXX IS FOXX ALL THE TIME.

REDD FOXX AND BOBBY SCHIFFMAN ARE CLOSE FRIENDS AND **PRANKSTERS**.

Both avid hunters, they even appear together on television on *American Sportsman.*

FOXX, YOU'RE GOING TO HAVE TO TAKE OUT THE **BLUE** STUFF.

I'M NOT GONNA DO IT.

BLUE = DIRTY

PLEASE DON'T SCREW ME OVER, THIS IS A FAMILY THEATER. I CAN'T HAVE YOU JOKING ABOUT FILTHY STUFF . . .

I'M NOT GONNA TAKE IT OUT.

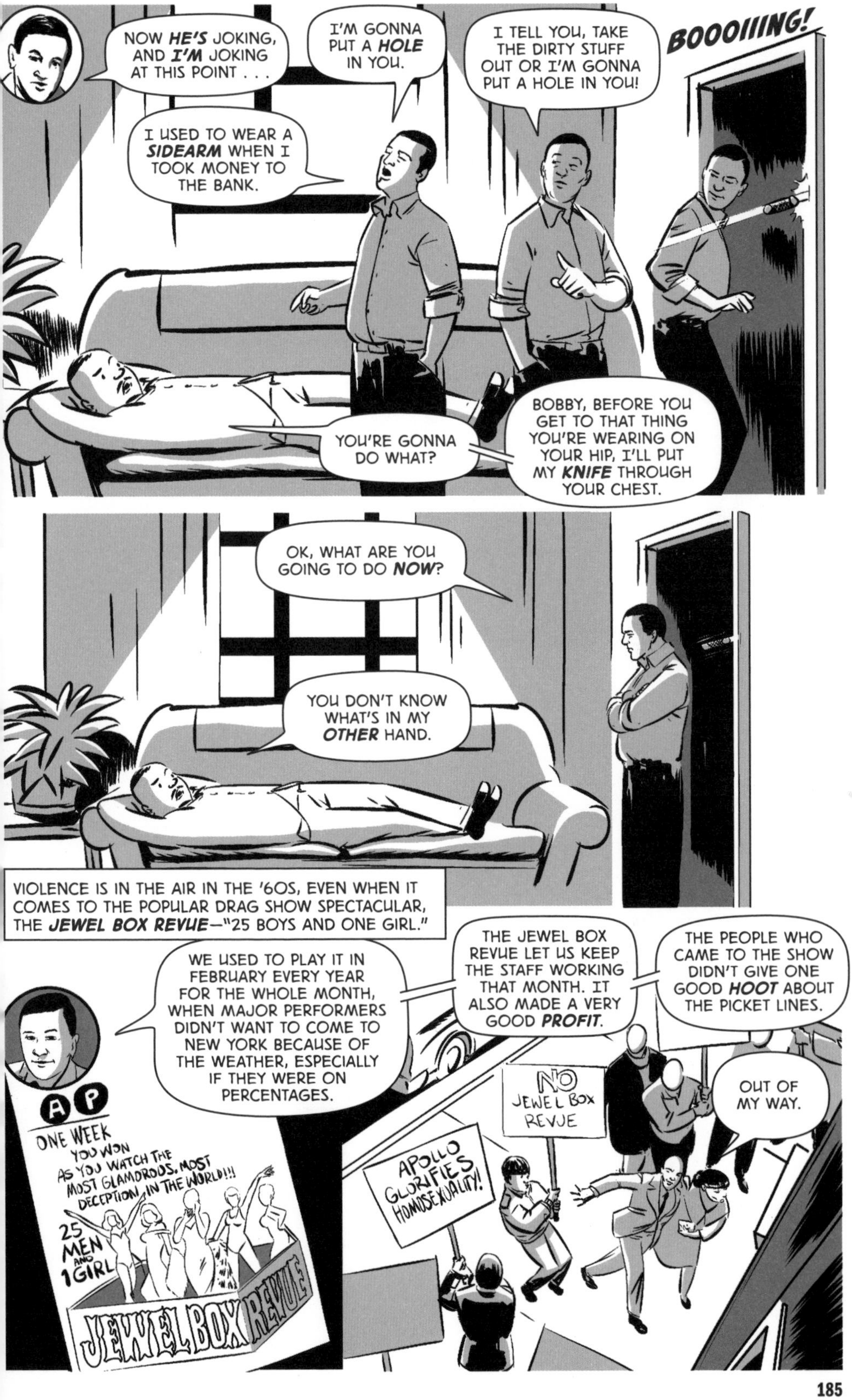
BOOOIIING!
NOW HE'S JOKING, AND I'M JOKING AT THIS POINT . . .
I USED TO WEAR A SIDEARM WHEN I TOOK MONEY TO THE BANK.
I'M GONNA PUT A HOLE IN YOU.
I TELL YOU, TAKE THE DIRTY STUFF OUT OR I'M GONNA PUT A HOLE IN YOU!
YOU'RE GONNA DO WHAT?
BOBBY, BEFORE YOU GET TO THAT THING YOU'RE WEARING ON YOUR HIP, I'LL PUT MY KNIFE THROUGH YOUR CHEST.
OK, WHAT ARE YOU GOING TO DO NOW?
YOU DON'T KNOW WHAT'S IN MY OTHER HAND.
VIOLENCE IS IN THE AIR IN THE '60S, EVEN WHEN IT COMES TO THE POPULAR DRAG SHOW SPECTACULAR, THE JEWEL BOX REVUE—"25 BOYS AND ONE GIRL."
WE USED TO PLAY IT IN FEBRUARY EVERY YEAR FOR THE WHOLE MONTH, WHEN MAJOR PERFORMERS DIDN'T WANT TO COME TO NEW YORK BECAUSE OF THE WEATHER, ESPECIALLY IF THEY WERE ON PERCENTAGES.
THE JEWEL BOX REVUE LET US KEEP THE STAFF WORKING THAT MONTH. IT ALSO MADE A VERY GOOD PROFIT.
THE PEOPLE WHO CAME TO THE SHOW DIDN'T GIVE ONE GOOD HOOT ABOUT THE PICKET LINES.
AP
ONE WEEK
AS YOU WATCH THE MOST GLAMOROUS, MOST DECEPTION IN THE WORLD!!!
25 MEN AND 1 GIRL
JEWEL BOX REVUE
NO JEWEL BOX REVUE
APOLLO GLORIFIES HOMOSEXUALITY!
OUT OF MY WAY.

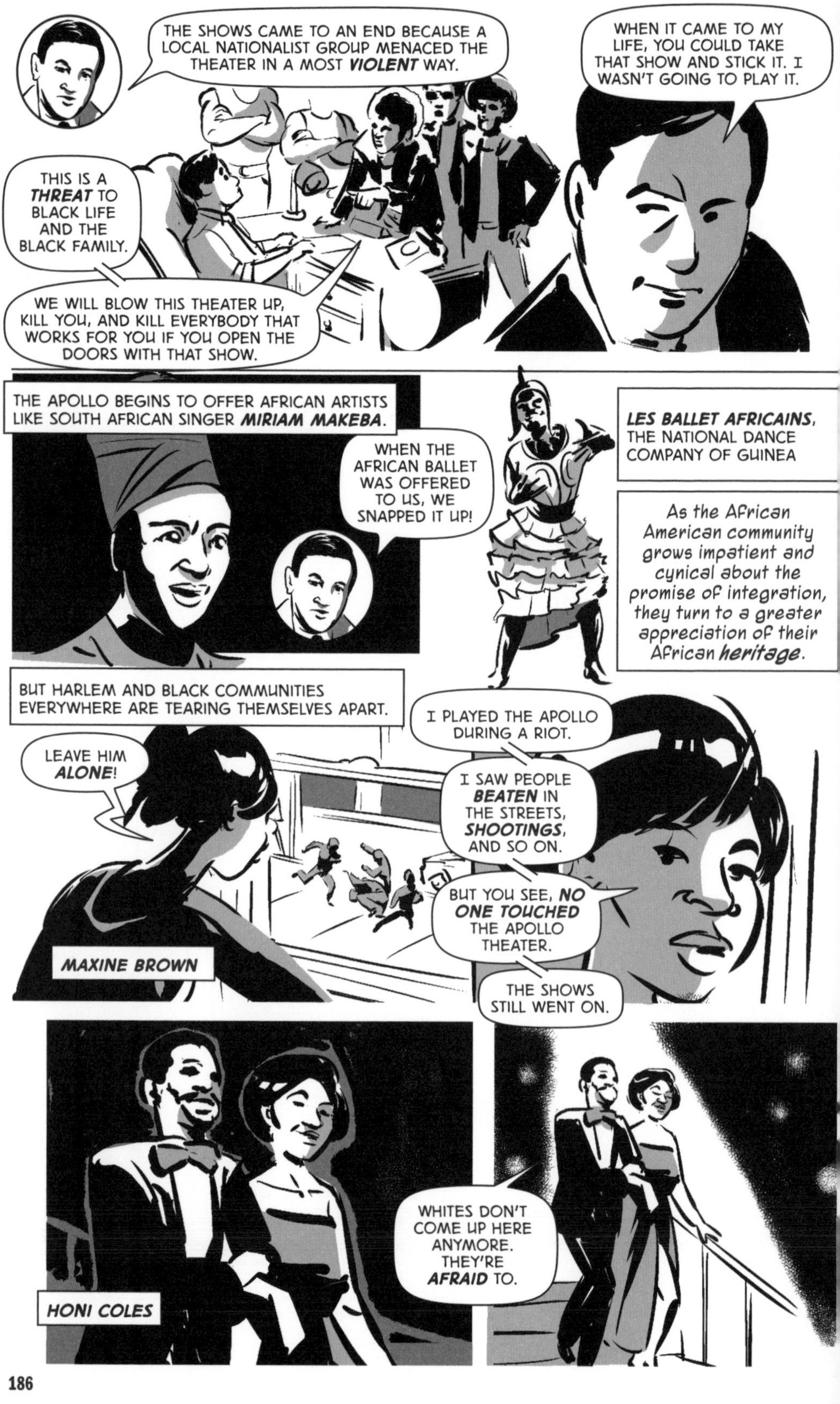

THE SHOWS CAME TO AN END BECAUSE A LOCAL NATIONALIST GROUP MENACED THE THEATER IN A MOST VIOLENT WAY.
THIS IS A THREAT TO BLACK LIFE AND THE BLACK FAMILY.
WE WILL BLOW THIS THEATER UP, KILL YOU, AND KILL EVERYBODY THAT WORKS FOR YOU IF YOU OPEN THE DOORS WITH THAT SHOW.
WHEN IT CAME TO MY LIFE, YOU COULD TAKE THAT SHOW AND STICK IT. I WASN'T GOING TO PLAY IT.
THE APOLLO BEGINS TO OFFER AFRICAN ARTISTS LIKE SOUTH AFRICAN SINGER MIRIAM MAKEBA.
WHEN THE AFRICAN BALLET WAS OFFERED TO US, WE SNAPPED IT UP!
LES BALLET AFRICAINS, THE NATIONAL DANCE COMPANY OF GUINEA
As the African American community grows impatient and cynical about the promise of integration, they turn to a greater appreciation of their African heritage.
BUT HARLEM AND BLACK COMMUNITIES EVERYWHERE ARE TEARING THEMSELVES APART.
LEAVE HIM ALONE!
MAXINE BROWN
I PLAYED THE APOLLO DURING A RIOT.
I SAW PEOPLE BEATEN IN THE STREETS, SHOOTINGS, AND SO ON.
BUT YOU SEE, NO ONE TOUCHED THE APOLLO THEATER.
THE SHOWS STILL WENT ON.
HONI COLES
WHITES DON'T COME UP HERE ANYMORE. THEY'RE AFRAID TO.

Throughout the '60s, the Apollo is *protected*, even when the rest of the community is *devastated*.

In July 1964, the worst riot in Harlem in more than two decades breaks out when an off-duty cop shoots and kills a Harlem teenager.

One dies, 140 are injured, and 500 arrested. The violence spreads to the black neighborhoods of Brooklyn.

Trouble continues in the '60s, culminating in more rioting in the aftermath of the assassination of *Martin Luther King Jr*. in Memphis on April 4, 1968.

Yet, as the Civil Rights movement alters the *consciousness* of the nation, other areas of *opportunity* become available at last to African Americans.

The system the Apollo works within and against for so many years *collapses*.

The general acceptance of black culture into American popular culture is the beginning of something *new*, but it is also the beginning of the *end* for the Apollo Theater.

Ironically, it is the Apollo itself that becomes a *casualty* of this revolution.

CHAPTER 9

The 1970s: Funky

Billboard HOT 100 SINGLES — JAN. 31, 1970

THIS WEEK			TITLE Artist (Producer), Label & Number	
3	3	4	**I WANT YOU BACK** The Jackson 5 (The Corporation), Motown 1157	12

THE FIRST PORTENT OF ONE OF THE GREATEST MUSIC SUCCESS STORIES EVER . . .

The Jacksons had approached James Brown about hiring the then unknown group.

THE *JACKSON 5* WITH THEIR FATHER, JOE—A COUPLE OF YEARS EARLIER

JAMES WOULDN'T DO IT.

SAM MOORE

WE COULDN'T HANDLE THEM AS AN ACT ON THE SHOW WITH US.

WE DIDN'T HAVE THE MONEY BECAUSE WE HAD JUST STARTED MAKING MONEY, AND HAD JUST BOUGHT A BIG OLE BUS.

SO THEY CAME TO TALK TO *US* AT THE APOLLO.

BUT WE TALKED TO HONI COLES, AND HE PUT THEM ON THE AMATEUR SHOW.

DAVE PRATER OF SAM & DAVE

PROBABLY FEBRUARY 1968—SOME SAY IT WAS AUGUST 1967, BUT THE APOLLO WAS CLOSED FOR SUMMER RENOVATIONS THEN.

THE YOUNGSTERS ARE BROUGHT BACK FOR TWO ENCORES AND THEY EASILY WIN.

GLADYS KNIGHT SENDS THEIR DEMO TAPE TO BERRY GORDY AT MOTOWN, BUT HE *PASSES*.

THEIR FIRST PROFESSIONAL APOLLO ENGAGEMENT STARTS THE WEEK OF MAY 24, 1968.

The unknowns are mistakenly called the *Jive Five* in the *Amsterdam News* preview.

DAMN!

ABOUT SIX MONTHS LATER, BERRY GORDY HAD A HIT OUT WITH THEM!

THE NEXT THING I HEARD, DIANA ROSS HAD THEM.

DAVE PRATER

If ever one can say the rest is history, *this* is that time!

JAMES BROWN IS AS BIG AS THEY GET IN THE EARLY '70S.

- IN 1971, JAMES BROWN IS THE HIGHEST-PAID BLACK ENTERTAINER IN THE WORLD.

- BETWEEN 1969 AND 1971 HE HAS SEVENTEEN TOP-TEN HITS ON THE RHYTHM-AND-BLUES CHARTS.

- THE MEDIA CALL HIM THE "BLACK MESSIAH" AND "THE MOST POWERFUL BLACK MAN IN AMERICA."

- HE OWNS THREE OF THE ONLY FIVE BLACK-OWNED RADIO STATIONS IN THE COUNTRY.

- HIS EMPIRE IS OVERSEEN BY A STAFF OF EIGHTY-FIVE WITH AN ANNUAL PAYROLL OF A MILLION DOLLARS.

- HE FILLS YANKEE STADIUM FOR A CONCERT ON JUNE 22, 1968.

AND THE APOLLO IS THERE FOR HIM, TOO, WHEN THINGS GO SUDDENLY, WILDLY **BAD**.

YET JAMES BROWN **NEVER** FORGETS THE APOLLO, EVEN THOUGH HE MAKES MUCH MORE ELSEWHERE.

JAMES BROWN

JAMES BROWN ENDORSES NIXON IN 1972 AND IS BADLY **SHAKEN** BY WHAT HE SEES AT HIS FIRST APOLLO SHOW AFTER THE ELECTION.

James Brown Nixon's Clown

Right On!

Get the Clown Outta Town!

ONE OF BROWN'S ENTOURAGE APPEARS ONSTAGE AT THE OPENING SHOW TO DEFEND THE SINGER.

AFTER THE NIXON THING— IT WAS LIKE A BIG **BOMB**.

BLAH BLAH BLAH

WE WAS CATCHING **HELL**.

DANNY RAY

IT **HURT**. EVERY LOCATION ON THE CIRCUIT SUDDENLY BECAME ALREADY "BOOKED," UNAVAILABLE TO US, NO OPEN DATES FOR US TO PLAY.

ST. CLAIR PINCKNEY

Yet even with all the controversy, the usual lines of James Brown fans *throng* 125th Street all week.

IF THE APOLLO IS TO KEEP GOING IN THIS NEW ERA, IT NEEDS TO BE ABLE TO BOOK THE **SUPERSTARS** WHOSE CAREERS IT HAS ALWAYS SUPPORTED AND ENCOURAGED . . .

YOU HAVE TO PLAY FOR THE PEOPLE OF **HARLEM**!

SMOKEY ROBINSON, JAMES BROWN, SAMMY DAVIS JR., DIONNE WARWICK, GLADYS KNIGHT, AND **NANCY WILSON**

. . . EVEN IF THEY CAN NOW MAKE **MUCH** MORE MONEY ELSEWHERE WITHOUT DOING AS MANY SHOWS.

BOBBY SCHIFFMAN

TOWARD THE END, IN THE '70S, AN ACT THAT WAS IN DEMAND COULD MAKE MORE MONEY IN **ONE NIGHT** IN A BIGGER AND BETTER LOCATION THAN THEY COULD MAKE AT THE APOLLO IN A **WHOLE WEEK**.

AND, IF YOU HAD AN ACT IN THE **APOLLO** FOR SIX DOLLARS, THAT ACT COULD SELL TICKETS FOR SIXTEEN DOLLARS **DOWNTOWN**, OR TWENTY DOLLARS OR FIFTY DOLLARS.

The Apollo: 1,683 seats

Carnegie Hall: 2,800

Lincoln Center: 4,500

The Felt Forum: 4,500

Madison Square Garden: 20,000

The Nassau Coliseum: 19,000

The Byrne Arena: 22,000

WE ASKED ACTS TO WORK AT A GREAT FINANCIAL **SACRIFICE**.

Many top stars are happy to come home and help keep the Apollo going.

SELLING OUT AN ENTIRE WEEK *IN ADVANCE* HAS NEVER HAPPENED BEFORE.

APOLLO

Gladys Knight and the Pips
ENTIRE WEEK—SOLD OUT!

Gladys Knight and the Pips
ENTIRE WEEK—SOLD OUT!

OUT

Jam-packed, big star shows are very profitable.

I GET GOOSE PIMPLES THINKING ABOUT IT NOW . . .

EARLY ON, WE GAVE PERFORMERS A SHOWCASE WHERE THEY COULD NURTURE THEIR TALENT . . . AND THEY *OWED* US.

THE FIRST TIME I PLAYED GLADYS KNIGHT AND THE PIPS, I PAID THEM $800 FOR THIRTY-ONE SHOWS OVER SEVEN DAYS.

THE LAST TIME, I PAID $80,000 FOR SIXTEEN SHOWS.

That is a lot of money for the Apollo, but she can make that in one or two shows in a larger venue.

THERE WAS NO WAY, BASED ON THE LONGSTANDING PERSONAL RELATIONSHIP I HAD WITH THEM, THAT THEY COULD SAY NO TO ME IF I SAID *I NEED YOU.*

BOBBY SCHIFFMAN

DIONNE WARWICK *COMES BACK* EVERY YEAR, STARTING IN THE LATE '60S.

I PRACTICALLY PAID MONEY TO GO IN AND DO IT THE WAY I WANTED TO DO IT.

AND THEY MADE AN AWFUL LOT OF MONEY, WHICH IS GOOD, BECAUSE IT KEPT THE DOORS OPEN.

YOU WILL *NEVER* CLOSE THE APOLLO. NOT AS LONG AS I LIVE!

THE APOLLO WANTS DIONNE TO FEEL APPRECIATED, AND THEY PULL OUT ALL THE STOPS.

IT GAVE THEM THE *LEVERAGE* THEY NEEDED TO ATTRACT OTHER PERFORMERS.

THE THEATER WAS *GORGEOUS*. THEY BUILT SCENERY FOR ME. WE DID LIGHTING.

THE SOUND HAS ALWAYS BEEN IMPECCABLE IN THAT THEATER.

AFTER THAT, LOU RAWLS WENT BACK IN, NANCY WILSON, THE TEMPTATIONS . . .

I BROUGHT *EVERYBODY* BACK TO THE APOLLO!

NANCY, IT'S GETTING REALLY *TOUGH* TO GO ON. YOU CAN PLAY ANYWHERE YOU WANT NOW.

YOU HAVE TO KEEP THE APOLLO GOING! IT'S *NEEDED*!

BOBBY SCHIFFMAN

NANCY WILSON

I PLAYED THERE BECAUSE I FELT I SHOULD.

I PLAYED THERE BECAUSE THE SCHIFFMANS WERE THE KIND OF PEOPLE YOU SHOULD GO PLACES FOR.

I PLAYED THERE BECAUSE IT MADE THEM FEEL GOOD.

AGAIN, THE APOLLO DOES EVERYTHING IT CAN TO MAKE IT *SPECIAL*.

NANCY WILSON

THE AUDIENCE AND THE PEOPLE OF THE COMMUNITY NEEDED US PERFORMERS.

I PLAYED THERE BECAUSE I KNEW THEY *WANTED* ME THERE.

EVERY PERSON WHO WORKED THE APOLLO HAD A TUX ON.

THAT WAS QUITE A NIGHT.

IT'S GREAT FOR THE APOLLO WHILE IT LASTS.

IN ALL THE YEARS THAT THE APOLLO WAS IN BUSINESS, 1970 TO 1974 WERE THE *BANNER YEARS* FINANCIALLY.

The Apollo can also thank a new crop of hit-makers for that.

If Detroit is the capital of black music in the '60s, *Philadelphia* becomes the star-making center of black America in the early '70s.

THE *PHILADELPHIA INTERNATIONAL* RECORD LABEL LAUNCHES IN 1971.

KENNY GAMBLE, LEON HUFF, AND *THOM BELL*

THE NEW PHILLY STARS KEEP THE APOLLO BUSY.

THE SOUND OF PHILADELPHIA

TSOP

THE DELFONICS

THE THREE DEGREES

THE O'JAYS

SOME, LIKE THE SPINNERS, WHO WERE APOLLO OPENERS FOR YEARS, COME BACK AS BIG STARS IN THE '70S.

THE STYLISTICS

Hey Mister Big Man, you're killing me!

PHILADELPHIA NATIVE *PATTI LABELLE* AND HER VARIOUS BLUEBELLES HAVE BEEN PLAYING THE APOLLO SINCE THEIR STRUGGLING DAYS IN THE EARLY '60S.

I REMEMBER WHEN WE WERE NOT MAKING VERY MUCH MONEY, WE'D BUY HOT DOGS AND KEEP THEM ON THE LIGHTBULBS ALL DAY!

They *treasure* the Apollo.

THE SPINNERS

If you don't know me by now...

ONE OF THE BIGGEST PHILADELPHIA INTERNATIONAL GROUPS IS *HAROLD MELVIN AND THE BLUE NOTES,* FEATURING *TEDDY PENDERGRASS.*

Even when the giant 1974 hit, "Lady Marmalade," makes Patti's Labelle the first African American group to play the *Metropolitan Opera House.*

PENDERGRASS PLAYS THE HARD-LUCK SEXPOT.

THEIR 1975 APOLLO ENGAGEMENT STARTS OUT STRONG.

BUT AFTER *ARGUING* WITH HAROLD AT THE APOLLO, TEDDY DOESN'T SHOW UP FOR THE SUNDAY SHOWS.

LADIES AND GENTLEMEN, WE REGRET TO INFORM YOU THAT TEDDY PENDERGRASS WILL *NOT* BE PERFORMING WITH THE GROUP . . .

The Apollo takes a big hit at a precarious time for the theater.

THE BUSINESS STARTED *CHANGING* A LOT.

BLACK PERFORMERS STARTED GETTING PLAYED ON WHITE STATIONS, AND THE CAREERS AND THE MONEY STARTED GROWING.

This great *breakthrough* for African American artists is *bad news* for Harlem's High Spot.

LESLIE UGGAMS

A LOT OF PEOPLE FELT, "I'M AT THE POINT WHERE I DON'T HAVE TO DO FOUR OR FIVE SHOWS A DAY."

THEY HAD SO MUCH OTHER INCOME FROM RECORD ROYALTIES, AND LATER ON TELEVISION SHOWS, AND FURTHER ON EVEN MOTION-PICTURE PRODUCTION.

WHEN THEY DECIDE TO WORK LESS AND LESS, THEY ARE *NOT* GOING TO WORK 125TH STREET.

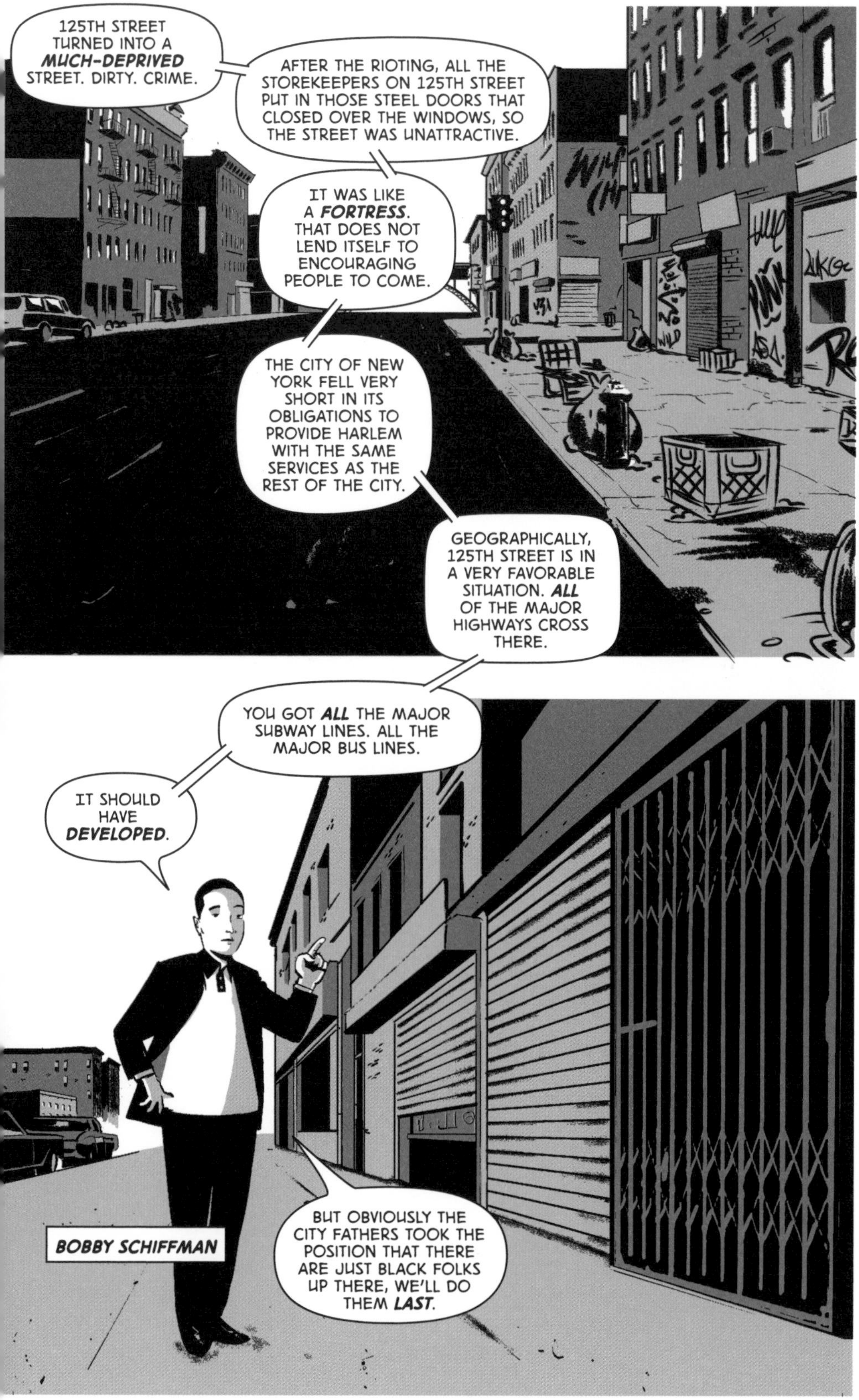
125TH STREET TURNED INTO A ***MUCH-DEPRIVED*** STREET. DIRTY. CRIME.
AFTER THE RIOTING, ALL THE STOREKEEPERS ON 125TH STREET PUT IN THOSE STEEL DOORS THAT CLOSED OVER THE WINDOWS, SO THE STREET WAS UNATTRACTIVE.
IT WAS LIKE A ***FORTRESS***. THAT DOES NOT LEND ITSELF TO ENCOURAGING PEOPLE TO COME.
THE CITY OF NEW YORK FELL VERY SHORT IN ITS OBLIGATIONS TO PROVIDE HARLEM WITH THE SAME SERVICES AS THE REST OF THE CITY.
GEOGRAPHICALLY, 125TH STREET IS IN A VERY FAVORABLE SITUATION. ***ALL*** OF THE MAJOR HIGHWAYS CROSS THERE.
YOU GOT ***ALL*** THE MAJOR SUBWAY LINES. ALL THE MAJOR BUS LINES.
IT SHOULD HAVE ***DEVELOPED***.
BOBBY SCHIFFMAN
BUT OBVIOUSLY THE CITY FATHERS TOOK THE POSITION THAT THERE ARE JUST BLACK FOLKS UP THERE, WE'LL DO THEM ***LAST***.

AT THE HEIGHT OF HOLLYWOOD'S BRIEF ENCHANTMENT WITH BLACK FILMS, THE APOLLO CAN ONLY BOOK CHEAP B-GRADE QUICKIES OR PLAYED-OUT MOVIES.

By the mid-'70s, the Apollo is only presenting twenty-two weeks of live entertainment a year.

To fill in *empty* weeks, the theater turns to *movies* that might appeal to the African American community.

A story of Southern hospitality.

a WILLIAM WYLER film
THE LIBERATION OF L.B. JONES

UPTOWN SATURDAY NIGHT

THE APOLLO FIGHTS TO GET A MAJOR BLACK MOVIE *PREMIERE*.

Nearly every *Uptown Saturday Night* star has appeared at the Apollo, even director and co-star *Sidney Poitier*.

Instead, Warner Bros. opens the film on Broadway and shuttles premiere-goers up to Harlem for an *after-party*.

You can still go uptown without getting your head beat in by going downtown to see Uptown Saturday Night.

ADDING GREAT *INSULT* TO THIS INJURY IS A HORRENDOUSLY *TONE-DEAF* AD.

THE APOLLO *FIGHTS BACK*, PROTESTS, AND EVEN FILES A RESTRAINT OF TRADE SUIT AGAINST HOLLYWOOD.

Cleopatra Jones and the Casino of Gold

WARNER BROS. AGREES TO OPEN ITS NEXT BIG *"BLAXPLOITATION"* FLICK SIMULTANEOUSLY AT THE APOLLO AND ON 86TH STREET.

JIM CROW LIVES! 125th IS STILL THE BACK OF THE BUS, MOVIEWISE THAT IS.

"IT'S A GREAT VICTORY FOR THE PEOPLE OF THIS COMMUNITY! MOVIE TIMES AT THE APOLLO ARE . . ."

VARIETY

New York, Wednesday, August 6, 1975

BLACKS SHUN PIC AT HARLEM SITE
"Apollo Experiment" Fails to Pull Locals

BUT IT DOESN'T WORK OUT.

Peril is knocking on the Apollo's door.

OH, COME IN . . .

OH, JESUS, **NO!**

WE GOT ROBBED TWO OR THREE TIMES AT THE APOLLO.

I WAS JUST GLAD THEY DIDN'T **KILL** US.

WELL, YOU KNOW WHAT IT IS, ALL RIGHT . . .

GLADYS KNIGHT

SMOKEY ROBINSON COMES BACK FOR AN SRO SHOW IN DECEMBER 1975.

The Apollo and the great stars who continue to make it their home are no longer *immune* to the violence and despair in the streets.

You've really got a hold on me...

SOME FOOL LIGHTING FIRECRACKERS?

The outside world *crashes in* on the Apollo.

AN EIGHTEEN-YEAR-OLD RECENTLY PAROLED FOR ROBBERY IS **SHOT DEAD** AND TWO OTHERS WOUNDED.

It is said the victim knows enemies are trying to get him. But he probably thinks he's *safe* at the Apollo.

It is a place that is respected and revered; to hurt it would be to hurt oneself, to commit violence there would be to commit violence in one's own *home*.

LIKE A **PRO**, SMOKEY ROBINSON FINISHES OUT A SUCCESSFUL WEEK, BUT SAYS HE WON'T COME BACK.

The gunman obviously doesn't feel that way.

WITHIN A MONTH, IN JANUARY 1976, THE APOLLO THEATER **CLOSES** ITS DOORS.

THE APOLLO HAS BEEN QUIETLY UP FOR SALE SINCE THE MID-'60S.

WITH THE ADVENT OF MALCOLM X AND THE STRONG GROWTH OF NATIONALISTIC PRIDE IN THE BLACK COMMUNITY . . .

. . . WHICH WAS A VERY VALID AND WORTHWHILE FORCE . . .

CLOSED
Thanks for the Memories

BOBBY SCHIFFMAN

IT WAS WITH THE GREATEST HEARTACHE THAT I RELINQUISHED MY INVOLVEMENT WITH THAT COMMUNITY.

. . . THERE CAME THE FEELING THAT THE BLACK COMMUNITY SHOULD OWN AND OPERATE THEIR **OWN** INSTITUTIONS.

WE HAD SEVERAL OFFERS FROM WHITE BUSINESSMEN WHO WANTED TO BUY THE APOLLO, BUT WE ALWAYS TURNED THEM DOWN.

FOR YEARS, THE AIM OF MANAGEMENT OF THE APOLLO WAS TO SELL IT TO A BLACK ENTREPRENEUR.

Ads appear in the classified sections of the *Wall Street Journal*, the *New York Times*, and the *Village Voice* in 1975.

WE WERE WAITING FOR A BLACK ORGANIZATION TO COME ALONG THAT HAD THE KNOWLEDGE, WISDOM, AND MONEY TO BUY THE APOLLO.

Classifieds

For Sale; Harlem's World Famous Apollo Theater.

ASKING PRICE: TWO MILLION DOLLARS, INCLUDING AN "OFFICE BUILDING"

Since 1972, plans and deals have been floated by prominent African American figures.

Nothing works. Bobby takes a job at booking agency, *Universal Attractions*.

UNIVERSAL ATTRACTIONS
BOBBY SCHIFFMAN
BOOKING AGENT

MANHATTAN BOROUGH PRESIDENT **PERCY SUTTON** AND *AMSTERDAM NEWS* OWNER **CLARENCE JONES**

NEW YORK Amsterdam News

A Detroit promoter mounts a successful 1977 Christmas show in the theater, which has sat largely empty and unused for two years.

Millie Jackson
The Manhattans
Harold Melvin and the Blue Notes

IT LOOKS LIKE A *RATHOLE*.

Not coincidentally, this show package includes all Universal Attractions acts.

Billboard

Apollo Theater Purchased

The Apollo has been purchased by an unnamed group of individuals. The new owners are reported to be from the Harlem area."

MARCH 1978. ONE ELMER T. MORRIS IS THE ONLY PERSON PUBLICLY ASSOCIATED WITH THE LISTED OWNER—THE 253 REALTY CORPORATION.

THEY SAY IT'S *NICKY BARNES* WHO BOUGHT IT.

THE BIGGEST DRUG DEALER IN HARLEM?

The theater needs a $350,000 *overhaul* to be operational.

YEAH MAN, WORD IS HE HAS SCHIFFMAN'S OLD OFFICE.

1978

All New Apollo Welcomes
RALPH McDONALD MAY 5 6 7

THE HARLEM-BORN AFRO-LATIN PERCUSSIONIST'S ROLLICKING "CALYPSO BREAKDOWN" IS HEATING UP BOTH THE DISCO AND JAZZ SCENES.

THIS IS THE BIGGEST THING UP HERE IN *YEARS*!

YEAH, MAN, THE STREET'S BEEN *DEAD* SINCE THEY CLOSED THE APOLLO . . .

TICKETS

199

The crowd is so *happy* the Apollo is back that, after waiting through *problems* with the theater's new reserved seating system . . .

GLADYS KNIGHT, WILSON PICKETT, WILLIS REED, PAUL SIMON, HARLEM REP. *CHARLES RANGEL*

. . . they don't even mind waiting again as the show starts nearly an hour late . . .

. . . and again as two banks of speakers fail.

I USED TO LIVE EIGHT BLOCKS FROM HERE. THIS COMMUNITY GAVE ME THE *FUNDAMENTALS* I WENT OUT INTO THE WORLD WITH.

NOW I CAN BRING SOMETHING *HOME* TO THE COMMUNITY.

RALPH MCDONALD

WE ARE FAMILY!

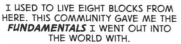

SISTER SLEDGE

1978 is a *hopeful* year as the Apollo once again presents the latest thing— disco—

—and brings back old *favorites.*

I'D RATHER PLAY FOR MY FOLKS HERE THAN AT THE WHITE HOUSE!

JAMES BROWN

IT IS HARD TO REGULARLY BOOK TALENT, THOUGH, AS MARTIN TELLS THE *AMSTERDAM NEWS* . . .

WE'RE OFFERING THEM *TOP DOLLAR* FOR A HOUSE OUR SIZE FOR THEM TO PLAY HERE FROM THREE TO FIVE DAYS.

THE *O'JAYS* COLDLY REJECTED OUR $40,000 OFFER.

APOLLO TALENT COORDINATOR *SPARKY MARTIN*

I DON'T KNOW WHO THESE NEW OWNERS ARE, AND I'M NOT TAKING ANY *CHANCES*.

AND, I HEAR THEY OWE BACK TAXES, TOO.

The O'Jays

APOLLO

Bob Marley and the Wailers

Now only the *toughest* aren't afraid to play the Apollo . . . to still make it home.

THURSDAY, OCTOBER 25, 1979, THE BEGINNING OF A FOUR-NIGHT STAND

It's Marley's first time back in the city since surviving an assassination attempt in Jamaica.

Unsatisfied with being the darling of white hipsters, Bob Marley wants to *reach out* more directly to African Americans . . . and he knows where to do it.

RITA MARLEY AND *JUDY MOWATT* AS THE *I-TWOS*.

BOB MARLEY & THE WAILERS

SURVIVAL

I SHOT THE SHERIFF

IT IS A *PROPHETIC* TITLE FOR THE THEATER, TOO.

The Wailers become the first *reggae* band to play the Apollo as Marley proclaims a pan-African message with a militant new album.

THE IRS MAKES ITS MOVE THE VERY NEXT MONTH AND **SHUTS** THE APOLLO FOR FAILURE TO TURN OVER PAYROLL TAXES.

NEVER DID TRUST THOSE NEW OWNERS.

OLE NICKY BARNES GOT LIFE AND THEN **RATS** THEM ALL OUT TRYING TO GET A PRESIDENTIAL PARDON! BUNCH OF THEM GUYS GOT ARRESTED.

HE SAID THAT ELMER MORRIS USED TO BE A COP AND TAUGHT NICKY'S BOYS HOW TO SHOOT!

DOLL THOMAS, MARCH 1, 1980

DECLARED **BANKRUPTCY** OF COURSE. SAW THAT COMING . . .

BUT MAN, THE APOLLO AIN'T DONE YET.

IT'S **NEVER** GONNA BE DONE!

GEORGE CLINTON AND "P-FUNK" ARE HEROES IN HARLEM--FUNK ROYALTY.

P-Funk!

Their shows, over the weekend of March 1, 1980, are the *last* live Apollo shows of the original era . . . spectacles of abandon perfectly in keeping with the theater's grand tradition.

GEORGE CLINTON . . .

I KNEW HIM BACK IN THE '50S WITH THE PARLIAMENTS. JERSEY BOY, STARTED SINGING IN HIS BARBERSHOP . . .

TAKES . . . ME . . . *BACK* . . .

Clinton, leader of *Parliament Funkadelic*, bypasses *Madison Square Garden* to help keep the Apollo going.

THE P-FUNK SIGN STANDS FOR CLINTON'S MOTTO: "ONE NATION UNDER A GROOVE."

HEY, WE GONNA SEE FUNKADELIC!

DAMN, WHAT WOULD MR. SCHIFFMAN THINK OF ALL THIS *REEFER* SMOKING?

DOLL THOMAS

NOT MANY *WHITE* PEOPLE . . . WHEN I FIRST GOT HERE WEREN'T HARDLY NO *BLACK* PEOPLE!

LET'S HEAR IT FOR THE *BRIDES OF FUNKENSTEIN!*

A NEW GOLD CURTAIN.

SOME THINGS *NEVER* CHANGE . . .

He is *home*.

There isn't a kid in the house who doesn't envy this guy. He's a star. He's the *show*.

It's Saturday night at the Apollo!

It's Saturday night at the Apollo!

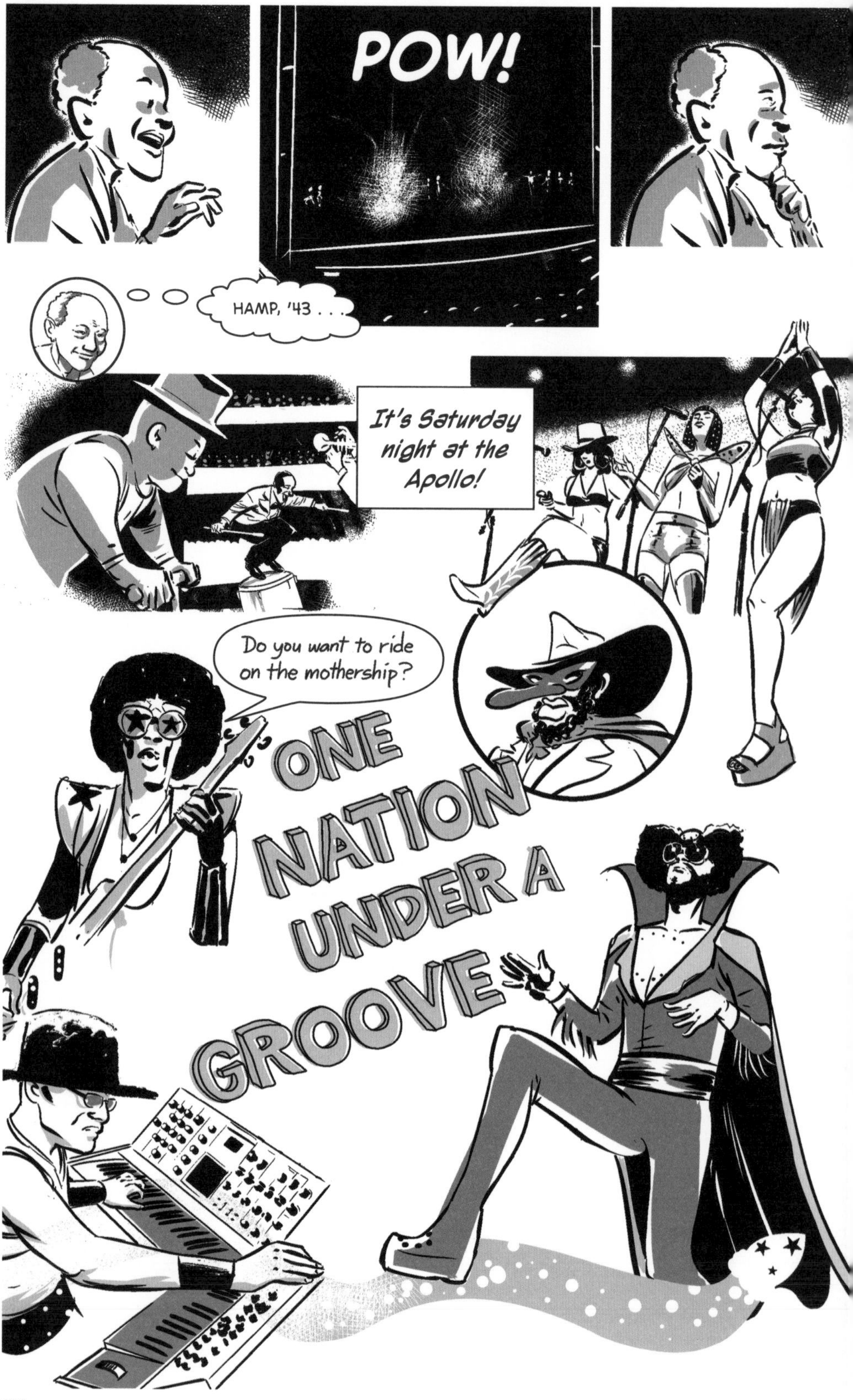
POW!
HAMP, '43 . . .
It's Saturday night at the Apollo!
Do you want to ride on the mothership?
ONE NATION UNDER A GROOVE

It's Saturday night at the Apollo!

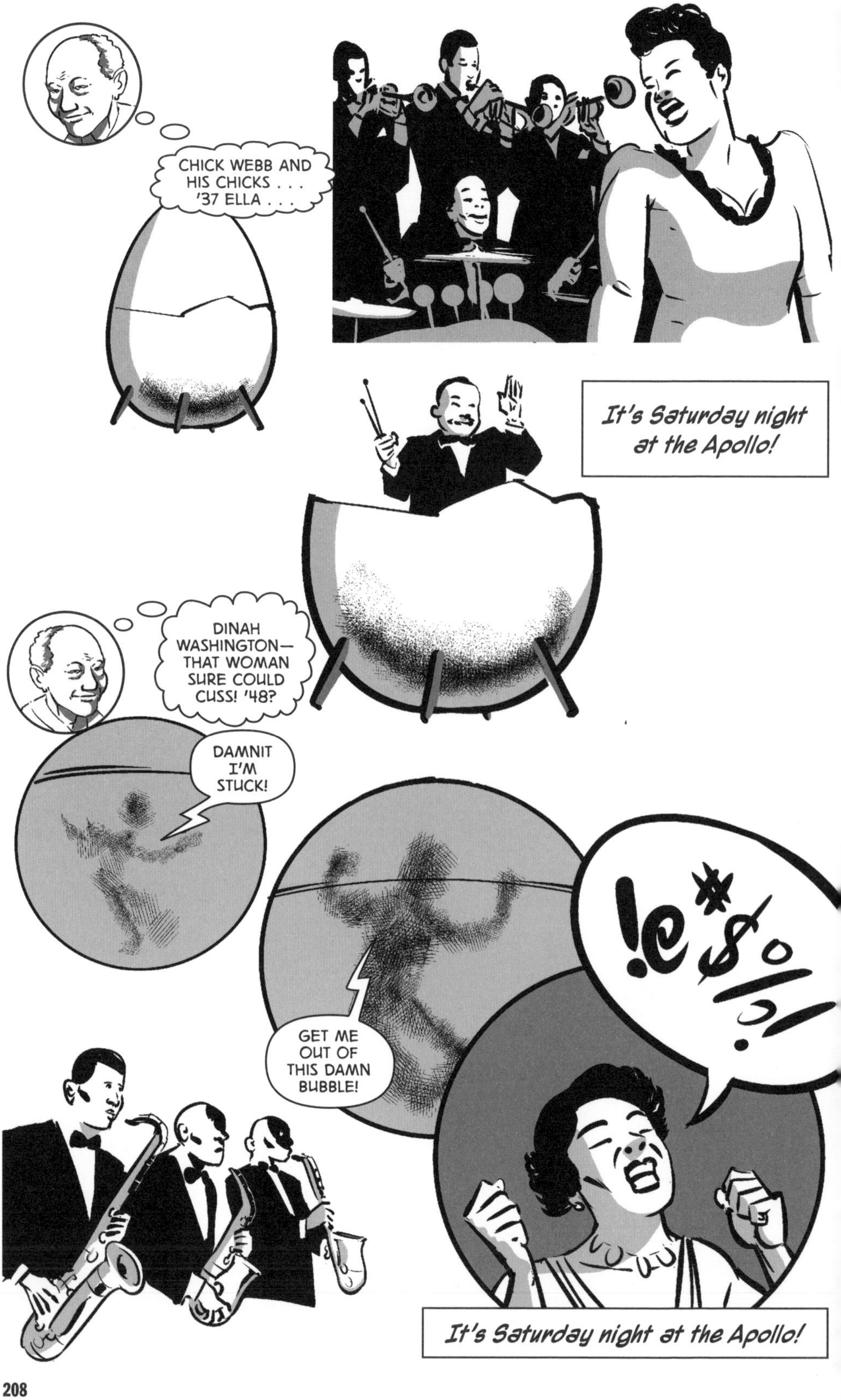
CHICK WEBB AND HIS CHICKS . . . '37 ELLA . . .
It's Saturday night at the Apollo!
DINAH WASHINGTON—THAT WOMAN SURE COULD CUSS! '48?
DAMNIT I'M STUCK!
GET ME OUT OF THIS DAMN BUBBLE!
!@*$%!?!
It's Saturday night at the Apollo!

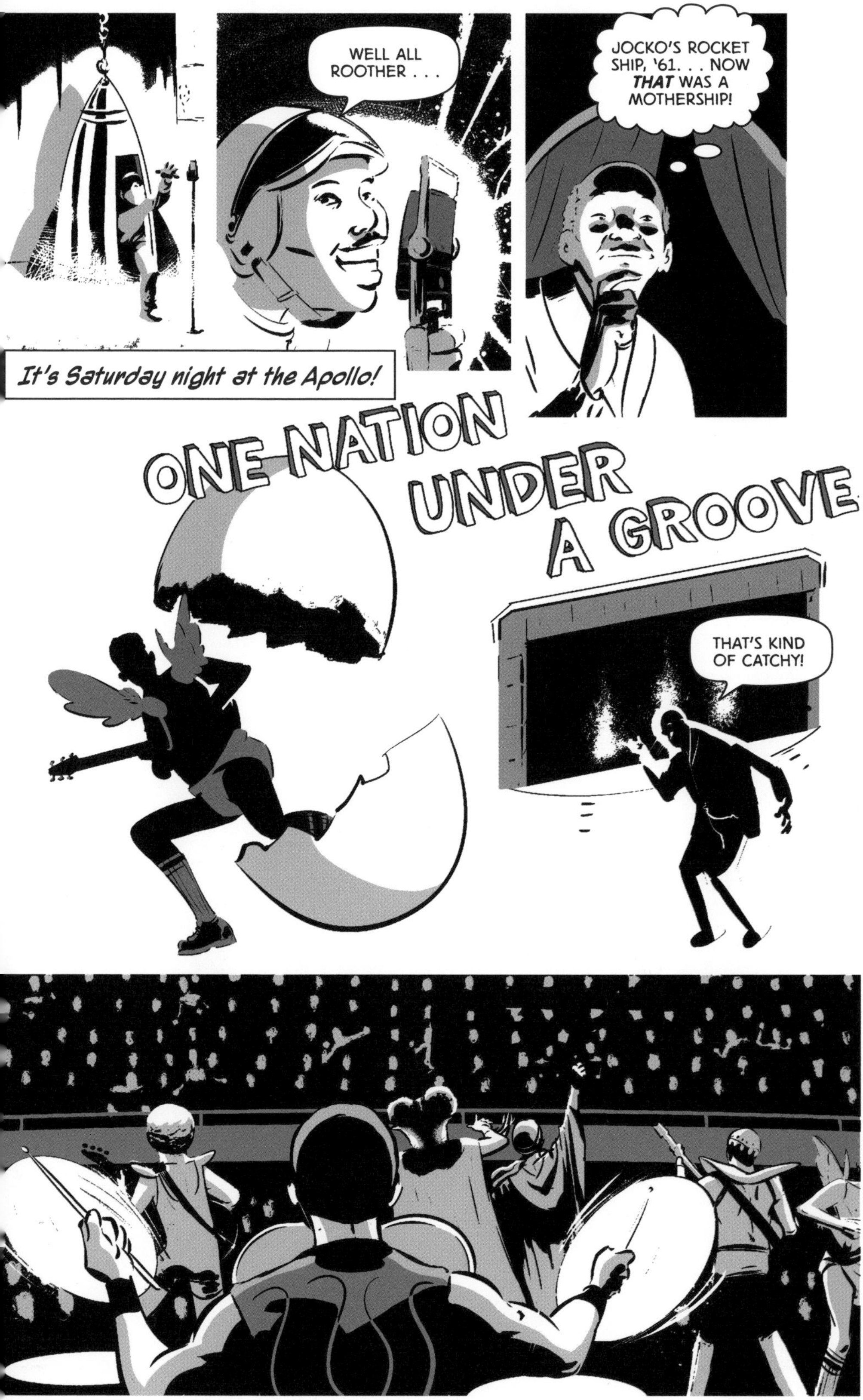
WELL ALL ROOTHER . . .
JOCKO'S ROCKET SHIP, '61. . . NOW THAT WAS A MOTHERSHIP!
It's Saturday night at the Apollo!
ONE NATION UNDER A GROOVE
THAT'S KIND OF CATCHY!

ONE NATION UNDER A GROOVE

As the Apollo will always be . . .

Afterword

How the Apollo Got Its Groove Back

(The End—and a New Beginning)

A LONGTIME FRIEND OF THE APOLLO STEPS IN TO TRY TO GET THE THEATER'S GROOVE BACK AFTER 253 REALTY'S BANKRUPTCY.

Percy Sutton's Inner City Broadcasting Corporation takes over in 1981.

MAY 1983, WORK BEGINS ON A *TOTAL OVERHAUL* THAT WILL ULTIMATELY COST SIXTEEN MILLION DOLLARS.

On June 29, 1983, the Apollo is designated a *cultural landmark*.

BILLY MITCHELL IS A NEWLY HIRED USHER IN 1984 AS SUTTON SEEKS TO BREATHE *NEW LIFE* INTO THE APOLLO.

It takes some effort to *win back* the people of Harlem.

THE APOLLO'S OPENING BACK UP!

YEAH, RIGHT, HEARD *THAT* BEFORE.

THEY AIN'T GONNA MAKE IT.

IT WAS SO *DISHEARTENING.*

WE COULDN'T GET PEOPLE TO GO THROUGH THE DOORS THE FIRST FEW MONTHS.

THE THEATER HAD BEEN CLOSED FOR QUITE AWHILE.

THE ECONOMY WAS SCREWED UP.

THE MUSIC HAD CHANGED AND DIDN'T APPEAL TO OLDER FOLKS.

BEFORE YOU KNEW IT, THIS WAS THE PLACE TO *BE* AGAIN.

IT WAS A REAL PARTY!

THEN PEOPLE STARTED *TRICKLING* IN.

IT WAS SOMETHING *NEW* TO A NEW GENERATION.

Billy Mitchell becomes the Apollo's tour director, and over the years inherits the name "*Mr. Apollo*" from Doll Thomas.

BEFORE RENOVATIONS ARE EVEN FINISHED, THE APOLLO *REOPENS* WITH A CHRISTMAS EVE AMATEUR NIGHT SHOW IN 1983.

An active Apollo becomes a good thing for 125th Street once again.

ON A BEAUTIFUL MAY NIGHT IN 1985, THE RENOVATED APOLLO *SPARKLES*.

It boasts new purple carpet, crystal chandeliers, and red-and-gold trimmed box seats.

213

DOWNTOWN, A SPECIAL RECEPTION FOR 500 GUESTS IN THE SUBWAY STATION AT 57TH STREET AND SIXTH AVENUE IS IN FULL SWING.

57 Street

AT 7 PM THE GUESTS BOARD A *1948-ERA A TRAIN* FOR THE RIDE TO THE 125TH STREET STATION.

SIR BOB GELDOF

ANDY WARHOL

DICK CAVETT

REV. JESSE JACKSON

CORETTA SCOTT KING

TONIGHT
Motown Returns to the Apollo

BILL COSBY HOSTS THE LIVE TAPING OF NBC'S *THREE-HOUR SPECIAL*.

ENTERTAINMENT WAS WHAT THE APOLLO WAS ALWAYS ABOUT AND WHAT IT IS STILL ABOUT.

SPEAK OUT IF SOMETHING MOVES YOU . . .

Stevie Wonder revives twelve-year-old Little Stevie playing "Fingertips."

AL GREEN, PATTI LABELLE, LITTLE RICHARD, AND MAVIS STAPLES, BACKED BY A NEW JERSEY GOSPEL CHOIR

LITTLE RICHARD, WILSON PICKETT, AND CHUCK JACKSON

Didn't it rain...

SIXTY ARTISTS, FROM SARAH VAUGHAN TO GEORGE MICHAEL, PERFORM.

You'll never walk alone...

SUTTON POURS MILLIONS INTO MAKING THE APOLLO A STATE-OF-THE-ART VIDEO AND AUDIO PRODUCTION FACILITY.

THE SHOW IS A SMASH, AND THE TELEVISION SPECIAL GARNERS TEN EMMY NOMINATIONS AND WINS FOR OUTSTANDING VARIETY, MUSIC OR COMEDY PROGRAM.

BARBRA STREISAND SHOOTS HER MUSIC VIDEO, "SOMEWHERE," AT THE APOLLO IN 1985.

Soooomewhere...

Dozens of music videos for acts such as Stevie Wonder, Whitney Houston, and U2 are shot there.

PATTI LABELLE AND B. B. KING RECORD *LIVE ALBUMS*.

LL COOL J HOSTS THE FIRST EPISODE OF THE *IT'S SHOWTIME AT THE APOLLO* TV SHOW IN SEPTEMBER 1987.

The show is the theater's greatest broadcasting success, syndicated nationally.

The theater continues to respond to the new music of the streets.

It runs for nearly 1,100 episodes over twenty-one years in various iterations . . . so far.

RUN-DMC

DOUG E. FRESH

ICE CUBE

PUBLIC ENEMY

MANY OF THE GREATS OF **RAP** PERFORM AT THE APOLLO AND MAKE IT HOME.

Rapmania
The Roots of Rap

THE DEBUT PERFORMANCE OF THE *JUICE CREW ALL-STARS* WORLD TOUR, NOVEMBER 18, 1988

Leave the crack alone!

The Juice Crew All-Stars, a Queens, New York, collective of hip-hop musicians, features Big Daddy Kane, Roxanne Shanté, Marley Marl, Kool G. Rap, and Biz Markie

TWO SOLD-OUT NIGHTS IN 1987

Sutton runs into many of the same problems the theater experiences in the 1970s, as well as new **challenges**.

Live at RADIO CITY
TONIGHT! SMOKEY ROBINSON

REAGAN CUTS ARTS FUNDING
RECESSION HITS NEW YORK!

AUDIO AND VIDEO OUTFITS ALL OVER THE CITY GO OUT OF BUSINESS.

The Apollo still finds it difficult to compete for established talent.

The Apollo's production business *dries up*.

IN JUNE 1991, PERCY SUTTON, UNABLE TO CONTINUE BY HIMSELF, ASKS THE STATE TO **STEP IN**.

"WORKING WITH CONGRESSMAN CHARLES RANGEL, SUTTON TODAY ESTABLISHED THE NONPROFIT APOLLO THEATER FOUNDATION WITH RANGEL AS CHAIRMAN."

YEAH, NEVER-WAS-PROFIT.

NONPROFIT, HAH!

THE ANNUAL SHORTFALL, MADE UP BY SUTTON AND HIS COMPANY, IS SAID TO REACH TWO MILLION DOLLARS.

Ralph Cooper Sr.
We Love and Miss You

In April 1998, the *Daily News* initiates a series of hard-hitting articles and editorials criticizing the Apollo's financial dealings and decrying the dilapidated condition of the theater.

DAILY NEWS

SHOWDOWN AT THE APOLLO

RALPH COOPER'S FUNERAL AND WAKE ON AUGUST 10 AND 11, 1992, IS AN EMOTIONAL AND SYMBOLIC **BREAK** WITH THE APOLLO'S PAST.

BY THE LATE '90S PROBLEMS **MOUNT**, AND FINGER-POINTING BECOMES NEARLY AS COMMON AS FOOT-TAPPING AT THE APOLLO.

THE NEWSPAPER WINS A *PULITZER PRIZE* FOR ITS COVERAGE.

Sutton settles a state lawsuit, pays the Foundation one million dollars—with Time Warner kicking in half—and Congressman Rangel resigns as chairman of the Apollo Board.

IT'S NOT AN AWARD MANY IN THE COMMUNITY ARE PROUD OF, OR HAPPY ABOUT.

CHARLIE RANGEL CARES MORE ABOUT HARLEM THAN ANY OF THEM!

EVERY TIME A BLACK MAN TRIES TO SUCCEED THEY TEAR HIM DOWN.

AND PERCY SUTTON SPENT HIS OWN DOUGH TO SAVE THE APOLLO.

IN 1997, SUTTON AND RANGEL HAD REACHED OUT TO *RICHARD D. PARSONS*, TIME WARNER'S PRESIDENT, THE CORPORATE ANGEL WHO WOULD ULTIMATELY BECOME THE APOLLO'S SAVIOR.

Parsons, who later becomes CEO of AOL Time Warner, is not only one of the most *powerful* African American executives in the world, he is also chairman of the Upper Manhattan Empowerment Zone.

CORPORATE PATRONAGE AND LARGESSE—ENJOYED BY OTHER CULTURAL INSTITUTIONS LIKE CARNEGIE HALL AND LINCOLN CENTER FOR YEARS—HELPS TURN THE APOLLO AROUND.

BEVERLY SILLS, OPERA STAR AND FORMER CHAIRWOMAN OF LINCOLN CENTER, BOARD MEMBER UNTIL 2002. *PHARRELL WILLIAMS*, SUPERSTAR, BOARD MEMBER STARTING IN 2014.

Happy!

Ah, reidi ancora qual eri allora quando il cor ti diedi allora, ah, reidi a me,

Parsons begins the tradition of attracting a wide array of *heavy-hitters* from the highest levels of culture and business to the Apollo Foundation board.

THE NEW MILLENNIUM STARTS WITH A GORGEOUS NEW FAÇADE AND MARQUEE.

Begun in 1999, another restoration project is unveiled in December 2005.

The marquee and sign look as much as possible like the original . . . only now powered by thousands of programmable LEDs.

Final *price tag* for the outside renovation is said to be 17.9 million dollars.

Total new renovation costs for the theater at this point: 65 million?

AT TODAY'S APOLLO, A LOT OF ATTENTION GOES TO THE BIG STARS AND CELEBRITIES WHO WANT TO EXPERIENCE THE APOLLO *MYSTIQUE* AND PAY TRIBUTE TO ITS HISTORY.

PRESIDENT OBAMA

PRESIDENT CLINTON

These are mostly exclusive, invitation-only affairs.

JAY-Z

METALLICA

BUT THERE IS A REAL EFFORT TO REACH OUT TO ALL.

Chris Rock does a special low-price show for the community while at the theater taping his 1999 HBO special.

WHO AND WHAT THE COMMUNITY IS IS *EVOLVING*.

Gentrification is pricing out some longtime Harlem residents, while bringing welcome new amenities and life to the neighborhood for others.

ACTUALLY, THE APOLLO IS JUST DOING WHAT IT'S ALWAYS DONE . . .

. . . FIGURING OUT WAYS TO KEEP THE DOORS OPEN!

DOLL THOMAS

APOLLO THEATER WALK OF FAME

BILLIE HOLIDAY

KIDS, THIS IS *OUR* THEATER, *OUR* CULTURE.

APOLLO PRESIDENT AND CEO *JONELLE PROCOPE* AND *CASSANDRA WILSON*

219

WE HONOR OUR PAST, BUT ALWAYS THINK ABOUT WHERE THE APOLLO IS GOING IN THE FUTURE . . .

JONELLE PROCOPE

The Apollo stays at the forefront with series like "Africa Now!", celebrating contemporary African music.

It also presents a robust education program.

BUT THE HEART OF THE APOLLO PERHAPS BEATS STRONGEST ON WEDNESDAY NIGHTS.

AMATEUR NIGHT

BOO!!

BOO!!

COMMON

ANGELA BASSETT

BLACK THOUGHT

IN APRIL 2018, A STELLAR CAST STAGES *TA-NEHISI COATES*'S BRILLIANT BOOK *BETWEEN THE WORLD AND ME*, DIRECTED BY THE APOLLO'S *KAMILAH FORBES*.

Amateur Night is where locals *still* rule, even as gaggles of Wall Streeters and tourists help pack the place weekly.

PULL BACK THE CURTAIN AND IT IS *STILL* THE APOLLO.

IT'S *HARLEM'S HIGH SPOT*.

THE APOLLO WILL *ALWAYS* BE THAT.

A NOTE ON SOURCES AND METHODS

I've been describing the scenes and telling the stories in *Showtime at the Apollo: The Epic Tale of Harlem's Legendary Theater* for decades. To see them depicted so beautifully in the vibrant art that pops off these pages is a thrill for me. It has also been a wonderful opportunity to revisit this great and complex story—to distill it into a narrative that carries readers along from the earliest days of Harlem to the present.

Work on my book, *Showtime at the Apollo: The Story of Harlem's World Famous Theater*—originally published by Holt, Rinehart and Winston in 1983—began in 1980 when I was twenty-five. Over the years there have been a number of editions, including a revised version that I published with my own Mill Road Enterprises in co-operation with the Apollo Theater Foundation, timed for the Apollo's 70th anniversary in 2004. It is currently available as an e-book, updated in 2014.

It may be puzzling for younger readers to realize how different times were for writers and researchers when the original work on this book took place. I wrote the manuscript on my father's hand-me-down, tanklike, gray metal Underwood Five manual typewriter. "Cut and paste" meant just that: cutting pages apart with scissors and pasting edited, rearranged sections together with library paste—or in my case, tape—over and over again. Changes were made by hand in pencil. New versions had to be retyped.

Before the Internet and the computer age, there was no instant and widely sourced information available with a few quick clicks. I spent many months over a couple of years in the New York Public Library's main branch; at their Library for the Performing Arts at Lincoln Center; and at the NYPL's Schomburg Center for Research in Black Culture in Harlem, digging into clip files—manila folders filled with photocopies or actual "clips" cut from the pages of newspapers and magazines.

The core of my early research—and absolutely essential to understanding the true course of history of the Apollo—something that had not been fully or veritably written at the time—was the immersive year I spent in Columbia University's Butler Library, poring through roll after roll of microfilm of the old Harlem newspaper the *New York Age*.

People's memories are not always the most reliable sources of actual dates, and their recollections, while wonderful for telling the story and providing context, cannot always be relied on for specifics. Furthermore, I knew that the only way for me to truly understand the Apollo's history would be to create an accurate time line, since one didn't exist. The Apollo did not have records of who played there and when. I did not then know about the Schiffman family's performer booking note cards and business logs, which at any rate were far from complete nor completely chronological, and did not emerge until nearly twenty years after my book was initially published.

As I looked through the *New York Age* microfilm, I realized that the Apollo ran detailed advertisements listing each week's lineup of performers in every issue. From these ads I transcribed—by hand, in script, on yellow lined pads—every show (with very few gaps) and most performers for each week of the Apollo's history, from its inception in 1934 until the early 1970s. This 300-plus-page document formed the indispensable, original Rosetta stone of the Apollo's history. Just transcribing and reading it, week by week and year by year, was an incomparable way to understand the Apollo's development and to imprint the theater's history in my mind.

Armed with that essential knowledge, I reached out to interview the people who lived that history. It is their stories and experiences that matter most and are invaluable in telling the story of the Apollo.

In addition to the countless hours spent with former owner Bobby Schiffman, who had never before been so thoroughly and relentlessly interviewed, I spoke with Estrellita Brooks-Morse, Maxine Brown, Ruth Brown, Benny Carter, Carol Carter, Deborah Chessler, Harold "Stumpy" Cromer, Jimmy Cross, Sammy Davis Jr., Billy Eckstine, Ahmet Ertegun, "Little Anthony" Gourdine, John Hammond, Lionel Hampton, Screamin' Jay Hawkins, Andy Kirk, Gladys Knight, Beverly Lee, David McCarthy, Herbie Mills, Billy Mitchell, Scoey Mitchell, Johnny Otis, Esther Phillips, St. Clair Pinckney, Dave Prater, Jonelle Procope, Danny Ray, Leonard Reed, Timmie Rogers, Thurman Ruth, Sandman Sims, John "Bubbles" Sublett, Percy Sutton, Francis "Doll" Thomas, Big Joe Turner, Leslie Uggams, Eddie "Cleanhead" Vinson, Dionne Warwick, Tom Whaley, and Nancy Wilson. Harold Cromer and Sandman Sims were also very helpful personal guides for me.

I taped most interviews on my trusty Sony Walkman Professional and transcribed them myself using a cassette transcriber with a foot pedal, allowing me to reverse and fast-forward. It also had a nifty speed adjustment knob to slow down difficult-to-understand passages—state of the art for the early 1980s!

To organize my research, I created index cards with important pieces of information, each with a subject head. This collection grew to a couple of thousand cards. After sorting them by subject, I spread them out in piles on the carpet of my living room in the upstate Owego, New York, apartment where I wrote the book. I arranged and rearranged the piles of cards into chapters and then arranged the cards within each chapter to lay out the plan of the book. After that, all I had to do was write it.

A number of books proved invaluable in my research, especially *Blues People* by LeRoi Jones (Amiri Baraka), *Honkers and Shouters* by Arnold Shaw, *The Gospel Sound* by Anthony Heilbut, *The Sound of Soul* by Phyl Garland, *Jazz Dance* by Marshall and Jean Stearns, *This Was Harlem* by Jervis Anderson, and *Uptown: The Story of Harlem's Apollo Theater* by Jack Schiffman. Newer books published after mine include Schiffman's *Harlem Heyday* (1984) and *Amateur Night at the Apollo* (1990) by Ralph Cooper. I contributed two essays and the time line for *Ain't Nothing Like the Real Thing: How the Apollo Theater Shaped American Entertainment* (2010), the companion publication to the exhibition of the same name produced by the National Museum of African American History and Culture in collaboration with the Apollo Theater Foundation.

The Frank Schiffman Apollo Theatre Collection, 1935–1973, Archives Center, National Museum of American History at the Smithsonian, is a fascinating treasure trove comprised of material donated by Bobby and Jack Schiffman in 1996 and processed in 2002. There are boxes filled with letters and telegrams, financial ledgers, phone books, accounting documents, Frank's booking cards with notes on hundreds of performers, print media, pamphlets, scrapbooks, flyers, promotional broadcasts, publicity shots, and more.

The Apollo's indispensable tour director and in-house historian, Billy Mitchell, generously gave me and James a thorough and informative backstage and all-around tour of the theater in October 2017, which helped James more accurately picture the place he was about to illustrate.

Today, thanks to the wonders of the Internet, I have been able to further check, double-check, and just surf endlessly through information and images that have helped corroborate *Showtime at the Apollo: The Epic Tale of Harlem's Legendary Theater*.

Ted Fox

INDEX

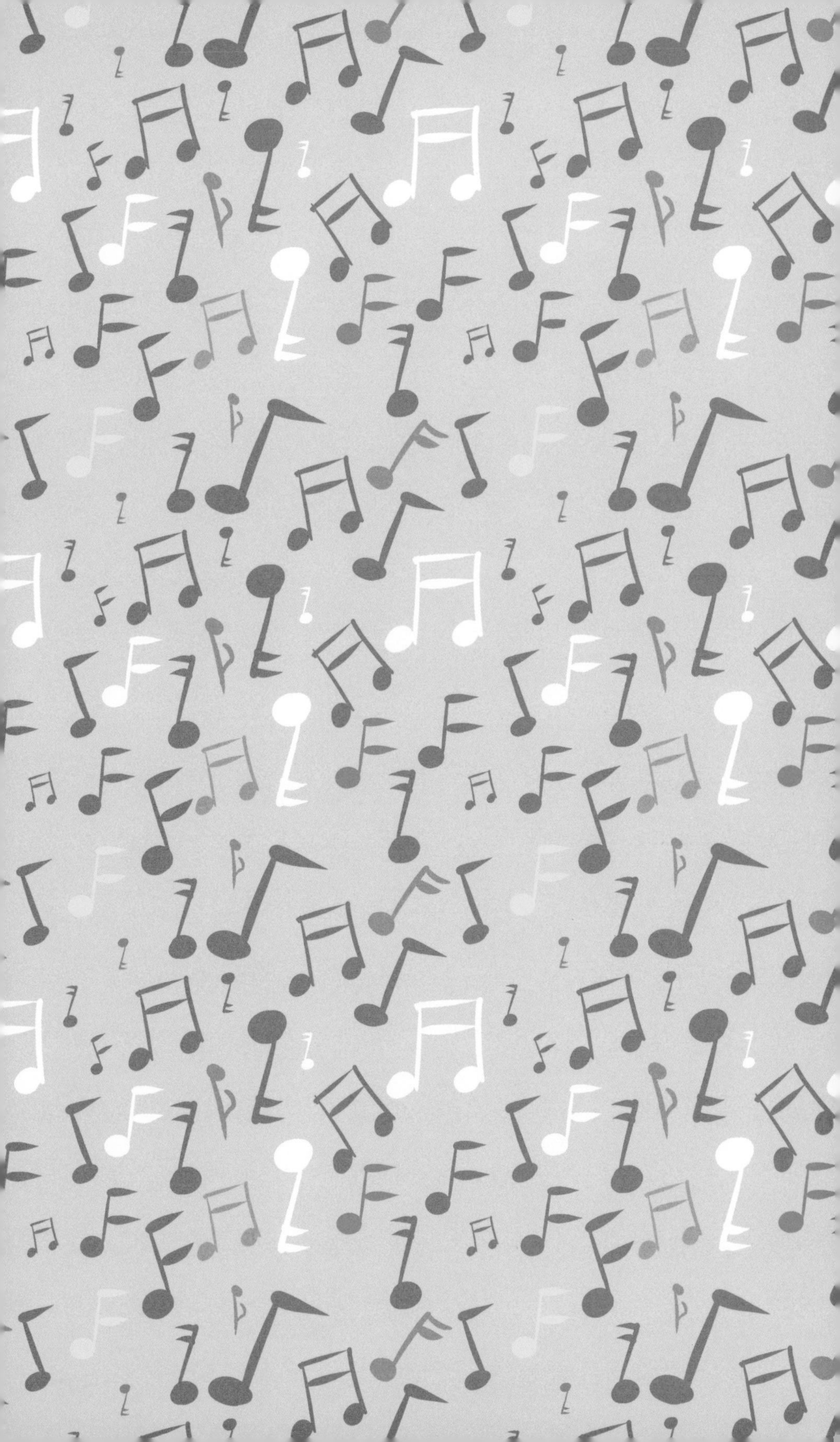

31901064004262

The world is in peril.

A long-forgotten evil has risen from the far corners of Erdas, and we need YOU to help stop it.

Claim your spirit animal and join the adventure now:

1. Go to scholastic.com/spiritanimals.

2. Log in to create your character and choose your own spirit animal.

3. Have your book ready and enter the code below to unlock the adventure.

Your code:

N69D43X2X3

By the Four Fallen,
   The Greencloaks

scholastic.com/spiritanima

He raised the flask to his lips
and gulped down the Bile.

It was like drinking death
itself. But within that
blackness, he felt something
vast and strong and dark.

SPIRIT ANIMALS™

HUNTED

HUNTED

Maggie Stiefvater

SCHOLASTIC INC.

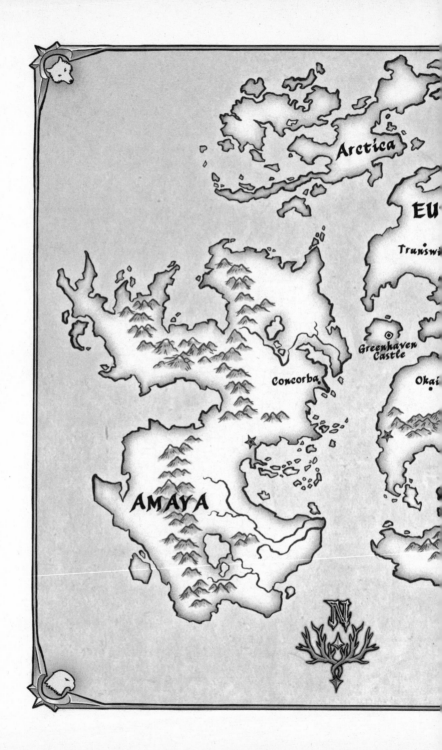

Arctica

EU

Trunswi

Greenhaven
Castle

Concorba

Okai

AMAYA

N

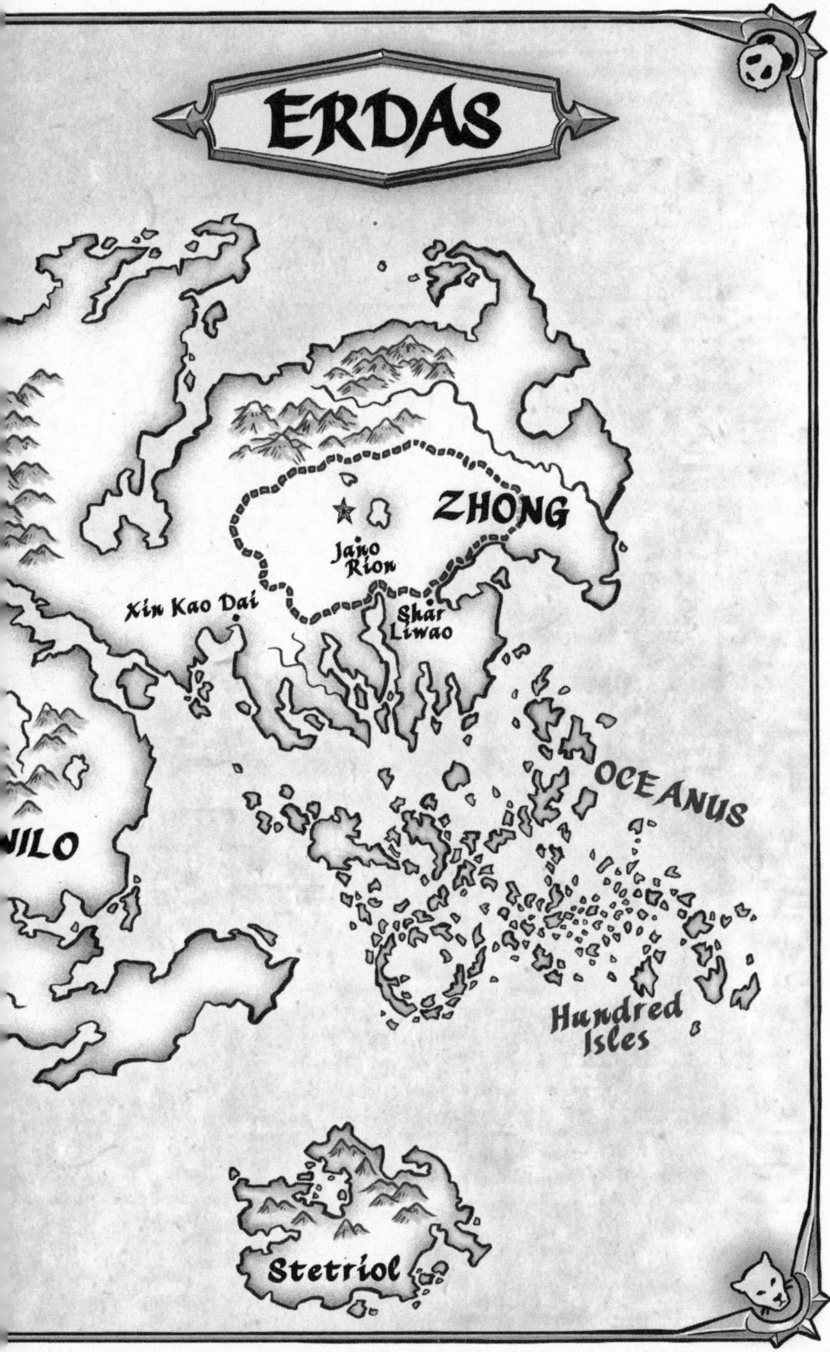
ERDAS
ZHONG
Jano Rion
Xin Kao Dai
Shar Liwao
OCEANUS
NILO
Hundred Isles
Stetriol

For Victoria and William
— M.S.

Copyright © 2014 by Scholastic Inc.

All rights reserved. Published by
Scholastic Inc., *Publishers since 1920.*
SCHOLASTIC, SPIRIT ANIMALS, and associated logos are
trademarks and/or registered trademarks of Scholastic Inc.

No part of this publication may be reproduced, stored in a
retrieval system, or transmitted in any form or by any
means, electronic, mechanical, photocopying, recording,
or otherwise, without written permission of the publisher.
For information regarding permission,
write to Scholastic Inc.,
Attention: Permissions Department,
557 Broadway, New York, NY 10012.

Library of Congress Control Number: 2013947126

ISBN 978-0-545-52244-1
10 9 8 7 6 5 4 3   14 15 16 17 18

Map illustration by Michael Walton
Book design by Charice Silverman
Book illustration by Keirsten Geise for Scholastic

First edition, January 2014

Printed in the U.S.A.   23

Scholastic US: 557 Broadway • New York, NY 10012
Scholastic Canada: 604 King Street West • Toronto, ON M5V 1E1
Scholastic New Zealand Limited: Private Bag 94407 • Greenmount, Manukau 2141
Scholastic UK Ltd.: Euston House • 24 Eversholt Street • London NW1 1DB

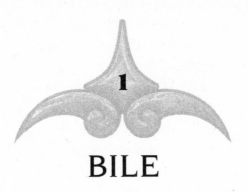

BILE

THE FOREST WAS DARK AND FULL OF ANIMALS. THE NIGHT between the trees clicked and growled and fluttered.

In the small light of a lantern, a man and a boy stood and stared at a tiny flask. Although the flask itself was unimpressive, the solution inside was remarkable: a powerful substance that could force a bond between a human and a spirit animal.

"Will it hurt?" the boy, Devin Trunswick, asked. He was handsomely dressed, and there was an arrogant, cruel tilt to his chin that fear couldn't erase. A lord's son, he would never admit he was afraid of the dark. Even if there was plenty to be afraid of.

The man, Zerif, pulled back the embroidered blue hood of his cape so the boy could see his eyes more clearly. Holding up the flask, he said, "Does it matter? *This* is a privilege, little lordling. You'll be a legend."

Devin liked the sound of that. Right now, he was the opposite of a legend. He came from a long line of Marked individuals—people who had bonded with spirit animals.

But when his turn had come, he had failed, breaking a chain that was generations long. At his Nectar Ceremony, the event where children who came of age drank from the Greencloaks' Nectar of Ninani and hoped for the appearance of a spirit animal, he had summoned nothing.

As if that wasn't bad enough, his own servant, a lowly shepherd boy, had called up a wolf. A *wolf*. And not just any wolf. The boy had summoned Briggan the Wolf, one of the Great Beasts.

Devin was stung by humiliation.

But that humiliation was going to end. Now an even more powerful animal would be delivered to him. He had prepared his whole life for this – it ran in his *blood*. This destiny had only been delayed, not destroyed.

"Why is it called Bile?" Devin asked, his eyes on the flask. "That doesn't sound great."

"It's a joke," Zerif replied tersely.

"I don't see what's funny about it."

"You've tasted the Nectar, right?"

Devin nodded, his face sour despite memories of its exquisite taste.

"Well," Zerif said, nose scrunching, "you're about to taste the Bile. Then you'll get the joke. I promise."

The boy looked hurriedly over his shoulder as a growl muttered from the trees. Beside him, a spider with a hard, shiny back lowered itself down on a thread. He tried to stay out of its path.

"Whatever animal I call will have to listen to me, right?" he asked. "It will do whatever I say?"

"Bonds with the Bile are different from bonds with the Nectar," Zerif informed him. "The Nectar might taste sweeter, but the Bile is more useful. *We* can control much more of the process. For instance, you don't have to worry about bonding with that spider you've been so desperate to avoid."

Devin bristled, annoyed that Zerif had noticed his terror. Loftily, he said, "I'm not worried."

But his eyes darted to the covered cage that waited for them. Beneath that cloth was the animal he would bond with. He tried to guess what it could be from the size of the enclosure. The cage was large, up to his chest. Occasionally he could hear scratching noises from underneath it.

This was the animal he'd spend the rest of his life with. The animal that would make him triumph.

Zerif handed the flask to the boy. His smile was as wide and encouraging as a jackal's. "Just one sip will do it."

The boy wiped his sweaty palms on his shirt. This was it.

Nobody would ever question him again.

Nobody would ever doubt his strength.

He was not the Trunswick family's first failure. He was its first legend.

Through the open top of the flask, the Bile smelled dreadful. Like hair burning.

He remembered the glorious taste of the Nectar, like butter over honey. It had been so remarkable, until it had gone wrong.

Now he raised the flask to his lips, and without another thought, gulped down the Bile. He had to fight hard not to gag — it was like drinking death itself, and the ground that death was buried in. But within that blackness, he felt

3

something coming alive within him – something vast and strong and dark. His body could barely contain the thing that grew inside him. In that instant, he felt no terror. He only felt that he could create terror.

Still smiling, Zerif whisked the cover off the cage.

2

GREENHAVEN

"I'M NEARLY READY, URAZA," ABEKE SAID, SLIPPING A BRACELET over her slender brown hand. Her words were directed at the leopard that paced the floor of her room. Because the room was much too small for a leopard, or because the leopard was much too large for the room, the big cat could only take a few steps in each direction before she huffed and twisted the other way.

Abeke could sympathize.

In just a few short weeks, their world had shrunk from their home in wide-open Nilo to a tangled training camp, and then shrunk again to this island fortress: Greenhaven, the headquarters of the Greencloaks, guardians of Erdas. Abeke supposed that the fortress was impressive – a sprawling stone castle built on top of a waterfall – but both she and Uraza were of the mind that the forest surrounding it looked more appealing.

Outside the window, a bell sounded from a distant tower. Three tolls: the call to training.

Uraza paced even harder, making low, grunting sounds.

"All right, we'll go!" Abeke tightened her bracelet so it wouldn't slip off. Although its strands looked like wire, they were actually boiled elephant tail hair. Four knots in the strands symbolized sun, fire, water, and wind. Her perfect sister, Soama, had given it to her as she'd left home. It was supposed to bring good luck.

But Abeke wasn't sure if *good luck* was really what she had been having since she left Nilo. She'd summoned a Great Beast as a spirit animal, which seemed like good luck. But almost immediately after that, she'd been recruited by people who were secretly in cahoots with the Devourer, enemy of the known world. Definitely bad luck.

The Greencloaks had agreed to take her in once she'd discovered her mistake; Abeke knew that she was probably supposed to consider that as good luck. After all, they hadn't had to let her switch sides. But it didn't feel very lucky at the moment. She'd made one friend since this whole thing began – Shane – and he was still on the other side, with the Conquerors. She'd traded her only friend for three kids who didn't trust her.

Really, Abeke would settle for the good luck of not getting lost in the giant Greencloak fortress again.

As she opened the door, she donned the green cloak that meant she had sworn to defend Erdas. The dim hallway was full of sound. A monkey screamed a laugh somewhere out of sight, and a man's voice rumbled low beneath it. A donkey brayed. Something like hoofbeats or pattering footsteps resonated through the stone walls. Abeke ducked as a bird the color of a banana soared overhead.

At the sight of the bird, Uraza, however, leaped skyward with a gleeful and rather threatening growl. The banana-colored bird shrieked. Just before the leopard slapped her paws together, Abeke grabbed her tail. The leopard's leap was brought up short with a yowl.

Uraza spun. For a moment her teeth were instinctually bared and menacing.

Abeke's heart stopped.

Then the leopard realized it was Abeke's hand on her tail. Her lips lowered. She gave Abeke a deeply wounded look. The bird flapped away.

"I apologize," Abeke said. "But that was someone's spirit animal!"

One would think a Great Beast would understand why it wasn't right to eat someone else's spirit animal, but with Uraza, sometimes the beast part outweighed the great part.

"Maybe we should do this," Abeke told Uraza, holding out her arm as a request. All spirit animals had the ability to enter a dormant form. If Uraza chose to enter it now, she would become a tattoo on Abeke's skin until they got to training. And tattoos had never eaten anyone else's spirit animal.

But Uraza was tired of being cooped up. She considered Abeke's outstretched arm for one long moment, and then she turned and stalked down the hall.

Abeke didn't press the issue. They were going to be late. As she hurried down the hallway after the leopard, various Greencloaks waved and greeted her by name. Abeke felt bad that she couldn't return the favor, but they all knew her more than she knew them. All four of the newcomers at the fortress—Abeke, Rollan, Meilin, and Conor—were well-known. The four kids who had somehow summoned the Four Fallen.

Uraza made a curious trilling sound as she leaped down a circular stairwell in front of her. At the bottom, both Abeke and Uraza hesitated. They faced two identical halls, each with plaster-white walls and exposed timber ceilings. Only one led to the training room.

"Uraza?" Abeke asked. Uraza's violet eyes darted from the floor to the ceiling, her long tail thrashing slowly.

Suddenly, Abeke didn't think she looked so much like a leopard deciding which way to go. Instead, she looked like a leopard about to—

Uraza lunged. She was a muscled blur of gold and black as she pushed off the wall. A thrumming, heart-chilling growl burst from her. For one moment, Abeke just thought, *What an amazing animal!*

Then she realized that Uraza was on the hunt. The leopard's unlucky prey crouched on a notch in the plaster wall. It was a small, squirrel-like animal with pink feet, a striped back, and large eyes. Abeke thought it was a sugar glider.

Uraza thought it was delicious.

"Uraza!" Abeke snatched for the leopard's tail again, but missed. The sugar glider leaped toward the opposite wall. As it flew, its tiny limbs stretched out from its body. There was skin webbing between all its legs, making its body into a furry sail.

Uraza pounced. The sugar glider darted out of her way. The two of them careened down the hall. The sugar glider soared onto a side table. Uraza knocked the furniture over. The sugar glider scrambled up a tapestry of Olvan, leader of the Greencloaks. Uraza clawed the fabric from the wall. Tatters of Abeke's dignity fluttered to the ground.

Helplessly, Abeke ran after them. She managed to get ahold of Uraza's back leg, but the leopard tugged free easily. Abeke was left with a handful of black and yellow hairs.

The chase hurtled on. The three of them crashed through the hallway into a small eating room Abeke hadn't seen before. People filled the benches. Abeke took the long way around the diners as the sugar glider and Uraza tore across the long table. Plates flew. One man got a faceful of his oatmeal. Another diner shut her eyes against an onslaught of fruit.

Outrage had just been added to the breakfast selection.

Abeke felt the Greencloaks' eyes. She wanted to shout: *It's her fault, not mine!* But she knew what their responses would be.

It is up to you to control your spirit animal.

Can't you control her?

This is your responsibility!

This is your failure.

Maybe you don't belong here after all.

There was no time for her to apologize or clean up the damage. She panted after the animals as they darted and clawed through several twisted hallways and a large room full of chairs, ending up in a foyer with an arched doorway on the other side. The sugar glider was making panicked, pitiful noises that sounded like a squeaky rocking chair.

Abeke was gasping too. Back in Nilo, she could track animals for hours without feeling she had taken a breath. What was this castle doing to her?

"Uraza," she said, grabbing a stitch in her side. "We are supposed to be here to *save the world* . . . so save your appetite!"

This made Uraza pause. The sugar glider had just enough time to hurl itself to the safety of the chandelier. Both Abeke and the sugar glider breathed a sigh of relief.

Uraza circled below, but the chase was over.

Now, Abeke thought with dismay, *we are really lost.*

Being lost wasn't the worst consequence either. Being *late* was. Not because it came with a steep penalty – her instructors were fairly understanding. But she knew her tardiness would only deepen the problems between her and the other three kids. They had begun their training together, while Abeke had still been in the clutches of the Devourer. She was not only the outsider, she was the suspicious ex-enemy. She could only imagine what they thought she was doing right now – spying somewhere in the castle. Sending secret messages to Zerif, the Conqueror who'd taken her away after her Nectar Ceremony. Letting Uraza eat someone else's spirit animal.

She had to get to that training room.

Maybe there was someone inside that arched doorway who could help her find her way. Even if the room was empty, there was something tempting about the curved entry. Although it surely led to another room, something about it felt as if it led to the outside instead. Abeke couldn't quite explain the sensation to herself.

Cautiously, she pushed the door open. Inside was a dim room she'd never seen before. It was cluttered with musical instruments, mysterious pieces of art, and mirrors. There was a pile of drums as tall as Abeke, a piano-like instrument the size of a dog, and a bin full of flutes and recorders. A portrait of a girl smiled at her from one wall, while a mural of a man leading dozens of unfamiliar animals through a field covered another. The room smelled like dust and wood and leather, but also, to Abeke's delight, like the outdoors, though, again, she couldn't explain why.

A single man stood inside, partially turned away.

It was possible his spirit animal was in its passive state, but Abeke realized quickly that she wouldn't be able to tell. Apart from his face, every inch of visible pale skin was covered in tattoos: inked mazes, circles, stars, moons, knots, stylized creatures. The mark of his spirit animal wouldn't stand out from the rest of the designs all over his body.

Abeke was suddenly impressed. Whether it was the man's intention or not, he had very cleverly hidden the identity of his spirit animal.

Even though what she could see of his face seemed young, his hair was gray. Nearly white.

He didn't seem to have noticed her silent entrance. His eyes downcast, he continued whispering to himself. Abeke couldn't quite make out the words, but it sounded like coaxing. She suddenly felt like she'd interrupted something quite secret, almost sacred. And in that dim, mirrored room, it was also just a little eerie.

She backed out. She'd find her own way back to training.

In the foyer, Uraza waited, her tail curled tidily around her own feet.

Abeke didn't have to tell the leopard she was upset with her. Uraza knew.

Without a word, Abeke held out her arm. And without a moment's hesitation, Uraza became a tattoo on her skin. It only stung for a second. Abeke started on her way. Back in Nilo she had been known for her tracking skills, hadn't she? She would find the training room. And she would make it her business to not get lost again.

———◈———

The training room was the second-largest room in Greenhaven Castle. It was bright and inviting and had a dazzlingly tall peaked ceiling for the high-flying spirit animals. One end of the room was devoted to weapons' storage — spears, maces, slingshots. Anything you might hope to find, so long as it would leave a mark. Stained-glass windows lined the walls, each one featuring a different Great Beast.

As she stepped in, Abeke was uncomfortably aware of suspicious eyes on her. Rollan, the scruffy orphan who had summoned Essix the Falcon, frowned at her. Meilin, standing near the panda Jhi, kept her striking face intentionally expressionless. Only Conor, the blond boy with pale skin who had summoned Briggan the Wolf, offered a faint smile in Abeke's direction.

Tarik, the Greencloak who was in charge of their training and their futures, stood in front of a folded fabric screen. His weathered, lean face was only a little lighter than Abeke's. Right now it wore a perplexed frown. "Abeke, didn't you hear the training bell?"

There was no point blaming it on Uraza. She knew what Tarik would say: *You're going to have to learn to work with Uraza in far more difficult situations than our hallways.* And she didn't want to give the others more reasons not to trust her.

Abeke said, "I'm sorry. I got lost." She hurriedly released Uraza from her arm.

"Lost?" Meilin rolled her eyes. She turned to Tarik. "Now can we start? Every minute we stand here doing nothing, a city in Zhong falls to the Conquerors."

"That's a lot of cities," Rollan interjected. "Do you mean eleven cities have fallen while we've stood here? How many do you think fell during *breakfast*? That was nearly twenty minutes! How—"

"Rollan, that is no joking matter," Tarik said. "And Meilin is right. Time is precious. But I think it will be more efficient if we train together. Today, you'll engage in hand-to-hand combat with other Greencloaks."

Meilin smirked, certain of her abilities.

"I call dibs on the mace," Rollan said. "And the brass knuckles."

"Not so fast," Tarik said. As he spoke, four other Greencloaks entered the room. Though their spirit animals were in passive form, the four newcomers held their arms in such a way to display their tattoos to the four kids—like the Greencloaks were introducing the animals, even though they weren't physically present. There was a llama, a fruit bat, a lemur, and a mountain lion.

Tarik continued, "You won't always have access to weapons. In fact, an attack will more often come when you're not ready—while you're sleeping or eating. So you will not be using those weapons."

He pulled aside the folded screen behind him. The wall behind it was hung with frying pans, broomsticks, plates, pillows, and other ordinary objects.

He said, "You'll be using these."

"Oh, I did that every day in my old life," Rollan joked.

"This is ridiculous," Meilin argued. "Maybe a street urchin is willing to fight with these crude tools, but I could do better with my bare hands."

Abeke exchanged a look with Conor. They both moved to the wall to get weapons. Neither bothered complaining.

"Grab the first one you come to," Tarik said. "And when I whistle, change to another object."

Abeke took a broomstick. Conor took a fork.

"Here," Rollan said, offering Meilin a handkerchief from the wall. "This one won't scratch up your noble hands."

Meilin smiled prettily. Removing the frying pan, she handed it to him. "And here's one for you. Doesn't require much brains to figure out how to use it."

Rollan pretended to bow.

"Everyone to their marks," Tarik ordered.

They took their places, the other Greencloaks opposite. Abeke faced a middle-aged man with a lemur tattoo and friendly-looking, wide eyes. The sword he held was not quite so friendly looking.

"I'm Errol," the man said, touching his chest.

"My name is Abeke," Abeke replied.

He smiled warmly at her. "I know."

Tarik's voice rose above the introductions. "Older team: Keep your spirit animals in passive form. Younger team: You may use all powers you have at your disposal. The object is to disarm your opponent. And if you manage that, to pin them to the ground."

"For how long?" Meilin asked. "How will we know if we've won?"

"There is no win or lose here, Meilin," Tarik replied. "We don't have time for games. What I want is for you to show me that you can neutralize an opponent so I feel more comfortable putting you in a real-life dangerous situation. Now. Are we ready? Three, two?"

Putting his fingers to his lips, he let out a sharp, piercing whistle. The training battle began.

Right away, Abeke knew that her broomstick would be no match for Errol's sword. So, drawing on her past in Nilo, she hurled her broomstick like a spear. The stick bounced harmlessly off his chest. Grinning at her, he picked it up.

"I'll let you have one free pass," Errol said, offering her the broomstick. In the background, iron clanged and Rollan swore joyously. "But remember that thing doesn't have a point on it. If you tossed it at me in a real fight, you'd just end up empty-handed as I came at you with my blade."

Abeke's cheeks felt warm. "Of course."

"But well-thrown," he said. "Here's a hint: Use that broomstick defensively, and count on your spirit animal as your weapon. And the other way around, if you find yourself with a real weapon."

"Thanks," she said. Then, suspicious of his kind smile, she added, "Don't go easy on me."

"That wouldn't be a favor," Errol said. "We want you prepared when you get out there. Don't go easy on *me.*"

Abeke stole a glance at the others. Meilin sat on the shoulders of her opponent, the silk handkerchief wrapped around her assailant's eyes. *If Meilin can do so well with just a scrap of cloth,* Abeke thought, *I have to be able to work with a broom!*

This time, when Errol came at her with the sword, she used the broom like a long staff instead, blocking his blows as best as she could. His strikes became steadily harder, though, and the broom handle began to splinter.

"Sorry!" Abeke said.

He looked confused. "For what?"

"For this!" With a pang of conscience, Abeke thrust the broom bristles into the swordsman's face. Sneezing, he swatted at the noxious cloud of dust, hair, and animal fur surrounding his head. He blindly windmilled his sword.

Well, he said not to go easy on him.

"Uraza!" Abeke called. "Now!"

Just as Errol's sword split her broomstick in two, shards flying, the leopard pounced. Her paws clapped on his chest. With a grunt, he fell back, catching himself with his hands. His sword clattered away.

Uraza licked a paw serenely.

Errol gave Abeke a thumbs-up from his place on the floor.

Abeke smiled at him. It was nice to feel accepted.

Tarik's whistle sounded.

"New weapon!" he shouted. "Now, this round, I want you fighting as a team. Hurry! Grab something, quick."

Abeke snatched up a heavy wooden mixing bowl. Conor took a spoon. Meilin and Rollan argued over a vase. Meilin ended up with the porcelain bottom and Rollan ended up with the dry flowers inside it.

"Wait—" Rollan said.

Tarik let out his shrill whistle. "As a team, go!"

This time, all four Greencloaks attacked at once, and the four kids moved as one against them. Abeke's wooden bowl served well as a shield. Out of the corner of her eye, she saw Conor and Briggan working together, darting forward and back.

Smart, thought Abeke. *Conor's been taking his training to heart. He would be prepared even if he was surprised out in the open, with no weapon at all.*

In fact, she was awed by their progress. Although he and Briggan had been gradually improving at each training session, this was a huge leap forward.

Suddenly, the older Greencloaks changed tactics, turning to Abeke at the same time. She found herself facing two swords, a spear, and an axe—impossible to hold off on her own, even with Uraza.

Uraza snaked beneath a Greencloak, her flexible body low to the ground. One paw darted out, claws sheathed safely away. The Greencloak with the llama tattoo careened to the ground, unbalanced. Abeke used her bowl to knock back the bat-tattooed Greencloak. Uraza sprang onto his shoulders effortlessly. The weight of the big cat brought him to his knees.

But the success was short-lived. The other two Greencloaks came at her while Uraza was occupied. Errol's sword smacked her bowl right out of her hands. As it flew up into the air, the other Greencloak slammed her with the broad side of his training axe, hard enough to throw her to the ground and knock the breath out of her.

Abeke gasped as her palms scuffed over the floor.

Tarik's whistle shrieked. It sounded a little irritated, louder and longer than usual.

"What was *that*?" Tarik demanded. "This was not a spectator event! Where were you three? How could you let her go down like that?"

Conor had the good manners to look ashamed. Rollan acted like it simply hadn't occurred to him to help. Meilin's carefully painted face remained haughty. They didn't explain themselves, but they didn't have to.

They don't trust me, Abeke thought, her eyes prickling with tears. The days of the others' distrust piled up inside her along with the ache of her scuffed palms and the humiliation of having been so badly beaten. She wouldn't cry in front of them. Especially not in front of Meilin. She was sure Meilin didn't cry over anything.

"I'm deeply disappointed," Tarik said. "Part of good strategy is making good use of all your assets. Abeke is one of your assets, and you should have protected her."

Conor offered his hand to Abeke. She hesitated before accepting it. He hauled her up.

"Sorry," he said.

On the other end of the room, footsteps rang out through the uncomfortable silence. It was Olvan, the regal leader of the Greencloaks. As always, his movements were slow and deliberate. There was something imposing about him, even when his spirit animal, a moose, wasn't visible.

Rubbing his beard, he surveyed the wreckage: shattered glass, broken broomsticks, dried flower petals. "Tarik, I don't like to interrupt. But this is important."

"Go ahead," Tarik said. He was still frowning at three of his four pupils. When he nodded at the four Greencloaks, they nodded back and exited. Errol waved to Abeke as he left. It was kind enough that it made her want to cry again.

"We've confirmed that one of the Great Beasts is in the north of Eura," Olvan said. "Rumfuss the Boar. It's not a far journey from here. The four of you and the Fallen must travel immediately to find out more. Tarik, you will lead them again."

"*Yes,*" Rollan said. "*Finally.* Let's leave all this cutlery behind."

Tarik's brow furrowed. "I don't know much about the North."

Olvan seemed unconcerned. "I'll be sending Finn with you. He's from that area and can act as a guide."

"Finn?" Tarik echoed. He didn't add anything else, but the single word was enough to make Olvan raise a thick eyebrow. It was unlike Tarik to question Olvan.

"Concerns, Tarik?" Olvan asked brusquely. But his tone didn't seem to encourage a confession. Tarik merely shook his head.

"It will be good to have another set of hands," Meilin said.

"Finn was once a great warrior, but now he's seen too much battle," Tarik answered carefully. "He will only be useful as a scout."

"But a very good scout," Olvan insisted. "He will not fight for you, but he will stand by you. There can be no question of that. Here he is."

Finn entered the room with footfalls much softer than Olvan's had been. Abeke's head darted up. At once her humiliation was forgotten, replaced by interest.

Finn was the tattooed man from the mirrored room. And their lives would soon be in his hands.

3

LETTER

THE FIRST THING CONOR DID TO GET READY FOR THE journey was head to the kitchen. He didn't have a problem existing in dirty clothing or without weapons as long as he had enough food to last the trip. The cool basement kitchen was dug right into the rock foundation of the fortress, and it was very full. Greenhaven required quite a lot of cooks – not only were there a lot of Greencloaks, there were more than a few spirit animals with very strange diets. So Conor tried to grab jerky, crackers, and dehydrated fruit from under elbows and over shoulders and around hips. He had to keep saying, "Excuse me," and "I'm sorry," and "Oh, was that your eye?!"

"Oh, love," said one of the cooks, a woman who looked a lot like a decorative pillow, "we will do that for you. You are too good to be in the kitchen!"

"Oh, *no*," Conor protested fervently. The kitchen was one of the only places in Greenhaven where he felt remotely comfortable. He came from a shepherd family and, until the last year or so, had grown up in fields. It wasn't the easiest life, but it was simple, and he'd been good at it. He knew his place, and it wasn't this magnificent fortress. This kitchen was closer.

"Oh, *yes*," the cook replied with a laugh. "You've bonded with a Great Beast! You're destined for greatness!"

With a hint of panic, Conor shoved some more jerky into his pack. The idea that he was destined for greatness was not a cozy one. His former noble employer, Devin Trunswick, would certainly have argued against it.

"Look, the messenger boat's come in!" called an older, bearded cook. Peering out of the small window, he beckoned for Conor to join him. The fortress sat up high above the shore, and though the beach was not close, the building's lofty vantage point let Conor see all the way down to where a small boat had scuffed onto the rocky sand. In the afternoon light, two messengers climbed out. One walked purposefully toward the castle, but the other began to run, heading for the main entrance of the fortress.

Why run? Conor wondered with a frown. *What is the hurry?*

As Conor watched the two messengers, the cooks took advantage of his distraction to pack his bag full of food, including a large bone for Briggan. A few minutes later, the running messenger disappeared around the side of the fortress, and the other, to his surprise, came right to the kitchen. She had a mailbag. And one of the letters was for Conor.

Conor accepted the letter, trying to keep the shock off his face. He knew very few people who would write to him.

Although he was close to his family and their small farming community, none of the peasantry could read or write very well. In all the time he'd served the Trunswicks, he'd only received a single letter from his family. They'd paid a week's earnings to hire the Finley girl, who was training to be a scribe, to scratch it all down. The younger Trunswick brother, Dawson, had read it aloud to him — when he wasn't too busy laughing at the penmanship.

Devin Trunswick was very capable of writing a letter, but it was impossible to imagine him writing one to his former servant. Conor could still remember the open hatred in Devin's gaze as Tarik led Conor away from the crowd during their Nectar Ceremony.

Which was why Conor was surprised to see what looked like Devin's handwriting. It was a little more jiggly and uneven, but the capital letters looked the same.

"Letter from home?" asked the pillow cook. Somehow figuring out from his hopeless expression that he couldn't read it, she added kindly, "Shall I read it to you?"

"Yes, thank you."

Wiping her hands on her apron, the cook took the letter and scanned to the bottom. "It's from your mother!"

Conor's heart soared for just a moment before crashing back to the earth. It couldn't be true. Conor's mother couldn't read or write.

Dear Conor,
I have wanted to send you a letter for a long time, but as you know, I could not write. Devin Trunswick's little brother, Dawson, has kindly agreed to write

it for me. He says he needs the practice with his handwriting anyway. He is a fine boy!

I do not have much time before my evening duties, but I wanted to let you know that we are proud of you. Sadly, things have gotten worse since you left. I have had to take your place as Devin's servant, as our debt to Lord Trunswick was still large when you left. Also, a very cold spring killed many of our lambs and the wolves have been getting desperate. We lost two of our dogs to them this season. Food is scarce. We must hand over almost everything we earn to the Trunswicks to pay our debt. I do not mean to scare you, but it is hard to make ends meet without your labor. Please ask the Greencloaks if they could send food for us this winter. Surely it is the least they can do for us as you work with them now. I would not ask if it was not dire.

With all of my love, Your mother

P.S. This is Dawson. I am sorry that your family is so hungry. My father will not forgive their debt. I asked him.

Conor didn't say anything. It was bad enough to imagine his mother as Devin's servant, but also to imagine his family starving? He didn't want to picture it, but he couldn't help seeing disaster striking. They had been close enough to it when his father had asked him to go work for Devin. Even as he'd hated leaving for Trunswick, even as he'd wondered why *he* was the sibling who had to go, he'd known that otherwise they would have starved. Suddenly the bag of food he'd packed felt like a luxury.

"I'm sure they'll be all right," said the pillow cook, draping her arm over Conor's shoulders and giving him back the letter. "Giving you up to Briggan is just their sacrifice to save Erdas. You heard what she said! She's proud of you!"

One of the other cooks handed Conor his bag. "As are we," she added. "Now, off with you. Briggan's lad doesn't belong in a kitchen, no matter where he came from."

But if I don't belong in a field or kitchen anymore, Conor thought, *and I don't feel like I belong in a castle, then where* do *I belong?*

4

MOON TOWER

O N THE OTHER SIDE OF THE FORTRESS, MEILIN PACED IN THE map room. As she moved around the room, her hands behind her back, she did her absolute best to avoid looking at the three-hundred-pound panda in the room with her. It wasn't that she didn't like Jhi. It was just that looking at her reminded Meilin of precisely everything that was angering her at the moment.

In front of Meilin was a map of Erdas. All the continents were neatly drawn in burgundy ink: Amaya, Nilo, Eura, and Zhong. Someone had lightly drawn in another continent, Stetriol, near the bottom of the map. Meilin put her finger on it. This was where the Conquerors were coming from. Where the Devourer was coming from.

Meilin traced her finger to Zhong. It wasn't very far at all. No wonder Zhong was the first to be attacked.

Is my father still alive? she wondered. If she closed her eyes, she could still see the general's face.

Meilin dragged her finger from Zhong to Eura. It seemed like a much farther distance than Stetriol to Zhong.

Why am I here? she thought furiously. *Why am I not there fighting? And why do I have such a useless spirit animal?*

She wished the others were ready to go. Meilin had selected her weapons and supplies and packed with the efficiency her father had taught her. She wasn't surprised that the others were slower. They probably weren't used to having enough belongings to even learn how to pack.

It felt a little better to be going on a mission, but doubt chewed at her. How was chasing down the other Great Beasts supposed to do anything to help Zhong *now*?

Meilin spun. Jhi sat silently behind her. The black spots around her eyes made her look a little sad. She was so slow. So peaceful. Sure, she had some healing powers, but not enough to save someone mortally wounded. Jhi would be a very useful ally if the Devourer needed to be cuddled to death.

Fury bubbled in Meilin.

The door opened. Immediately, Meilin composed her face. She wouldn't let anyone see her truly upset. Especially not if it was Rollan.

And it *was* Rollan, along with Conor, Abeke, and Finn. They seemed in high spirits, apart from Finn, whose youthful face was as masked as Meilin's. In the lamps of the map room, his gray hair looked nearly white.

"It's a little late to be studying up on geography," Rollan said to Meilin. Essix sailed in behind him, tucking her wings to keep from singeing them on the torches.

"I was bored," she replied stiffly. "I finished packing hours ago."

"Let me guess," Rollan said. "You took a class in it. Four tutors taught you how to fold your clothing."

"For the record, I traveled a lot with my father. I taught myself." Meilin turned to Finn. "Tell me again why our mission is so important?"

Quietly, Finn explained, "If we truly can find Rumfuss the Boar, we might be able to persuade him to give up his talisman. I understand you four retrieved one from Arax the Ram. The Devourer seeks these talismans to use them in the war, and we must beat him to them."

"*If*," Meilin echoed. "If we find the boar. If we persuade him to give us the talisman. What if we don't?"

Finn gave her a very long look. "I don't think we should bank on failure so early, do you?"

Suddenly Tarik flew into the room, cloak swirling, face grim. "I'm sorry to be late, but I have very bad news."

Meilin's stomach lurched. She felt like Tarik was looking at her in particular.

Father!

Sure enough, Tarik's eyes held hers a moment longer. He said, "Zhong has fallen to the Conquerors."

"No . . ." she whispered.

"I'm afraid so," Tarik said. "The capital city has been taken over. And, Meilin — your father is missing."

Meilin folded her arms to hide their shaking. She wanted to cry, but she wouldn't let herself do so in front of the others, all of whom were trying very hard to look at anything but her. Instead, as devastation burned behind her eyes, she shouted, "I should have never come here! There's absolutely no point to having me along on a — a *treasure hunt* across the globe! I should've been fighting by his side." She shot a poisonous look at Jhi. "And *you* – !" The panda met Meilin's glare with her own gentle gaze, cutting the girl short. Jhi's presence was a painful reminder of home.

All Meilin could think of was the colorful roofs of Jano Rion burning. Zhong fallen! Her father missing!

"Meilin," started Tarik. "I know that this is terrible news, but finding Rumfuss is really the most helpful step you can take right now."

"I don't believe that!" she snapped. She thought she could feel some sort of emotion coming off Jhi, but she pushed it away. "There's no guarantee that we'll find him, and there's no guarantee that he'll give us the talisman, and even if he does, there are more than a dozen left to go! Zhong needs me *now*."

"You're only one girl," Tarik said. "Here, you're part of a team."

Meilin's cold gaze flitted across Conor, Rollan, Abeke, and Finn. The servant, the orphan, the traitor, and the warrior who had given up war.

Not much of a team, she thought.

"You cannot force me," she said. "I'm going back to Zhong."

"You can't," Conor said, an unbearable concern in his voice.

"Watch me," Meilin shot back.

Conor stuttered, "B-but we *need* you."

"Zhong needs me." Turning to Jhi, she added, "*You* can stay here."

Storming from the room, she slammed the door behind her. She hurried down the hall so fast that the flaming lamps flickered as she passed. She hoped no one tried to come after her. All she wanted was to get her bag and a horse and go. She'd follow the main trade road back to Zhong.

She was nearly back to her room when a hand caught her arm.

"Meilin."

She spun. It was Finn. She didn't know how he caught up to her so silently.

Meilin's expression darkened. Trundling behind him was Jhi. Slower, of course. Not much louder, though.

"You can't keep me here," she said.

Finn tossed her arm away. Almost contemptuously, so she could see how he never intended to physically contain her. In a way, it made her feel better that he wasn't trying to spare her feelings, like Tarik or Olvan might have. She didn't want to be coddled.

He said, "I left a place once in anger. Leaving in anger means returning in regret. I don't want that for you."

I'm not returning, Meilin thought. *So the regret won't matter.* But something about the way he spoke, calm and measured, reminded her a little of her father. So she said, "I'm listening."

"You did your spirit animal a bad turn back there," Finn continued. "Has she ever done the same to you?"

Glancing at Jhi out of the corner of her eye, Meilin felt a little stab of guilt . . . but not enough guilt to change her mind. Out loud, she said, "No! She does practically nothing. The bond was wrong. I'm sure she'd be happier with a different girl." Actually, Meilin thought that Jhi would have been perfect for the girl everyone back in Zhong had *thought* she was. Very few had known about her combat lessons or her interest in strategy. Most saw only the carefully made-up girl who looked so pretty as she strolled in the tea garden or handled the cocoons for silk-making. Jhi would have looked right at home with that public Meilin.

"I don't know if you're so different," Finn said. "Will you come with me? I'll show you something. If it doesn't interest you, you can leave and I won't be the one to stop you."

Meilin reluctantly followed him to a foyer with an iron chandelier, and then through an arched doorway. The room inside was cluttered with dusty mirrors, musical instruments, and objects Meilin saw no use for. It reminded her of all the useless weapons at the morning's training exercise. This room was piled with things that would serve as shoddy weapons. The mess of it irritated her. What was the purpose, she wondered, of a room full of disorganized junk? Even if there was something useful in here, no one would be able to find it.

"What is this place?"

"This is the Moon Tower," Finn said. "It's a place where Greencloaks can form deeper bonds with their spirit animals."

"My bond is fine," Meilin replied crisply. Jhi sat down heavily beside a dusty gong. "She would go into passive form on the first day. Rollan is still struggling."

Finn raised his eyebrows. "I wouldn't compare myself with Rollan. We are our own competition."

Shocked, she said, "My father said that very same thing to me."

"Well then," Finn said with a ghost of a smile. "He must be very wise. Now, this tower isn't for training. It's more like play, or meditation. Sometimes music, art, or logic games will encourage a stronger bond and reveal hidden skills."

Meilin sighed in frustration. "I know her skills. But she's nothing like me."

Finn's expression sharpened. "You do everyone a disservice when you forget who you really are. Is combat all there is to you?"

She opened her mouth and then closed it. The question was maddening in its silliness. "Of course not. But my home has already been taken. It's what Zhong – what my father – needs of me at the moment!"

"And at the end of all this?"

Meilin raised her hands in a helpless gesture. "We'll see about that once we get there. If we get there."

"Take my word on it: That might be too late. Balance, Meilin. Surely your father told you that. Look at this." He pulled up his sleeve, looking for one tattoo among the tangle of tattoos. Finally, he pressed his finger to a symbol inked between a tangled thorn tree and a collection of pictograms. It was a circle, divided in half with a wavy line. One half was light. The other half was dark.

Meilin was again shocked. "That's a Zhongese symbol. How do you know it?"

"I was one of the Greencloaks' greatest warriors. I have been all over Erdas in my time. So you know this symbol?"

Of course she did. "One side is light, one side is dark. One side is active, the other is passive. Day and night."

"Opposites," Finn said. "But both part of the same whole."

Meilin worked hard to quell her indignation. She was getting tired of Greencloaks telling her she needed to make more of an effort to bond—as if she hadn't been trying. "How does that do me any good?"

Finn gestured to the things around them. "This is a place to find out." When she still looked unconvinced, he said, "I'm using this room myself. Would you like to hear the story?"

She merely raised an eyebrow in response.

He began, "My final battle was near Zhong, in Oceanus. My brothers and I were ambushing a small band of the Devourer's allies. There were fifty of them and only five of us, but we had fought worse odds with our spirit animals. Five Marked siblings in one family, yes," he said in response to Meilin's puzzled look. "The Greencloaks told us we were *chosen*. I was supposed to accomplish so many great things." Finn said this last part with a bitter smile that gave Meilin a stab of anxiety. The Greencloaks were saying the same thing about her.

"I was known to be clever with the making of things, so my brothers asked me to build a trap. It was a cunning one, a great pit with young trees bent this way and that over it. Over the top of their flexible trunks, I'd woven in brush with the roots still hanging, so the plants would stay green. When I was done it looked just like a grassy bank. Just another hill to climb. It was strong enough to support one man, but the trees would give way under the weight of more than one. Then all we'd have to do is wave at the enemy from up above after they'd all fallen through.

"Half of the Conquerors were meant to fall in it before the other half even knew what was going on. But then something went terribly wrong. They discovered the trap – or rather, their spirit animals did. Somehow, all fifty of them had bonded with spirit animals. That's impossible, but they had. So it was not only fifty Conquerors, but fifty Conquerors aided by fifty spirit animals."

Meilin made a soft noise of disbelief – bonding with spirit animals was so rare that it was hard to imagine fifty Marked individuals in one place, outside of the Greencloaks.

But Finn's face was serious. "You doubt it. I doubted it myself. Like I said: impossible. But *you're* also impossible. No one can summon a Great Beast, and yet the four of you have. It seems we have entered impossible times."

Meilin inclined her head. True enough.

Finn continued, "The spirit animals discovered the trap easily, making it useless. There's nothing danger-ous about a hole no one falls into. My brothers and I tried to hold them off, but it was no use. There were too many of them. Imagine if you can, Meilin: fifty spirit ani-mals. Animals we'd never seen before. Rhinos. Cougars. Anacondas. Scorpions. My brothers were slaughtered. It was – I barely . . . My youngest brother, Alec, distracted them so I could get away.

"Recovering has been difficult. It was horrific. Not just for me, but for my spirit animal, Donn. I nearly lost him. During the battle, he entered the passive state and now he will not come back out."

Meilin's eyes were wide. "Your brothers. That's terrible. And your spirit animal . . . I didn't know that could happen."

Finn looked around the Moon Tower. "My spirit animal, Donn, and I had a very difficult bonding. I lived in a very remote village and the Nectar didn't make it in time – I was the only child of age and the Greencloaks found me too late. The Moon Tower helped us to find a measure of peace. I know it will help us again."

Meilin said, "I want to ask a question, but it might be rude."

Finn smiled a tiny smile. "I won't be offended. There's not much that can hurt me in this world anymore."

"Was your hair always that color?"

Now Finn smiled ruefully as he patted the crazy gray-white spikes. "No. It changed after the battle. I woke up and my hair had gone completely white. Now – will you try to connect with Jhi here in the Moon Tower?"

Slowly, Meilin nodded. She didn't think it could really change her mind, but after his terrible confession, she felt she owed it to him to try.

"What's the right way to do this?" she asked.

"It's play," Finn said. "There is no right way."

Meilin had never been a playful child. There had always been combat to train for, languages to learn, skills to conquer. There might have been time for play, but she hadn't been interested. *Play* had never changed the world.

She took another look around the room. Before, she had found it disordered and useless. But with deeper examination, she saw a kind of organization. Drums gathered near paintings that had to do with earth and objects made of leather and wood. String instruments were near metal sculptures and mirrors and paintings of water. Woodwinds, paper objects, and anything having to do with air seemed to be grouped together.

Somehow this made her trust the room's purpose more. She had been educated in the usefulness of the arts. She would never be convinced there was a purpose for chaos.

Her eyes landed on an erhu, a traditional instrument from Zhong. She had received hours of lessons, but it had been months since she'd played. Taking up the bow, she crossed back to Jhi. Standing this close, Meilin could feel the heat radiating from the panda's body and smell the wet bamboo scent of her coarse fur.

Jhi rolled her gaze toward Meilin.

"I'm trying," Meilin said. "I'll try if you'll try."

Feeling a little foolish, she began to play. At first, she could only remember her instructor correcting her finger position and her bow technique. But after a few measures, she began to feel something else. A wide-open peace. Meilin knew that the emotion was coming from Jhi. This was part of the panda's power. Ordinarily this was where Meilin lost patience – she had no interest in being calm.

But she had promised Jhi she would try. Slowly the peace focused.

A very strange thing happened then. Meilin imagined she was surrounded by small, floating planets. Tinier moons circled some of them. She knew in a fuzzy, dreamy way that these orbs were her options. As the erhu sang sweetly in the background, Meilin realized that the closest little sphere represented the path back to Zhong. It was certainly the closest option, but it was also the smallest.

And there were no other moon-choices floating around it.

With her decisions hovering outside of her mind, it was easy to tell that her plan to return to Zhong was logical, but reactive. And it was easy to see too that it left her with nowhere else to go.

Jhi's power kept pushing at Meilin. She glimpsed the orb that represented the choice of going in search of Rumfuss. It was a troubled, stormy planet, but it was surrounded by more choices, and each of those was surrounded by even more. It wouldn't be an easy choice, but it had more possibilities close by.

Meilin strained her neck to see it closer. Suddenly, in one of the orbs, she saw her father's proud face. *You've made the wise decision*, he said, *instead of the smart one. Well done.*

Meilin stopped playing all at once. The mysterious orbs vanished. Jhi blinked quietly at her.

"What happened?" Finn asked. Meilin had forgotten he was there.

Meilin didn't know how to explain it. The panda had helped her to *think*.

"I made a decision," she said. "I'm going with you."

JOURNEY

IT STARTED TO RAIN. IT RAINED AS THEY FETCHED HORSES FROM the stables. It rained as they left Greenhaven Castle. It rained while they loaded supplies onto the boat to Eura. It rained as the ship shoved off from the pier and into the storm-gray water.

It rained on everyone, but it especially rained on Rollan. He didn't get along with boats, so he stood at the railing and tried not to focus on his churning insides. He could bear being drizzled on if it meant he didn't throw up on anyone. Essix found a perch on one of the masts, looking a little unsettled herself. Stuffing her head under her wing, she quivered sickly.

It was strangely quiet; he could hear the rain falling on the ocean. Although the ship had sails, they were tied tightly away on the masts. He couldn't quite work out what propelled the ship. Far up ahead, though, he saw two odd waves breaking again and again. Water pushed by the ship's hull, maybe? It didn't seem very likely.

"Whales." Abeke's clipped voice startled him as she

joined him. The rain dribbling down her nose matched the rain dribbling down Rollan's. Uraza sauntered behind her, ears pinned in the damp, tail thrashing.

"Whales what?"

Abeke pointed. "Rockback whales. They're pulling the ship."

She indicated the odd waves. Now that Rollan focused on them, he could tell that they were indeed whales, not water. The beasts were as mottled gray and black as the stormy sea, and their spines were studded with stones and boulders. Like moving cliffs just beneath the water. They must have been longer than the ship itself.

Rollan was deeply impressed, but would have never admitted it out loud.

He asked, "How did you know?"

She didn't seem as if she wanted to answer, but she pressed her lips together and replied, "When I accompanied the Conquerors to look for the first talisman, we traveled in a ship like this. I'd never seen anything like it. There is not much opportunity to travel by ship in Nilo, much less a rockback-whale ferry."

For a few minutes, they both watched the rocky backs rise and fall. In the eerie hush, one of the whales called to the other. It was a hollow, echoey sound that seemed both very close and very far.

"Wow," Abeke breathed.

"Creepy," Rollan corrected. "Speaking of creepy, let's talk about those Conquerors."

It wasn't the most tactful way to bring it up, but Rollan wasn't really known for his tact.

Abeke raised an eyebrow but said nothing; it was hard

to say if she was hurt by his words or hiding something. Rollan glanced toward the mast where Essix perched, her head still beneath her wing. Her intuitive power would have come in handy right about now, but she showed no signs of helping out.

"Well, you were fighting for them and all," Rollan said. "I figured you might have the inside track on all things Conqueror."

"I already told you how it happened," Abeke replied stiffly.

"Tell me again. I love happy endings."

She sighed. "Rollan, don't you remember what it was like when you called up Essix? Was she what you expected?"

Of course she hadn't been expected. Rollan hadn't been expecting much of anything, as he had been sitting in a prison at the time, and in prison, disappointment was generally the most practical thing to expect. And even if he hadn't been incarcerated, he couldn't have expected Essix to appear. Nobody called up Great Beasts.

"Sure," Rollan replied easily. "Miracles happen to me all the time."

Abeke made a face. She touched the tuft of coarse fur at Uraza's shoulders, as if for comfort. "Don't you remember how uncertain everything was? Nobody knows if they are going to call up a spirit animal at all. And the rituals make it so nerve-racking. Everyone is looking at you. There is so much pressure."

"I didn't have a ritual," Rollan said. "I had a homeless guy and a rat. But I get the idea."

Abeke stopped. "Do you want to talk about it?"

"No. Actually, I don't. That's basically the beginning, middle, and end of it, anyway: homeless guy, rat, magical falcon. Happy ending. Told you. I love those things. Go on with your story."

She said, "My ritual was very well attended. We desperately needed rain, and there was hope that a new rain dancer would be named. Then, all of a sudden I had a spirit animal, and it was a *Great Beast* and then it began to rain! My father had never looked at me like that before. My sister had never looked at me that way before—*no one* had. Everyone thought I was the new rain dancer. I was still trying to understand that I'd summoned a spirit animal! And then in the middle of the commotion, Zerif appeared and told me that he needed me to help save the world. Maybe you would have done better, Rollan, but during all that, I really didn't think to ask him, *Are you telling the truth?*"

Rollan thought back to his own summoning. Zerif had appeared not long after Essix had. But Rollan *had* doubted him. And then taken off running.

To be fair, that was how Rollan approached most situations in life. He'd pulled the same stunt for the Greencloaks too: doubt and run. Never a *bad* plan.

Abeke broke in ruefully, "You did ask him, didn't you? Or at least, you didn't trust him." When he looked at her, surprised, she added, "I could tell by your face. You were thinking I was foolish to go with him."

"A fool's better than a traitor."

Very serious, she nodded. "Rollan, I want you to know that I won't let the Greencloaks down."

I'm not a Greencloak, he thought. But he didn't say it out loud.

Instead, he watched Uraza slink damply after Abeke as they retreated to the ship's cabin. After they had gone, Essix flapped down to join him, her talons tight on the wet wood.

"Thanks for your help back there," he told her. "What do you think about her?"

Essix stretched out a leg and chewed on one of her talons.

"That," Rollan said, "is exactly how I feel about it."

<hr/>

It kept pouring. Once they made landfall, they transferred the supplies to the horses and set off through the damp evening. Technically, the horses were supposed to be a privilege. A way to make the long journey faster and more agreeable.

But practically, Rollan wished they were walking. Neither he nor Essix got along with his horse. For starters, Rollan wasn't the best of riders. Life as a street urchin hadn't exactly prepared him for hours in the saddle. Back in Concorba, if he'd wanted to go somewhere, he'd gone on the bottoms of his own two feet. It was only because of their last mission that he'd had any experience on horseback at all. In fact, after that ride across Amaya, he still had blisters in all kinds of places where blisters shouldn't be.

Also, his horse was a terrible animal. Terrible to look at, with its flecked gray coat, and terrible to be around, with its habit of biting Rollan. If he relaxed his hold on the reins at all, the creature would bend itself almost in half to nip at his legs. It hated Essix too. If the falcon got anywhere near, the horse would rear and snap toward the bird.

"Maybe it's hungry," Conor suggested as they rode side by side through the drizzle.

"Hungry for human flesh, maybe," Rollan replied.

Overhead, Essix cried out; the horse pinned its ears back angrily. "Falcon flesh too."

"If you treat him with respect, he'll treat you with respect," Tarik called.

Easy for him to say, Rollan thought as Tarik and Meilin began a conversation about the pleasures of being taught horseback riding before one could walk.

After a few hours, Rollan was wet to the skin. His scruffy hair stuck to his forehead. The rolling, treeless countryside was already soaked green and black. Even if they'd wanted to stop, there was no shelter.

"Oh, yeah," he said, "this reminds me of home." He'd spent countless evenings on the streets, pressed against a wall, barely out of the rain. Stomach growling, always hungry.

Well, at least now his stomach was full.

"Too tough for you?" Meilin asked sweetly. Her black hair was slicked on either side of her face.

"Oh, no," Rollan replied. "I'm great at being cold and wet. One of my finest skills."

Meilin shot back, "Did you have tutors for that?"

"I taught myself."

She smiled at that, then hid it, fast. But Rollan had already seen. *Ha! Score one point for me.*

He was a little worried at how much he was getting used to *not* living on the streets, actually. He still hadn't made up his mind over whether or not he wanted to work with the Greencloaks permanently, but if he left now, he'd have to get used to being hungry and dirty and mostly dead all over again. Just a few weeks ago, all he'd cared about was whether or not he'd get to eat once every three days. Now he had stopped worrying about meals and was instead concentrating on getting a smile out of a snotty general's daughter.

Slippery slope, Rollan, he reminded himself. *Don't forget how to be on your own.*

"It will be better once we get in the trees," Tarik said, gesturing to a small copse of oaks ahead.

"We'll need to be on our guard," Finn spoke up, the first thing he had said since they mounted the horses. "Eura is not as safe as it once was. You all should remember the lessons you learned in training before we left."

The main lesson Rollan had learned in training was that Meilin was dangerous with a handkerchief.

Taking advantage of his distraction, Rollan's horse stopped in its tracks and tried to take a bite out of his leg.

"No way!" he told it, jerking the opposite rein. "That's my favorite leg."

From down the road, Tarik said, "Your horse used to be a spirit animal. His human fell in battle. That's why he's so irritable."

Rollan worked to save his favorite leg and then the other one. "Pretty shoddy reason."

Abeke said thoughtfully, "I hear it's unbearable if the bond is broken."

"It's true," Tarik said. "As you four know, the bond is a powerful thing, and it gets stronger the longer you're together. To lose your bonded partner is like losing a limb."

Rollan's horse made another grab at him. Yellow teeth snagged fabric and narrowly missed bone.

"I'm right on track to know what that feels like," he muttered.

"Do you think the horse is jealous of Rollan and Essix's bond?" Abeke asked.

There was not a lot to be jealous of. Essix would come to Rollan in a pinch, but they both seemed to be loners. Rollan couldn't figure out a way to get through to the falcon – or even if he really wanted to. He'd gotten along fine before she came along, and he figured he could probably manage fine after too. He guessed she felt the same way about him.

Tarik lifted a shoulder. "Possibly. Or it could just remind him of what he once had."

Rollan twisted to look at Abeke. Her bond with Uraza seemed pretty great. The leopard followed her as if the two of them were thinking the same thoughts. Wanting the same things. With Essix, Rollan felt they wanted the same thing about as often as any bird and boy would . . . which wasn't much at all.

Tarik's horse spooked, hooves stamping and scraping on the ground. Rollan couldn't immediately see what had startled it. Then he glimpsed a small, furry animal scrabbling up the horse's side. Tarik swiped at it with a surprised, hoarse laugh. He called out, "It's a weasel!"

Rollan curled his lip. He hated weasels more than his horse. They were like rats, but longer. Like snakes, but furrier.

"What's going on up there?" Finn asked from his position at the rear.

"I've got it under control!" Tarik called back, swatting at the biting and clawing animal. It looked like he was being attacked by a scarf. Behind him, Conor and Abeke clearly couldn't decide if they were allowed to laugh.

The weasel lunged for Tarik's eyes. Tarik blocked the animal—barely. His horse reared again.

Suddenly a surge of intuition jolted through Rollan, certain and overpowering and ferocious. His eyes found Essix in the sky without having to search for her. The falcon's gaze was fixed on him as well. This was one thing they had in common: an uncanny ability to read people and situations. And when they worked together, the connection was—well, it was easy to see why Essix was called a *Great* Beast.

Now Rollan knew the truth as clear as if someone had shouted it to him.

Something was wrong.

This was an ambush.

"Watch out!" he shouted. "It's a trap!"

Finn scanned the woods, his expression sharpening. "Conquerors! Arm yourselves!"

Two men plunged out of the brush, a fox on their heels. In a decisive move, one seized the bridle of Finn's horse and the other threw himself at Tarik. Lumeo, Tarik's spirit animal, an otter, twisted suddenly out of his dormant form. A third man charged from the trees, a badger on his heels.

Rollan's stomach dropped.

These new animals were no ordinary animals.

They were spirit animals.

Conquerors' spirit animals.

"Don't just stand there!" Meilin ordered, voice clear and ringing. "Attack!"

Rollan realized he had been frozen by the chaos. Up ahead, Tarik jumped off his horse and drew a knife against his human attacker, even as the weasel dug its teeth into his shoulder. The Conqueror easily avoided Tarik's knife – the bond between him and the weasel was giving the man superhuman agility. More Conquerors emerged – too many to count. Everything was a mess of people and spirit animals. So many spirit animals.

Rollan kicked his horse to get closer to the fray. The action promptly caused the horse to swing its head to snap at him.

"No!" he said furiously. "You grass-burning chump! Look! They're in trouble! Go that way!"

The horse bucked. Rollan clutched its neck to keep from flying off. Briggan loped by him, Conor close to his heels, dagger in hand. Abeke was right behind, wielding a large tree branch like a weapon as Uraza pounced. They all looked gloriously useful.

Overhead, Essix cried out. In falcon language, it clearly meant *Do something!*

"I'm *trying!*" Rollan said. "Where's your sense of loyalty, horse?!"

The horse reared. This time, Rollan slid right off the back of his rain-slick saddle. Both his pride and his tailbone shouted angrily as he landed. The horse was gone faster than you could say *traitor*.

He clambered to his feet. Essix swooped low to see if he was okay.

At least somebody is loyal around here, he thought. He gave her a thumbs-up. He didn't know if she understood. Falcons didn't have thumbs.

Two other Conquerors were closing in on Tarik. One of them was bald and had a snake wrapped loosely around his arm. The other was dramatically mustached and had a small cat at his feet. As Tarik parried their blows with astonishing precision, Lumeo pounced on the cat in a chaos of fur and tooth. The cat's Conqueror was momentarily distracted and Tarik took advantage of this, delivering a roundhouse blow to his foe's midsection. The Conqueror stumbled back into Tarik's horse, who delivered a kick of its own, knocking the attacker unconscious. The cat fled to the woods.

Conor and Briggan were holding off the Conqueror who'd been joined by the badger – the man seemed to weaken as soon as Briggan got the badger clamped in his jaw. Finn stood in the shadows, head bowed, holding his side tightly. He seemed to be fighting a battle that existed behind his own closed eyes. The Conquerors hadn't noticed him yet. Close by, Meilin had been drawn farther away to fight with two other Conquerors. When Abeke approached with her tree branch to give aid, Meilin shouted to her, "I don't need *your* help!"

Abeke looked shocked, but she wasn't deterred. She leaped to rescue Finn as a Conqueror discovered him. It wasn't ideal, but Meilin, Abeke, and Finn looked like they were handling themselves. Tarik, on the other hand – he faced not only the persistent weasel, but also the bald Conqueror with the snake wrapped around his arm.

Rollan ran toward him. The weasel scrambled up Tarik's face. In that moment, the bald Conqueror tossed the serpent. Blinded by the weasel, Tarik didn't immediately understand this new threat.

"Tarik!" Rollan shouted. "It's the snake!"

The Greencloak's hands tightened around the serpent. Too late. The snake's fangs sank into his arm. Tarik shook off the weasel and ripped the snake from himself, but he staggered. In this moment of vulnerability, the bald Conqueror raised his sword, about to deliver a killing blow.

There wasn't enough time for Rollan to reach him before the sword fell.

"Essix!" he yelled. Surely she would come through for him when it was really important.

The falcon dove, claws outstretched. She landed on the enemy's bald head a moment before he swung the sword. As the Conqueror flailed, nothing but feathers in his view, Rollan scrambled to seize the man's sword.

"Get it off of me!" the man screamed. His eyes were shut tight; Essix's talons were inches away from them.

Rollan clutched the sword threateningly. "If I do, will you leave us alone?"

"Anything!" the man said. "Trust me!"

Out of the corner of his eye, Rollan glimpsed the snake slither into the bald Conqueror's open hand.

"Unfortunately for you," said Rollan, "I don't trust anyone."

The Conqueror threw the serpent forward, but Rollan was ready. He swung the sword. The heavy blade sliced the snake neatly in two and kept on swinging.

Right into the Conqueror's leg.

Both Rollan and the bald man howled – the Conqueror in pain, Rollan in surprise. It was the first time Rollan had ever struck a human with a proper sword, and unbelievably, no one had been around to notice it. *Well, except Essix,* Rollan thought as the falcon flapped into the air with a dry, approving cry. He gave the falcon a hasty one-finger salute as he spun to deal with the remaining spirit animal. The weasel, however, had slunk into the trees. It must have been looking for its human partner.

The Conqueror continued wailing.

"Don't move a muscle," Rollan warned, sword still pointed at him. "You try to slither your way out of this one, you might lose something precious to you – like your life."

A cry pierced the air from where Conor had been fighting his foe. Without removing the sword's tip from his prisoner, Rollan glanced toward the commotion. Briggan held a Conqueror's spirit animal in his jaws – the badger Rollan had seen earlier. The Conqueror watched anxiously from the edge of the woods. With a growl, the wolf opened his jaws; the badger fell lifeless to the ground.

The Conqueror threw up his arm, trying to call the badger back to him. Nothing happened. He tried again. Still nothing. No tattoo would form. The man let out an anguished cry. No one moved against him as he shifted to claim the badger. Without even a glance for the others, he disappeared with it into the forest.

Conor did not follow. There was a curious sadness in his face.

Rollan was unsympathetic. The Conqueror should have known: Don't bring a badger to a Great Beast fight.

Rollan turned his attention to Tarik, whose clothing was tattered and bloodstained.

"It looks worse than it is," Tarik muttered, teeth clenched in pain.

"That snake—" Rollan began.

"A Euran adder. I need to get the herbal antidote for the venom. Unfortunately, it will only get worse."

This sounded alarming to Rollan. "Have you been bit before?"

Tarik answered calmly, "No. But I have seen others."

"Can you walk?"

The Greencloak winced. "Is my horse gone?"

Nearby, Conor nodded grimly. Gone. In fact, aside from the Conqueror's groans, which Rollan thought were uncalled for, the forest had fallen uneasily silent.

Rollan called out for Meilin, Abeke, and Finn.

There was no reply.

"Where'd they go?" he asked Conor.

Conor pointed. "The others galloped that way. But we'd never catch up. Our horses are gone." Even Tarik's well-behaved steed had vanished, spooked by the combat.

"Well, this is a grand adventure," remarked Rollan. "Three missing and one chewed on. What do we do now?"

With a grimace, Tarik pushed himself onto an elbow. In a low voice so that the Conqueror couldn't hear, he whispered, "There's a Greencloak near here. An old informant. I think that's the best place to go. Finn knows her, and she will have the antidote. I'm afraid you'll have to help me walk, though."

Conor and Rollan each took one of Tarik's arms and hauled him up. Lumeo stood by his side, his coat uneven and sodden from the fight in the damp underbrush. His normally playful expression was keen, trying to anticipate what Tarik might need from him.

"It's all right, old friend," Tarik said to his spirit animal. He was shivering in an alarming sort of way. "Don't worry."

"Do you think the others are okay?" Conor asked. "You said Finn was just a scout. He doesn't fight, does he?"

"But Meilin does," Tarik said. "Very well, as we keep finding out. And Finn still has his wits. I am optimistic. But we'd better get going. It's not far. But with me like this, it will probably feel that way."

Tarik tried to be valiant, but it was clear that his condition was darkening with the evening. By the time night had fallen, he was quivering and clammy. Rollan wondered just how fast this antidote would work.

Finally, Tarik breathed, "There. There it is."

Conor exclaimed, "That's a castle!"

Rollan squinted at the single tower, gray and ghostly in the rainy dark. There was only one very short door and no discernible window openings. It looked like the sort of building an unimaginative child would build. "If it's a castle, where's the rest of it?"

"Beggars can't be choosers," Tarik said. "Help me down the path."

At the small door, he did a complicated knock.

Nothing happened.

He did it again. He told them, "Sometimes she pretends to be deaf."

The door opened. An old woman, tiny and as wizened as an ancient fruit tree, stood on the other side. She said, "I *am* deaf."

Rollan and Conor exchanged a look behind Tarik's head.

"Tarit," croaked the old woman. She had a voice like wood shavings. A faded green cloak hung on a peg just beside the door, but it looked as if it hadn't been moved for quite a while. "It's been a long time."

"Tarik," corrected Tarik.

"That's what I said," she replied. "There seems to be less of you than last time I saw you."

"A snake and a weasel ate the rest," Rollan said. "A Euran adder, to be precise. I'm not sure what kind of weasel."

The old woman noticed Conor and Rollan for the first time. "And two new Greencloaks, I see." Really, her voice sounded more like someone eating pebbles.

"One," corrected Rollan. "By which I mean, not me."

"Lady Evelyn," Tarik said faintly. "These are the ones you must have heard about. The children who summoned the Fallen Beasts."

The lady eyeballed them closely. It was not an entirely comfortable experience. She had a little bit of a mustache. Just a few white hairs. Rollan tried not to stare.

"Oh, no, Tarin, you must be mistaken," she crackled. "There are four of *those* children. This is certainly only two."

"*Tarik*," he corrected again. "There was a scuffle on the road. We have lost touch with the other two for the moment."

"You lost half of the Fallen? That seems careless,"

the old woman – Lady Evelyn – said. Now her voice was more like stepping on a very large beetle. "Well, come in before you lose another half."

Inside the tower was the opposite of the grand Greenhaven Castle. Straw covered the floor. Threadbare tapestries hung over the narrow window slits to keep the wind out. Something thin and gray boiled in a pot hanging over the fire. Circular stairs led up to nowhere. Rollan could see clear up into the blackness that must be the top of the tower; Essix had already soared up there to explore.

"I know what you're thinking, not-a-Greencloak," Lady Evelyn said. She was already puttering around in a collection of glass bottles and dried herbs, fingers searching across the cluttered windowsill. "Not a very pretty castle, that's what you're thinking. It wasn't meant to be pretty. It was just a place to keep cattle after you stole them."

"Who steals *cattle*?" Conor asked.

She cackled. "Who doesn't?"

"Me," he said.

Turning, she sniffed him. "Ah, you're a shepherd's son, though. You're a guardian, not a thief."

Conor, surprised at her intuition, sniffed his wet sleeve as if he possibly still smelled like his old life.

A soft whicker interrupted them.

"Ah," said Lady Evelyn. "This is my spirit animal, Dot."

Rollan grimaced. Another horse. Dot was a sway-backed black-and-white miniature horse the size of a dog. She also had a bit of a mustache. Just a few white hairs.

He whispered to Conor, "It's the opposite of a Great Beast."

Lady Evelyn chose that moment to be deaf. She instead

knocked several plates and scrolls off the table and said, "Why don't you lay Tarbin down here, so I can get to mending him? You boys can dry off by the fire and help yourselves to dinner."

The boys hesitantly stripped off their cloaks to dry by the fireplace and peered into the bubbling cauldron. Every now and then, something white and shapeless would boil up to the surface and then descend into the gray liquid again. Conor whispered, "I don't know if that's food or laundry."

Rollan's stomach growled. It didn't care. "I ate my fair share of laundry on the fine streets of Concorba."

Conor poked it with a ladle. He scooped something brown and stringy from the bottom.

"Food," Rollan declared. "Laundry is never stringy."

Conor didn't seem eager to sample it. Apparently shepherds' sons had more refined palates than street urchins. Rollan tried the stew, or whatever it was. It tasted like a puddle in the bad part of town.

"How is it?" Conor asked.

"Delicious."

Conor looked over to where Lady Evelyn was ministering to Tarik.

"Do you think he'll be okay?" he asked.

Rollan didn't want to lie. So he answered, "I don't know."

They ate in silence for a short time. Tarik was not entirely successful in stifling his pain. Eventually he quieted too. Neither Rollan nor Conor was sure of what this meant.

"Greencloak boy," Lady Evelyn ordered from behind them. "And not-a-Greencloak boy. I need to talk to you. About your quest."

They joined her at the table.

"Taril is fine now," she told them in a low voice. "I gave him something to help him sleep. He will recover. But it will take some time. He is lucky the serpent didn't strike closer to his heart. As it is, the venom will be hard to counteract. He will need constant rest and even more constant attention. Luckily, I never rest and am constantly attentive. However, he won't be able to travel with you."

"What?!" Conor cried. Both he and Rollan peered at Tarik. Though their mentor's face was more peaceful now, his skin looked strange and slack, and his lips were oddly parched. His breath came unevenly and his fingers still shook with the tremors Rollan had felt on the journey here. It was obvious he'd used the very last of his strength bringing them all here.

Rollan struggled with how to feel. Since he wasn't a Greencloak, he technically didn't owe Tarik any allegiance. But still—Tarik had trained him and protected him; he'd never been anything but kind to Rollan, even if Rollan wasn't sure if that was only because of Essix. It was difficult to see him like this. Utterly vulnerable. So close to death.

"He tells me another elder Greencloak—Fonn? Finn? Fann?—should find his way here with the remaining Fallen. If they don't get here by morning, though, you need to set off alone."

"Alone?" echoed Conor, dismayed.

"Time is of the essence. The Greencloaks are not the only ones who seek Rumfuss."

"But we don't know where to go," protested Conor.

A gaping chasm of uncertainty opened in Rollan's stomach, and it only grew wider and blacker the more he considered. They had just barely survived an encounter with a few Conquerors. Tarik had been doing this a lot longer than either Rollan or Conor, and now he was flat on a table being fed gruel. The last time the boys had faced off against a Great Beast, they'd had the help of adults. Even if by some crazy stroke of luck they managed to meet back up with Finn, the other Greencloak didn't fight. Which meant that the plan on offer right now involved Rollan and Conor heading into the wilderness and then taking on Rumfuss on their own.

"I have a map," Lady Evelyn said. When neither of them looked excited by this confession, she added, "Do you children know what a map is?"

Rollan and Conor exchanged another dismal look.

Lady Evelyn spread a map over Tarik's sleeping chest. She pointed to a town near the top. "This is Glengavin. The rumor says that Rumfuss is near here. Now, I know what you're thinking. You're thinking, that's far north, and up there they paint their faces blue and eat foreigners."

That hadn't been what Rollan or Conor was thinking, but it sure was what they were thinking about *now*.

Lady Evelyn continued, "But the Lord of Glengavin is amicable toward the Greencloaks. He should provide a welcome, or at least no hindrance. The surroundings are quite wild and I doubt you'd be able to find it without this."

"Where are we now?" Rollan asked.

Lady Evelyn traced a line southward. "Here."

"Oh!" Conor said in a surprised, glad sort of yelp. "We're near Trunswick. It's on the way."

"What's Trunswick?" Rollan asked. "And why does it make you say 'oh!' like an overexcited pigeon?"

"It's where I used to be a servant," Conor said. "And my family works the land near there."

"You don't have time for detours, Greencloak boy," Lady Evelyn said. "Stick to the task."

Conor's face fell. "Right. Sure. Of course."

Rollan couldn't help it. He hated to see Conor looking so crestfallen. "Maybe we could still spend the night in Trunswick tomorrow. Not home, but close, right?"

Immediately Conor's face brightened. "I'm sure they'd give us a warm welcome. And my mother—"

Lady Evelyn interrupted with a vague frown. "I feel as if I have heard a rumor about Trunswick."

"Good or bad?" asked Rollan.

She tapped her remaining teeth with a stick. "Something about Greencloaks and the Devourer. Or maybe it was Trynsfield. Or Brunswick. Trunbridge? Was that the one we were talking about?"

Conor pointed to the map. "Trunswick. Right there."

She said, "Lovely place, I'm sure."

6

HAWKERS

THEY—FINN, MEILIN, AND ABEKE—WERE HIDING.
Along with Uraza, they were tucked between two boulders. As far as the eye could see, which wasn't very far in the darkness, there were man-sized, teeth-shaped stones pressed shoulder to shoulder. While Abeke marveled over the strangeness of the landscape and listened to the night, Meilin and Finn argued.

"Tonight is not a night to die," Finn whispered hoarsely.

Meilin's voice was cross. "I wasn't suggesting we die. I was suggesting we go back for the others."

"At this point, both of those things are the same," he muttered back.

"Shh," Abeke shushed them as quietly as she could. She jabbed a finger into the darkness.

Finn and Meilin turned to look where she pointed. Uraza was already looking, her ears swiveling to and fro. The black night kept most of its secrets, but Abeke could hear the wet squelch of a man's footprint on stone. One of the Conquerors. Close by.

Meilin opened her mouth. Abeke held her finger to her lips.

It had taken them hours to rid themselves of the group they'd first encountered in the forest. By then they had lost track of Conor, Rollan, and Tarik, and would have lost their way as well, if not for Finn's knowledge as a guide.

The sound of the man's footsteps came closer. Uraza stiffened. Abeke felt the vibration of an inaudible growl through the leopard's ribs pressed against her. Finn stretched out a hand: *Don't move.*

Holding their breath, they listened to the man climb over the boulders near them. All he had to do was clamber over two or three more, and he would discover them and alert his allies.

The Conqueror scraped over another boulder. His breath huffed out noisily as he landed at the base of it. Abeke suspected that he wasn't truly looking for them, or he would've minded how loud he was. But then again, maybe not. Abeke was always surprised by most people's ignorance of their own noisiness. It was one of the reasons why Finn's deliberate stealth impressed her.

Suddenly the Conqueror's breath was quite near. He was on the other side of the boulder Abeke knelt behind. If there had been any light at all, she probably would have been able to see his face through the gap between the rocks.

Every muscle in Uraza's body was knitted solid.

Abeke's heart pounded so loudly in her ears that she could barely hear anything else. She pressed her fingers into Uraza's fur. Slowly, her pulse calmed. Now she heard the sound of the man's palm as he felt his way along the stone.

He was so close.

Finn closed his eyes. Strangely enough, he looked quite serene. One of his arms hugged his chest so that his fingertips could touch his upper bicep. *Is that where his spirit animal is?* Abeke wondered.

Needle-fine claws scritched on stone as the Conqueror's spirit animal joined him. Abeke heard the click of hungry jaws. Somehow, a small, hungry spirit animal seemed more terrifying than a large one in this darkness. As if you maybe wouldn't notice it until it was right on you.

Then the Conqueror's voice sounded roughly. "Come on, Tan."

His footsteps receded as he headed away with whatever sort of animal Tan was. After a very, very long silence, Finn blew out a relieved sigh. Abeke released her handful of leopard fur. Uraza's tenseness oozed from her.

Meilin turned to Finn. "Do we have a regroup point? To reconnect with Tarik and the others?"

Abeke was unsurprised to hear her sounding efficient and strategic. That girl's heart was a battlefield.

"We did," Finn said. "A local Greencloak waypoint. But we've passed it, and we'd have to risk fighting back toward it. I think we should continue on to Trunswick. Even if the others aren't there, we can try to get a message to Greenhaven."

Abeke thought of the terrible fight in the woods and shuddered. She hoped the others were all right. "Message? How?"

"Gilded pigeons carry messages from many large towns in Eura," Finn answered. "Most Greencloaks know where to find someone who runs the birds."

I wonder if I could send a message to my family, Abeke thought.

Finn must have sensed her interest, because his expression softened and he added, "I will teach you how to send messages if it comes to that."

Meilin eyed Abeke suspiciously, but said nothing.

What? What did I do? Oh, Abeke thought dismally. *I wonder if she thinks I want to send messages to the enemy.*

She wished there was a way that she could reassure the other girl, but there didn't seem to be a way to without sounding even more suspicious. So she just said, "So we go now to Trunswick?"

"It's still quite a ways from here," Finn said. He pushed to his feet stiffly. "Let's find a place to sleep. Someplace a bit more comfortable."

By *more comfortable*, Finn meant sleeping under rocks instead of on top of them. They spent a rather brittle night beneath a rock overhang on the edge of the boulder field. It wasn't cozy, but at least it was dry and out of the wind. Abeke and Uraza curled up together like siblings and fell asleep.

———◆———

In the morning light, their surroundings looked quite different. Coming from Nilo, Abeke had never seen anything like the landscape. Behind them was the expanse of strange, square boulders, and before them was a flat, purple-green field that went on and on. Finn looked somehow at home here: All his green-purple tattoos matched the colors of the grass, and his silver hair matched the clouds that pressed low.

"Those rocks are called the Giant's Chessboard. And this is a moor," he explained to them. "It looks quite innocent, but it can be treacherous. The ground is soft in places and will happily swallow a person. Or a panda."

Meilin, stretching elegantly, said, "I'll keep Jhi in passive form today."

"Do you think it's safe to let Uraza walk?" Abeke asked, resting her fingers on the leopard's shoulder blades. "She prefers to run when she can." *Like me.*

"I think so," Finn said. "Cats are careful. But if we see anyone coming, it would probably be best to hide her."

"I guess there is no mistaking her for an ordinary leopard," Abeke said. Uraza preened at the admiration in Abeke's voice.

"Not many ordinary leopards in Eura anyway," Finn noted. "Much less extraordinary ones."

They set off across the moor. The ground beneath them shifted from hard-packed rocks to watery silt without warning. If Abeke hadn't been paying attention, she could've been in hidden water above her head before she had a chance to cry out.

In fact, only a few moments had passed before disaster struck. It wasn't that Abeke heard something—it was that she suddenly didn't hear something. A second later she realized that it was Meilin's breathing. She didn't hear it anymore because Meilin wasn't *there* anymore.

Abeke spun this way and that, but there was only motionless moor ahead and behind her.

"Finn!" she cried.

Finn understood immediately. "Where?"

"I don't *know*!"

They both scanned the moor for any sign of the other girl, but even Uraza couldn't pinpoint where she had gone. Abeke was too aware that every second that passed was a second Meilin couldn't breathe.

"Uraza," Finn said urgently, "any ideas?"

Nothing.

Then Meilin's arm burst into sight. It looked as if it grew from the tufted grass. Her fingers felt for the foliage, seized it. There was no way she would be able to pull herself out, but she was going to try. Leaping forward, Finn gripped her forearm with one tattooed hand. He stretched out his other hand to Abeke.

"Don't let us both go in," he warned. Grabbing his hand, Abeke braced herself. Then she hauled, and Finn hauled, and the moor gave Meilin up like a newborn calf. She sprawled across the grass rather unbeautifully and spat out some muddy bits of water.

"Welcome back," Finn told Meilin, a little out of breath.

"I was doing fine," she retorted, spitting out another glob of dirty grass.

Finn's mouth made a crafty shape. He said, "Abeke and I will know better next time."

Abeke hid a smile.

Meilin was already retrieving the bag she'd dropped

when she'd disappeared. She seemed completely unfazed by the experience. As she took down her damp hair and shook her head, she muttered, "It is going to take *forever* for my clothing to dry in this climate."

"I did say to be cautious," Finn said. "Let's use our heads."

The image of Meilin's hand extended from the hungry moor did keep Abeke careful for quite a bit of their journey that day. But then she began to notice how gifted Uraza was at finding dry spots to leap from. She also discovered that if she really focused on the leopard, she could sense them too. Soon the two of them were dancing across the moor.

Laughing, they outstripped the others. After a few minutes, however, Abeke and Uraza hesitated. Up ahead, Abeke got the *sense* of people. Then, a second later, she caught a glimpse of distant figures.

"Uraza!" she called. She held out her arm and the leopard vanished onto it without pause. The sting of it was more like a flush of heat now. It felt good. Powerful. Like Uraza was somehow becoming a part of her. She felt as if she could still feel the leopard beside her.

"What is it?" Meilin asked as she and Finn caught up.

Finn followed Abeke's gaze to the approaching silhouettes. As they grew closer, Abeke could see that one of them carried a pike with a stubby red-and-white flag on it.

"I don't like this," he said. "I think they're Hawkers."

Meilin's eyes narrowed. "What's a Hawker?"

"They're scoundrels who sell fake Nectar." Finn's

voice had turned dark. "They also sell the pelts of spirit animals."

"What?!" Abeke exclaimed. "Why?!"

Finn's fingers rested lightly on his complex tattoos. "There is a dirty superstition that wearing the pelt of a spirit animal will give you their powers, even if you weren't able to summon one yourself. You two *must* hide the fact that you have spirit animals or the Hawkers might be tempted to attack you."

Meilin and Abeke wordlessly tugged their sleeves down.

As the figures approached, dragging a small cart behind them, Meilin dropped her gaze and slumped her shoulders. She was transformed immediately to a docile and shy farm girl. Abeke ducked her head hurriedly. She wasn't sure she was as gifted an actress as Meilin, though.

"Hello, hello, hello!" said the first of the Hawkers. He had a very winning smile. It looked made out of rubber, like it could stretch and stretch and never break. If Finn hadn't been uneasy before, Abeke probably would've trusted this newcomer.

"Fine morning to you," said the woman beside him. She also appeared friendly, though she seemed to be made out of porridge instead of rubber. All soft dimples and warmth. "On a journey with your . . . daughters? Servants?"

Abeke and Meilin shot irritated glances at each other.

Finn replied in his quiet, unaffected way, "Foster daughters."

"Oh and oh," the man said. "I hear in your voice you're from the North too."

The Hawker said it aggressively — a taunt or a dare — but

Finn did not waver. "That's where we are headed. They will learn to sing for those with troubled bonds."

"A noble calling," the woman said.

"Noble," agreed the rubbery man. "Troubled bonds and troubled bonds, eh? How old are you lot? Old enough! Do you have spirit animals, little daughters?"

Meilin actually managed a blush as she turned her face away, looking too bashful to even *think* of answering. Abeke kept her head ducked and hoped they'd think she was too shy as well. She was beginning to change her mind about trusting the smiling man.

"Do you know the legend of the black wildcat?" the rubbery man asked.

Finn's mouth thinned. Meilin shook her head imperceptibly. Abeke didn't move at all.

"Going to the North and don't know the legend of the black wildcat!" exclaimed the porridge woman. "For years, the North has had its stories of giant black cats wandering its moors. Wondrous things, these wildcats. Big as a horse. Fierce. Full of magic!"

Finn said, his voice flat, "There are no black wildcats in the North anymore."

"Oh, you and you!" said the rubbery man. "Have faith! There's a prophecy that says a boy will bond with the black wildcat and deliver the North from persecution and poverty! That will lead us all to a glorious, peaceful future!"

"Maybe one of you is the child of the prophecy!" the porridge woman exclaimed.

Abeke forgot to be bashful. She said, "I'm not a boy."

The rubbery man grinned and pointed at her. "Well

spotted. But we can sell you a potion that will force the bond! We don't have to wait for the legend to come true—we can make it come true."

Finn said, "There's no such potion. And there is no black wildcat of the North. Not anymore."

"Oh, that is where you are wrong, funny little man!" said the porridge woman. She grandly let the door to their small cart fall open, revealing a rainbow of bottles, books, and colorful flotsam. A caged black animal peered out. When it saw Abeke's face, it mewled.

Meilin was unable to disguise her scorn. Her voice was anything but demure. "That's a house cat."

"It's a baby black wildcat," the rubbery man said.

"It's a full-grown house cat," Meilin insisted.

"It will get larger."

She scoffed, "I think it's plenty large enough for a house cat."

The cat stood on its back legs and pressed the small black pads of its feet against the cage bars. Abeke's heart and Uraza's tattoo stirred.

"Oh," Abeke said suddenly. "It's cruel to keep it locked up. You should set it free."

"And lose our livelihood?" the rubbery man said. "Indeed no."

Abeke burst out, "Can we buy it from you? Not to bond with, just to have. It really is only a cat."

Finn and Meilin stared at her. So did the rubbery man and the porridge woman.

"What will you buy it with?" the rubbery man asked.

Abeke had no money. They'd packed everything they needed, and anyway, back in Nilo, everything was bartered and traded for. There was no need for money.

Hesitantly, she said, "I will trade you for my bracelet. It's made of real elephant tail hair, all the way from Nilo, and it is good luck."

"Oh, Abeke," Meilin said with disgust. "It's a *cat*."

Finn said nothing, just crossed his arms.

Rubbery man and porridge woman consulted. Abeke knew it sounded crazy. She couldn't explain her affinity for the cat, but it felt a little like her bond with Uraza.

"All right and all right," agreed the rubbery man. "For the price of your good luck charm. That seems fair."

So Abeke handed over her bracelet, thinking, *I'm sorry, Soama, I hope you will understand!* The porridge woman unlocked the cage and gave the little black cat to Abeke.

As Abeke accepted it, the sleeves of her cloak slid to her elbows. For just a moment, her bare skin was exposed and her tattoo was revealed to the air. Hurriedly, Abeke shook her sleeve back down.

Maybe they didn't see it, she thought.

But she knew from the rubbery man's suddenly sharp expression that he had.

"So you *have* bonded," he said, grabbing her wrist. Every ounce of friendliness had drained from his voice.

Quick as anything, he had a knife in his hand. The knife was the opposite of his smile in every way. It was thin and unforgiving and as black as a lonely night.

And it was pointed right at Abeke.

"Produce your spirit animal," he ordered. "Or I will cut your throat."

Abeke *couldn't* give Uraza to these people, but she

didn't know what else to do. Finn was motionless, his gaze fixed hypnotically on the knife. It was as if the true Finn had gone somewhere else and left just his body behind. Abeke didn't know what was wrong with him, but she knew she didn't have a chance without the help of Finn or Uraza.

Suddenly there was a blur of motion. The rubbery man released Abeke's wrist. He fell backward with a tremendous *whoof* as the air was knocked out of him.

Meilin stood over him, pointing his own knife at his throat. She was glorious and fierce, loose strands of her black hair snaking around her angry face. "It's insulting enough that you sold us a stray cat. But this is beyond insulting. Here is my bargain: Give this girl back her bracelet and *I* won't cut *your* throat."

The porridge woman started to move and Meilin threw up her other hand. With a flash of blue light, Jhi appeared. The rubbery man and the porridge woman stared, mouths agape. The little cat in Abeke's arms clung to her neck. It was a very clawsome hug.

"*Here* is a legend," Meilin snapped, gesturing to Jhi. The panda looked imaginary and grand in the gray-green surroundings. "The Four Fallen have returned! We will defeat the Conquerors and we will be the ones to usher in a peaceful world. I suggest you find something other than lies to sell."

There was absolute silence.

"Jhi," whispered the porridge woman.

Meilin gestured toward Abeke.

Abeke released Uraza in another flash of green light.

The massive leopard *did* look legendary, her violet eyes ablaze.

"Uraza," murmured the porridge woman. "Impossible."

The rubbery man held out the bracelet. Finn took it from him without a word.

Meilin smiled sharply at the Hawkers. "Spread the word. The Great Beasts are back."

Then she turned to Finn and Abeke. "What are we waiting for? We have work to do."

7

TRUNSWICK

CONOR REALLY WAS DOING HIS BEST TO BE A GOOD PARTNER with Briggan. Sometimes it was easy. He'd grown up with sheepdogs, and Briggan could be quite doglike. He liked for Conor to toss clumps of sod for him to fetch. He played gleeful tug-of-war with vines. He always let Conor lead, to show that he trusted him to be in charge.

But sometimes he was nothing like a dog, and Conor was never sure if this was because he was acting more like a wolf specifically or acting more like a Great Beast in general. For instance, the family sheepdogs had always been eager to curl up to sleep beside Conor. But Briggan, no matter how cold the night, slept at least a few feet from him. The sheepdogs had absolutely hated to be stared at, but if Conor caught Briggan's gaze, the wolf held it unblinkingly until Conor became uncomfortable.

And he really did howl at the moon.

Conor had spent so many nights being terrified of that sound. Wondering when the wolves would appear.

Wondering if he'd be able to keep them from killing any sheep. Wondering if he'd be able to keep them from killing *him.*

If he was being honest, he tried so hard with Briggan to hide the fact that he was still a little afraid of him.

"Home sweet home, eh?" Rollan asked, shielding his eyes.

They had made it to Trunswick. Finally.

The others had never made it to the tower, so Rollan and Conor had started across the fields alone. They had walked and walked and walked, jumping at the slightest noise, fearing Conquerors, dangerous animals, or Conquerors with dangerous animals. They had stopped to snatch a few nervous hours of sleep – long enough for Conor to have a fuzzy dream of both Rumfuss and a large, wild-looking hare sleeping in a patch of wisteria – and then walked some more.

Now the town rose up above them; the castle stood at the highest point of the hill. Blue-roofed houses made of sandy-colored stone crowded below it. Brilliant blue flags and banners flew from nearly every roof, as if the town were waving a frantic greeting to the boys. Conor knew that all the standards would feature Briggan, Eura's patron beast. He felt a warm flood of relief: It had been such a nerve-racking journey without either of the older Greencloaks. But now here was familiar old Trunswick. Everything would be all right, surely.

"So this is Trunswick," Rollan observed. "Where you have fond memories of being sold into servitude by your father?"

Conor's cheeks heated. "I wasn't sold."

"Loaned, then," Rollan corrected warmly. "Oh, don't look so beaten up over it. My father rudely up and *died* on me, so I reckon he's the worse parent. Oh, hey. You did say 'a warm welcome,' right?" He pointed toward the town. "Did you mean warm like 'burning'?"

A plume of smoke rose from the opposite side of the town. Vaguely uneasy, Conor said, "Sometimes the farmers burn their fields to kill the thistles and heather. Come on, we'll go in a side way."

A sandy-colored wall that matched the sandy-colored houses surrounded Trunswick. There were several unguarded gates. The main gate was always crowded, so Conor led them toward the nearly hidden one nearest to the castle. He paused, tipping his head back.

Two blue flags flew over the gate, just like before. But unlike before, Briggan's silhouette was missing. In its place was the outline of a bulky black cat. The change was so absolutely unexpected and so *wrong* that Conor couldn't immediately process the truth of it.

Slowly, he asked Rollan, "Am I awake?"

"Is this a trick question?"

Conor had grown up under the image of a gray wolf on a blue field. Briggan's iconic image had flown over every state event. Every family had a wolf figure on their mantel or a howling wolf carved into the wood above the doorway. Briggan *was* Eura.

But now there was a blue flag with a wildcat flying over the gate.

It seemed like it should be a dream. Or a hallucination.

Rollan had noticed Conor's goggling at the flag, so Conor stammered, "That's supposed to be Briggan."

"What? The cat? Looks a little like Uraza."

This cat was far more muscled than Abeke's leopard, but Conor saw the resemblance. If he hadn't known any better, he would've thought it was supposed to be the silly wildcat from the children's stories he'd grown up with. Hadn't every child in Eura heard about the hero who would rise up with a black cat? It had been an inspiring sort of myth.

But Trunswick didn't need a myth. They had Briggan. He was back. He was real.

Before Conor had time to wonder about this out loud, a huge mastiff burst from the other side of the entrance. It bayed, jowls slobbery. The noise rumbled in their feet. Its threatening bark called out a second dog. Conor knew these were no ordinary hounds. The Trunswicks' mastiffs were infamous for their fight-to-the-death training. It wasn't their bite that was deadly, although it was formidable. It was their *hold*. The mastiffs were trained to find a grip on their victims' throats and not let go until a Trunswick guard gave the order.

"Brace yourself," Conor warned.

"I don't get along with dogs," Rollan muttered, reaching toward the dagger he wore by his side. Briggan's ears pinned and his tail dropped.

But the mastiffs merely circled and pushed them forward. This wasn't an attack. It was an escort.

"Spirit animals?" Conor asked Rollan.

"Slobber animals," Rollan replied, holding his hands out of the way of their drooling mouths. "What's going on? Is this slimy greeting usual?"

Before Conor could reply, a guard shouted at them from his post at the gate. "Hey, you!" The mastiffs herded the two boys closer. A few feet away, Conor saw that the guard wore a blue Trunswick surcoat over his chain mail. But, as on the flag, the wolf insignia had been replaced with a black wildcat. Behind him, another three mastiffs emerged. The guard tugged Conor's cloak, rubbing mud off between his thumb and forefinger and revealing the color beneath. "Greencloaks!" The contempt in his voice when he said the word was as shocking as anything else that had happened. "You can come quietly to the prison, or you can make this difficult."

Of all the ways Conor had imagined this day would go, this had not been one of them.

Rollan said, "Keep your shirt on, old man. We haven't done anything wrong."

Stunned, Conor stammered, "Please. I'm not a stranger. I used to be Devin Trunswick's servant. I—I lived here."

How foolish he felt. Just a bumbling shepherd facing these castle guards, unable to explain himself.

"Quietly," the guard repeated. A few people had gathered behind him, anticipating drama. "Or difficult?" As he moved toward them, Briggan let loose a rippling snarl.

"No, Briggan," Conor said. There were five of the dogs and only one Briggan. Although Briggan was superior in most ways to each dog, if one of the mastiffs got him by the throat, he'd be powerless against the other four. "We're not here to fight."

He felt Rollan's attention on him, waiting for him to somehow sort this out; this was his hometown after all. But this was no Trunswick Conor knew. Not with that strange animal on the blue flag. Not with this guard, this strangely bloodthirsty crowd, these mastiffs.

A familiar voice rang out. "What's the commotion?"

Inside the gate, people and animals parted for the newcomer. An animal led the way: a large black cat, waist-tall. Its eyes were golden and its pelt was silky, inky black with even blacker spots that showed in the sun.

A black panther.

As it stalked dangerously down the cobblestones, a boy stepped out behind it.

Devin Trunswick.

His posture was even haughtier than before. His clothing was impeccable. Everything about him shouted that he was a lord's son. Conor felt so foolish for thinking anything might have changed between them because of Briggan.

How ridiculous, Conor thought. *I'm still a shepherd's son and he's still a noble. We won't ever be equal.*

Devin's eyes found Conor's and held them. He seemed to be thinking the same thing.

Devin held out his arm. Without a second's pause, the panther vanished. A tattoo appeared on Devin's arm.

Conor inhaled audibly.

Impossible. It was absolutely impossible. Conor had been at the Nectar Ceremony where Devin had failed to call up a spirit animal. He had been standing right beside him. Close enough to see the disappointment painted on his mouth.

His mother hadn't mentioned this in her letter. Conor's pulse fluttered.

Where is my mother?

"Devin!" he called, trying to cover his surprise. "It's me, Conor."

Devin said, "I know." Then he called to the guards, cool and imperious, "What are you waiting for? *Seize them!*"

Rollan grabbed Conor's elbow. Together they jumped away. One of the guards snatched at Conor, but he rolled out of the way. Briggan snapped at the mastiffs. They were stronger, but slower. And there was absolutely no reason to engage them: they had no purpose here in Trunswick. Conor knew these streets. If he could get to the smaller alleys, he might be able to lead Rollan and Briggan out of danger.

He ran down an alley. Beside him, Briggan jumped on top of crates, his powerful hind legs sending them crashing behind him. Essix coursed overhead, her shadow shrinking and growing as she ducked beneath clotheslines and over jutting roofs.

A girl shouted out a window, "*Run*, Greencloaks!"

Conor barely had time to look up before the girl's mother dragged her inside and clapped the window closed. The mother's expression was frightened.

Farther ahead, more windows opened. A boy and a girl waved at Conor, and then, just after Conor and Rollan had passed, they tipped buckets of scalding-hot water into the alleyway. The pursuing guards yelled in pain. Steam curled up the walls. The children were helping Conor and Rollan escape.

Conor had no breath to thank them, but he waved and hoped they understood.

"I'll remember that!" one of the guards shouted at the windows, his hand clapped over his scalded face. Conor and Rollan left them behind, not slowing. Conor knew that there was a hidden weakness in the wall nearby. If they could just make it there, they could leave Trunswick behind and escape across the moors.

But as Conor darted down a side street, a huge lizard – as long as Briggan – suddenly loomed from the darkness. Its face and clawed feet were black, but the rest of its bumpy hide was a checkerboard of orange and black. Everything about it looked poisonous. It hissed like something out of a nightmare. Conor scrabbled in the other direction. Behind him he heard snarls and cries. He couldn't see Briggan or Rollan. It felt like there were walls and people everywhere – an older girl with a flat frog in her hands, another girl with the giant lizard, and Devin with his leering smile.

As he spun, Conor was brought up short by a fourth person: a tall, dark-skinned boy and his spirit animal, a long-legged chestnut bird with a big, stork-like head. The bird was tall enough to look right into his eyes. Possibly it was adrenaline, but the hair on Conor's arms felt charged, like when lightning had struck very close.

"I'd suggest giving in," the boy said. "My hammerkop here has a very short temper."

"Also," added the girl holding the flat frog, "because we have your spirit animal."

The mastiffs had pinned Briggan to the ground. Conor's heart sank when he saw that one of them had bracketed its jaws loosely around Briggan's windpipe. The wolf's eyes flashed, full of rebellion, but he had no choice but to submit.

"Also also," Devin said, "we have this one. His cloak seems slightly less green than yours."

He pointed to Rollan, who squirmed and thrashed in a guard's hands. Behind them, a tall, handsome man in a richly embroidered cloak watched the proceedings with an approving smile.

"Two little piggies," the man said. "And one not-so-big, not-so-bad wolf."

Rollan sneered and spat at him.

The man seemed unconcerned. If anything, Rollan's rage pleased him. "You had your chance to choose sides, Rollan. We both see you chose poorly."

This man knew Rollan? Conor tried to place him. Was he from the castle? A guard?

No.

His mind returned to the mountains of Amaya, where Barlow, their ally, their *friend*, had been slain — stabbed through the back while saving Abeke's life.

This was Zerif.

A Conqueror.

We've delivered ourselves to the enemy, Conor thought, cursing himself. *All because I wanted to come back here. Why? This isn't home. This place has always been a trap. All because I wanted to return to a place where I'd always been trapped. Now I'm trapped all over again.*

He couldn't explain to Rollan how sorry he was.

The crowd parted for the earl himself. He looked exactly like his son Devin, only he had a pointy, neatly trimmed beard. He surveyed them coldly. "Put them both in the Howling House. We'll decide what to do with them later." To Conor and Rollan he said, "Place your spirit animals in passive form now."

"Yeah," Devin agreed. "It'd be too bad if we had to hurt a Great Beast." His nasty smile indicated he didn't think it would be too bad at all.

"Wait," Rollan snapped. "What are we being imprisoned for?"

"We've done nothing," Conor said. He unsuccessfully searched the earl's face for any trace of compassion. "And you know I'm not a stranger to Trunswick."

The earl barely glanced at them. It was obvious he didn't find Rollan or Conor worthy enough to get the full attention he'd give a *proper* enemy. He said, "The cloak you wear here condemns you, boy. Trunswick has had enough of the Greencloaks' iron rule. We're weary of all their talk of Erdas's destiny." He lifted a lazy hand toward a blue flag bearing the wildcat. "Erdas, indeed. All this talk of our destiny. Trunswick will make its own destiny."

Conor protested, "My lord, we only came to—"

The earl held up his hand as if he were calming a dog. "Please be quiet. I will no longer tolerate hearing the voices of the likes of you."

The likes of you.

His voice oozed dismissal.

It was like a slap. Conor had not been hit, but he felt the same urge to sink to his knees. The same rush of blood to his cheeks. The same thud of his heart in his rib cage.

Devin was trying very hard to hide a smile. Zerif nodded approvingly. As if he was so pleased the earl had finally stopped letting those Greencloaks push him around.

The earl turned to the guard beside him. "If the boy won't put his animal into passive form, have the dogs kill it and burn the body with the rest."

Rollan's eyes widened, his cool facade dropping.

Conor wordlessly stretched his hand toward where Briggan was pinned to the ground. The wolf immediately vanished from beneath the mastiffs and appeared on Conor's arm. Rollan, however, had no such success. With a scowl, he called to Essix. But the falcon flew high overhead in ever wider circles. Every so often the bird looked down so that it was clear she was listening, just not obeying.

Devin and the girl with the frog snickered. Zerif yawned. It was a glorious yawn, his hand elegantly covering his mouth and his laugh at once. Behind them, Conor could see Devin's little brother, Dawson, averting his eyes. He'd always been the best one in the family. It was hard to imagine him taking any joy in this horrible scene, but he was too young to help now.

"The boy's bond is weak," the earl said. "So the bird's no threat anyway. Just leave it and lock the others up."

"Welcome home, shepherd," Devin sneered.

8

THE HOWLING HOUSE

IT DIDN'T TAKE ESSIX LONG TO FIND MEILIN, ABEKE, AND FINN. They were just climbing a grassy bank that afforded a view of Trunswick when Finn spotted the falcon circling. He waved one arm, and then two. Abeke and Meilin joined in. Essix wheeled toward them.

"It's Essix. Does that mean something's happened to Rollan?" Meilin asked. The thought annoyed her. If someone was going to hurt that boy, she wanted it to be *her*.

"Essix doesn't seem alarmed enough for him to be dead," Finn said. Abeke winced, but Meilin appreciated that Finn didn't try to sugarcoat the possibilities for them. Lives were at stake. It would do them all well to remember that.

Finn shielded his eyes to better see the falcon. "But she seems agitated. It's hard to say if Rollan sent her to us or if she's come on her own accord. Do you see a message tied to her leg?"

"Nothing," Meilin verified.

"Are they in Trunswick?" Finn called up to Essix. The bird shrieked back, three times.

Meilin said, "I think that means yes."

Finn asked the falcon, "Should we meet up with them right now?"

Essix cried out once. It was an angry, ferocious bark of a sound. Quite clearly: no.

"Imprisoned, I would guess," Finn said. "Or working secretly to get information. Either way, we'll have to be cautious."

Meilin considered. She touched the tattoo where Jhi waited in passive form. It wasn't nearly as effective as the meditation sessions, but the gesture reminded her of that clarity of thought. She asked, "Should we circle the town to see if we can learn any more?"

Finn nodded. "Probably a wise idea. I shouldn't really go marching into town without some strategy anyway. The Earl of Trunswick and I had a disagreement not too long ago."

"What sort of disagreement?" Meilin demanded.

Finn narrowed his eyes in the direction of the castle. "He tried to kill me."

That seemed like a valid reason to avoid going into town.

"In any case, it would be advantageous to have a plan," he added.

Abeke made a little pained noise. At first Meilin thought it was because of worry, but then she saw no — it was because the Hawkers' ridiculous black cat thought Essix was going to eat her. The cat had affixed its claws rather securely into Abeke's hair. It looked as if the animal was actually growing directly from the other girl's head.

"You could let that cat down," Meilin said scathingly. "You wanted to free her, and now she's free."

Abeke tried to remove the cat from her head. Reams of her own hair stretched from her scalp to the cat.

"She's scared," insisted Abeke, still tugging. The cat let out a rattling wail that oscillated in time with the tugs. "She won't slow us down."

Meilin narrowed her eyes, but it was hard to argue. Abeke had been seeming a little more feline lately, more like Uraza. Maybe this was part of it. "Good. Keep it that way. The others need us, whether or not they're in immediate trouble. The sooner we find out more and meet back up with them, the sooner we can get to Rumfuss. Now, let's get out of here, unless you *want* the Conquerors to catch us."

Before Meilin could stop herself, the insinuation slipped out—the prospect that Abeke might not mind the Conquerors finding them at all, since she might still be working for them. Finn leveled a very heavy look at her. Tarik or Olvan would have probably scolded her for talking to Abeke like that, but she thought they also would have understood why deep down, Meilin still didn't trust Abeke. And it was hard to be very kind to someone she didn't trust, now more than ever.

But Finn simply turned away and, under his breath, said something only Meilin could hear. "Trust must be practiced."

Meilin wanted to roll her eyes and ignore him, but his words – and his quiet disapproval – rankled her. Somewhere along the way, she had started wanting to impress him. This annoyed her for reasons she couldn't quite find words for. Why should she care for the respect of a man who wouldn't even lift a sword to save himself at that forest battle?

But he had led them across the Giant's Chessboard and the moor, and had pulled her from the waste. And without his advice in the Moon Tower, she would have never learned about Jhi's problem-solving abilities.

What is a warrior's heart? she wondered. *Does it always carry a sword?*

Grudgingly, she said out loud, "Abeke, I'm sorry if . . . my words seemed harsh. I didn't mean them that way."

Abeke's eyebrows shot up. She appeared so surprised by this miserly kindness. Was it possible Meilin had been a little too uncaring the past several days? Just because she sometimes doubted Abeke's loyalties didn't mean she had to be so cruel about it.

Finn looked over his shoulder.

He didn't say anything. Not a word. But he nodded, and Meilin's heart felt lighter.

They climbed over the bank, down toward Trunswick, keeping enough distance to avoid attracting any unwanted attention. Meilin searched the town's appearance for any clues as to what kind of place this could be and what their friends could be up to inside it. The town's structure was straightforward: castle crowning the hill, buildings huddled around it. It stank of beeswax smoke, coal, and the peculiar scent of horse hooves, so

Meilin could tell already that it had more than its fair share of blacksmiths. The blue flags that flew from nearly every roof flapped listlessly, made of heavy wool rather than the silk and linen flags that Meilin had grown up under. The entire town seemed crude and disheveled in comparison to Zhong's elegant cities, and Meilin felt a pang in her heart.

She pushed it down.

No time for weakness or second-guessing her decision to stay now.

"Ah, Trunswick," said Finn. His voice had gone a little flat. It was a bit like his face had gone when the Hawker had brandished the knife.

"What is that over there?" Meilin asked. Over a nearby knot of trees, a patch of sky was dark with smoke.

Lifting her chin, Abeke sniffed the air. "I think it's a bonfire. It's not just wood they are burning, anyway. Do you smell it?"

Abeke was right. There was something a little off about the odor of the fire. Something a little unpleasant that made her feel anxious.

Zhong, burning . . . She pushed the thought away as her eyes stung.

Finn interrupted her thoughts by saying, "It doesn't feel like a good sign."

"Finn . . . I think Essix is trying to tell us something," Abeke said. She pointed in the other direction, toward Trunswick. Or rather, since she was holding the cat with both hands, she pointed with the cat to where Essix circled over a large building partway up the hill. "Do you think the others are in that building?"

"It would be bad luck if they were," Finn said. "That's the Howling House. It's where they keep people and animals who bonded without Nectar, and developed the bonding sickness. Well, one sort of bonding sickness – it's for those who went mad. It's part hospital and part prison."

Meilin's mind turned over his words: *those who went mad.* She had heard of the bonding sickness, of course. Everyone learned about the dangers of bonding without the Nectar. In the days before Nectar, some bonds went well, and other bonds didn't. Human and animal were tied to each other, and yet couldn't connect. Sleepless nights piled one upon the other. Some were able to work through it on their own, or learned to live with the difficult bond. But others, as Finn noted, went mad.

This was why even the most remote village in Zhong had a designated authority to notify the Greencloaks when a child came of age. It was hard to imagine anyone bonding without Nectar these days – harder still to imagine enough difficult bonds to warrant an entire prison.

Meilin asked, "You think they're being kept prisoner there?"

"It is the only place that would hold them and their spirit animals, yes. Everything inside that building is reinforced to prevent spirit animals from escaping."

Meilin said, "How do you know so much about that place?"

Finn didn't answer. He'd gone all quiet and faraway again. Suddenly she remembered what he had said in the Moon Tower. He had bonded to Donn without the Nectar. What had he called his bond? *Difficult.*

Difficult enough to be locked up in the Earl of Trunswick's house for insane humans and animals?

Difficult enough that the Earl of Trunswick might have tried to kill him?

"So now what?" Abeke demanded.

All three of them looked toward the sun in the sky.

Finn said, "We wait."

He held out his arm, and Essix coasted smoothly down to land heavily on it. Abeke settled to the ground, opened her bag, and pulled out some jerky to munch on. They all seemed content to wait.

Waiting was Meilin's least favorite thing.

Trunswick was a silent place after dark. When night fell, Abeke, Meilin, and Finn crept closer to town. Unlike the cities of Zhong, which were lit and beautiful even at night, Trunswick was nearly as black as the moor. Only a few lanterns illuminated the main street up to the castle. There were no candles in any of the windows. No voices rose from the bars and no stragglers moved through the streets. Even Trunswick's famous and industrious blacksmiths completely disappeared as night fell, leaving behind only a few glowing embers in their forges. Guards stood in vigilant silence at each of the gates.

Finn whispered, "There's something very wrong with this town."

Meilin, Finn, and Abeke crouched around the back of the wall. There were no gates here; no one to see them. But that meant there were no easy entrances either. In a low voice, Abeke asked Uraza, "Can you find us a weakness in the wall?"

The leopard galloped away, low and silky. She returned a few minutes later to lead them to a bricked-up gate. Some of the barrier had crumbled, leaving an opening just large enough for a person to crawl through.

Meilin kept Jhi in passive form. The gap was *not* large enough for a giant panda.

On the inside of the wall, the soundless nature of the town was even more pronounced. Meilin was very aware of their footfalls on the uneven cobblestones as Finn led the way up the narrow roads toward the Howling House. Uraza trailed behind, ears swiveling as she listened for threats. Overhead, Essix's dark form flitted from roof to roof, confirming they were headed in the right direction.

At the Howling House, torches blazed, their fiery reflections thrashing in the puddles of last night's rain. Out front, guards moved restlessly. At least three large mastiffs lay just inside the door. It was a hive of activity in comparison to the quiet town.

"This seems impossible!" Meilin whispered to Finn.

"Patience," he whispered back.

Meilin wasn't very fond of patience.

Abeke whispered to Uraza, and the two of them danced quietly through the shadows, finding an invisible path around the side of the fortified barn. The leopard led them to a hiding space in a blacksmith's shop directly across the narrow road from the Howling House. It was full of the things one would expect to find in a smith's shop – anvil, furnace, wrought iron firedogs for holding wood – but was also cluttered with cabinetry and farming equipment.

In the smith's, Abeke crouched behind a half-built cabinet. Finn took a place behind a large harrow. Meilin hid beside the still-warm forge. The blacksmith was on the higher side of the road, and from their hiding places they had a clear view into one of the only rooms with a normal-sized window. Inside, there were five people eating a not insubstantial meal. One very handsome, oily man and four kids.

The last time Meilin had seen the man with his tidy beard and expensive clothing, he had been stabbing one of her allies in the back during the battle for the last talisman. Just the sight of him placing a spoon in his mouth was enough to close off her throat for a moment. She barely checked her first impulse, which was to leap across the road and engage him in combat on the spot.

"Zerif," Meilin and Abeke snarled at the same time. Their voices were equally harsh, which surprised Meilin. She still didn't trust Abeke, but her rage at Zerif sounded genuine. Uraza's tail thrashed at the abrasive tone.

Finn said, "I'll stand watch here. You two go listen."

Abeke handed Finn the cat and Meilin shook her head with annoyance.

"What are you planning to do with that thing anyway?" she demanded. "Throw it at Rumfuss?"

But Abeke merely smiled, cool and catlike, before following Meilin to the window. The voices inside were mumbled, but audible.

"Don't be foolish," Zerif was saying in between bites of dinner. Meilin was disgusted to watch him eat – not because he wasn't careful, but because of the opposite. For some reason the care he took to place each bite in his mouth and then wipe his lips infuriated her. *How dare he eat like there is nothing wrong in the world. How dare he wipe his beard clean as if it matters if he is handsome!*

"No one will care about the Great Beasts when we're done," he continued. "Did you see any of the townsfolk caring a whit for Briggan today? They only had eyes for Elda."

Devin preened as he admired his wildcat tattoo. "She is everything the people want."

"That's what I am telling you children," Zerif said. The older blond girl with the flat frog looked rather annoyed at the word *children*. "For decades, the Greencloaks lured in most people with their talk of Erdas's Great Beasts. By making every village everywhere reliant on the Greencloaks and the Nectar, they denied the power every country already has. Briggan serves no one but Briggan! But you, Devin. You serve Eura with their black wildcat. And you, Tahlia, serve your people with Tiddalik, Stetriol's beloved water-holding frog. Ana, with Amaya's glorious and fearful gila monster, Ix. And of course Karmo with Impundulu, Nilo's lightning bird. How long have your people been waiting for these legends to release them from hardship? Now they don't have to wait for the future. We *make* the future."

Devin nodded enthusiastically as Meilin silently fumed.

"How long do we have to deal with people like *them*, then?" demanded Karmo, jerking his chin toward the interior of the barn. He was a handsome, dark-skinned boy already as tall as Zerif. "As long as we battle the

Greencloaks, we are distracted from our true purpose of aiding our people."

People like them. Meilin was sure he must mean Rollan, Conor, and Tarik.

"Once we get the talismans, they will be powerless to stand against us," Zerif said. He was briefly distracted by his reflection in the spoon. He admired it.

Tahlia looked vexed. "Just how can you be so certain? There are four other *children* with Great Beasts out there, looking for the *exact* same thing as us."

"Two," corrected Devin with a smirk. "These two we already have aren't getting out any time soon. My father built the Howling House to be the best."

Abeke and Meilin shot each other a look. Two? Who was missing?

"And I chose all of *you* to be the best," Zerif said. "The four returned Great Beasts were summoned at random to rather unworthy human partners, as I think you saw earlier today. Each of you, on the other hand, was hand-picked to be a hero. Excellent breeding—" He smiled at Devin. "Exceptional intelligence—" He pointed his spoon at Tahlia. "Exceeding connections—" This was directed to the girl with the lizard. "And exacerbating strength," he said to Karmo.

The table was quiet, probably because none of them knew what *exacerbating* meant, including Zerif.

"With the Bile," Zerif continued, "we can create even more worthy heroes. It creates bonds even when the Nectar fails. And the bonds are superior. The human has complete control! We choose the animal! No follower of the Reptile King needs to worry about bonding with a field mouse. Long live the Reptile King!"

The table was quiet again, and the faces of the children indicated that they had heard Zerif give this speech before.

Finally, he cleared his throat, moved his plate, and produced a piece of parchment. "Here's the map we got from the two urchins. Devin, you and Karmo will use this to follow them to their destination. Get the talisman. I will come find you."

Karmo said dubiously, "You are not joining us?"

"Karmo," Zerif said. He stood and draped an arm across the tall boy's shoulders. "Karmo, Karmo, Karmo. Now that the first stage of your training is done, it's time for me to return Tahlia to Stetriol and Ana to Amaya, where they can begin to inspire their people. Devin remains here in Eura where he is most influential. And you, as we've discussed, have more work that you can do on Nilo's behalf before you go home as a hero. There are two of you. Two of them. I think we can all agree that Elda and Impundulu are more than a match for that panda, even with Uraza helping her."

Meilin gritted her teeth. There was no point in staying any longer. Punching Abeke's arm lightly, she indicated for the other girl to follow.

When they returned to Finn, Meilin said grimly, "They're definitely Conquerors, handpicked by Zerif. He says they have some sort of version of Nectar that can *force* a bond. And they have Rollan and Conor there in the Howling House."

Finn's expression went very dark. He said, "At Greenhaven, we had heard rumors. . . . There's no time

94

to spare. We have to get the others out. What we need is a diversion. Havoc. So they don't have time to attack us."

Meilin felt an idea prickle. She whispered, "Keep a lookout. I need to have a moment of silence."

She released Jhi from her dormant state. The panda was dreadfully conspicuous in the dark. Not the black bits, of course. But everything white. And the blacksmith shop was not designed to fit a panda. Jhi shifted her weight so that the anvil would stop poking her in the flank.

Meilin asked, "Jhi, will you help me? I think I have an idea, but I need to focus."

The panda actually looked happy to be asked – ears pricked forward, eyes brighter, mouth less tense. Meilin hadn't realized before that Jhi's face was capable of holding such expression.

The moment Meilin closed her eyes, the panda's calming influence washed over her.

It would be easy to fall asleep, she thought. She could curl up in the panda's soft fur right here. Suddenly she missed Zhong so badly that she could cry.

This was all part of the panda's power, she knew. Pushing down all her logical barriers. She didn't have time for it. Focusing, she shoved away the emotion.

Choices swirled into view. This time they were more like stars than planets: bright and hard to look at directly. When Meilin considered some of them – causing a commotion with the mastiffs, sneaking in another window, attacking the guards directly – they fizzled and died out.

But one choice stayed bright. Meilin let it circle her as she studied it from all sides, looking for dull areas or weakness.

This idea isn't an easy one, she thought.

Jhi's encouragement washed over her. Of course she was right. Meilin had never needed the easy way.

She opened her eyes.

"Well?" Abeke asked.

Meilin said, "I'm going to need you to cover for me. This idea is going to take a bit of time."

ESCAPE

"W ELL, THIS IS BRILLIANT," ROLLAN SAID. "EVERYTHING I imagined our second mission would be."

Their captors had taken all their things and thrown them in a stall in the Howling House, fifteen feet wide and fifteen feet long, with bars and fine wire over a single, tiny window high up on the wall. The stone floor was covered with claw marks. Deep ones. Some of them were at the edges, like an animal had tried to dig itself out. But some of them were randomly gouged into the middle of the wall. Like the animal was just angry. Or crazy.

Conor was halfway to crazy himself after being in the stall for only an hour. He didn't do well being contained. All he could think about was how wrong Trunswick seemed, and how he didn't know if his mother was trapped here—or even if she was still alive. He couldn't be sure of anything in a world where he was thrown into prison on sight.

Rollan lolled on the opposite wall, scruffy and indolent, picking his teeth with a piece of straw. He looked rather at home here in prison. But Conor was beginning to realize that Rollan worked very hard on looking at home anywhere.

"I just don't understand how Devin has a spirit animal," Conor said. "I was there, Rollan. I saw him at the Nectar Ceremony. There was no trick."

Rollan mused, "Did you see how tight he and the spirit animal were? They were the best of friends. It did just what he asked. I mean, why would it do that? Clearly it's not because of Devin's dazzling personality."

In between this line of thinking and remembering the encounter with the Trunswicks earlier, Conor suddenly felt awfully tired . . . and an awful lot like a shepherd's son. "Look, Rollan. I'm sorry. We wouldn't be here if it weren't for me."

The other boy wordlessly lifted an eyebrow.

"It wasn't that it was ever home," Conor confessed. "Home was the fields. But . . . it was different, at least, before. My mother sent me a letter and said she was working here now that I was gone, and that things weren't going so well. I just wanted to see her, see how bad things were. And I thought it would make her proud to see . . ."

He trailed off. He didn't want to think about where his mother might be. His heart felt as low as it could go.

"We all make mistakes," Rollan said. "For instance, that laundry I ate last night. That was a mistake. I can still taste it."

Conor sighed. At least he had apologized. It didn't make him feel much better, though. He knew only weakness had brought him here. Why in the world would someone like him have summoned Briggan? What a waste.

"You're driving me crazy with the pacing," Rollan said. He frowned. "Did you just hear something?"

Conor listened. He heard the sounds of animals moving in the stall next door, and night birds cooing outside, and the sound of his own breathing. "What sort of something?"

Rollan cocked his head. "A screaming sort of something?"

They both listened.

Outside, a thin shout pierced the quiet. Then another. Then a higher scream, far away.

"Yep," said Rollan. "See, screaming. I'd recognize that sound anywhere. I'm a bit of a connoisseur of it. That, to me, sounds like high-quality surprise right there."

They both jumped as something struck the fine wire of the window. It was Essix, perched precariously on the ledge. She dragged her talons across the wire.

"She's trying to get in!" Conor exclaimed.

"Sadly, that's not going to happen, my friend," Rollan told Essix, who cried thinly.

Outside, the shouts grew more numerous. They were followed by a peculiar crashing noise that Conor couldn't quite place.

Suddenly Finn was at the door, a small square of his face visible through the wire-covered view hole by the latch. He worked busily at the lock.

"Finn!" Conor said happily.

"Get ready," Finn warned. His fingers trembled as he worked at the lock, but his voice was steady. "You might have to fight your way out."

Rollan yipped in surprise. Water pooled around his feet.

Alarmed, Conor lifted a damp boot from the ground. "Where's that water coming from?"

"The water tower," Finn said. He kept digging at the lock. His hands kept trembling, but the rest of him stayed steady. Voices rose outside.

"What's that sound?" Conor asked.

"Greencloaks, and their supporters," Finn replied. He kicked the lock angrily. "The earl's locked up dozens of people who spoke out for the Greencloaks."

Rollan joined Conor at the door. "What's wrong with your hands?"

Finn's eyes cut up to Rollan. "Nothing."

Rollan's eyes narrowed as if he knew there was more to the story, but he just asked, "What's wrong with the lock?"

"It's jammed somehow," Finn said. He pulled on the door, hard. It jumped on its hinges but didn't give way. "I need more force. Can you push from the inside?"

Conor and Rollan threw their shoulders against the wood. The door jumped unsuccessfully. They couldn't push hard enough. There was shouting from not very far away.

"Are the other locks like this?" Conor asked.

"No. It's only this one that seems jammed! I've unlocked it, but the bolt won't give."

"Then free the others," Conor said. "Maybe they can help hold off the guards. We'll keep pushing. Go!"

Finn hesitated. "I'll come back when I'm done if you haven't escaped yet."

As he hurried away, Conor and Rollan tried the door again. Water wicked up their legs. Straw floated on the water seeping through the walls and under the door.

"How much water can there be in that tower?" growled Rollan through gritted teeth.

"How *stuck* can this door be?" Conor said. "They just put us in here! If we just had a bit more weight—"

A voice came through the door. "You *do*. Release Briggan!"

"Meilin!" both boys said at once.

Her angular eye appeared in the opening. What was visible of her hair was soaking wet. She said, "Trust you two to need to get rescued! Conor, why are you just standing there? I said, release Briggan! Hurry up. Where's Tarik?"

"It's a long story. He's safe, but not here. Meilin, the guards—" Conor started.

"They're busy for the moment. I've knocked over the water tower."

"Knocked it over!" Rollan said, shocked. "It's not a *goblet*. You can't just *knock it over*."

"Well, I did. Conor!"

With a flash, Conor released Briggan. The wolf instantly appeared beside him. He lifted his damp paws with distaste.

"Can you help, Briggan?" Conor asked. "You're heavy!"

Without hesitation, the wolf jumped up onto the door. His weight hit it just as Meilin pulled on her side. Conor and Rollan hurled themselves against it as well. Meilin groaned. Briggan groaned. The boys groaned. The door groaned too. And then it fell open.

"That's it!" Conor clapped his hands on either side of the wolf's muzzle. The wolf let out a thrilled, resonant cry.

"All right, all right," Rollan said. "Enough of the happy reunion."

They splashed down the dim corridor after Meilin. Half of the torches had been extinguished in the commotion.

Rollan's voice was tinged with awe as he asked, "How did you knock over the water tower?"

Meilin glanced over her shoulder. Without a hint of a smile, she replied, "I had tutors for it, back in Zhong."

The three of them suddenly grinned at each other, relieved that they were back together again, even if they weren't out of trouble.

"Prepare yourselves," Meilin added at the end of the corridor. "It's wild out there."

Outside, the courtyard was lit erratically by fretful torchlight. Trunswick guards fought with over a dozen people without uniforms — the former prisoners of the Howling House. Spirit animals skirmished and galloped around the edges of the yard. Mastiffs milled underfoot.

Briggan pressed up against the back of Conor's leg, pushing him outside, and Conor thought: *This is madness.*

Finn and another man ran up to them. Even in the dim light, Conor could see that the other man was tattered and haggard. Conor had been imprisoned for just a few hours. It was clear the other man's imprisonment had lasted much longer.

"Hurry," Finn urged. "Follow me! They can't cover us long."

"Cover us?" Conor echoed. His eyes roamed over the fighting. "We have to help!"

The haggard man shook his head. "No. Briggan and the others must escape from here. You are meant for more than this."

Just then, one of the mastiffs jumped, lurching heavily into the haggard man's side. As he turned to face it, another savagely bared its slobbery teeth before lunging for his neck. Meilin immediately turned to help him, but Finn seized her arm.

"You heard what he wanted. Don't make him fight for nothing," he snapped. "Our goal is the talisman. Their goal is to allow us to pursue that goal."

Another man ran up to attack the mastiffs. But the haggard man didn't get back up.

"They want you out of here," Finn hissed, dragging Meilin away. "I'm getting you out of here. I said *follow me.*"

It felt wrong to leave the Greencloak supporters behind, even if they wanted the Four Fallen to escape.

This is wrong, Conor thought. *If we're so important, why can't we make a difference now? What makes us any better than these men and women?*

As they threaded through the fighting, Meilin blocked blows and Rollan ducked under swinging staffs. Everything smelled like burning wood and sweat. A rabbit bounded by them. A small bear clawed on another side. Conor realized that these must be the spirit animals of the captured Greencloaks and their supporters from the Howling House. Individually, the animals wanted to help. But as a group, they had no plan or order. It wasn't like Conor and the others — at least they'd had some training to work together.

If only they'd had a way to formulate a plan before all of this, Conor thought.

Just then, a guard dragged Conor to a stop by his cloak. Conor jerked and tugged, but the guard kept pulling him closer. Conor's boots skidded across the dirt courtyard. He was much smaller than his assailant.

"Rollan! Meilin!" he shouted. But the commotion drowned out his voice. The others hadn't even noticed that he'd been apprehended.

The guard flipped out a stubby, sharp sword. The look on his face was branded in Conor's mind.

This was not a training exercise.

This man was about to kill him.

But I'm just a boy, Conor thought.

There was no trace of mercy in the guard's eyes.

"Briggan!" Conor cried out desperately.

The wolf pivoted. But he was too far away—

A woman struck the guard with a soaked piece of wood. For a bare moment, his expression didn't change. His sword was still poised over Conor. But then the guard's eyes went blank and he slumped to his knees.

All of the breath escaped from Conor's lungs.

The woman with the piece of wood threw her arms around Conor and dragged him to her in a hug.

"Conor!" she said. Her voice was so familiar. As Briggan bounded breathlessly to Conor's side, Conor got a good look at his savior's face. His mother!

Like all the prisoners, she was tattered and careworn, but her appearance couldn't get in the way of Conor's relief. She was alive.

"Mother!" He hugged her tightly. His head was a clutter of images: that man's face as he prepared to kill Conor, the Greencloak supporter being attacked by the mastiffs, and even Finn's hands trembling as he tried to open the lock. His mother was so skinny too. "I—"

"I know," she replied. "But there's no time. You need to go! It isn't safe here for Greencloaks anymore. They even . . . even Isilla is gone."

"But th-this is wrong," Conor finally stammered, shocked to hear of the gentle Greencloak who had presided over his Nectar Ceremony. She'd been a revered figure in Trunswick for as long as he could remember. "I don't want to leave you behind. Come with us."

"I can't," his mother said. "Your father and brothers still need me."

The others had finally noticed Conor's detainment, and they struggled to fight their way back to him. Nearby, Abeke and Uraza fought with two of the mastiffs. Overhead, a seagull, someone's spirit animal, circled and screamed.

Madness, Conor thought again. Their odds were technically better than in that forest battle, but in this chaos, the Greencloaks were doomed.

"How can I help?" he asked desperately.

"Did you get my letter? You've made us all so proud, Conor! You called Briggan, and surely there was a reason. Briggan was a great leader. You're good and wise. Do what you feel is right. You always do what's right."

"But I don't *know* what is right!"

His mother hugged him again. "Do what is right in your heart, Conor."

Conor hesitated. He was certain that if they left, all these Greencloak supporters would give their lives to shield them. Maybe they were okay with that. But he wasn't. He couldn't be. He just couldn't. Like Lady Evelyn had pointed out, he was a guardian. He couldn't just stay, though, either. Then they would all die. What was right in his heart?

He didn't know.

"Briggan," Conor said. He buried his hand in the wolf's ruff. "Can we help them? They *need* us."

What this group needed was a leader, he knew. He just didn't know if he and Briggan were ready to be leaders yet. Well, he knew Briggan was ready. He just didn't know if *he* was.

The wolf's ears pricked. He surveyed the chaos. Conor did too, and as he did, he saw that even worse was in store for them. The Earl of Trunswick's white horse was making its way jauntily down the streets toward the courtyard. The earl sat high on its back, his powerful lynx spirit animal lumbering beside him. He was riding in a leisurely fashion, as if he had come to the same conclusion Conor had: The Greencloak supporters had no chance.

This was the Fallens' last chance to run.

Conor and Briggan met each other's eyes. This time, neither of them looked away.

Cupping his hands around his mouth, Conor shouted, "Meilin! Rollan! Abeke!"

When he was sure he'd caught their attention, he gestured wildly for them to join him.

Meilin reached him first. "Come on! Let's go."

"We're helping," Conor said. "It's what we're meant to do."

Conor's mother nodded. She stepped back, tightening her hands on the piece of wood she'd used to hit the guard.

"What did you have in mind?" Rollan asked.

"Training room, like we practiced. Find weapons where we can and fight as a team."

He didn't have to say it twice. Rollan brandished his knife, Meilin put up her fists, and Abeke crouched low beside Uraza. Briggan tipped back his head and let out a long, cool howl. The sound pierced the fighting. It raised the hair on the back of Conor's neck and on his arms. Every spirit animal there turned all attention to the wolf.

In that brief silence, Conor shouted, "Greencloaks! Attack!"

They moved forward as one creature. Uraza slunk low before them, Briggan charged beside them, and Essix swept by overhead. They threw themselves into the battle. But not as four people fighting four separate targets. As a single entity dispatching one enemy at a time and then moving on to the next.

Rollan fought with his dagger. Abeke brandished a torch. Conor swept up a shovel from a cart near the black-smith's. Meilin still preferred to fight bare-handed.

It didn't take long for their efforts to catch the eyes of the other Greencloak supporters. The first to catch on had been fighting with only the help of her spirit animal, a goat. But when she saw the four of them battling as a team, she leaped in behind them. Then a man with an owl. Then a young man with no visible spirit animal. When they saw how the Fallen had found weapons and worked together, they began doing the same.

It was working. The cacophony was dimming. The guards were falling back. The mastiffs were finished.

We're doing it, Briggan! Conor thought fiercely. He

could feel the wolf's power surging through him, giving him strength. It was like he was a wolf himself. He was faster, stronger, sharper. This was what the bond could be.

They were winning.

Then the Earl of Trunswick's voice rang over the courtyard.

"If you want this man to live, I suggest you lay down your weapons!"

In the uneven torchlight, the Earl of Trunswick stood on an auction block at the other side of the courtyard. Finn stood in his grasp. The earl's sword was pressed against his throat, and his lynx prowled the block, as if daring anyone to intervene.

The fighting stopped. The only sound was that of several people trying to catch their breath.

Finn's voice was softer than the earl's, but in that ragged quiet, it was just as audible. "Go. Don't listen to him! Just go!"

Conor's heart ached. His mother nodded at him. *Just go!*

All the other Greencloak supporters were watching Conor, Rollan, Abeke, and Meilin to see what their next move was. There were few enough guards that the supporters would have been able to take them on easily if the earl hadn't had Finn hostage.

"If you go," the earl warned with the familiar Trunswick jeer in his voice, "I won't just kill him now. I'll put him back where he belongs. In the Howling House! Don't worry, Finn Cooley! We'll burn that troubled bond out of you yet!"

Finn's hands shook, just as they had inside the Howling House. But when he spoke it was with a steady voice. "*Go.* This is bigger than me!"

Meilin hissed, "We can't leave him."

The earl traced the edge of his sword against Finn's skin. A shallow wound appeared, a few beads of blood drawing a line across his neck.

Finn pressed his lips together. He looked straight at Conor. "Take the rest of them out of here."

Conor needed a plan, but there was no plan. Meilin's agonized face meant that she didn't have one either. Rollan and Abeke shook their heads. His mother's eyebrows pulled together. She was in over her head.

Was this how it had to end? Handing Finn over to their enemy?

Suddenly a wall of flame appeared. It roared and spat and devoured as it hurtled across the cobblestones. Straight in the direction of the earl and Finn. It was so out of place that it took Conor a long second to realize what it was. A cart, piled high with burning straw. Smoke rolled off it in great, choking clouds.

Conor searched the courtyard's edge to see who had set the cart in motion. A small figure caught his eye. Dawson Trunswick, Devin's younger brother. When he saw that Conor had spotted him, he nodded in a nervous way and vanished into the blackness.

The cart blasted toward the auction block. The earl and his lynx leaped off the side to save their skins. Finn leaped the other way. He plunged through the blinding smoke toward the kids while the earl cursed on the other side of the cloud.

"Run!" Conor's mother shouted as Finn reached them. She touched Conor's face. "Now's the time to run, my son! We'll cover you. Take Finn and go!"

Blaring through the smoke, the earl roared furiously. There were words in it, but they were lost in his rage.

"Thank you . . ." Conor whispered to his mother. "Thank you!" he called louder, turning to the Greencloak supporters.

"Long live the true Great Beasts!" someone shouted.

The rest of the supporters echoed it. His mother's smile was a proud thing indeed.

Conor's heart swelled.

Then the supporters turned back to the smoke, weapons out, ready for the remaining guards.

The kids ran for it. In the back of Conor's head was the thought that it was lucky, or strange, that Zerif and the other children hadn't made an appearance to help the Trunswick guards, but he was too relieved to be making a getaway to think long on it. If they got out of Trunswick alive, he could devote more time to wondering if their absence was due to cowardice or strategy.

But for now: They ran.

The sounds of battle rose again in the courtyard, but no one emerged to follow them. Their allies were holding back the guards.

Soon there was no sound except for the noise of their footfalls slapping on the stones. Then the scuff of their boots on the bare ground beside the Trunswick wall. And then, as they ran into the surrounding pastures, there was no sound at all.

Finn made a wordless gesture, and they all followed him into the blackest of nights.

10

GLENGAVIN

FINN CONTINUED TO SAVE THEIR LIVES. ROLLAN, HAVING
considerable experience being chased, was fairly
certain that the group's escape from Trunswick was
thrilling but temporary. After all, he'd seen the smug
Earl of Trunswick. More important, he'd seen the Earl
of Trunswick's horse. Despite Rollan's testy relationship
with his former mount, he was well aware that most
people were faster on horseback than on foot.

But the Trunswick guards didn't catch up with them.

This was because Finn led them on an untraceable path.
Close to Trunswick, he walked them through rivers to keep
from leaving scent trails for hounds to track. After they'd
put some distance between Trunswick and themselves, he
led them into a strange, boulder-filled forest that no horse
could enter. Tree branches hung as low as Rollan's waist.
The rocks were covered with perpetually damp moss that
ripped free if he wasn't careful as he climbed.

They walked and walked, over stranger and stranger
trails. The more foreign the surroundings grew, the more

comfortable Finn seemed to become. After he seemed satisfied that their path had been obscured enough, he scratched maps in the dirt with a stick and constructed shortcuts, mumbling to himself as he thought.

Which was how Rollan found himself hiking through deceptively friendly-looking green mountains, a rope around his waist connecting him to the next person in line, who also had a rope around *their* waist to the *next* person in line, and so on. The idea was that if Rollan fell, he'd have a safety catch. Rollan thought it was more likely that if he went down, they were all going down. But he guessed there was some comfort in the promise of company on the way down the mountainside.

As they traveled, Finn taught them an ancient Northern Euran method of sending coded messages.

"This is how you spell *Abeke*," Finn explained. He'd tied a mysterious number of knots into a ribbon. It didn't make much sense to Rollan, nor, Rollan noticed with some satisfaction, to Conor (who had been moping about since they left Trunswick anyway). Abeke and Meilin looked on very keenly, however. Finn continued, "You would just tie this ribbon onto the legs of a gilded pigeon from Trunswick and let it go. It will fly back to its home with your message."

Rollan couldn't think of anyone at the moment that he would send a message to. Possibly he could just write *Dear Mother, thanks for nothing*, and send that bird in the general direction of Amaya.

They also talked about what Zerif had said about the Bile. At the news that the spirit animal bond could be forced, Conor's face became pensive, but Rollan wondered if it would really be such a bad thing if people could choose what sort of animal they had to live with for the rest of their lives. He didn't say it out loud, though. He could tell by the others' faces that it wouldn't be a popular opinion.

They hiked for what felt like weeks, although it was really just days. Rollan ate all the interesting food in his pack, and then all the boring food, and had finally started in on the unappealing food. Meanwhile, the landscape grew harsher and more unforgiving. The mountains became more gray and less green, with savage rocks biting up through the grass. The fields that stretched below turned dry gold and purple, beautiful but unsatisfying for any livestock. They passed no towns, no farms, no houses, no people.

As the food ran low and the landscape became more bleak, Finn became straighter and stronger. His chin was up and his white hair seemed to mark him as different and special instead of defeated and war-torn. This part of Eura seemed to feed him.

It wasn't feeding Rollan, though. He reckoned it was probably time to make peace with the probability of starving to death.

Then, on the day Rollan ate his last piece of jerky, they came to Glengavin.

Like Trunswick, it was surrounded by a stone wall, which they could see over from their high vantage point. But that was where the similarities between the cities ended.

For all its old-fashioned details, Trunswick had reminded Rollan a lot of the cities in Amaya. Those cities were all skinny streets and crowded buildings, and people using the roads to relieve themselves, and flies collected on top of things that used to be food. Merchants and thieves and drunkards. And bundles of filthy orphans like himself, of course. Cities were full of opportunities, most of them opportunities for bad things to happen to you. And they all sort of looked the same to Rollan. No matter how different a city's architectural flesh was, he could see the bones of desperation underneath.

But not Glengavin. In the center was a massive stone building. A fortress, or castle. Or perhaps *palace* was the best word for it. An older central bit had clearly been built with defense in mind. But the extensive stone wings on either side had clearly been constructed for beauty and luxury. They were studded with stained-glass windows like jewels. Gargoyles and carvings hung from every stone overhang. Deep blue flags flapped from poles and hung beside doors.

It was shockingly different from the rugged landscape outside the wall.

"Am I really awake?" Conor asked. "It looks like a dream."

Rumfuss, Rollan just thought. This looked like a place a Great Beast would be.

Abeke, the small black cat perched on her shoulders and Uraza standing by her side, just shook her head wordlessly.

Meilin and the panda regarded Glengavin pensively. "The gardens remind me of home," she said with uncharacteristic wistfulness.

The stone manor was surrounded by acres of manicured plants and crushed gravel paths. Every bush was trimmed into a geometric shape. Every rose was pleasingly groomed. Lavender plants cut into squares led the way to the front entry.

The entire thing made Rollan feel a little strange inside. Since he'd become a full-time orphan, he had worked pretty hard to never be impressed by anything—hard to get disappointed that way—but he thought, maybe, he was impressed. Or excited even. Or possibly he was just hungry.

"Lady Evelyn said the Lord of Glengavin would welcome us," Conor said dubiously.

"Yeah, we saw how well that went back in Trunswick," Rollan replied.

"Maybe you could send Essix ahead," Finn suggested. "She might be able to let us know if she thinks something is amiss."

Rollan tipped his head back. Essix was sailing around overhead as usual. Within earshot. Not that that guaranteed she'd comply.

Meilin had crossed her arms and turned to stare at him expectantly.

Great, he thought. *An audience always makes this easier.*

Really casually, he said, "Hey. Essix."

The falcon kept circling. Her head was turned a little bit toward his voice, though. She heard him. But she wasn't going to do anything about it.

A little louder, Rollan called, "Essix."

Still more circling.

Now they were all looking at him.

"Problems?" Meilin asked, sweetly sarcastic.

"No," Rollan replied. He twirled his hand as if this is how he had meant it to go. "I don't tell her what to do. She doesn't tell me what to do. We have a great bond. Awesome. You know what? I'm going to go check out Glengavin myself."

Hiding his annoyance, he ripped loose the knotted rope around his waist and began to slip down the slope toward the wall. He only made it a few feet before Essix cried out and flapped off ahead of him.

Finn laughed – a rare sound from him. "Well, you two contrary animals are well matched, aren't you?"

"Oh, you know," Rollan said. "We like to keep the relationship fresh."

"It seems pretty fresh all right," Meilin murmured.

With a wrinkle of his nose, Rollan replied, "I'm going to choose to be the better man here and not say anything about how *fresh* you and your spirit animal smell." Meilin actually didn't smell – Rollan suspected girls didn't sweat – but the panda did have a distinct musky odor.

Rather arch, she countered, "Really? That's what you have? *Smells* bad?"

"We all could use a bath," Finn cut in. "Hopefully the welcome at Glengavin will be warm enough to afford us such luxuries."

It seemed as if that might be a possibility too, because when Essix returned, she looked unconcerned. Reassured, they approached the gate. Over it stretched a plaque that read: THREE UNDENIABLE TRUTHS: LOVE, DEATH, AND THE LAW OF GLENGAVIN. KNOW ALL THREE WELL.

Rollan felt it wasn't the most inspirational of mottos. Love was all right, he thought, but death wasn't incredibly tempting. It was hard to say which side the Law of Glengavin came down on, but he guessed it probably wasn't the hugging one.

The three guards, however, were not just pleasant, but actually excited to see them. After only the briefest of explanations from Finn, the group was brought inside.

"We are proud to welcome you to Glengavin," one of the guards said. He had an enormous red beard and equally enormous red eyebrows. Rollan thought that they could all take cover in his facial hair in the event of an emergency. Even more impressive than his beard, however, was his leather armor. It was more intricate than any leatherwork Rollan had ever seen. Every inch was etched with tangled artwork, much like Finn's tattoos. It seemed like the sort of thing that should be displayed on a shelf, not worn every day. Both guards also wore tartan kilts and leather sporrans—fancy pouches that hung low around their waists. Short knives rested in scabbards tied at their ankles.

War is so pretty here, Rollan thought. He thought again of that plaque over the gate.

"We had heard rumors of four heroes," the hairy guard said. "But we'd heard that one of them had summoned a black wildcat."

"You heard wrong," Meilin said coldly. "As you can tell, these animals are the Four Fallen."

Finn, in a much milder voice, said, "There is much darkness on the move too. Where there are heroes, there are always villains. We'd all be wise to be wary of opportunists."

"Oh, aye," agreed the red-bearded guard, quite amiable. He reached to pet the black cat Abeke held. "This isn't a Great Beast."

"No," Abeke said. "Her name is Kunaya."

"You *named* her?" demanded Meilin, pressing her hand to her face.

"Does she have special powers?" the guard asked.

Meilin made a sour face. "Shedding. Clawing. Being heavy."

Abeke merely smiled mysteriously. She was good at that. So was Uraza. Actually, so was the little black cat Kunaya. Smiling mysteriously was a rather feline magical power.

Rollan didn't trust cats, but he thought they were all right. Better than weasels.

A messenger made his way to them, a little out of breath. "Lord MacDonnell is pleased to welcome the heroes! He is throwing a banquet in your honor tonight. Would you like to see your rooms?"

The four kids looked at each other, surprised. They couldn't have asked for a more opposite experience from Trunswick.

Rollan's stomach growled. Banquet!

The messenger mistook their silence. "They are quite nice rooms," he promised quickly. "No comfort is wanting!"

"Oh, no," Finn said. "It's just . . ."

Rollan finished, "It's nice to have such a *warm welcome.*"

As they were led toward the main castle, Rollan glanced over his shoulder. The plaque about the three truths wasn't visible from this side, but he hadn't forgotten it.

It was indeed a warm welcome. Rollan and Conor were given a room to share. Though they were from very different backgrounds, both of them were equally stunned by the size of it. And the beds! – great poster beds, with a pillar at each corner supporting a draping fabric ceiling. One for each boy. Most inns in Amaya didn't even have two beds in a room, and when they did, it was only to cram five or six people – sometimes strangers – into the same space. And there was a private washbasin with soft cloths beside it. Fresh clothing had also been laid near the washbasin, two choices of outfits for each boy. One was a deep green surcoat and kilt that matched the guards. The other was a more standard-issue Euran surcoat and leggings.

"No way am I wearing that kilt," Rollan observed.

Conor touched the tartan wool fabric. "I think it's interesting. Why not?"

"Too much like a uniform. You know how I feel about those. What did you think of that plaque over the gate?"

"Er, remind me what it said again?" Conor asked sheepishly, and Rollan remembered with a pang of regret that the boy was not a talented reader.

"Something about the Law of Glengavin. Death and hugging."

Conor shrugged. "Seems like an orderly place. Makes sense they'd want people to obey the law. Why, are you feeling anything about it?"

After the dismal experience of asking Essix to check out Glengavin, Rollan had almost forgotten about her otherworldly powers of observation. It felt like a long time since they'd had a moment of connection.

"I just don't like rules," Rollan answered finally. "They're like uniforms."

The boys continued poking around in the room. All the furniture was very fancy, and probably expensive, but that impressed Rollan less than the pillows.

"Probably one thousand geese were plucked to fill this thing," he told Conor, burying his face into it. It was a cloud of indistinct perfection.

"Two thousand," Conor replied drowsily. Neither boy had had a decent night's sleep since well before Trunswick. "Did you see the washbasin? You can get rid of your fresh smell."

He made a face as he said it so that Rollan knew he was joking about Rollan's comment to Meilin earlier.

"Oh, sure, I'll get right on that."

But neither of them did. Instead, they let the pillows suffocate them for a few hours until a messenger woke them for the banquet. They washed and dressed before following another servant. The great hall was as richly decorated as the gardens. A woman in a brilliant dress played a skin-headed drum. A man in a matching tunic played a set of humming bagpipes. A younger teen played a carved wooden harp. The sound beat up the tapestry-covered walls.

"Look at this place," Conor said to Rollan.

"Look at *you*," Rollan replied. Conor had opted for the kilt. Rollan had not.

Flushing, Conor said, "It seemed polite."

Polite was never really on Rollan's list of priorities.

"If we have to make a speedy escape and you have to do it in that skirt, that's all on you," Rollan whispered.

As the bagpipes buzzed a merry jig, Meilin and Abeke entered the hall. Both looked startlingly different in the lush green surcoats that had been provided. Meilin in particular looked stunning and odd. It took Rollan a moment to realize that it was because it had been a long time since he'd seen her *clean*.

The two girls joined them. Meilin's eyes lingered on Rollan for a long moment before finding Essix. The falcon perched on an unused torch holder and ran her beak through the feathers on her leg.

"Rollan, you look *clean*," Meilin said. Her gaze still seemed to linger on him a little longer than usual, a fact that didn't bother Rollan a bit.

"Hey," Conor protested.

"Oh," Meilin added hurriedly, "you do too. The green, uh, brings out your eyes. It's nice to be staying somewhere *civilized*."

"More civilized than I'm used to. Any sign of Rumfuss?" Conor asked.

Rollan said, "Yeah, any boars running around the castle?"

"Actually," Abeke pointed out, "there is a tapestry with a boar on it in the hall near our room. I think it is Rumfuss. I asked the servant who led us here, and she said he was the boar in the gardens – but nothing more."

"Boar in the garden?" Meilin echoed. "She wouldn't say anything more?"

"She said it was against the law for servants to carry on with guests."

"That's a funny law," Rollan said.

"This place seems to have a lot of them," Abeke agreed. "I tried to leave our door open for some air and one of the guards told me that only the lord or the lord's family was allowed to leave their doors open. They said it was a privilege."

Rollan sniffed indignantly. "That seems stupid."

Meilin broke in. "It's exotic. But I'm sure Zhong's customs would seem strange to an outsider as well."

"That's true," Abeke agreed. "Nilo is quite different from Eura or Amaya, especially some of the more remote villages. At least it is pleasant here."

It was indeed pleasant. Conor asked, "Where's Finn?"

"Talking to Lord MacDonnell, I believe," Meilin answered. "The Lord of Glengavin."

Rollan's stomach growled loud enough for it to be heard over the music.

Abeke looked sympathetic. "Have you seen the food?"

Long tables lined the edges of the room. One sat higher than the others on a raised platform. All the chairs were fancy at that higher table, but the fanciest was a gold-painted one, like a throne. The other tables were piled with food. There were cakes soaked in sugar syrup and potatoes glazed with butter. Fruit swam in cream. Oatcakes formed teetering stacks. Sausages lay in savory pyramids. Blushing lumps of carrot and rich knobs of beef floated in tureens.

None of the many people in the hall had touched the food yet. They all seemed to be waiting for a cue.

Finn entered the hall with a big, jolly-looking man – Lord MacDonnell. He had a tidily trimmed dark beard and wide-spaced, amused eyes. He wore a kilt and tall wool socks. A great tartan sash draped one shoulder and was pinned at his hip with a dagger-shaped brooch.

Everything about Lord MacDonnell seemed cheerful. A little too obviously cheerful, perhaps. As a street rat, Rollan had learned that a smile could sometimes hide wicked thoughts better than a sneer.

He didn't trust him.

He didn't know why. Probably because he didn't trust anybody. In any case, something in Rollan whispered, *Maybe not everything about him is jolly.*

As if confirming this suspicion, Essix swung down suddenly to perch on Rollan's shoulder. Her talons clung tightly to his leather jerkin. Leaning close to him, her beak parted as she made a soft noise in his ear.

"I know," he hissed. "I'm watching."

But she made another soft noise. And this time, Rollan's vision suddenly clicked into sharper focus. It was as if he had been observing the world in black and white before, and now it was in color. He saw how the servants' postures became more tense now that Lord MacDonnell and Finn had entered the room. He noticed how the musicians hesitated, confirming that they were still wanted. He saw how the two children, a boy and a girl, who walked behind MacDonnell were spitting images of him – the lord's children, surely. He noted that there was no Lady MacDonnell in evidence. He noticed the wrinkle between Lord MacDonnell's eyebrows. He saw the dais where the lord was meant to sit with his children and wife, and he noticed that there was a raised seat for the lord of the castle's spirit animal to rest on. And he noticed that seat was covered with dust.

It was almost too much to notice all at once. He could see with Essix's great eyes, but he still had to process it with Rollan's less-than-great brain. He staggered a bit. Conor grabbed Rollan's arm (how clearly Rollan could observe even Conor, with his worn shepherd's hands). As Rollan swatted at him in protest, Essix flapped from his shoulder. Immediately everything became ordinary again.

The sudden ordinariness was as overpowering as the stunning vision had been. It seemed impossible to go back to seeing things in the usual way after observing the world with Essix's amazing power.

If our bond was better, Rollan wondered, *is that how I'd see things all the time?*

Finn, Lord MacDonnell, and the two children walked up to Rollan and the others.

"Welcome! I am Lord MacDonnell, and this is my home!" The man had a big, jolly voice to match his big, jolly body. "Greencloaks are always welcome here. Glengavin is a home to all heroes."

Finn murmured a noise of polite gratitude.

"This is my son, Culloden," Lord MacDonnell said, gesturing to the boy behind him, "and this is my daughter, Shanna."

Both children bowed. Conor, Meilin, and Abeke bowed back, with Rollan quickly chiming in with a sort-of bow-like movement of his own. Finn then introduced the four kids, adding, "The four Great Beasts need no introduction, I'm sure."

"No, indeed! Where's your green, lad?" Lord MacDonnell asked as Rollan glanced around, trying to spot where Essix had suddenly gone to.

Meilin elbowed Rollan. Lord MacDonnell was talking to *him*.

"Oh, that," Rollan said. "I'm less a member of the Greencloaks and more a member of Let's-Save-Erdas."

Lord MacDonnell laughed heartily. "Aren't we all. Aren't we all! Shall we eat?"

He clapped his hands.

Instantly, every sound in the hall went silent. Conversation stopped. Not a single footstep shuffled on the stone. The musicians' hands slapped to dampen their strings.

The quiet was eerie.

Then Lord MacDonnell smiled hugely again and clapped once more.

The musicians scrambled to play a more stately march as he made his way to the feast. Lord MacDonnell plucked a single grape from a platter. Every eye in the room watched as he dropped it in his mouth.

The moment he'd eaten it, conversation buzzed back up again and everyone moved to collect food for themselves. This must be another law. How tense that silence had been. Rollan wondered what the penalty was for finding yourself on the wrong side of the Law of Glengavin.

Rollan and Meilin hung back as Finn, Conor, and Abeke helped themselves.

"This is weird," Rollan said.

"I think it's great," Meilin said. "Look how well-run this is. Most banquets and parties are disasters. This runs like an army. And his children are perfect."

"Perfect minions," replied Rollan, watching them. The

two children followed just behind Lord MacDonnell, nodding when spoken to.

"That's respect," Meilin said. "I wouldn't expect *you* to recognize it."

"Oh, don't pull rank on me now –" started Rollan. He broke off as Lord MacDonnell headed back their way.

"Aren't you two going to enjoy the feast?" Lord MacDonnell boomed in a pleasant baritone. "The salmon is divine."

"We were just admiring it," Meilin said smoothly. "And also how well your children obey."

Rollan was about to open his mouth to point out that he had not been admiring that particular aspect of the night, but Meilin pinched his elbow, out of sight of Lord MacDonnell. Rollan swallowed his words.

"Well, my castle, my law!" Lord MacDonnell said with a laugh.

The image of the perfect guest, Meilin asked him, "Will you tell me more about how you run this banquet?"

She was so clever at disguising her true emotions that even Rollan couldn't tell if her interest was manufactured or genuine. She and Lord MacDonnell went to get food together, chatting the entire way.

With a frown, Rollan took a single sausage from the very end of the table and ate it, while simultaneously looking for Essix and surveying the banquet.

His attention was snagged by the musicians. A singer had joined them and they were singing a song that he knew. It was a street song about the Great Beasts that all the urchins in Concorba could sing in their sleep. The verses went through all the Great Beasts in order, the tune annoyingly monotonous, until by the fifteenth and final Great Beast, most listeners were ready to pummel whoever had decided to start the song in the first place.

The musicians played so skillfully, changing up the harmonies in each verse, that Rollan didn't even realize that he had forgotten to be bored until it was over. In fact, it stirred that same strange part in him that the first sight of Glengavin had. This place sure was getting to him.

He told the musicians, "Usually I hate that song."

"Oh, I'm sorry," the singer said.

"But not this time," Rollan finished. "You guys are great."

The singer smiled graciously. "Thank you."

The teenage harpist piped up, her voice annoyed: "But no one can hear us on the other side of the room. It's too noisy."

The musicians and Rollan gazed around the great hall. The arched ceiling should have been a good soundboard for the music, but the thick tapestries on the wall swallowed all sound.

"If you were higher," Rollan suggested, "the sound would carry better. Above the tapestries. There?"

He pointed to a small, disused balcony.

"Oh, but—" started the singer in a small voice.

"Probably not," replied the drummer.

"Not this time," the harpist added.

Rollan was about to comment on their apparent fear of heights when he realized he could see movement on the balcony. It was Essix. At first he thought she was just flapping for a takeoff. But then her wings fluttered even more violently, and he realized she was trapped somehow. It made him feel strangely fluttery himself. Anxious.

The musicians' gazes followed Rollan.

"Is that Essix?" breathed the harpist.

"Yes," Rollan said, a little grim. "And she seems to be trapped. I need to know the way up to that balcony."

"Oh, but—" started the singer.

"Probably not," replied the drummer.

The harpist said, "No. No, you shouldn't go up there."

"I have to," Rollan said. Their attitude toward the balcony was beginning to make him feel a little uneasy, though. "Why, is it unstable?"

"No," the singer said. He glanced urgently at Lord MacDonnell, who was engaged in conversation at the raised table at the end of the hall. "No one is supposed to stand higher than the lord of the castle. It's the law."

Rollan thought all laws were stupid, but this one was stupider than most. He said, "But I won't be standing. I'm freeing a bird and then coming right down."

The musicians conferred among themselves.

"No," the harpist said finally. "I'll go free her. You're a guest. You shouldn't have to risk it."

"*Risk* it?" echoed Rollan. The sight of Essix flapping was making him feel even more uneasy. "She has to be freed! What if she's hurt? If I'm not supposed to be up there, is he going to do it himself?"

This made all the musicians glance anxiously at Lord MacDonnell.

"I'll just go," the harpist said. Her voice was brave, but her face looked sick. The other musicians placed their hands on her shoulders and nodded. She moved down the wall to a small door. When she opened it, Rollan saw the steep stairs that led up to the balcony. She disappeared inside.

The other musicians muttered, twisting their hands. Rollan didn't get it.

The harpist reappeared on the balcony above them.

The musicians kept fretting.

In just a moment, Essix flapped free of whatever had trapped her on the balcony.

It was barely a minute. No time at all.

The harpist moved back toward the staircase at the wall.

Just then, Lord MacDonnell looked up sharply from his gilded chair. His eyes went right to the balcony. The harpist's face was pale as the moon.

Without taking his gaze from her, Lord MacDonnell clapped. Just once.

Immediately, all sound ceased.

Lord MacDonnell said, "Do my people not know my law?"

The hall was quiet.

"Scribe, what is the sixteenth rule of the hall?"

A squirrelly boy at the end of the raised table spoke up. "No one shall sit higher than the lord of the castle."

Everyone's eyes were now on the harpist on the elevated balcony.

"Oh, my lord, I didn't mean it as a dishonor!" she cried. "I was just trying to –"

"My castle," said Lord MacDonnell. "My law."

"Please—"

"Demoted!" Lord MacDonnell shouted. "You are no longer the court harpist. Ten years in the kitchen, then beg for my forgiveness."

"My lord," begged the harpist as the guards approached the doorway to the balcony. "That harp was made by my father."

"And you will destroy it right now," Lord MacDonnell ordered.

"My lord—"

"Did you know my law?"

The harpist hung her head. As Rollan's heart charged in his chest, she stood there until guards climbed the stairs to fetch her. Limply, she accompanied them and stood before the harp.

"My castle," repeated Lord MacDonnell. "My law."

Rollan didn't need Essix's supernatural eyesight to see how much the instrument meant to the harpist. He couldn't bear that she'd known this might happen, and risked it anyway for Essix and him.

Swiftly, Rollan stepped in front of the high table, his hands burning with anger and guilt. He held his chin up high. "It was my fault. She climbed there to free Essix for me."

Lord MacDonnell raised a dark eyebrow. "Ah, it is the boy who walks by himself." He didn't say anything for a moment, and then he said, "There are three true things in this place: love, death, and the Law of Glengavin. Her punishment remains. But for your bravery in taking responsibility, join me here at the knights' table. Glengavin is a home to heroes and I see that you are becoming one."

Rollan gritted his teeth. The last thing he wanted was to accept a reward for his stupidity. This was all his fault.

But Meilin, seated at one of the other tables, found his gaze. Her eyes flashed. It was the visual equivalent of her pinching him before. It meant *Just do it!*

She was probably right. A nobleman who just ruined a girl's life for climbing onto a balcony probably could think of something worse for an orphan who refused to sit at his table.

Rollan looked over his shoulder at the slump-shouldered singer. His blood was starting to boil, but he tamped it down. *One day,* he thought, *nobles won't be able to do this to us.*

But until then, he sat at Lord MacDonnell's right hand, three seats away from him. Directly next to the noble was his son, Culloden, eating quietly. And then was Shanna, making shapes in her potatoes. Then Rollan.

In front of them, the guards stood by as the harpist smashed her own harp. Tears ran down her face and the splinters of the instrument cut her hands, but she didn't complain anymore.

Then, as she was led away to the kitchen with slumped shoulders and bloody hands, Lord MacDonnell muttered, as if to himself, "My castle. My law."

11

WINDOW

THAT NIGHT, IN THE WEIRD QUIET OF A BEAUTIFUL, VAST guest room in Glengavin, Conor dreamed of falling out the window into the garden. He heard the tune the musicians had been playing right before Lord MacDonnell had punished the harpist. The song turned discordant and suddenly he saw an animal moving between the manicured perfection of the green gardens. A boar. It was huge and terrifying, all bristles and tusks. When it looked over its shoulder at him, Conor instinctively knew it was no ordinary boar.

"Rumfuss!" he called. "I need to talk to you!"

The boar immediately ran through the bushes and into the brushy wild outside of the gardens. The landscape here was scruffy and rocky, with lots of nooks and crannies for smaller animals to hide in. But Rumfuss didn't seem interested in hiding. Instead, the boar broke into an ungainly gallop and led Conor in a lopsided figure eight, past part of the castle.

"Wait!" Conor called again.

Suddenly another animal darted in front of him, through a curtain of purple wisteria. It was an enormous hare – even in the dream it felt familiar, as if Conor had dreamed it before. Its powerful hind legs propelled it one way and then the other. It was running away from Glengavin. When Conor turned back to Rumfuss, the boar was gone.

"Wolf boy, wake up!"

It took Conor a moment to realize the hissed voice came from Rollan in the next bed over. He blinked in the darkness.

"Are you awake?" Rollan whispered. "There's something outside the window."

Conor quietly rolled over to listen. Rollan's eyes glistened in the faint light from outside. Heavy curtains blocked most of the light and all the landscape, but the other boy was right. Something was shuffling outside the window. It couldn't be anything good – their room was four stories above the ground and there was no balcony.

Sliding out of bed, Conor gestured to Briggan. The wolf climbed to his feet and faced the window. His hackles prickled as another scraping sound came from outside.

The window was cracked and the curtains moved slightly.

Rollan swung his feet silently over the edge of his bed and pulled a dagger from under his pillow. He held up five fingers, then four, then three. Counting down.

When he got to one, both he and Conor grabbed a curtain and pulled them open.

A figure stood on the sill, wild-haired and ferocious. Wind tore at the person's clothing. The figure balanced precariously on the window ledge. There was nothing behind but dozens of feet of open air.

Conor gasped, "Meilin?"

Because it *was* Meilin. She swayed on the edge of the window. Her eyes were fast shut, her mouth moving. Tears coursed down her cheeks. She barely looked like herself.

"She's sleepwalking!" Conor exclaimed, horrified. "Grab her!"

Rollan and Conor each seized an arm, pulling her into the room. When she landed on the floor with an unceremonious crash, she moaned and shook her head.

"Wake up," Conor said gently, shaking her shoulder.

It was strange to see her face with tears on it. It must be difficult to know your father was missing and your home city was destroyed. To belong somewhere, and then suddenly to not.

Rollan leaned over her too, concern written on his face. But when he caught Conor looking, Rollan quickly slapped a smirk on his face and quipped, "Yep, wakey wakey."

Retrieving a pitcher of water from beside his bed, he dumped it over her. With a muffled shriek, Meilin leaped from the ground. She pinned Rollan against the wall, her hand against his throat, her hair dripping.

"I was *awake*," she snapped. "Conor woke me."

Rollan grinned saucily. "I know."

She slapped him. Then, to Conor, she said, "Thank you for pulling me inside."

"Hey, I helped," Rollan protested, but she ignored him.

"What happened?" Conor asked uncertainly. "What were you doing out there?"

Meilin stoked the fireplace to give them some more light, and then returned to the window. Now that she was inside, she seemed a little undone by the dizzying height. She gestured to the next window over. "Our room is over there. I must have been sleepwalking. I was dreaming . . ."

"Were you dreaming of being a spider?" Rollan asked. He joined them at the window, Meilin's slap mark bright on his cheek. "Because you must have had sticky feet to get from there to here."

"No, there's a tiny ledge," Conor pointed out. "You're lucky you didn't fall, Meilin. I can't believe you did that while asleep." He didn't want to remark on the tear marks still visible on her face, because the idea of pointing them out seemed embarrassing to both him and her. But he was certain that Meilin would never cry while awake.

Rollan opened his mouth and then shut it again. Meilin's furious face dared him to say anything.

"I am going back to my bed," Rollan said, "because it is good and true and would never lie to me. You two can do what you like."

"That's a good idea," Meilin said as he climbed back into his bed. "Tomorrow we have a long day ahead of us, looking for Rumfuss." She placed her hand on the doorknob.

"Be careful," Conor warned.

Rollan jerked his blanket down from his chin. "Are you sure you don't want to crawl back out of the window?"

Meilin gave him a withering look and slipped back out into the hall.

Rollan disappeared back down into his pillows. He muttered, "My castle, my law."

12

VOICES

THE FIRST THING ABEKE NOTICED WHEN SHE WOKE UP WAS that it was not quite morning. The room was still blue-edged and black-shadowed, though birds sang thinly outside. The second thing she noticed was that the door was cracked open, and what looked like Uraza's tail was disappearing through it. Presumably following the rest of Uraza.

As Abeke pushed herself up and blinked, trying to decide if she had seen the leopard leave, she heard a faint *pad-pad-pad-pad* and saw Kunaya's dark form trot out into the hall too.

"Uraza!" hissed Abeke, shooting a glance at the lump that was Meilin's sleeping form. This was not the place to go wandering. But the leopard didn't return.

"Mwuwuh?" Meilin asked the room sleepily.

"Uraza's in the hall," Abeke replied in a hushed whisper. "I'm going to get her."

"Mwuf. Need help?" Even half-asleep, Meilin sounded a little suspicious of Abeke creeping out of the room so early.

"I am all right!"

"Mwufay." The other girl turned back into her pillow.

Abeke headed down the hall. She could smell the faint scent of bread baking – the bakers up early. Maybe that was what had lured the big cat out of the room. It took her a moment to glimpse the forms of the two cats disappearing around a corner.

"Uraza!" she hissed once more. But she didn't dare to do it again. If there was a law against leaving your bedroom door open, surely there was a law against sneaking around while no one else was up. She had no choice but to slink after the two cats.

Closed doors lined the high-ceilinged hall, and every few yards was an alcove containing something unexpected and magical: a delicate water fountain trailing water over carvings, a cage of sleeping canaries, a pillowed chair with lion's paws, a tree covered with white blossoms.

Uraza paused at the next corner, her lavender eyes keen. She wanted the girl to know that she wasn't trying to be disobedient. This was no helter-skelter chase through a castle. This time, Uraza was leading her.

Crouching low, Abeke silently caught up to Uraza. Together, the two cats and the girl made their way past the black rectangles of closed doors. From the way the leopard stalked – pausing every few steps – it seemed she wasn't quite sure where she was going or what she was looking for.

The hall grew lighter. Gradually Abeke realized she could hear the dull murmur of voices coming from inside one of these many rooms. From the thrashing of Uraza's tail, this was what she had been looking for. They scouted back and forth, trying to get closer, until Abeke found a long, skinny room full of washbasins. Morning light came in a large window at the end, suddenly strong and bright. One wall was lined with animal-headed fountains, each faucet carved with a different species. Cloths, perfumes, and draping robes sat on a long shelf opposite.

Abeke pressed her ear to the washbasin wall, and suddenly the voices came into focus.

"Look," said a familiar voice, "clearly Lord MacDonnell is a little crazy. But we aren't going to be here long. All we need to do is find Rumfuss and then find the girl and get out of here before he does any more of his crazy 'my castle, my law' stuff."

"How will we persuade Rumfuss to give up his talisman?" asked another voice. This one also sounded familiar, and had a Niloan accent. Suddenly Abeke knew who they were — and why Uraza had been so intent on finding them. Devin and Karmo!

"Give up?" Devin scoffed. "Look at our beasts! We'll take it."

They must have made it to Glengavin in the night! Abeke leaped back from the wall and out of the washroom. She needed to tell the others immediately.

But as she rounded the corner back to the hall, she was brought up short. She stood face-to-face with Devin Trunswick. Uraza stood nose-to-nose with his black panther, Elda. Behind him stood tall, dark Karmo, and beside him was his huge hammerkop stork, Impundulu. The bird's head and beak were nearly as long as Karmo's arm.

In just a second, Abeke had snatched a large glass bottle of perfume from the table beside her. Makeshift weapon. She *had* been paying attention in the training room back at Greenhaven.

"Ah, Abeke," Devin said with a clever smile that he seemed to have learned from Zerif. He didn't seem at all concerned by the prospect of getting hit over the head with a perfume bottle. "I don't intend to murder you. We were just talking about you."

"How did you get in here?" Abeke demanded.

"Glengavin is a hall for heroes," Devin boomed, clearly mocking Lord MacDonnell. He gestured to his spirit animal, who thrashed her tail. "Elda makes me very popular in Eura."

"Not in this particular corridor," Abeke replied. She jerked her chin toward Karmo. "Who is he?"

"This is my friend Karmo," Devin said. "He's from Nilo too."

I know, thought Abeke, with a pang of homesickness. *I heard.*

Karmo's eyes were narrowed, as if Devin and he weren't particularly friendly. He said, "I've come to see if I can change your mind. Come back to us. Come back to Nilo. Our people need us to be beacons of hope."

Taken by surprise, she blinked. Was *she* the girl she had heard them talking about? "*What?* I am not coming back. I have seen enough to know who fights for what I believe in. The Greencloaks are the good guys."

Karmo raised a dark, handsome eyebrow. He was the sort of boy that her sister, Soama, would have been silly over back home. "Are they?"

Abeke nodded. "I am very fortunate that they allowed me to switch sides. They understand the value of mercy, unlike your master, Zerif."

Devin scoffed. "They would not have killed you, Abeke.

You know that. You walk with Uraza. The Greencloaks want you alive."

Abeke didn't like this conversation. There wasn't any chance that she would fight with the Conquerors again, but it awoke all kinds of unpleasant tangled feelings inside her. For a pained moment she thought of Shane, the friend she'd had to leave behind. "You won't convince me, Devin. My spirit animal chooses the Greencloaks."

"But is she right?" Karmo broke in gently.

"Of course she is! She's a Great Beast!" The fierceness of Abeke's reply made Uraza growl beside her. Abeke could feel the power of Uraza seeping into her, preparing her for a fight. Her nerves danced. Next to Devin, Elda dropped down, tail thrashing even harder, her black fur scuffed up threateningly. Impundulu clawed the floor with one foot. The atmosphere felt charged and dangerous.

"The Great Beasts aren't always right," Karmo said. "They may mean well, but just like humans, their decisions are fallible. After all, aren't you and I here in search of a Great Beast who flees us both?"

Abeke didn't want to admit that he was right. But Uraza was not like Rumfuss. She'd died standing up for what she believed in.

"Abeke, I came to bring you back so that you and I could lead Nilo to a better future," Karmo said. He held out a hand. "Come with me?"

He asked in such a mild, kind way. Not at all as if his hammerkop stood threateningly beside him, one foot raised, giant beak parted.

"I have chosen my side," Abeke said harshly.

Devin shrugged. "Well, you're coming with us either way. Karmo?"

Abeke swung the perfume bottle just as Uraza sprang at Elda. Devin let out a muffled cry as he blocked the blow. Karmo stood by quite calmly. As Abeke reached up to swing again, Impundulu flapped its wings. Lifting from the ground, the bird punched its legs into Abeke's abdomen.

There was an arcing flash of light as the bird's feet touched Abeke. The contact was more than a blow – it was a jolt. Her limbs suddenly went numb. Karmo was on her in a moment, pinning her arms behind her. Kunaya had appeared from nowhere and she wound around Abeke's legs, mewing piteously. Uraza and Elda fought in the hall, making soft thumps when their bodies hit the walls. Elda was larger, but Uraza was greater. She would win a battle against the black panther . . . but then what? There were still two humans against Abeke, and another spirit animal with strange abilities.

Abeke opened her mouth to shout for help. Devin stuffed one of the cloths into her mouth.

"Put her in passive form," he told Abeke, "or I will cut your throat."

She had no choice. She held out her arm pleadingly, and Uraza disappeared in a blitz of light, forming a tattoo on Abeke's arm, right next to where Karmo's hand held her in place.

"There was an easier way," Karmo said into Abeke's ear.

Devin held out his arm, and Elda immediately vanished into passive form. It was like an instantly obeyed order.

"Don't look so angry, Abeke," he said. "You're going home."

13

LORD MACDONNELL

BECAUSE MEILIN LIKED ORDER, SHE LIKED GLENGAVIN. Although the others were horrified by what had happened to the musician the night before, Meilin could see where MacDonnell was coming from. The harpist had known the rule. She could have approached MacDonnell with their predicament and asked for a solution.

"If you like him so well," Rollan said over an impressive breakfast, "why don't you convince him to let us go see Rumfuss?"

Meilin daintily bit into a crumpet. She chewed it and swallowed it entirely before answering, "That is my plan."

Finn, on the other side of the long and mostly empty table, looked up from his own meal. "Hospitality is very important in the North, and if we hope to impress Lord MacDonnell into allowing us access to Rumfuss, we must convince him that we are worthy. Where's Abeke?"

Meilin had just been wondering this herself. Abeke had not returned after going after Uraza this morning. It was possible she'd gotten into trouble. But it was also possible that Abeke was hunting for Rumfuss on her own or otherwise doing something for the Conquerors.

Meilin didn't know how long it would take for her to trust Abeke. All she knew was that it hadn't happened yet.

"She went out this morning and hasn't come back yet."

Finn narrowed his eyes. "That seems troubling. Meilin, why don't you, Conor, and Rollan go speak to MacDonnell while I look for Abeke? I can move about the castle more safely than you three; I know more of the customs."

"And what is it you want us to do?" Rollan demanded. "Be *charming*?"

As Lord MacDonnell entered the room, Meilin stood up and patted her hair. "I don't have a problem with that." She called loudly, "Lord MacDonnell! Good morning!"

Behind her back, she gestured for the others to join her.

MacDonnell seemed pleased to see them. He boomed, "How are you liking that kilt, Conor? It looks fine on you! You'd be a good addition to Glengavin. You and your wolf."

"Briggan is not really mine, my lord," Conor said. "If anything, I suppose I'm his."

"Where is he at this fine morning?"

Conor held up his arm. Briggan was frozen in midflight in the tattoo.

"Let that wolf loose!"

Conor released the wolf with a brilliant flash. Immediately Briggan frisked around him. Playfully, the wolf took Conor's hand in his mouth. He looked ferocious when he pretended to bite Conor, but he meant it all in good fun.

Meilin glanced up to MacDonnell to see what he thought of this.

The older man's expression had gone very un-jolly, but it snapped back into good cheer when he noticed Meilin watching. "What's your surname, boy?"

"You mean my last name?" Conor blushed, and Meilin felt bad for him. "I don't have one. I'm just a shepherd's son, my lord."

"No shame in that," Lord MacDonnell said. "What's your father's name?"

"Fenray."

"If you were from Glengavin, you'd be Conor MacFenray," Lord MacDonnell said. "*Mac* means son of."

Conor tried it. "Conor MacFenray."

"You could pick any old last name, you know," Rollan said from just behind them. "Who says you have to have your father's name? I'd pick something like SuperStrongGuy. Rollan SuperStrongGuy. Or Rollan FALCONMASTER."

Both Meilin and Conor raised their eyebrows. Rollan was a long way away from being a falconmaster.

With a booming chuckle – always the booming! – Lord MacDonnell led them to an open courtyard in the center of Glengavin. On the grass and under the covered stone walkways, more than forty soldiers in kilts were training. Only, Meilin would not have guessed it was training if Lord MacDonnell hadn't told them. Because instead of engaging in mock battles, the men copied music into decorated books, practiced harp and lute, and recited ballads at each other. Only a few of them had spirit animals, but when they did, the spirit animals seemed content to help them with these strange tasks. Next to one man, a shaggy Highland cow stood patiently as her human partner used her massive horns to hold her elaborate knitting. Another man was aided in his harp-playing by a stoat. It plucked the low notes. He plucked the high ones.

Rollan said, "Sweet merciful chicken. What are they training for? Becoming a princess?"

"War," Lord MacDonnell said.

"War against princesses?"

"War's useless if you don't know how to live with peace," Lord MacDonnell boomed. "Not very long ago, Glengavin had the best soldiers in Eura. But our skill was meaningless. We were almost destroyed by war. All we did was murder each other, and for nothing. Cattle! Glory! We were great warriors, but we didn't know what to do if we weren't fighting."

Meilin raised an eyebrow. Finn would have liked to hear this description. "So you turned to the arts."

"Exactly," Lord MacDonnell said. "Now we spend equal time on training in the arts as we do keeping our muscles fit."

"That's a sweet story," Rollan spoke up. "But what about those musicians last night? The ones that are now scrubbing pots?"

Cheeky, Rollan, Meilin thought. *Be careful.*

But Lord MacDonnell merely said, "Disorder leads to war, and I won't risk more war. My castle, my law. It's not difficult to follow the rules."

They stopped to watch two men who were laughing and playing chess.

Lord MacDonnell said, "Will you young heroes know what to do when the battle is over? You're spending your childhood saving the world. What happens when it's saved?"

"We should be so lucky," Meilin said.

Conor said, "I know what I will do. I will return to my family's farm with enough money to pay off our debts, and then I will take my place among my brothers as a shepherd, just like my father before me."

No, Conor, Meilin thought. *You're forgetting Briggan. You can't take a wolf among the sheep.*

Rollan's eye briefly caught hers, and Meilin knew that he was thinking the same thing.

"My lord," Meilin said, "speaking of saving the world — the Great Beast, Rumfuss. There's a rumor he's locked in your gardens."

MacDonnell continued to stare at one of the chess players for a moment, then turned to Meilin. "Indeed he is."

He said this very simply, the same way one might say, "It's a touch rainy today," or "I'm wearing new shoes."

She tried to sound quite collected. "We really would like to speak with him."

MacDonnell shook his head. "Only I am allowed to hunt in the gardens. Even if your hunt is just for a word with the Great Beast. It's for the best — he's a miserable, grumpy creature. He'd likely trample you."

"Sir, it's important," Conor said. "It's why we've come all this way."

"To collect the talismans. To recapture the power of the Great Beasts. To destroy the invaders." MacDonnell said all this dismissively, like he didn't believe it. "Finn told me last night why it is you seek Rumfuss. The Greencloaks are wrong, if you ask me. No man-made machination could possibly fix soured relationships with spirit animals. Sometimes, things have simply gone too wrong."

"How can you believe that with such conviction?" Meilin asked.

MacDonnell frowned for a moment, then drummed his fingers together. "I'll tell you a story. When I was a boy, I was cruel and proud. I was the son of a warrior lord. I knew who I was. I knew what I had coming to me." Lord MacDonnell's gaze was far away. "I dreamed of the animal I would summon to be my spirit animal. The North is full of animals that would increase my glory. And yet, when my summoning ceremony happened, I didn't call a hound or a horse or even a fighting badger. I called a hare."

Meilin remembered her own Nectar Ceremony. She had been so stunned and disappointed to see a panda instead of a more agile animal.

"I was furious," Lord MacDonnell recalled. "A hare! An overgrown rabbit!" Now he ducked his head, and Meilin realized that his expression was one of shame. He had to consider for a long time before he could continue. "I tormented my spirit animal. At best I dismissed him. At worst I taunted him. I knew I was being terrible, but I didn't care. Part of me wanted him to lash back at me. To prove his mettle. But he was loyal to a fault—he swallowed my harsh words and did my bidding like a servant rather than a spirit animal.

"One morning, I woke and he was gone. I had driven my spirit animal away." Lord MacDonnell closed his eyes. "Since then, there is a hole in my heart that nothing can fill. All joys and entertainments seem empty, and I'll never know what the hare and I might have accomplished together. I am going through the motions of leading my people, but nothing truly matters to me. I'm a shell. A creature that was Lord MacDonnell."

I will never let that happen to Jhi and me, Meilin vowed. *I must treat her better.*

"But part of being a leader," MacDonnell said, straightening a bit, "is thinking about what you want in the future, not what you wanted in the past." He motioned to the chessboard. "This game teaches that strategy. I train my men to be masters of it, so they might succeed where I have failed."

"Chess?" Rollan scoffed. "All chess ever taught me is that I should always play cards."

MacDonnell ignored this and turned to Conor. "Play a round with me?"

Conor's head jerked up, utterly horrified. He stammered, "Oh, I don't . . . I'm not really good at chess."

Lord MacDonnell was already pulling out a chair at one of the unoccupied chess tables. He arranged his kilt all around the chair so that nothing too embarrassing was showing. "As I said, Briggan is a great leader. And this game is a lesson all leaders should learn."

Meilin, not at all convinced, offered, "You can do it." But she was thinking: *Not him!* Conor was the least schooled of any of them, except for maybe Rollan. And at least Rollan had street smarts. What had Conor ever learned of strategy and leadership in a sheep pasture? He was going to blow their chance to hunt Rumfuss.

"You summoned Briggan, Conor. That means your destiny *demands* that you become a great leader," Lord MacDonnell said. "Begin."

Conor moved a pawn across the beautifully painted chessboard. Lord MacDonnell charged out with a knight. Conor inched out another pawn. Two moves later, one of his pieces fell to Lord MacDonnell. Conor slid his queen out to defend himself. Lord MacDonnell peacefully murdered one of Conor's bishops. Conor threw more pieces in the direction of Lord MacDonnell's king. Lord MacDonnell took several more victims.

Just like that, it was over. Lord MacDonnell checkmated Conor's king. He stood up.

"Not quite, Conor," he said.

I knew it, Meilin thought miserably. *I could have done this with my eyes shut! What is the point of being on a team if you are the strongest one?*

"Please, my lord," Meilin broke in. "We desperately need to speak to Rumfuss. If I could—"

"No," Lord MacDonnell said. "Do not ask me again today."

Just then, Finn burst from the fortress onto the grass of the courtyard. To Meilin's surprise, he didn't have Abeke with him. Instead, he had that absolutely ridiculous black cat, Kunaya.

"Abeke is gone," Finn said. "All I could find was the cat."

Meilin snapped, "I knew it!"

"Look," Finn interrupted. He touched the cat's neck. A piece of string was tied around it – no, not string. Abeke's elephant hair bracelet. Several frantic knots were tied along its length. "A message."

"What does it say?" Conor asked.

Finn's face was serious. "'Help.' And then: 'Devin hunts Rumfuss.'"

14

HUNTING

"**H**E *HUNTS*?" MACDONNELL ASKED, VOICE CURIOUS, LIKE HE thought he'd misheard the punch line of a joke. Finn repeated what the knot code said. MacDonnell's face didn't change, but when he spoke again, his voice had gone dark. "Hunting. In my castle's gardens, where I alone am permitted to hunt." He pursed his lips. "They take advantage of my hospitality and break my law."

"And they have Abeke!" Rollan added, irritated that MacDonnell seemed to find hunting more offensive than kidnapping. He turned to the others. "Why are we standing here? We've got to help her."

"I'm certainly not allowing *more* people to break my law and hunt on my land," MacDonnell said, as if this should have been obvious. "My soldiers will stop them. Trunswick won't be allowed to leave Glengavin."

"He has the wildcat," Finn said quietly. "Even if you manage to take him, it won't be without significant losses to your soldiers." He motioned to the soldiers, who were pretending not to eavesdrop, though they were doing a terrible job – in his distraction, one soldier had knitted his sleeve into the Highland cow's hair.

MacDonnell, who had already lifted his hands to clap and signal his soldiers, hesitated.

"You wouldn't want to be down men, should you have to defend Glengavin from the Conquerors, sir," Conor said, then reached down to the chessboard. He put his fingertip on MacDonnell's king piece and slid it toward MacDonnell himself.

MacDonnell took a deep breath, one that seemed to make his already broad shoulders even broader. "A wise move, Conor – Briggan is indeed making you a good leader, even if you aren't a good chess player. But what will my people think, if I allow you and your friends to break my law?"

"What if we did you some sort of favor in return for permission to break the law? A – a boon?" Conor said.

"Such as?" MacDonnell asked, and Conor furrowed his eyebrows in thought. "I have no need for your money –"

"The hare," Meilin said, stepping forward. "What if we find your spirit animal?"

"The hare for Devin Trunswick and Rumfuss?" MacDonnell's eyes widened. "Deal. But I warn you – he's not a friendly boar. Even if you find him, I doubt he will speak to you. You may arm yourselves from my stock, just in case."

"We'll figure it out," Rollan said. He spun around. "Hey, can I borrow this?" he asked, diving toward the soldier knitted to the cow. He grabbed the soldier's sword; when the soldier moved to stop him, the cow mooed irritatedly and shuffled away, dragging the man with him.

MacDonnell, who looked a bit overcome with the prospect of the hare returning to him, had a soldier lead them through the palace and down a wide staircase to the gardens. As they came into view, Rollan had to hide his surprise. When Rollan thought of gardens, he thought of little patches of grass with flowers. Maybe a fountain. Maybe even a tree, if it was a really fancy sort of garden. And what lay before him was exactly those things – except times a thousandfold.

The gardens stretched out toward the horizon. The section farthest away was a swath of gray almost the same color as the late morning sky. Somewhere was the wall that kept Rumfuss contained – but Rollan certainly couldn't see it among the thick trees, climbing vines, and flower beds so ruffled and colorful they looked like ladies' dresses cascading from their boxes.

"All right, what's first?" Rollan asked. "The hare, Abeke, or Rumfuss?"

"I had a dream about the hare," Conor said. "I think I know where he is. Finn, come with me, we'll go after the hare. Meilin and Rollan, you guys go find Abeke."

<hr />

After Conor and Finn had hurried into the garden in search of the hare, leaving Rollan and Meilin on the steps, the two began searching the perimeter of the castle for Abeke.

Meilin was already clacking around with plans and possibilities. "There's no place to keep Abeke locked up in a garden, is there? She has to be inside somewhere."

"Surely not in their rooms – even Devin Trunswick isn't that stupid," Rollan said.

Kunaya wrapped herself around Meilin's legs several times. Meilin looked down, clearly annoyed at the distraction. "Maybe a closet? Or another guest room? I wish every door in this castle wasn't closed – Kunaya, stop rubbing on me!"

Kunaya bit Meilin on the leg, an action that made Meilin hiss and Rollan grin.

"You ridiculous *cat*!" Meilin snapped.

Suddenly Rollan felt a flash of intuition so strong that he knew Essix must be near. He said, "What if she's not just a ridiculous cat? Kunaya was the last one to see Abeke."

"Follow a cat?" Meilin said. "That is the stupidest idea you've ever had."

Rollan said, "Oh, trust me, it is not. Let's go."

He started after Kunaya, and the little cat, looking pleased that they understood the game, bounded down the path ahead of them.

They rounded the corner of the castle. The carriage house came into view, a small but tidy building with a thatched roof. Kunaya shot into the dim interior, where carriages were lined up. The cat wove around the wheels, a blur of motion, ever faster. Meilin and Rollan had to hurry to keep up with her.

And then she stopped. With her tail crooked into a curl, she meowed smugly.

"Kunaya?" a voice called out, sounding just a little tearful.

Abeke! Rollan was stunned, even though the suggestion to follow the cat had been his. He vowed to make sure that Kunaya got a cat banquet thrown for her when this was all over.

He ran to one side of the carriage; Meilin ran to the other. Resting in the center of the carriage's floorboard was a massive wooden trunk with a heavy lock.

Meilin leaned over the edge of the door. "Abeke! We're here to save you!"

"Meilin?" Abeke's startled voice came from inside the trunk. "Is that *you*?"

"And Rollan is here too," Rollan said indignantly.

"I didn't think anyone would find me!" Abeke cried, her voice muffled. "I managed to knot my bracelet onto Kunaya, but I ran out of cord before I could spell out where—"

"Great story," said Rollan. "Tell us later. After we get you out."

He grabbed ahold of the lock on the trunk and gave it a tug. Frowning at Meilin, he shook his head.

Meilin pursed her lips. "Perhaps there's a spare key? Or—I bet Jhi could crush this entire thing if she sat on it!"

"Jhi is going to *sit on me*?" Abeke cried, voice panicked.

"Well, the trunk, not—"

"Jhi isn't sitting on anyone," Rollan said calmly. Clambering up on the carriage back, he grabbed for the canopy. It ripped easily, and with it came the thin pieces of metal that gave the canopy its shape. In a heartbeat, Rollan had pulled one from the fabric. He jammed it into the trunk's lock and wiggled it around in a practiced way. Looking over his shoulder at Meilin, he grinned cheekily.

"What?" she said, flushing. "What are you smiling at me for? The lock—"

"What lock?" Rollan said. At that instant he twisted his makeshift pick a final time. The lock popped open and clattered to the ground.

Never has a poorly spent childhood paid off so well, Rollan thought with satisfaction.

Meilin laughed, a bright, honest sound that she swallowed as soon as she realized he had noticed it.

"Let me guess," Meilin said. "Tutors?"

Rollan grinned.

In the carriage, the trunk's lid flew open. Abeke and Uraza leaped out in motions so identical they looked like two of the same animal rather than one human and one leopard.

"How did you find me?" Abeke asked breathlessly.

"Kunaya's not a spirit animal," Meilin answered, looking down at the cat, "but she's still a pretty great beast." Meilin tugged the bracelet off Kunaya's head and held it out to Abeke.

"Have Devin and Karmo found Rumfuss?" Abeke asked as she took the bracelet from Meilin and put it back on her wrist. "They've been looking for hours now!"

"I don't think so," Rollan said. "We can still find him before they do. Although I don't have a clue where to look. What do boars like? Mud?"

Meilin and Abeke exchanged a look of exasperation.

"We could go ask MacDonnell?" Abeke suggested.

"By the time we find *him* and then look for Rumfuss—" Meilin began.

She was cut off by a sharp cry from the top of a nearby carriage. Essix was perched on a driver's seat. When she caught Rollan's surprised look, she cocked her head as if to say, *What? I showed up, didn't I?*

"What is she trying to say, Rollan?" Meilin asked.

Rollan muttered, "Like I would know."

But the falcon ruffled her feathers at him and cocked her head. He felt the familiar sensation of her intuition trickling into his own mind. *If it was like this all the time,* he thought, *things would be a lot easier.*

Meilin and Abeke were waiting for his verdict.

"Essix is the answer," he said. "She can guide us from above. Come on!"

15

THE HARE

I HOPE THEY'VE FOUND ABEKE, CONOR THOUGHT AS HE AND Finn rushed down a path that snaked along the castle's east wall. Their search for the hare had consumed more time than Conor liked, and still they'd seen no sign of their friends. Around them, the garden darkened as morning faded into afternoon, and afternoon into late afternoon. Losing the talisman to Devin would be awful, but losing another one of their team after Tarik . . . it would be unthinkable. Briggan glanced over at Conor, as if he'd overheard the boy's thoughts.

"Convincing the hare to rejoin MacDonnell won't be easy," Finn said from behind them, startling Conor back to the moment. "Not after the way MacDonnell treated him."

"Remember Rollan's horse when we left Greenhaven?" Conor said, looking back at him. "He used to be a spirit animal. He was jealous of Rollan and Essix's bond. Maybe when the hare sees Briggan and me, he'll be jealous—

jealous enough to want his bond with MacDonnell back."

"Maybe so," Finn said. "I know that *I* find your bond inspiring."

It was high praise coming from the quiet Greencloak, and Conor felt a surge of hope too. They pressed on. Then, suddenly, there it was: a curtain of wisteria.

This was in my dream, Conor thought.

He dove for it, pushing the cascade of purple flowers out of the way. Beside him, Briggan snorted and rubbed his nose against the ground, protesting the flowers' overpowering scent.

The three emerged in a small clearing of trees. There was a stone bench on one side; on the other, the castle's stone wall. The branches arched overhead, leaving only a tiny circle of the darkening sky visible.

Finn made an uncertain noise. "The horse's partner died," he reminded Conor. "He had no choice but to go on alone. The hare knows MacDonnell is still alive – what makes you think he misses the bond so much?"

Conor took a deep breath before stepping toward the castle wall. He extended a hand to a rosebush planted alongside the stone.

"Because," he said. "Do you know what's on the other side of this wall?"

"I don't," Finn admitted, voice cautious.

"It's MacDonnell's bedroom," Conor said. Careful to avoid the thorns, he brushed the rosebush to one side.

With a soft whine, Briggan lay down. Finn sucked in a sharp breath. In the dark, two tiny, beetle-colored eyes shone, peering up at Conor. The hare had clearly been sleeping, curled up in a ball in the soft dirt. He looked surprised to see someone, much less someone so clearly looking for *him*.

"Hello," Conor said gently. "I'm Conor, and this is Briggan, one of the Great Beasts. We're, uh, hoping to convince you to return to Lord MacDonnell."

The hare blinked. He did not look convinced. His ears sagged—not so much sleepy as hopeless.

Conor wished he'd worked out more to say. He had really just thought the invitation, combined with the image of Briggan and him together, would be enough.

Behind him, however, Finn exhaled before speaking. "I know what it is to lose your spirit animal. The pain I feel, I see in Lord MacDonnell's eyes. I see in *your* eyes."

The hare blinked again, his ears sagging further.

"Please," Conor said. "Come with us. Come back to Glengavin. Give MacDonnell another chance. I know you miss him. You sleep beneath his bedroom window."

"He wants you back," Finn added. "He's changed."

This time, the hare did not blink. He sat still, his giant front legs locked in place. Only his nose moved, twitching with each breath. They were so close. Once they had convinced the hare to go back to MacDonnell, they could concentrate on Rumfuss. Time was running out. Conor finally reached toward the hare, palm open and promising, growing closer, closer to the animal—

The hare bolted, gone so fast into the underbrush that even Briggan couldn't have outrun him. It would be impossible to find him in this huge, dark garden.

"Well," Finn said, sounding defeated. "There goes that."

Conor gritted his teeth. Why had he reached out? He

should have been more patient, given the animal more time. He was a shepherd — he knew better than to rush an animal slow to trust.

Well, he reminded himself glumly. *You* were *a shepherd.*

Finn lifted a hand to touch a spot on his bicep — where his spirit animal, whatever it was, stayed dormant. "Perhaps sometimes a relationship is just too broken to fix."

Briggan walked to Conor's side and sat down, letting Conor run a hand over his fur for comfort. As soon as his hand came down on Briggan's ruff, he felt something shift in his head. His mind cleared, and the feeling of hopelessness that was threatening to overpower him was washed away. He had to lead. He had to make a decision.

"We can at least stop Devin from getting the talisman, even if MacDonnell won't let us take it for the Greencloaks," he told Finn. "Let's go find Rumfuss."

16

RUMFUSS

AFTER A FLYOVER OF THE GARDEN, ESSIX WAS ABLE TO GUIDE Rollan and the others toward the fruit orchards. The journey had taken the remainder of the day, but finally Essix had landed in the branches of a thick apple tree, and seemed to announce with a churr that they were close. Now, Meilin, Abeke, and Rollan hid in the shadow beside the apple tree, while Uraza peered across the orchard from the tree's branches itself. Abeke was impressed – perhaps Rollan and Essix really were working on their bond.

"My legs are cramping," Rollan complained. "Let's keep looking somewhere else."

Abeke looked up at Uraza, whose lavender eyes met hers with disappointment. Leaving Kunaya sitting in the tree, Uraza slunk down to join the rest of them. Her movement caused a few apples to shake loose, one of which knocked Meilin on the head. She caught it on the bounce and held it up to the leopard accusingly.

"Sorry," Abeke said for Uraza.

Meilin looked irritated for a moment, then tossed the apple into the darkness. "Don't worry about it. Let's go—"

Meilin didn't finish her sentence, because Rollan had grabbed her arm in an uncharacteristically serious way. Essix, who was perched on his shoulder, stared in the same direction—the area where Meilin had thrown the apple. It was through grapevines and fruit trees, a part of the orchards that seemed more wild than the rest of the garden.

Under his breath, Rollan said, "It's too dark and there's all that stuff in the way. But I think it's Rumfuss."

Meilin started in that direction. "Well, let's go."

"Wait," Rollan said, snagging her cloak. "Do you really think we should just go blowing over there like a hurricane? He might run, or worse. Remember Arax?"

Abeke shuddered. The image of the gigantic ram bearing down on her would be with her for the rest of her life.

"If you were Rumfuss and crazy MacDonnell had locked you up in his garden, would you be excited about talking to humans?" Rollan continued.

"Well . . ." Abeke said as her gaze landed on Uraza. "Who better to approach one of the Great Beasts than fellow Great Beasts? Uraza, could you go see Rumfuss?"

Uraza's ears tilted forward and she sat down, tail twitching behind her. Rollan gave Essix a nervous look, but the falcon made a soft clicking sound and jumped to the nearest branch. Meilin held out her arm and Jhi tumbled out, crunching loudly onto the ground. Everyone cringed as Rollan peered back through the trees to make certain the noise hadn't sent Rumfuss running.

"All right," Rollan said. "Good luck, guys."

Uraza was the first to go, letting her tail swing playfully in Abeke's face as she walked off. She was every bit as silent on the ground as Essix was in the air. Jhi took a step forward—

"Maybe wait a moment?" Meilin said, putting an arm in front of the panda. The panda obliged, giving Uraza and Essix time to reach Rumfuss before she started off. Jhi rumbled off into the trees, crushing leaves and sticks under her heavy paws. When Abeke could no longer see the bright white bits of Jhi's fur, she worriedly rubbed the spot on her arm where Uraza usually waited in her dormant state.

A growl came from the trees, then a falcon's cry. There was then a huge, roaring sort of noise, almost human in its expressiveness—the boar. None of the noises were sounds of alarm, but it still made Abeke's eyes widen.

Funny, she thought. *A few months ago I'd never even met Uraza. Now I'm nervous when I lose sight of her.*

"Oh!" Meilin said, reaching forward and touching her temple. "We . . . we can go speak to Rumfuss now."

"Jhi told you that?" Rollan asked, sounding impressed.

Meilin shrugged. "Not told, exactly. But I felt calmness. Safety."

They crept through the trees—despite Meilin's spirit animal, she was able to go rather quietly, though it was Abeke who truly moved like the leopard without even trying. Suddenly they broke through the darkened area into a copse of peach trees. Light now poured down from the heavy moon, so Abeke could see Rumfuss clearly. Perhaps *too* clearly.

Abeke thought Arax the Ram was rather frightening, but he was nothing compared to Rumfuss. The boar was more than twice her height and had narrow, dark eyes. His hide looked more like armor than skin, and the hair that jutted out from either cheek looked like it would cut her hand if she touched it. Most dangerous looking, however, were the two thick tusks on either side of his snout. They gleamed yellow-white and looked like the sharp corners of two glowing stars. Several huge mounds of chewed apples, each as tall as Abeke, surrounded him on all sides.

Rumfuss grunted, stamped at the ground, and then he spoke with a resonant voice that seemed to boom from both inside and outside Abeke. "You . . . want?"

His words were filled with the hesitation of someone who does not speak a language fluently. Abeke thought it had probably been a long time since he'd spoken to any humans.

"Rumfuss," she said politely. "We seek your talisman — the Iron Boar. We need it to defeat the Devourer."

"Talisman?" Rumfuss grunted warily. He flicked his tail back and forth, the bundle of hairs on the end whishing at his legs. "Why . . . give it to you?"

"The Conquerors will come for it otherwise," Meilin spoke up. "They've already taken my country, Zhong. And they've taken over Trunswick. *And* two Conqueror recruits are here, in this garden, looking for you — for the talisman."

"Can . . . handle . . . recruits," Rumfuss said. Abeke didn't doubt that he'd be a match for Devin and Karmo, even with their powerful spirit animals.

"*We* still need the talisman, though," Abeke pleaded. "We can't handle the Conquerors on our own."

"In return?" Rumfuss grunted.

"Um . . ." Abeke frowned. She looked to Meilin, who was equally lost.

"Freedom," Rollan said. They turned to look at him. He was leaning against one of the peach tree's branches, arms slung across it casually. He lifted his eyebrows at the girls. "That's what anyone who's in a cage wants most, no matter how big the cage is. Right, Rumfuss?"

The boar stamped the ground and nodded his head; Rollan smiled a bit in understanding.

"Wall," Rumfuss said, turning his head and jutting his snout toward the edge of the peach trees. There was indeed an immense stone wall, which rose up high above even the Great Beast's head. With all its jutting stones, it would have been nothing for an animal like Uraza to escape, but for a creature more lumbering, even one as huge as Rumfuss, it might as well have been a thousand feet tall.

"Not so fast," a voice jolted through the dark. A voice Abeke knew. A voice she knew too well.

They whirled around. Uraza hunched and hissed, showing her impressive teeth. Rumfuss stamped the ground and gave a throaty, rolling growl. Even Jhi hunched forward and flexed her muscles.

"What a reception," Devin said, grinning like this was all a fantastic game. "Abeke! I see you managed to escape. My own fault — I always underestimate how wily vermin can be when they're cornered." Karmo, standing beside Devin, looked sour at the joke, though Devin snickered hard at his own genius.

"Rumfuss, we're going to need that talisman," Devin continued. He whistled sharply; the wildcat appeared at his side. Karmo's hammerkop flapped out from the trees, thick bill open and menacing.

Rumfuss looked unimpressed—and Abeke couldn't blame him. The three of them, their spirit animals, and Rumfuss the Great Beast against Devin and Karmo? They could handle this.

But then Devin grinned even wider, and whistled again. Now the trees were alive with footsteps, footsteps of all sizes, skittering sounds, crunching sounds, the sounds of hooves and paws and human feet on the ground. Conquerors—a dozen or more, and all with spirit animals—poured from the foliage. There was a man with an iguana around his shoulders, and another with a meerkat crouched at his feet. There was a giraffe, a lemur, and a bobcat, each paired with a human who looked armed and ready for combat.

Devin had snuck Conquerors into Glengavin.

"Well, Rumfuss? The Iron Boar Talisman?" Devin said, holding out his hand.

Rumfuss studied Devin for a moment, so long a moment that Abeke began to worry he was going to give in. But then the boar lowered his head. He huffed, nostrils flaring, and his hackles lifted.

Then he charged.

17

BATTLE

"I HEAR THE OTHERS! THEY'RE UP AHEAD!" CONOR SHOUTED back to Finn. Briggan was in the lead and howled as he blasted through the orchard, leaping over grapevines and dodging tree trunks. Conor wasn't exactly sure who *they* were just yet—but he knew they were either *in* trouble or they *were* trouble. Animal sounds rose up like a storm in the night—roars, chirps, growls, snarls, hoots, and cries. Overhead, a falcon shrieked.

"That's Essix!" Finn shouted.

Conor's heart thrummed frantically. Briggan howled again, guiding them through the vines, until . . .

Conor's pounding heart stopped instead.

Conquerors. Spirit animals. A boar as large as a carriage—that *had* to be Rumfuss. And in the middle of it all, Abeke, Meilin, and Rollan. Abeke and Uraza worked as a team, bounding off trees and tackling their opponents. Uraza knocked them down, with Abeke moving quickly behind her to fling the smaller spirit animals away and deliver a few well-placed kicks to her downed opponents' ribs. Jhi was safely in passive state, a tattoo on the same arm Meilin used to box a Conqueror in the nose. Rollan dove under arms and ducked through legs like someone with a bit of practice at evading authority.

"Conor!" Meilin cried desperately, somehow seeing him between Conquerors. Saying his name took Meilin's concentration away for a heartbeat too long – a macaw swooped down and blinded her with scarlet feathers and claws. It gave a nearby enemy enough time to grab her by the leg and pull her down.

"Briggan!" Conor shouted to the wolf, who darted into the crowd and heaved the Conqueror off Meilin. Another one, however, took his place in an instant – there were too many. Far too many.

A bobcat leaped for Conor's face; he threw his staff into the air just in time to knock it away. He bashed it a second time in the head, rendering it unconscious, then ran forward, staff held horizontal so that it crashed into the backs of a few unsuspecting Conquerors. A baboon grabbed hold of his arm, yanking him down so hard Conor thought he might have dislocated his shoulder. Wincing through the pain, Conor whirled around and punched it squarely in the face. Rollan was suddenly there, offering him a hand up, but he'd no sooner found his feet than he realized a group of Conquerors were surrounding the two of them.

"Any ideas?" Rollan said. Essix swooped down, clawing at the eyes of a few Conquerors, but it wasn't enough to stop the horde. Briggan was still helping Meilin; Uraza and Abeke were being forced farther and farther into the orchard. Conor gripped his staff; Rollan, his sword.

Suddenly a pile of men were lifted into the air with a chorus of screams – Rumfuss! The boar smashed through them, sending fur and bodies flying. Conor wanted to pause and marvel at his size and strength, but there was no time. He spun forward, bringing the staff down hard on a nearby Conqueror's head.

Conor turned to see who needed help; there were still so many enemies, at least another half dozen, and mostly the ones with the sizable spirit animals. Meilin leaped from a branch and, midair, released Jhi from passive form. The panda slammed to the ground, butt-first, crushing a woman beneath her, and then in a flash was back to being a tattoo on Meilin's arm. Finn was by her, fending off a man with a giraffe who used its muscled neck like a battering ram –

Conor suddenly felt the unmistakable pain of teeth slicing into his shoulder. Devin's black wildcat had leaped on him from behind. Its claws and teeth were tearing into Conor's skin. He couldn't stop himself from screaming in pain, and turned in a wide circle, flinging the beast off. Conor grabbed his shoulder, and his hand came away sticky with blood.

"Not so great now, are you?" Devin hissed at him, and stalked forward. He tilted his head toward the wildcat, who raced back to him and threaded herself around his legs. Devin started forward; Conor lifted his staff but winced. He couldn't hold its weight with his injuries.

"You thought you were so special, didn't you, Conor? You thought you were better than me. You thought Briggan made you greater. Briggan's just a shadow of the Great Beast he used to be. Elda, however, is still a legend."

Conor backed up; strong hands grabbed his shoulders — a Conqueror. The man dug his fingers into Conor's fresh wound until he shrieked in pain. *Briggan, I need you*, he thought desperately.

Then he saw the wolf. Briggan was being held down by several Conquerors, one of whom kicked him sharply in the stomach. Briggan yelped loudly, and Conor could feel the noise in his skull.

Seeing this, Devin snorted. "Great Beast? Sure." He turned back to Conor. "Elda. Take him down."

Conor closed his eyes, but then immediately opened them again — he was scared, but he wasn't going to face his death with his eyes shut. Elda yowled, deep, sharp, and rumbling, and sprang forward.

Something else grabbed the wildcat in midair, crushing her to the ground. Something sleek and black, almost like a shadow rather than an animal. It bounded away quickly. Elda didn't get up, but her chest continued to rise and fall weakly. Devin's eyes widened and he rushed to her side. With a flash, she disappeared into a tattoo on his arm. The Conqueror holding Conor's shoulders released him, drawing a knife to fight off whatever this new creature was. But the animal was too fast — it pounced on the man, slashing his neck with what must be massive teeth. Then it shot off toward Meilin and Finn.

Devin was roaring angrily, shouting at the others. Karmo, who had been fighting Abeke, turned to look — just long enough for Rollan to tackle him to the ground and then hold him at swordpoint. Abeke dove for the hammerkop, which narrowly avoided her grasp and flapped for the trees. Conor ran for Briggan and shoved his staff deep into the stomach of the man kicking *his* wolf. It gave Briggan just enough time to bound to his feet and leap back into action.

The Conquerors were realizing how dangerously low their numbers had fallen – three left, no, two, since Rumfuss had just tossed one over the wall.

The dark shape, still moving too fast for Conor to see clearly, pounced on another man. Finn tossed his blade to Meilin, who held it aloft toward the final Conqueror. The man looked at her, then at the others. He then turned and fled.

"Coward!" Devin screamed. "Come back and fight!"

It was not very wise for Devin to draw attention to himself – Uraza heard him. She bounded across the orchard and pounced, slamming Devin into the ground with her front paws. She bared her teeth at the boy, flexing her claws out so that they pricked Devin's shoulders.

"Is everyone all right?" Conor finally asked, panting.

"I'm fine," Abeke said. "Just hold him there, Uraza –"

"Get your stupid cat off me!" Devin barked.

Abeke shook her head. "Never mind, Uraza. You can eat him."

This shut Devin up, at least for a few moments, while the others called out. Meilin had a bad cut on her arm, and maybe some broken toes. Essix was missing more than a few tail feathers, and it was making her fly all wobbly. Rollan had a black eye, though Karmo, lying on the ground with his palms up in surrender, had two.

They'd survived. Not only survived . . . they'd won. Conor could scarcely believe it.

And Finn – where was he?

"Finn?" Conor called out. "Where'd he go?"

"He was just here!" Meilin said, looking around in a panic.

"I'm fine," Finn said. His voice was hushed and thick with awe. It took them a few moments to work out where it was coming from. When they did, their jaws dropped in unison.

"Finn!" Abeke finally said. "It's you!"

Finn smiled, really smiled, his face bright and open. Conor couldn't remember him ever smiling before. The Greencloak lowered his arm and ran it along the back of a spirit animal — *his* spirit animal — who stood by his feet. He touched the creature with nervous, shaking hands, like he was very afraid this was just a dream.

"Why didn't you say anything?" Meilin asked wonderously.

"I thought he was gone," Finn said. "I thought he didn't want me anymore." His spirit animal looked up at him, then forced his head into Finn's hand, nuzzling at him. He was beautiful — ink black, with even blacker spots that glowed in the moonlight.

A black wildcat.

18

BLACK WILDCAT

Finn was the boy from the North, the legend Devin only pretended to be. Abeke laughed loudly in shock, Meilin stared, and Rollan scoffed and shook his head like he still didn't quite believe it. Even Rumfuss looked impressed.

"The bond . . . never lost," Rumfuss said, so wisely that it was hard to think less of him when he dropped his head and ate a mostly rotten apple from the ground.

"Rumfuss," Conor said. The boar looked up, and Conor dropped his head with respect. "Thank you for fighting with us."

"Thank you," Rumfuss said roughly, "for . . . fighting for me." The boar paused for a moment, then also dropped his head to the ground. At first Conor presumed it was to eat another piece of fallen fruit. Instead, the boar dug his massive tusk into the dirt of the nearest tree. It only took him a few moments to emerge with something hanging from it.

"Is that —" Abeke began.

"The talisman?" Conor finished.

"Here," Rumfuss said, stretching his neck out. Conor reached forward and took the pendant from the boar's shining tusk, his muscles tensing at the animal's smoky breath on his forearm. The talisman — the Iron Boar — was very heavy, and a deep rust color similar to Rumfuss's hide. It was shaped like a boar, of course, and while Conor couldn't be certain, he suspected the miniature boar's tusks were made from bits of Rumfuss's full-sized ones. They were too perfect not to be.

"Thank you," Conor said. "Thank you so much." He slipped the talisman around his neck and turned to the others. Karmo rose, still at Rollan's swordpoint. Uraza reluctantly got off Devin, though Meilin was quick to brandish her own dagger right under his chin.

"Wait," Rollan said. "Rumfuss. We promised to free him for the talisman."

"I will . . . be fine," Rumfuss snorted, but Rollan shook his head.

"We've got to get him out of here," he said. He turned to Rumfuss. "Come with us. We'll tell MacDonnell how you fought off Conquerors on his grounds. He'll owe you a favor."

"Hopefully that favor will work for the rest of us too, because we don't have the hare," Conor said.

"Hare?" Rumfuss asked.

"MacDonnell's lost spirit animal. He ran off before Finn and I could convince him to return. What do you think MacDonnell will care about more — that we didn't hold up our end of the bargain, or that we stopped his castle from being invaded?"

No one answered. It was hard to tell with someone like MacDonnell. Conor tucked the talisman under his shirt. With a resigned sigh, he led the others back through the orchard groves, toward the castle. The trek back through the massive gardens took nearly as long as it had to find the boar. Rumfuss followed, uprooting entire trees when they got in his way rather than walking around them. The two prisoners sulked silently the whole way – or rather, silently until either Rollan or Meilin poked them a bit too hard with the tips of their blades.

They arrived back at the garden steps to see most of the castle staff waiting for them. The night sky was already brightening. Rumfuss had elected to wait within the boundary of the tree line. MacDonnell and his children stood ahead of the others.

"Kindly tell me, what sounded like a *war* going on in my garden?" MacDonnell barked at them, motioning toward the orchards.

"It was a war. Well, a battle, I guess. But it sure felt like a war," Rollan said, and Karmo made a sound of agreement.

"Lord MacDonnell," Finn said. "Devin and Karmo allowed other Conquerors onto your grounds to help them capture Rumfuss the Boar and take his talisman."

MacDonnell's eyes widened, and a vein on his forehead began to pulsate. Seeing this, his children stepped away. "You mean to tell me, these two not only insulted my hospitality . . . they *invaded* my home?"

"We didn't invade –"

"Silence!" MacDonnell roared. "Guards! Relieve me of the burden of Devin Trunswick's presence. Lock up him and his companion immediately. And force Devin to call his spirit animal into its passive state."

"It is in its passive state, sir," Conor said shyly. "*This* wildcat belongs to Finn."

Now all attention shot to Finn, and a ripple of shock and awe raced through the crowd. Even MacDonnell's lips parted in wonder as Finn stepped forward, his wildcat, Donn, moving regally beside him. Donn made Elda look like a kitten. He was all muscle, with eyes as bright and yellow as the sun reflected off water. His black fur was dark velvet.

"The wildcat? The one from the legends? That means . . . you . . ." MacDonnell said, lifting his eyes to Finn. Suddenly MacDonnell was laughing, voice booming. "The true legend! In my home! I knew it couldn't be that snub-nosed Trunswick child!"

Finn bowed a bit, though he seemed rather bashful of the attention. Conor could relate. As the tittering and excitement died down, Finn cleared his throat. "My lord, we did not stop the Conquerors on our own. We were assisted by none other than Rumfuss, the Great Beast."

At this, Rumfuss, who had been mostly lurking in the shadows of the garden, stepped ever so slightly into the dwindling moonlight. The sheer size of him was obvious, even from this glimpse. The boar's eyes landed hard upon Lord MacDonnell. A hush fell over the assembled crowd; a few people went indoors, wary of Rumfuss's ferocity.

Conor found himself wondering for the first time just how the Great Beast had ended up within these walls. A story for another time, perhaps.

"It would be very honorable, sir," Conor added, "for you to release him from captivity, in return for his heroics."

MacDonnell paused. He puffed up his shoulders a bit, and somehow managed to look nearly as large as Rumfuss. "The deal, if I recall, was my hare for Rumfuss and his talisman. I cannot allow lawbreakers to simply suggest new laws for their own convenience."

"Oh, come on!" Rollan snapped. "You'd be overrun with Conquerors right now!"

"My castle, my law!" MacDonnell barked, and there was a buzz of agreement among the crowd, though Conor suspected this was merely because no one wanted to disagree with a man like MacDonnell. He shook his head, furious with himself for not convincing the hare sooner.

Behind him, Rumfuss made a deep sound in his throat, one that was loud but strangely gentle, almost like a cat purring. Rumfuss inclined his large head, indicating over his shoulder with a perfect tusk, then stamped a foot on the ground softly.

A collective gasp rose from the crowd. MacDonnell's face paled and, even from afar, Conor could see his lower lip was trembling.

It was the hare. It hopped from behind Rumfuss slowly, cautiously. Rumfuss looked down at the hare, who peered back up at him. They were speaking, though whatever they were saying was beyond any of the humans present. The hare now turned and looked up at MacDonnell, who sank to his knees in one swift motion. The sight of the great Lord MacDonnell in such a position sent a chorus of gasps from the assembled servants.

Rumfuss looked up at MacDonnell. "Say . . . sorry."

"I'm sorry," MacDonnell said immediately. "I'm so very sorry."

"Say . . . never again."

"Never again!" MacDonnell said, voice pleading.

"Say . . . you want."

"What?"

"I think the hare wants to know you want him," Meilin said. She wore a pained expression that Conor couldn't quite figure out. "That you are satisfied with him."

"I do! I am!" MacDonnell bellowed. With this, the hare sprang forward. MacDonnell's face spread into a wide, teary grin as the hare leaped into the air and, with a flash, disappeared – only to reappear as a tattoo on the man's forearm. MacDonnell rose, tears falling freely, and placed a hand over the hare tattoo, like he was afraid it would melt away.

"You're free!" he called out to Rumfuss. "Free! I should never have locked you up. You have my gratitude and my apologies, Rumfuss. I beg you to forgive me."

Rumfuss didn't seem quite ready for forgiveness, but he patiently followed the guards around the edge of the castle. Then, when the gates had finally opened, he was patient no more. There was a sound that seemed to shake the entire castle, and suddenly the only Great Beasts left in the garden were the ones that had come with them.

19

IRON BOAR

WHILE MacDONNELL WOULD HAVE BEEN HAPPY TO HOUSE the Greencloaks as esteemed guests for another night, Finn had insisted time was of the essence. Though Rollan loudly protested—the boy had only slept a single night in that amazing bed—their group set off that very morning. Understandably, they bypassed Trunswick entirely, shaving several days off the return trip to Lady Evelyn's. There they found a rather embarrassed Tarik, much improved from his previous condition. He was tired, but healthy enough to travel with them the relatively short way back to Greenhaven Castle.

Finn, however, would not be going with them. After a hushed and intense conversation, Tarik returned to the group and announced that he would ask Olvan's permission for Finn to remain at Glengavin. Finn would act as a much-needed emissary for the Greencloaks in the North. He was, after all, supposed to be their long-awaited hero. It took a little convincing that the group wouldn't need his protection on the way back—Tarik was clearly not yet at full strength – but Rollan's enthusiastic and animated retelling of the battle in the apple orchard reminded the older Greencloaks that the Four Fallen had learned a lot on this trip.

Still, they were glad that the remaining leg of the journey was so short, with just a single night's stop between them and home. Soon they would be back in Greenhaven, enjoying a well-earned moment of peace and safety.

They had done it, really done it. The second talisman was in Greencloak hands.

That night, as Conor stood watch over the others, he reveled in the wide, starry peace of the Euran pasture for what might be the last time in a long, long while.

And just for a moment, he let his guard down.

A cloaked figure loomed out of the darkness. Immediately Conor scrambled to his feet, ready to cry out for the others. As he reached for a weapon, however, a low, familiar voice, said, "Conor, it's me."

Dawson. Conor blinked at Devin's little brother. He kept his voice quiet, so that he wouldn't wake the others. "Why are you here? Are you alone?"

Dawson pushed back his hood, revealing shiny, high cheeks and bright eyes. He nodded. "I have a letter for you."

Conor marveled that the younger boy had tracked them down just to deliver a letter, but he nodded. Bashfully, he admitted, "You know I won't be able to read it."

"I'll read it," whispered Dawson, taking the weathered sheet from his cloak with a sad expression. "But just . . . I'm sorry, Conor. It's from my father." He took a deep breath.

Conor, son of Fenray,

I know that we last met under unpleasant terms, and you will not want to listen to what I have to say. However, I would like you to imagine the starving faces of your family as Dawson reads you this letter. Then you should imagine all the worse things than starvation that can befall a woman charged with betraying her lord to his enemy — even if this enemy is her own son. I have a bargain for you. Give the Iron Boar to Dawson. As soon as it is in my hands, I will forgive your family's debt and your mother will go free. They will own the land they work, and all the sheep they tend. They will be freemen, no longer my serfs. All you have to do is give Dawson the talisman. And if you do not? I will hold them to every last copper that they owe me, and I promise you, they will starve this winter, and the fate of your mother will be far crueller. Rest assured this is the last you will hear from me either way. Devin has become involved in something that Trunswick can no longer afford to support openly, lest we collapse upon ourselves. Zerif tells me that if the Conquerors may have their talisman, then I may have my family back. And so you will have yours.

The decision is yours.

With regards, The Earl of Trunswick.

Dawson folded the letter and put it back in his cloak.

He at least had the grace to look horrified.

Conor's hands shook as he imagined his mother's thin face on the night they'd escaped from Trunswick. How proud she'd been of him! *Follow your heart!*

He glanced at the others. They slept soundly, trusting him to watch them on their way back to Greenhaven. They trusted him with this treasure of Rumfuss. But his family had trusted him to help keep them alive too, when they'd sent him to Trunswick to be Devin's servant. No matter how hateful he had found that position.

What was the right decision? Once the Greencloaks were victorious, surely his family would be free. But it would be too late then.

Conor was glad that Briggan was in passive form. He didn't want to see the wolf's expression as he crept to his saddlebag and removed the Iron Boar.

"I expect your father to keep his word," he whispered to Dawson. He gave the talisman to the boy.

Dawson nodded. "I'll make sure he does, Conor."

Tucking the Iron Boar into his cloak, Dawson ran into the night. The sound of his footfalls woke Meilin's horse, and Meilin sat up with a start.

"Conor, is someone there?" she asked. Her voice made the others stir as well.

When Conor, shattered with guilt, didn't answer, her eyes darted from his saddlebag, the flap hanging open, revealing the empty inside, to the place in the woods he still stared after.

"I'm sorry," he said.

"What happened?"

Conor hung his head. "I'm sorry."

20

CONSEQUENCES

THE NIGHT WAS DARK AND FULL OF ANIMALS.

Meilin lay in her bed, eyes wide open. Her mind was full of the gardens of Zhong, her father's wise face, and the Conquerors marching over the places she'd loved.

The four kids were finally back in Greenhaven. It had been a few days since they'd returned, and Meilin's mind had been troubled for each of them. Their journey seemed to have been for nothing; Conor had handed over the precious talisman to the enemy. For his family! Hadn't she wanted to go to Zhong for her family when she'd had the chance? Hadn't he been the first to tell her to stay with them?

Far off, down the hall, someone's spirit animal made a drowsy night noise. Meilin was far away from sleep.

Since they'd returned, the fortress had been abuzz with the changes happening all over Erdas. People were taking sides. For the Greencloaks and the Fallen. For the Conquerors and Zerif's new false heroes. Rumors were on everyone's lips: rumors of an advancing army, and of the strange promise the army had—a potion, stronger than the Nectar of Ninani, which could force the spirit animal bond for anyone who drank it: the Bile.

There was no more time for wasted missions.

"Jhi," Meilin whispered. The panda had been drowsing in the corner of the room, but when she heard her name, she lifted her chin. Her eyes were sympathetic. "Help me."

This time, when Meilin closed her eyes, searching for answers, the orbs around her were like droplets of water, brilliant, fragile, trembling. They spilled from her eyes and down her cheeks. Here were her choices: Stay. Go.

One was both wise and logical.

Stay. Fight alongside the Greencloaks: Build an army to fight this new threat.

Go. Be an army of one: Find her father before it was too late. It was neither wise nor logical. Jhi's intuition recommended against it.

But it was the choice Meilin was going to make.

She got out of bed and packed, silent and swift. The panda hesitated when Meilin held out her arm. She was offended, perhaps. After all, she'd offered her advice and Meilin wasn't taking it. Or maybe she was concerned. She'd never refused the passive state before. With a frown, Meilin focused on the request. With a whimper, Jhi vanished in a searing flash, reappearing on Meilin's skin, barely visible in the dark night.

Meilin stopped only to pick up a map from the map room and a bag of food from the kitchen.

Then she let herself out of the castle. She was going back to Zhong.

BOOK THREE:

BLOOD TIES

Lost and starving in occupied lands, Meilin
must seek out what remains of her home's
fragile resistance. Her friends aren't far behind
her, but they aren't the only ones.

Meilin is being hunted.

Each book unlocks in-game rewards.
Log in with your copy to help save Erdas!

The Legend Lives in You

scholastic.com/spiritanimals

Enter your code to unlock huge rewards:
N69D43X2X3

You've read the book — now join the adventure at **Scholastic.com/SpiritAnimals**!

Enter the world of Erdas, where YOU are one of the rare few to summon a spirit animal.

Create your character.

Choose your spirit animal.

CHARACTER CREATION

MALE
SKIN
EYES
HAIRSTYLE
HAIR COLOR
NAME
RANDOMIZE

Welcome to the world of the magical beasts.

This screen is where you create your hero to save the world (once again)!

Get creating!

ACCEPT

Henrik Freeking

THE LEGEND LIVES IN YOU